Twilight of the Belle Epoque

Twilight of the Belle Epoque

*The Paris of Picasso, Stravinsky, Proust, Renault,
Marie Curie, Gertrude Stein, and Their Friends
through the Great War*

Mary McAuliffe

ROWMAN & LITTLEFIELD
Lanham • Boulder • New York • Toronto • Plymouth, UK

Published by Rowman & Littlefield
4501 Forbes Boulevard, Suite 200, Lanham, Maryland 20706
www.rowman.com

10 Thornbury Road, Plymouth PL6 7PP, United Kingdom

Distributed by NATIONAL BOOK NETWORK

British Library Cataloguing in Publication Information Available

Library of Congress Cataloging-in-Publication Data

McAuliffe, Mary Sperling, 1943–
  Twilight of the Belle Epoque : the Paris of Picasso, Stravinsky, Proust, Renault, Marie Curie, Gertrude Stein, and their friends through the Great War / Mary McAuliffe.
    pages cm
  Includes bibliographical references and index.
  ISBN 978-1-4422-2163-5 (cloth : alkaline paper) — ISBN 978-1-4422-2164-2 (electronic) 1. Paris (France)—Intellectual life—20th century. 2. Intellectuals—France—Paris—Biography. 3. Paris (France)—History—1870–1940. 4. Paris (France)—Social conditions—20th century. 5. Social change—France—Paris—History—20th century. 6. Social conflict—France—Paris—History—20th century. 7. World War, 1914–1918—Social aspects—France—Paris. I. Title.
  DC735.M44 2014
  944'.3610813—dc23
                                                                    2013047607

♾™ The paper used in this publication meets the minimum requirements of American National Standard for Information Sciences—Permanence of Paper for Printed Library Materials, ANSI/NISO Z39.48-1992.

Printed in the United States of America

In memory of my parents

Betty F. Sperling and Godfrey Sperling Jr.

~

Contents

Illustrations

~

Acknowledgments

As always, my first debt of gratitude is to the City of Light itself, which for more than twenty years has nourished my sense of beauty and deepened my appreciation of history. No matter how much I research and write about this remarkable subject, there is still so much to discover. Paris is indeed a feast, and I have benefited immeasurably from the opportunity to partake of it.

I would like to thank the New York Public Library for providing me a place in its Wertheim Study Room, a quiet sanctuary for scholars in the heart of its vast research facilities in the renowned Forty-Second Street Library. In particular, I would like to extend my thanks to Jay Barksdale, the senior librarian in charge of the Wertheim Study Room, for his ever-ready assistance in solving the variety of problems that can confront a researcher.

Along the way, many people have generously provided a wide array of assistance. Gilles Thomas, who knows more about underground Paris than anyone can possibly imagine, has for years shared his vast historical as well as geographical knowledge of the city with my husband and me. It was Gilles who insisted that we come with him to visit the extensive caverns of Chemin des Dames, outside of Paris, because (as he put it) we are Americans and we should see them. He was right: the wall carvings made during World War I by lonely American soldiers on this front-line position—all too close to Paris—moved us deeply and added an important element to my understanding of the war and its impact on Parisians.

I would also like to thank Gérard Duserre and Jean-Luc Largier for their unflagging commitment to historical preservation and for their enthusiasm in sharing their discoveries with us. Our friend Ray Lampard has also generously shared his interest in Paris's past, going well out of his way to show us the Paris and its environs that he loves.

This is the third book that I have published with Rowman & Littlefield, and I have been blessed throughout with an extraordinary editorial staff. Special thanks to my editor, Susan McEachern, who has regularly held my hand along the road to publication, providing invaluable expertise and guidance along the way. My thanks as well to my longtime production editor, Jehanne Schweitzer, who has never met a problem or a complexity she could not master. I am also grateful for the assistance of my patient copy editor, Catherine Bielitz, and to assistant editor Carrie Broadwell-Tkach, who makes so many things happen, and so smoothly.

Last, a special thank-you to my husband, Jack McAuliffe, who throughout the gestation of four books and more than one hundred articles on Paris and France has unsnarled the inevitable travel snafus and provided valuable insights and photography along the way. I have had the joy of discovering Paris with him, and that is the best of all.

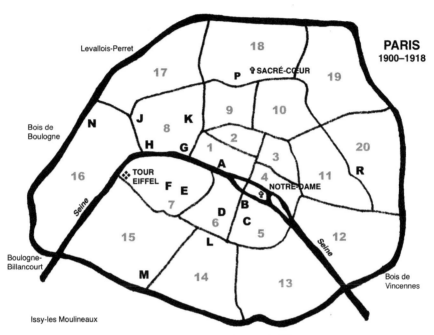

Paris, 1900–1918. © J. McAuliffe

Key:
A. Musée du Louvre
B. Sorbonne and Latin Quarter
C. Panthéon
D. 27 Rue de Fleurus (Gertrude Stein)
E. Hôtel Biron (Rodin)
F. Les Invalides
G. Place de la Concorde
H. Théâtre des Champs-Elysées
J. Etoile

K. 102 Boulevard Haussmann (Proust)
L. Café du Dôme and Café de la Rotonde
M. La Ruche (Chagall)
N. Porte Dauphine
P. Bateau-Lavoir (Picasso)
R. Père-Lachaise Cemetery

Paris's twenty arrondissements are indicated by number.

Introduction

My last book on Paris, *Dawn of the Belle Epoque: The Paris of Monet, Zola, Bernhardt, Eiffel, Debussy, Clemenceau, and Their Friends*, took the reader from the multiple disasters of 1870–1871 through the extraordinary reemergence of Paris as cultural center of the Western world, ending with the triumphal Paris Exposition of 1900.

It was not, of course, as if Paris and Parisians experienced no trials or tribulations during these years. The poor continued to suffer, and their advocates, such as Georges Clemenceau and Louise Michel, continued to have their work cut out for them. Moreover, a prolonged period of economic listlessness provided an ongoing undercurrent of anxiety, exacerbated by debacles such as the Union Générale bank crash and the Panama Canal scandal—thoroughly avoidable disasters that wiped out the life savings of so many who could not afford to lose a sou. In addition, the unsettled nature of the Third Republic itself undermined confidence. Monarchists and the Church continued to battle republicans of all stripes, while anti-Semites and nationalists, feeding upon the swirling undercurrent of fear, almost tore the nation apart in their victimization of an innocent Jewish soldier, Captain Alfred Dreyfus.

And yet, somehow, a remarkable series of artists and innovators emerged during these years, battling traditionalists and—at least for a substantial number—achieving success. Claude Monet, Emile Zola, Sarah Bernhardt,

1

and Gustave Eiffel were well-to-do or even wealthy by the turn of the century, as was that innovative founder of the Samaritaine department store, Ernest Cognacq. Auguste Rodin and Pierre-Auguste Renoir had also attained financial success, and others among their acquaintances had likewise left their years of poverty far behind. There would always be those such as Paul Gauguin who would die impoverished, and the market for paintings by Camille Pissarro, Alfred Sisley, and Paul Cézanne did not really take off until after their deaths. But a surprising number of the starving artists and entrepreneurs of the 1860s and 1870s had, by the turn of the century, found fame and fortune in Paris.

A new cast of characters greets the reader in this book, starting with nineteen-year-old Pablo Picasso, who arrived late in the year 1900 to visit the Paris exposition and glory in the fact that one of his youthful paintings was hanging in the Spanish pavilion. The new century would soon belong to Picasso, as well as to Henri Matisse, Igor Stravinsky, Claude Debussy, Maurice Ravel, Marie Curie, Gertrude Stein, Marcel Proust, Jean Cocteau, and Isadora Duncan. It would belong just as rightly to Louis Renault, André Citroën, Paul Poiret, François Coty, and all those innovators and entrepreneurs who created new technologies and far-flung businesses based in Paris, as well as to those magnificent men—and women—who added excitement and adventure to the Paris scene by piloting some of the era's earliest automobiles and flying machines.

This did not mean that the leading lights of the previous century had somehow stepped aside. Sadly, Edouard Manet and Berthe Morisot had departed, and Zola was about to make his dramatic exit, but Monet and Renoir continued to paint for wealthy collectors, and Sarah Bernhardt soldiered on, reaping accolades and gamely entertaining the troops during World War I despite her recently acquired wooden leg. Gustave Eiffel, disgraced in the aftermath of the Panama Canal scandal, would keep his word and never build another bridge or tower, but his experiments in radio communications and aerodynamics would keep him fruitfully active for the rest of his long life. Claude Debussy, after two decades of battling traditionalists, was about to emerge as a giant on the music scene, while Georges Clemenceau would eventually cap a roller-coaster career in politics by stepping in at the age of seventy-six to lead his country to victory in war.

These years, from 1900 for more than a decade, were remarkable ones—remembered in the Great War's aftermath as the Belle Epoque. They were years of extraordinary achievement in almost every field of endeavor, marked by a dizzying sequence of breakthroughs. Yet they were also years of shadows, and those shadows were growing longer as war approached—a cataclysm that tested the mettle of the City of Light, even as it brought the end of an era.

The Rolling Sidewalk, Universal Exhibition, Paris, 1900. Bibliothèque Nationale de France, Paris, France. Photo Credit: Snark / Art Resource, NY. © Art Resource, NY.

~

CHAPTER ONE

Enter the King

(1900)

It was mid-October 1900 in the City of Light when Pablo Picasso arrived from Barcelona at Paris's bustling new railroad station, the Gare d'Orsay.[1] He was almost nineteen years old and filled with bravado. After all, the Spanish pavilion at the Paris Exposition of 1900 had included one of his paintings in its exhibit. What a coup! And what a way to make his entrance into Paris! Scrawling on a self-portrait soon after learning that he would be making the trip, Picasso had euphorically written, "I, the king." Not once, but three times. It would prove to be amazingly accurate.

He arrived with his best friend, Carles Casagemas, an aspiring artist and poet who was similarly yearning to experience the Paris art scene and its famed bohemian life. The exposition was due to close on November 12, giving the young men little time to dally if they intended to see it.

Millions that centennial year had already flocked to the Paris exposition, which featured a virtual explosion of the newest and the most breathtaking, including its Palace of Electricity, which was gloriously illuminated by night, and an electrically powered moving sidewalk that magically carried hoards of delighted and possibly footsore visitors around the Left Bank portion of the exposition. This world's fair, like its predecessors, was meant to overawe, and it succeeded—much to the pleasure of the fifty million visitors who crowded into its acres of amusement and education for the months from April through early November.

Fantasy, futurism, and the exotic flourished there, but if there was a single style in architecture and decoration that prevailed, it was Art Nouveau—or what by then was referred to in Paris as *le style Mucha*, named after the Czech artist whose late 1890s posters of Sarah Bernhardt had set off a frenzy in the decorative arts.

Alphonse Mucha had survived years of poverty as a lackluster artist in Paris before unexpectedly creating something entirely new and vibrant when opportunity and emergency combined. Sarah Bernhardt wanted a new theatrical poster at an awkward time, and—like the diva she was—she wanted it immediately. There was no one else to do it but this unlikely artist, who had the sole recommendation of being available. Mucha later claimed to have drawn upon the Czech tradition of folk ornamentation, although it is more likely that a yeasty mixture of Symbolism, Japanese art, and the curved, organic elements of the emerging Art Nouveau movement guided his brush. Whatever happened, he struck gold, metaphorically and otherwise, and from then on his fortune was made.

Called upon in the months leading up to the Paris exposition to plan a grandiose Pavilion of Humanity (which never came to fruition) and to design the entire pavilion for Bosnia-Herzegovina, Mucha endured what he later remembered as a "nightmare of hard work." A notoriously intense worker, who usually started at nine o'clock in the morning and continued until one o'clock the following morning or later, Mucha suffered so much stress that he smoked incessantly and developed nicotine poisoning. That is, until (as his son tells the story) he decided in desperation to go cold turkey and threw all his smoking gear into the oven. This drastic change produced its own dire results, which impelled a doctor to prescribe what sounds like the ultimate Parisian prescription—a bottle of champagne a day!

Thus fortified, Mucha seems to have recovered. He and the jeweler Georges Fouquet successfully collaborated on the exposition's Bosnia-Herzegovina pavilion, and then Fouquet asked Mucha to design every detail of the new shop he was opening on the elegant Rue Royale, between the Place de la Madeleine and the Place de la Concorde. Mucha accepted and then proceeded to outdo himself, creating a luxurious little oasis of sinuously carved cabinets, intricate flooring, sculpted peacocks, and stained glass windows featuring his characteristically long-tressed maidens. This was in addition to designing the jewelry itself, and it was all done with extraordinary attention to detail and in the very best of Art Nouveau style. Laboring long and hard on this tiny bit of perfection, Mucha managed to complete Fouquet's jewel box of a shop by 1901.[2]

～

Work on a far different scale had already been proceeding for several years in the heart of Paris as engineers and construction workers created urban havoc by tearing up great swaths of streets and sidewalks and digging enormous holes in the most inconvenient places, all in the gigantic effort to build the city's new underground Métro system. Under the direction of Fulgence Bienvenüe, the eminent but sadly forgotten chief engineer for this difficult project, the first stretch of the new Métro (crossing the city from east to west on the Right Bank) was successfully completed in July 1900—not quite in time for the opening of the exposition, but soon enough to provide a satisfyingly impressive example of French engineering ability for the world gathered at its door. To the gratification of those concerned in this endeavor, the new Métro's first line carried some seventeen million passengers by the year's end.[3]

During the course of his career as a civil engineer, Bienvenüe, known as "le Père Métro" (Father Métro), had successfully supervised the construction of railway lines, aqueducts, and a funicular railway for the steep heights of Belleville in northeast Paris. From 1898 on, this elegant man with the neat white beard and smiling eyes directed a team of some two thousand workmen, who dug their way into and through the urban underbelly of Paris. With a goal of maintaining a distance between stations of no more than four hundred meters, and of keeping the number of necessary transfers down to a minimum of two, Bienvenüe and his army of workmen opened a series of spectacular construction sites during the years from 1900 to 1914—an endeavor that would turn out to be blessedly free from accidents, cave-ins, or other major delays.

Following the July 1900 opening of Line 1, Bienvenüe did not let up but continued to push the envisioned Métro network into reality. By October 1900, the completed section from Etoile to Trocadéro made it even easier for exposition-goers to reach the fair grounds—although it admittedly came a little late for the majority of attendees, since the exposition closed scarcely more than a month later. Also in October, Bienvenüe's army of workmen began Line 2, a partially elevated line that followed the circular northern, or Right Bank, course of the old Farmers-General wall. They completed a useful section from Etoile to Porte Dauphine in December, and then began on Line 3, which had to pass under the Canal St-Martin—an endeavor that would delay this portion of the line until 1901.

Onlookers, especially those inconvenienced by the lengthy disruption that the digs imposed, were at first less than enthusiastic about this intrusive newfangled piece of technology. Yet as it began to revolutionize their lives, many would not be able to imagine life without it.

∿

Among the multitude of decisions involved in creating Paris's new Métro system was the choice of the young architect Hector Guimard to design its many entrances—those small but important structures that would become the Métro's most recognizable face above ground.

It was in many ways an audacious choice. Guimard had trained at Paris's Ecole Nationale des Arts Décoratifs as well as at the Ecole Nationale des Beaux-Arts, where he earned a reputation as a rebel and, chafing at academic restrictions, failed to take his diploma. But his remarkable talent, coupled with a lively scorn for the mundane, soon attracted the attention of those with deep pockets and avant-garde taste. By the 1890s Guimard had emerged as a man to watch, with commissions to plan and build a number of mansions in Paris's well-heeled sixteenth arrondissement. His most famous was

The Hector Guimard "Dragonfly" Métro entrance at Porte Dauphine, Paris. © J. McAuliffe

the astonishing Castel Béranger (1895–1898), which its detractors referred to as the "Castel Dérangé—a daring and difficult concept and execution that placed him at the forefront of the Art Nouveau movement.

What the Métro's commissionaires wanted was something elegant but light, with iron (a nod to Eiffel's famed constructions) and glass (including ceramics) as the preferred materials. Guimard had rivals for the job who were far more conventional and who had the support of the municipal council, but he seems to have benefited from wealthy and powerful backers within the Métro commission itself. Whatever actually happened behind the scenes, Guimard's plans were finally approved in early 1900.

Guimard's models varied from simple enclosures to the full-scale stations at Etoile and Bastille (neither still in existence). In between was a type known as the "dragonfly," because of its glassy resemblance to dragonflies' wings. Two of these gauzy "dragonflies" still exist—at Porte Dauphine and the Abbesses station in Montmartre (the latter moved from its original placement at the Hôtel de Ville).

But it was Guimard's simple shelter that was most frequently used on the Métro's earliest lines. This structure, with open walls of cast iron rather than of solid stone, adapted well to the narrow sidewalks and typical crowding of urban Paris. Today, with their sinuous organic lines, Art Nouveau lettering, and lights like floral pods that seem to sway at the end of their long cast iron stems, Guimard's Métro entrances have become some of the most best-known images of Paris.

By the end of 1900, eighteen stations on Line 1 had opened, and more would soon follow. It looked like a dream commission for young Hector Guimard. But his hair-trigger temper and keen sense of self-worth was about to get him in trouble, and a Paris Métro without Guimard would soon become a distinct possibility.

～

One of the many visitors to the Paris exposition was twenty-five-year-old François Spoturno, a native of Corsica who had come to Paris to make his fortune. A born charmer, he already had proved his skills as a salesman in Marseilles. Now, using a connection he had cultivated during his military service, he found a position as attaché to the senator and playwright Emmanuel Arène. It was a tremendous coup. Young Spoturno may not have had money, but he now had access to the glittering upper reaches of 1900 Paris, with its salons, clubs, and fashionable gatherings. As he quickly realized, it was a world in which women played a key role, from the most elegant aristocrats to the grandest courtesans—a fact of great importance, as it turned out, since women would soon make Spoturno's fortune.

Spoturno's interest was not in clothing but in perfume. At the opening of the new century, the perfect perfume was as essential to the well-dressed Parisian woman as was the latest fashion in dresses, and the French perfume industry was booming, with nearly three hundred manufacturers, twenty thousand employees, and a profitable domestic as well as export business.[4] Naturally, perfume makers took the opportunity to display their wares at the 1900 Paris exposition, and Spoturno took the time to wander among their displays, including those of leading names such as Houbigant and Guerlain. Spoturno was not yet sufficiently knowledgeable to judge a perfume's quality, but he did note that the bottles containing these perfumes were old-fashioned and uninspired. It would not be long before it would occur to him that perhaps their contents were also a trifle outdated.

But first he had to find his way into the perfume business. After getting a job as a fashion accessories salesman and marrying a sophisticated young Parisian, Spoturno became acquainted with a pharmacist who, like other chemists at the time, made his own eau de cologne, which he sold in plain glass bottles. One memorable evening, Spoturno sniffed a sample of his friend's wares and turned up his nose. The friend then dared him to make something better, and Spoturno went to work. He hadn't the slightest idea of how to proceed, but in the end he managed so well that his friend had to admit that he was gifted.

Yet natural gifts were not enough in the perfume business, and soon Spoturno decided to go to Grasse, the center of France's perfume industry, to learn perfume-making from the experts. Along the way he would change his name to his mother's maiden name. Only he would spell it "Coty."

⌒

The 1900 Paris exposition, which was sufficiently grand in itself, shared the stage, if in a minor way, with the 1900 Summer Olympics, which were held as part of the exposition. In contrast with present-day extravaganzas, these early games were quite simple and even crude in production and execution.

The 1900 Paris games were the second in the history of the modern games (the first having taken place in Athens in 1896) and lasted from May through October. Track and field events took place on the far western side of Paris on a rough field at the Racing Club de France, in the Bois de Boulogne's Pré Catelan. Rowing, swimming, and water polo contenders splashed about in the Seine, while cycling, football (soccer), gymnastics (including weight-lifting), cricket, and rugby enthusiasts went at it on the far eastern side of the city, in the Bois de Vincennes. Shooters were relegated to the city outskirts, while fencers dueled on the Terrasse of the Jeu de Paume in the Tuileries gardens—reminding the more historically minded of the Three Musketeers' derring-do near this very spot.

Three women competed with men for croquet, and these women, sadly eliminated, were among the first to appear in modern Olympic games. Hé-lène de Pourtalès, a Swiss contender, became the first woman to win a medal, as part of the winning team (with her husband) in a yachting event on the Seine. Charlotte Cooper, a three-time Wimbledon champion, became the first woman to win an individual medal, defeating all comers in the women's singles tennis competition, and then went on to win in mixed doubles. For the record, she wore an ankle-length skirt, corset, and long sleeves as she demolished her opponents with what was described as a "formidable back-hand." But Margaret Abbott, an American studying art in Paris who placed first among ten women golfers, credited her success to the fact that she wore sensible clothing, while her French competitors wore restrictive dresses and high heels.

Alvin Kraenzlein of the United States won a glorious sweep of four indi-vidual gold medals in track and field, although this triumph may have been slightly diminished after he was punched in the face by a rival in the long jump. (In defense of the fellow who threw the punch, Kraenzlein had un-expectedly competed in this event after informally agreeing to stand solidly with other American contenders and not compete on a Sunday.)

Croquet would not survive as an Olympic sport, nor would cricket, tug-of-war, or motorcycle racing. But the marathon, the starring attraction of all Olympic games since ancient times, has continued, despite some storms, weather and otherwise, along the way. The marathon course for the 1900 games took the runners from the Bois de Boulogne onto the winding streets of Paris. Thirteen runners (five French, two American, three British, two Swedish, and one Canadian) braved a blisteringly hot July afternoon on what turned out to be a badly marked course. Runners became lost, wandered about, and had to contend with horses and buggies, occasional autos, and irate pedestrians. One of the American contenders claimed that a cyclist knocked him down just as he was about to overtake the lead runner.

The French managed to take first and second place, although the lead American runner argued that they must have cheated and taken a short cut, since he never saw them pass him. Adding further to the confusion, the

The Renault family driving three of their earliest cars (Louis Renault in the middle car), 1899. France, Private Collection. Photo Credit: CCI / The Art Archive at Art Resource, NY. © Art Resource, NY.

winner turned out to be from Luxembourg rather than France—although the Olympic Committee still credits this medal for France.

⌒

Montmartre's Rue Lepic starts at the Moulin Rouge, on Place Blanche, and then climbs steeply before swinging westward and looping back again, in all likelihood following an earlier footpath that wound its way up the Butte. It is a street with a memory. Pablo Picasso, on his first day in Paris, carted his belongings up Rue Lepic to temporary housing on the western side of the Butte. In time, Gertrude Stein would climb Rue Lepic on a regular basis to Picasso's Bateau-Lavoir studio, where she repeatedly sat for Picasso while he endlessly painted—and repainted—her portrait.

But it was on a chill Christmas Eve in 1898 that twenty-year-old Louis Renault made a different kind of history on Rue Lepic. Driving an automobile of his own construction, made largely from bicycle parts, he won a race up the street's steep (13-degree) slope, confounding those who thought it couldn't be done in such a lightweight vehicle. Automobiles until then had been heavy, noisy, and expensive, widely regarded as eccentric and dangerous toys for the rich. Renault, who soon patented the direct drive that made his victory possible, held a very different vision for the automobile. His own little two-seater, which weighed only 550 pounds and could reach thirty miles per hour, ran quietly and had been cheap to build. He foresaw a future for motorized vehicles that would be light, fast, quiet, and inexpensive to purchase and maintain.

Until now, Louis had been the black sheep of his family, the youngest of three surviving sons of a Parisian drapery dealer and button manufacturer. Born and raised in an atmosphere of bourgeois comfort and respectability (at 12 Place de Laborde, 8th, now Place Henri-Bergson), he found it difficult to persuade his father and brothers that his tinkering and puttering would ever amount to anything. But after his friends began to clamor for vehicles just like his, Louis's brothers (who had taken over the father's button and drapery business after his death) realized the potential of their little brother's mechanical abilities and decided to back him financially. As a result, Renault Frères made its appearance in 1899, with its workshops on the Ile de Séguin at the southwest edge of Paris. Louis, who was as good a carpenter and builder as he was a mechanic, constructed much of the first Renault works himself.

Germany's Karl Benz may have invented the gas engine (in 1880) and another German, Gottlieb Daimler, patented his first gas engine soon after, but it was a Frenchman, Armand Peugeot, who can be said to have built the first motorcar, beginning its manufacture (with his cousin) in 1892, and in 1896 setting up his own company in Audincourt to build cars with internal combustion engines. In 1895, the first motorcar race took place, from Paris to Bordeaux and back, and by 1900, what has been called the "heroic period of the automobile" had begun,[5] with the Renault brothers in the thick of it.

The most glamorous aspect of motoring in the early years of the twentieth century was the road race, and here Louis and his brother Marcel excelled. In France, road races between cities and across the countryside drew crowds of enthusiasts, as the racers achieved hitherto unbelievable speeds of up to sixty miles per hour. This was a dangerous sport, and Louis Renault and his brother soon made their mark, first in the 1899 Paris–Trouville race, and then in the Paris–Toulouse–Paris race of 1900, which was part of that year's Olympics.

In that race, Louis Renault competed with a supercharged engine whose grease pump soon broke. Unable to mend it, he bought a funnel and soup-spoon from a roadside peddler and continued the race, driving with one hand and using the other to spoon oil through the funnel into the grease-tube, which fortunately passed near the driver's seat. Unfortunately he encountered other misadventures en route (including an encounter with a passing wine cart, which knocked him onto the road, temporarily unconscious), but he managed to complete the course—something that only two other light cars in his class, both of them Renaults, succeeded in doing.

The publicity value of such races was tremendous, and the Renault brothers benefited greatly from this as they began to pile up victories. Unfortunately, though, road races were dangerous, and tragedy would eventually strike.

⌒

Maurice Ravel loved automobiles—and factories. After all, his Swiss father was an engineer, and during Ravel's youth the father played a major role at one of the fledgling automobile factories in Levallois-Perret, a manufacturing area just over the northwestern border of Paris.

Maurice and his younger brother, Edouard, both enjoyed music, and the father—a music-lover himself—encouraged their musical interests and talents. Yet the father also took his sons to visit factories, which fascinated them. Later in life Maurice Ravel would say that it amazed him "that musicians have not yet captured the wonder of industrial progress."[6]

Maurice's younger brother became an engineer, like their father, but Maurice—with the support of his parents—followed his love of music into a career. This meant attending the Paris Conservatoire, where he repeatedly failed to take the piano prize (which sunk his aspirations for a career as a pianist), and where his compositions ran into headwinds as he attempted to integrate his extraordinary sense of musical color with new harmonies and rhythms.

Many of his compositions were and would continue to be rooted in his mother's Basque heritage, but Ravel's own musical vocabulary had by 1900 developed in a unique direction, one that startled many of his less venturesome colleagues. By this time, Ravel had gravitated to an avant-garde group of friends who called themselves the Apaches or Outcasts. Here among these young poets, painters, pianists, and composers, he was free to reach for new musical horizons.

Yet Ravel, who dressed elegantly and showed little outer sign of his inner radicalism, still had dreams of glory that were defined by the conservative values of the Paris Conservatoire. In the spring of 1900 he prepared for the Prix de Rome, a hugely demanding and fundamentally restrictive competition with two stages, the first requiring the contestant to write, in the space of one week, a four-part fugue on a given subject in addition to setting a short text for mixed chorus and orchestra. The five or six contestants remaining after the first round had to compose (within a month of strict isolation) the setting for an extended cantata text for solo voices and orchestra. The winner received a four-year stipend and would spend at least two of the four years at the Villa Médicis in Rome. The promise of a stipend, not to mention the honor involved, seemed well worth the trouble, even to such a determinedly unconventional composer as Ravel was turning out to be. After all, even the pioneering Claude Debussy had somehow choked back his natural musical instincts and managed to jump through the required hoops.[7]

Yet Ravel would not be able to duplicate Debussy's feat. Earlier in the year, during a preliminary examination, he had "patiently elaborated" a scene given to him with music that was "rather dull, prudently passionate, and its degree of boldness was accessible to those gentlemen of the Institute."[8] The noted composer Gabriel Fauré, who by this time was Ravel's composition teacher, understood Ravel's talent and was warmly supportive, but to no avail. Ravel encountered a buzz saw in the person of Théodore Dubois, the powerful director of the Conservatoire, who gave Ravel's composition a zero, commenting that it was "impossible, owing to terrible inaccuracies in writing." Ravel found it particularly disturbing that Dubois' criticisms were not even directly addressed to the work under consideration, but to an earlier Ravel work (Overture to Shéhérazade) that Dubois had heard performed in 1899 and detested. "Will it be necessary," Ravel added, "to struggle for 5 years against this influence?"[9]

As it turned out, the answer most unfortunately was "yes." Ravel was eliminated after the first round of the 1900 Prix de Rome competition, and he would endure other such defeats in the years to come—leading to a scandal that would shake Paris's musical world and blast the hidebound Paris Conservatoire into the twentieth century.

⌣

Like Claude Debussy, who was twelve years his senior and whom Ravel greatly admired, Ravel was influenced by the music of Mozart, Chopin, Chabrier, and the Russian composers, especially Mussorgsky, Borodin, and Rimsky-Korsakov. Both Ravel and Debussy held strong reservations about the music of Beethoven and Wagner as well as the works of those French turn-of-the-century composers led by Camille Saint-Saëns and Vincent d'Indy. It should be noted that although Saint-Saëns once extended a compliment to Ravel,[10] this aging composer generally regarded the music of Debussy and Ravel as a serious threat to the future of music.

In another respect like Debussy, Ravel was deeply influenced by the poetry of Stéphane Mallarmé and the writings of Edgar Allan Poe. Through his friendship with Misia Godebska Natanson, Ravel entered the cutting-edge literary and artistic milieu of Thadée Natanson's *Revue Blanche,* while Gabriel Fauré provided entrée to the exclusive salons of Madame René de Saint-Marceaux and the Princesse Edmond de Polignac. Noted for his "ironic, cool humor,"[11] twenty-five-year-old Maurice Ravel may have been encountering major roadblocks at the Conservatoire, but he was becoming known in the right artistic circles.

It is not clear exactly when Ravel first met Debussy. By the late 1890s the two had many common acquaintances, and their professional and social lives may well have casually brushed them across one another. Ravel had been deeply moved by Debussy's *Prelude to the Afternoon of a Faun,* recognizing it for the revolutionary work that it was. For his part, Debussy was present, or at least heard about, the premiere of Ravel's *Sites auriculaires* in 1898 and found it sufficiently interesting to ask its young composer for a copy of the manuscript.

Yet no actual meeting between the two seems to have occurred until sometime in 1900, when Debussy invited Ravel and several others to his home, where he played excerpts from *Pelléas et Mélisande,* the opera on which he had been laboring for seven long years. It was the beginning of a complex relationship, begun in friendship, that would link the two composers more closely in the public mind than either in the end would have preferred.

~

As a youngster, the future fashion designer Paul Poiret was acquainted with the Renault family, who—like the Poirets—owned a country house in Billancourt, southwest of Paris. The Poiret retreat would eventually become the property of the Renault auto works, but during these early years Billancourt still remained a tranquil escape for members of the prosperous bourgeoisie such as the Renaults and the Poirets.

Paul Poiret was only two years younger than Louis Renault but did not know him well. Poiret later recalled that "the Renault boys never showed themselves to those who went to visit their parents." Instead they preferred to stay in their workshop, among "machinery, coupling rods and pistons." Moreover, "if by chance one caught sight of them, they were covered with oil and grease."[12]

This certainly was not something that the future fashion titan could or would enjoy. Paul Poiret, son of a Paris cloth merchant, had dreamed of women's fashion for as long as he could remember. "Women and their toilettes drew me passionately," he later recalled, remembering that he "went through catalogues and magazines burning for everything appertaining to fashion."[13] His father was alarmed by his spendthrift and dandyish son and apprenticed him to an umbrella-maker, where young Poiret was given the most menial jobs. To keep his spirits up, he pinched bits of silk that fell when the umbrellas were cut, pinning them to a small wooden mannequin that his sympathetic sisters gave him. From there, he began to design "fantastical ensembles," some of which he eventually took on a dare to one of the leading Paris *couturières*, Madame Chéruit.

Madame Chéruit, a beauty who dazzled Poiret, was one of the first women to control a major Paris fashion house. She saw his designs, liked them, and paid him twenty francs apiece for them. "It was a gold mine," Poiret enthused, and with this encouragement he began to visit the other great dressmaking houses, including Doucet, Worth, Rouff, Paquin, and Redfern. One day Monsieur Doucet proposed that Poiret should produce for him alone. The youngster, who was still in his teens, became head of the tailoring department. "I am putting you in as one throws a dog into the water to teach him to swim," Doucet told him. "You must manage as best you can."[14] Poiret managed.

He soon learned the fine art of cultivating the patronage of leading actresses, using them to introduce and advertise his fashions on stage and off. He had always been enamored with the theater ("It was Paradise"),[15] and now he had the opportunity to dress stars such as Réjane and Sarah Bernhardt. "I had stormed the ramparts on the shoulders of Réjane," he later recalled.

It was an era of spectacular actresses and just as spectacular courtesans, the two categories frequently overlapping. Reigning supreme among Paris's *grandes courtisanes* at the turn of the century was a flawless beauty with the acquired name of Liane de Pougy. Like her somewhat lesser rivals, Emilienne d'Alençon and Caroline Otero (known as La Belle Otero), Liane had experienced adventure en route to stardom, including stints at the Folies Bergère and two bullets permanently lodged in her lovely thigh (courtesy of a jealous husband in her past). Liane regularly held court at Maxim's, where she and her similarly bejeweled rivals specialized in entrances on the arms of their latest conquests—men of great wealth, whether aristocrats, businessmen, or even the occasional crowned head (the Prince of Wales being the prime example of this species, much to his mother's dismay). In this spirit, Paul Poiret now took a beautiful mistress, whom he took care to dress fabulously, and in her company he began to frequent the most chic cafés and theaters along that portion of the Grands Boulevards known as The Boulevard (from the Madeleine to Rue Taitbout, and encompassing the Opéra Garnier). It was an expensive lifestyle, but Poiret was earning good money (even though he spent it as rapidly as he earned it), and it helped establish his image as a fashion designer to watch.

After a spell at the House of Doucet, Poiret went to the venerable House of Worth, once patronized by the Empress Eugénie. There, following the death of Charles Frederick Worth in 1895, Worth's sons (Gaston and Jean) carried on their estimable and profitable trade. Jean Worth continued in his father's footsteps, but Gaston had a different vision. Today, he told Poiret, the House of Worth's clientele no longer dressed exclusively in robes of state: "Sometimes," he said, "Princesses take the omnibus." But his brother, Jean Worth, refused to make concessions to modernity. "We are," Gaston continued, "like some great restaurant, which would refuse to serve aught but truffles. It is, therefore, necessary for us to create a department for fried potatoes."[16]

Poiret immediately grasped Gaston's vision and signed on with Worth, but Jean did not like what he saw of Poiret's work, even though it sold well. "In his eyes," Poiret explained, "I represented a new spirit, in which there was a force (he felt it) which was to destroy and sweep away his dreams."[17]

From the outset, Poiret had the same confidence of conquering Paris as had Picasso, only in different fields. In time, Poiret would indeed become known as *Le Magnifique*, or the King of Fashion. Yet it would not be until 1903 that he would establish his own fashion house and at last get to do things his way.

Rue Cortot, Montmartre. © J. McAuliffe

CHAPTER TWO

~

Bohemia on the Seine

(1900)

From the outset, Picasso's parents had never envisioned his departure for Paris as a permanent move. In fact, they had dug deep into their pockets to pay for his round-trip railway fare, leaving them little to live on for the rest of the month. But how often did such an honor come to a family—especially one in such modest circumstances as Picasso's?

Born in 1881 in Andalusia, Pablo Picasso was the oldest child and only son of José Ruiz Blasco, a charming and easygoing artist and painting instructor who spent much of his life chatting in cafés and producing endless paintings of pigeons. Don José never was able to make enough money to support the family—a large one, which for years included Picasso's maternal grandmother and two unmarried aunts. Yet what the father lacked in talent and drive, the son soon abundantly provided. Although little Pablo may not have been a genius from the outset, he showed sufficient promise to prompt his father to enroll him in a series of art schools. Here Pablo learned the basics and, by his early teens, was creating a flow of technically impressive although entirely conventional works. One of these, *Last Moments*—a sentimental painting of a priest attending a woman on her deathbed (which he later painted over with a masterpiece, *La Vie*)—was the one that gave him his entry to the Paris exposition.

Not surprisingly, Picasso quickly became bored with this kind of painting and found his art instruction increasingly stultifying. Fortunately for him, his father's search for jobs had brought the family to Barcelona, where Pablo became a loyal Catalan and an enthusiastic member of Barcelona's young and vibrant artistic community. By his late teens Pablo had turned his back on the conventional and assured artistic career that his father envisioned for him. It was now that the young man began to sign his works as Picasso rather than Ruiz—from his mother's maiden name.[1]

In preparing themselves for their journey to Paris, Picasso and Casagemas outfitted themselves in identical black corduroy suits with loose jackets and narrow pants, vented and buttoned at the bottom—evidently the latest thing in fashion for young Barcelonans, although in Paris it clearly marked them as foreigners. They promptly set out for Montparnasse, an emerging hub for artists in southern Paris, where they rented a studio in a building recommended by a friend. Yet after visiting another friend on the Butte of Montmartre, located on the far northern side of Paris, they immediately regretted this decision, having decided that Montmartre was where the action was. This friend convinced them to take over his apartment in a few days, after he returned to Barcelona. They agreed and, to climax an already-long day, settled up with the Montparnasse landlord and carted their luggage across Paris and up Montmartre's steep Rue Lepic. There they temporarily settled into a dodgy hotel while waiting for their more permanent lodging to open up.

Once into their friend's studio, the two newcomers wrote home to describe how hard they were working. "So long as there is daylight," wrote Casagemas (with input from Picasso), "we stay in the studio painting and drawing." Nighttime, of course, was a different matter, and Casagemas proceeded to paint a lively picture of Montmartre night life, including café concerts and drinking bouts. In conclusion, they enthused that their letter's recipient must "rob, kill, assassinate, do anything to come."[2]

In this letter, Casagemas listed the meager furnishings of their apartment, down to "a kilo of coffee and a can of peas."[3] What he did not mention were the three young women that he and Picasso found virtually in residence there. The three were models, in the parlance of Montmartre, and while they indeed modeled for artists, they also provided ready companionship for the two newcomers plus another friend from Barcelona who soon joined them. Germaine and Antoinette were sisters and spoke some Spanish, which was a help in communicating with the trio of Spaniards, especially with Picasso, who spoke no French. The third, Odette, spoke no Spanish but must have been a live wire. Attractive and promiscuous as well as easygoing about Picasso's own promiscuity, she and Picasso quickly paired off, as did Casagemas and Germaine—born Germaine Gargallo but now known as Germaine Florentin, having casually acquired and disposed of a husband along the way.

Picasso was only dallying with Odette, but Casagemas soon fell passionately in love with Germaine. Unfortunately, he seems to have been an inadequate lover—at least by Germaine's standards. Whether he was impotent, as has been conjectured, or merely overwhelmed by inadequacy in such close proximity to his macho hero Picasso, the relationship between Casagemas and Germaine became increasingly strained.

In the meantime, the trio of artists managed to stay solvent, partly by drawing on Casagemas's resources (provided by his wealthy and indulgent parents) but also by selling drawings and paintings that they had brought with them. Of the three, Picasso was the most successful. Soon after arriving in Paris he introduced himself to Pere Mañach, a Catalan who had recently established himself in Paris as a dealer in modern art. Mañach was greatly taken by Picasso's bullfighting scenes, and he was even more impressed when another art dealer, Berthe Weill, bought three of them from him for 100 francs. She in turn quickly resold these for 150 francs, prompting her to request a meeting with Picasso, where she took a look at his stock and made several more purchases.

Weill, who would become legendary in the modern art world, was just beginning her career as a dealer in modern art (she had recently opened her first gallery at 25 Rue Victor-Massé, at the foot of Montmartre, in what amounted to a bric-a-brac shop). In time she would become a staunch supporter of artists ranging from Matisse and Modigliani to Maurice Utrillo. Picasso was one of the first of the modern painters that she spotted. Most importantly for him, this first encounter prompted Pere Mañach to offer him a contract that would provide Picasso with a monthly payment of 150 francs. This seems to have been in exchange for Picasso's entire output; yet given Picasso's traditionally limited financial resources, this modest stipend promised for the first time in his life to give him a degree of financial independence.

Mañach sold Picasso's remarkable painting of the Moulin de la Galette to one of the most forward-looking collectors of the day, Arthur Huc of Toulouse, for 250 francs—a princely sum for a work by the young artist. By this time Picasso would have been well aware of Renoir's famous painting of the same subject, which then hung in Paris's Musée du Luxembourg. Toulouse-Lautrec had also painted this scene, with an entirely different technique and sensibility. Yet Picasso, even at the age of nineteen, had no qualms about painting this celebrated spot, challenging these giants on their own ground by bringing a dark and threatening interpretation to the scene. Picasso never had qualms about his own worth.

Early on, amid this intense round of work and play, Picasso made his way to the Paris exposition, where he spotted his own painting (which he thought was hung much too high) and took in the exposition's huge display of French art, including its large selection of modern works.[4] He soaked up

French art wherever he could, whether at the Louvre or the Musée du Luxembourg, which had become the state repository for recent French painting. He also checked out the many commercial galleries, especially those of progressive dealers such as Paul Durand-Ruel and Ambroise Vollard. He even managed to take the time to decorate the walls of his shabby Montmartre studio with a frieze of the temptation of St. Anthony—a subject that would periodically occupy him.

It was a heady experience, but Picasso had promised his family that he would return in time for Christmas, and he thought it important to bring Casagemas with him. Casagemas's state of mind was worrying his friends, especially Germaine, whom he insisted was his fiancée—even though (to her bafflement and his evident frustration) their relationship was largely platonic.

Casagemas's behavior definitely was disturbing. And it just as definitely signaled trouble ahead.

⌒

When Picasso arrived there, Montmartre still was "a real village, almost unknown to the uninitiated," as the poet J. P. Contamine de Latour later recalled. The poet had lived there before the turn of the century with his friend the composer Erik Satie, and several decades later he nostalgically reminisced that "this was the real bohemian life, with its uncertainties and expedients, but free and happy."[5]

Montmartre had remained outside the Paris orbit until the middle of the nineteenth century, when Baron Georges Haussmann, in his capacity as prefect of the Seine, undertook to reshape and modernize the City of Light. Haussmann created wide and spacious boulevards, uniform and gracious housing, and an array of expansive parks—all at the expense of the undulating terrain, winding streets, and ancient but shabby neighborhoods of Old Paris. Hammering his vision into reality, Haussmann in 1860 removed one of the two last walls that still enveloped Paris—an act that brought down the barrier between the city and many of the villages surrounding it. Officially and physically incorporated into Paris, Montmartre now became the city's eighteenth arrondissement.[6]

Until then, the Butte of Montmartre had been predominantly rural, although poverty-stricken urbanization—the detritus of industrialization—was beginning to crowd in at its foot. The anything-goes atmosphere of the brothel-filled neighborhoods of lower Montmartre also fostered an array of nightlife that drew bourgeois pleasure-seekers northward from their more sedate quarters in the heart of the city. Cabarets proliferated, the most famous being Le Chat Noir and the Mirliton, while dance halls such as the Moulin de la Galette and the Moulin Rouge featured rowdy can-can girls and other delights.

The quarries that once tunneled deep into the steep hillside of the Butte for gypsum, or plaster of Paris, had closed years before, leaving place-names such as Place Blanche (recalling the white of gypsum) along with a treacherous network of quarries that destabilized much of the Butte's southern face. Builders of the dazzling white Basilica of Sacré-Coeur (erected during the last part of the nineteenth century on the locally revered site of the 1871 Commune uprising) found it necessary to sink more than eighty massive stone pillars almost one hundred feet to bedrock in order to support the basilica's bulk and weight. They succeeded in their daunting project, but the portion of Montmartre's southern face directly below the basilica would remain scarred and desolate until Sacré-Coeur undertook to change this desert into the steeply pitched garden one sees today.

Up to the turn of the century, much of Montmartre's poverty and the more raucous of its nightlife proliferated at its base, along the outer boulevards (Clichy, Rochechouart) and the Pigalle quarter, leaving the upper reaches relatively untouched. The presence of Sacré-Coeur at Montmartre's peak probably had little to do with staving off this decidedly irreligious invasion, since Sacré-Coeur relied on the fervent devotion of supporters elsewhere. The Butte's residents, who either were impious bohemians or staunch supporters of the bloody and failed Commune uprising, had heartily opposed the basilica's construction from the outset, and most of them continued to ignore or despise it.

Life in Montmartre was undeniably gritty for the poets and artists who increasingly congregated there, drawn by its cheap rents and a growing community of like-minded bohemians. Yet it also retained some of the bucolic aura of its past. As Contamine de Latour recalled, "Once you'd climbed its rough steps, you felt as though you were hundreds of miles away from the capital. . . . Everything about it was rustic and peaceful. Streams ran down the middle of the streets, . . . and birds twittered in the luxuriant greenery that covered the old, ruined walls."[7]

The oldest of these walls belonged to the mansion called the Maison de Rose de Rosimond (now the Museum of Old Montmartre). Located on Rue Cortot, behind Sacré-Coeur and near the top of the Butte, this splendid old house had by the turn of the century become a haven for impecunious artists. Renoir lived here during the early years of his career, when he painted his *Dance at the Moulin de la Galette*. He later recalled that his only belongings there were "a mattress (which was put on the floor), a table, a commode, and a stove—to keep the model warm."[8] It was also on Montmartre that Renoir painted Suzanne Valadon, the free-spirited former circus performer, who modeled for his famous *Dance at Bougival*. Valadon went on to become a respected artist in her own right, breaking hearts along the way—especially that of Erik Satie, who never offered his heart to another woman. She had affairs with Renoir and others, and after one of these gave birth to a son, Maurice Utrillo, whose paternity she never acknowledged, but whose paintings of Montmartre would in turn bring him fame.

⁓

Unlike Picasso, Henri Matisse was tired and dejected as he gazed on the Paris exposition. The exposition had turned down his one submission for the contemporary painting section, and he was reduced to taking a job gilding a kilometer-long swag of laurel leaves for the Grand Palais.[9] Even this job did not last very long, for after three weeks his resentment boiled over and he was fired for insubordinate behavior.

Floundering for direction, Matisse turned to sculpture, using the same model that Auguste Rodin had used for his *Walking Man* and *St. John the Baptist*. In the course of this work (*The Serf*), Matisse visited Rodin at his Rue de l'Université studios, bringing several drawings with him. This meeting was not a success; Rodin was not impressed with Matisse's work, which he found insufficiently realistic. For his part, Matisse was put off by what he regarded as Rodin's assembly line production methods and commitment to an exterior rather than an internal reality. Matisse never returned.

The life of an artist most typically was a hard one, as Matisse had discovered. Born in 1869 in an area of northeastern France dominated by textile mills and sugar beet refineries, Matisse was the son of a hard-working grain and seed merchant. His father's family were weavers, and by the 1870s the town of Bohain in which he was raised had become famous for its luxury textiles. Matisse would always retain his love for beautiful fabrics, but his parents—especially his father—had little time for or interest in beauty.

It was only by chance that Matisse discovered his artistic ability, in a school art class, and given his stern upbringing he promptly rejected any possibility that he could develop it. It took many years of false starts, including a stint at law, before he again encountered a paint box—this time in a hospital, where he was recovering from a breakdown. "From the moment I held the box of colours in my hand, I knew this was my life," Matisse later wrote. "I dived in, to the understandable despair of my father."[10]

Secretly enrolling in art classes at a nearby free art school (founded for training impoverished weavers), Matisse progressed rapidly and soon outstripped the school's capabilities. Eventually his mother coaxed his father to give him an allowance for a year's study in Paris. Once there, Matisse enrolled in the Académie Julian, in preparation for admission to the all-important Ecole des Beaux-Arts, but found the Académie tradition-bound and stultifying. Despairing that he never would be able to paint, because he did not paint like anyone else, he nevertheless persevered. En route to self-discovery, he discovered Goya, whose work convinced him that he could become a painter. He also discovered a pretty model, Caroline Joblaud, with whom he began to live and who bore him his beloved daughter, Marguerite.

By this time Matisse had twice failed his entrance exams to the Ecole des Beaux-Arts and had long overstayed the original year that his father had allowed him. The illegitimate child and the shame it brought to Matisse's deeply religious and conventional parents served as the breaking point with Matisse père, but life gradually began to change for the better as Matisse learned to paint in the accepted way and experienced some success. On his third try he passed his Beaux-Arts entrance exam, and around the same time he successfully submitted several paintings to the Salon de la Société Nationale des Beaux-Arts, where he was elected an associate member. The Ecole des Beaux-Arts awarded him a third prize for composition, and the state was beginning to buy his work. Suddenly fame and fortune seemed possible.

And then in the late 1890s, under the influence of van Gogh's friend John Peter Russell and the grand old Impressionist Camille Pissarro, Matisse made fundamental changes in his technique, adopting simplified shapes and bright color—a breakthrough that would influence his work for the rest of his life. Unfortunately this new direction earned him no plaudits among the traditionalists, and all possibility for commercial success quickly evaporated. His relationship with Caroline grew correspondingly rocky. She and his friends thought he had gone mad, and Matisse in turn had bouts of severe self-doubt.

It was after Caroline's departure that Matisse met and married Amélie Parayre. Amélie, who was from a politically and culturally progressive family of some prominence (although little wealth) in Toulouse and Paris, had always dreaded a conventional marriage. She need not have worried; her marriage to Matisse was hardly conventional. Not only did he have an illegitimate child, but his art was radically different and unlikely to sell. Yet Amélie believed in him, and her parents approved. Even Matisse's parents were pleased by the connection. The newlyweds honeymooned in London, where they viewed the Turner paintings, and then spent many months in Toulouse and Corsica, where Matisse painted with increasingly vibrant color—paintings that he did not show to any but his closest friends. Despite his fastidious appearance (complete with neatly manicured beard and gold-rimmed spectacles), Matisse was making a radical departure into the unknown.

Their son Jean was born early in 1899, after which the couple returned to Paris, where Matisse encountered the same old problems—no work and no sales. Still, despite his poverty he managed to buy a wonderful painting by Cézanne (*Three Bathers*) after Amélie, understanding the painting's importance to him, let him pawn a treasured ring. Many years later, when he gave this painting to the City of Paris, he said that it had "supported him morally at critical moments in my venture as an artist; I have drawn from it my faith and my perseverance."[11]

Amélie went to work by starting a hat shop, and she agreed to take in Marguerite when Caroline could no longer care for the child. In addition, their second son, Pierre, was born in the summer of 1900. Fortunately Amélie and Marguerite soon became close, and the six-year-old managed to help her stepmother significantly. Yet even though the babies stayed with their grandparents (Jean with Matisse's mother, and Pierre with Amélie's family), Amélie was greatly overworked and Matisse was at the end of his rope as the new century began.

∿

Unlike Matisse, by 1900 Auguste Rodin had achieved worldwide artistic renown. Reinforcing this at the Paris exposition, he set up a well-attended private exhibit of his own works, located right outside the exposition's main gates.

By this time Rodin had also acquired a well-earned reputation of another sort. His great love, the sculptor Camille Claudel, no longer was part of his life and, indeed, was rapidly sinking into paranoia, but there were many others eager to take her place. As Rodin's hundreds of erotic drawings showed, he had a huge appetite for sex and thoroughly enjoyed watching and drawing women in the most explicit poses. The Countess Anna de Noailles, who posed for her portrait bust, wrote that she was worn out "from the way he looks at me, the way he imagines me nude; from the necessity of fighting for my dignity before this hunter's gaze."[12]

Some have seen Rodin's intense and overwhelming love for women as a celebration of women's strength rather than as a declaration of their weakness and dependence. Others, like the keenly perceptive Anna de Noailles, sensed the dangers of his gaze—even though he seems to have maintained a prudent hands-off policy with upper-class women. The future fashion king Paul Poiret, who frequently took the Paris commuter boat with Rodin (Poiret going between Paris and Billancourt, Rodin between Paris and Meudon), described the famed sculptor as "a little thickset god."[13]

Whatever the correct view of Rodin, it was clear by the early years of the century that women found him exceptionally attractive. In 1900, at the age of sixty, he was involved with an appealing young artist and model named Sophie Postolska, who was his first lover after the end of his affair with Claudel. But Postolska was not the only woman in his life: Isabelle Perronnet, the former mistress and model of the sculptor Alexandre Falguière, made herself available to Rodin soon after Falguière's death in the spring of 1900,[14] and there were many more, including, of course, Rodin's first mistress, who had remained with him all these years—the much-neglected Rose Beuret.

∼

While Rodin had his own personal triumph at the Paris exposition, the Impressionists at long last received official recognition by being included along with the traditional artists of the Salon in a huge exhibit of French art.[15]

It amounted to a significant breakthrough, but at the moment Claude Monet had other concerns. In arranging for his departure to London in February 1900, he left explicit instructions for his gardener at Giverny: to sow about three hundred pots of poppies, sixty of sweet pea, sixty of white agrimony, and thirty of yellow agrimony, in addition to blue sage and blue water lilies (the latter in beds in the greenhouse). From February 15 to 25 the gardener was to "lay the dahlias down to root," planting those with shoots before Monet returned. "Don't forget the lily bulbs," Monet added.[16]

Monet's garden at Giverny was a focal point of his life, and he never overlooked any detail of its welfare and appearance, even when preparing for a major journey. Once in London, Monet painted from the balcony of his room at the Savoy Hotel and from nearby Charing Cross Hospital, delighting—and just as often despairing—at the fluctuations of the light, the mists' varying colors, and the abrupt changes in the weather.

Monet had been a penniless exile when he first visited London thirty years before, at the time of the Franco-Prussian War. Now he was a celebrity, and London society treated him as such. He enjoyed the adulation, but his first concern was for his painting, which he approached with a volatile mixture of joy and trepidation. His wife, the patient Alice, was accustomed to receiving letters from him that veered as rapidly from one mood to another as did the weather, and usually were directly related. Writing to Alice in late March, Monet told her that he had been productive—he would be bringing back eight full crates of his work, containing eighty canvases—but that she should not expect to see finished products. "If I'd had the right idea in the first place and had started afresh each time the effect changed, I would have made more progress," he wrote her. Instead, he added, "I dabbled around and altered paintings that were giving me trouble which as a result are nothing more than rough drafts."[17]

He badly wished to complete his unfinished work, but Monet, now sixty years old, was exhausted. Day after day of unrelenting painting on his feet, and the constant anxiety over whether he could correctly capture the fleeting effect, had taken their toll. The subtle light of the short days of winter now changed into the brighter light and longer days of spring, and he could do no more. He returned to Giverny in early April, where his wife and family—and his garden—awaited him.

⟶

Another indefatigable worker was Sarah Bernhardt. In 1899 the playwright Edmond Rostand, author of *Cyrano de Bergerac* as well as of *La Princesse lointaine*, in which Bernhardt starred, gave a description of a typical day for this phenomenon, who by then was well into her fifties.

Rostand takes Bernhardt from her fur-covered entrance to the theater, where she energizes a crowd of theater folk, arranges scenes, erupts in anger, insists on "everything being done over again," and then smiles, drinks tea, and "draws tears from case-hardened actors" before retiring to her dressing room, where the decorators are waiting. There she upends their plans, collapses, and then rushes to the fifth floor, where she startles the costumer by making up a costume before returning to her room and teaching the awe-struck extras how to arrange their hair. Not wasting a moment, she busies herself with various tasks while someone reads a proposed play and multitudes of letters to her, weeps over some of them, and consults with the wig-maker before returning to the stage and reducing the electrician to "a state of temporary insanity." From there she proceeds to demolish a blundering super, returns to her dressing room for dinner (which she does not have time to finish), and then dresses for the evening performance while listening to the manager's sales report from the other side of the curtain. She gives her all to the performance, while conducting business between acts, remains at the theater until three in the morning to make arrangements, and then returns home where, to her infinite amusement, someone is waiting to read her a five-act play. She listens, weeps, accepts it, and retires to bed. But then, finding that she cannot sleep, she gets up and studies the part.[18]

For almost twenty years this dynamo had managed a series of her own theaters, culminating in the Théâtre des Nations on the Place du Châtelet, which she unhesitatingly renamed the Théâtre Sarah Bernhardt. After all, why not? It was her theater, and as a star of her magnitude, she had no reason in the world not to name it after herself.

At an age when others would have been winding down their careers, Bernhardt continued to set new challenges for herself, including taking on the role of Hamlet—a most controversial role for a woman, and especially one well past her youth. There were critics who pointed out that she was twice the age of the young man whom Shakespeare envisioned, and added that the Bard most certainly had not contemplated a woman in the role. But audiences loved her, and the production was a huge success; she then took it on tour.

With the new century Bernhardt reached for yet more challenges and found them in Rostand's most recent play, *L'Aiglon*, the tragic tale of the son and heir of Napoleon—the young Eaglet, or *L'Aiglon*—who died at the age of twenty-one. Like *Hamlet*, this was a trouser role, requiring Bernhardt to dress in the tight-fitting jacket and breeches of the era. She did not hesitate, and in anticipation of the role wore her costume (designed by Paul Poiret), complete with boots and sword, for weeks before the play opened. She had always been slim, and to her credit she still managed to look creditable as a young man. Again audiences loved her, and the play was a hit, opening in March 1900 and continuing for 250 performances.

⌒

The family of young Charles de Gaulle was not accustomed to visiting the theater—any theater. It was a straight-laced family with roots in the dour textile town of Lille, in northern France. Charles's mother did not allow dancing in their home and considered the theater an invention of the devil. Any sort of frivolity ran counter to the family dictates of stern morality and conservative Catholicism. And yet, for his tenth birthday, young Charles's father took him to see Sarah Bernhardt in *L'Aiglon*.

The son of devout Catholics and monarchists, Charles was born in 1890, the third child of what would become a family of four sons and one daughter. Although France had not had a monarch for decades,[19] Charles's parents were among a staunch minority that yearned for the monarchy's return. Along with this brand of politics came a large helping of nationalism, patriotism, and respect for the military. All of these elements came together in *L'Aiglon*, which Bernhardt milked for all its worth of drum-rolling patriotism. In addition, *L'Aiglon* had a terrific death scene, Bernhardt's specialty. Charles's father, at least, must have been convinced that it would be worth seeing, and so little Charles de Gaulle saw Sarah Bernhardt in *L'Aiglon* as a birthday treat.

The de Gaulle family lived in the fifteenth arrondissement, near the border of the seventh arrondissement—not far from the Eiffel Tower, Les Invalides, and the Ecole Militaire, the elite military school that Bonaparte himself had attended. Charles's father often took the family to Les Invalides for outings, and Charles's life revolved around his parish church, Saint-François-Xavier (a substantial church in the 7th arrondissement), and his schools. Given his parents' ardent Catholicism, the first school he attended had been run by the Brothers of the Christian Schools of St. Thomas Aquinas. When he turned ten—about the time that he attended the performance of *L'Aiglon*—Charles began to attend the far-more-rigorous Jesuit Collège de l'Immaculée-Conception, on Rue de Vaugirard (15th), where his father was a teacher.

Despite the efforts of the Third Republic to oust the Jesuits and secularize education, nearly all of France's former Jesuit *collèges*, or secondary schools, were back to full strength by the time young Charles was entering their halls. They drew their support from those who, like the de Gaulle family, appreciated their staunch opposition to secularism and republicanism as well as to the more liberal and socially conscious Catholicism that was beginning to emerge. As the twentieth century opened, right-wing Catholics and fervent monarchists viewed the social order with increasing contempt and alarm. In their eyes, the Third Republic's anticlericalism was undermining the Christian faith and everything it supported. Consequently, the rigorous and conservative education that the Jesuits offered appealed mightily to those who appreciated the discipline and the tough moral code that it enforced.

The school that Charles was about to enter had managed to evade the Third Republic's attempts to eradicate it by clever maneuvering within the letter of the law. The Collège de l'Immaculée-Conception (often simply referred to as Vaugirard, after its street address) turned itself into a private company with sympathetic laymen in charge. This new company hired the administrators and teachers, and by the time Charles arrived, it was as if nothing had changed. Or almost nothing, since the memory of what had happened left a perceptible shadow over this endangered community.

Charles received a good education there, but he unquestionably was molded by the values—and fears—that surrounded him. As he grew to manhood he would exemplify the ramrod-straight values and upright life that had been instilled in him. Yet it would become increasingly apparent that these clear-cut values and unforgiving moral code would have an additional con-sequence, reinforcing a prominent authoritarian streak that he had displayed since childhood.

〜

In June 1900, the Third Republic's Senate passed a bill of general amnesty to all the participants in the wrenching Dreyfus Affair of the 1890s, in which the army had framed and court-martialed an innocent Jewish captain for treason.[20] The problem, though, was that both the guilty and the innocent would be forgiven, thus denying justice to the innocent. An anguished Dreyfus—released from prison but only pardoned rather than cleared of all question of guilt—wrote the Senate that the proposed legislation would only protect the guilty and derail his own prospects for justice. Freedom without honor, he protested, meant nothing to him. Emile Zola, who had suffered greatly as a result of his own efforts on Dreyfus's behalf, protested in a similar vein. But France's prime minister, Pierre Waldeck-Rousseau, was looking for peace rather than justice, in the attempt to quiet the passions that had ruptured France for so long.

"The view that one can save a people from the disease that gnaws it by decreeing that the disease no longer exists is myopic indeed," Zola protested, in a public letter to the French president, Emile Loubet, and published in the newspaper L'Aurore.[21] Yet the passions surrounding the Affair did in fact subside once Dreyfus was released from prison and amnesty took place. Indeed, most French quickly forgot. Unfortunately, as a consequence of these compromises, Captain Alfred Dreyfus would not receive justice for many more years.

〜

Marcel Proust, that delicate asthmatic with refined sensibilities, seemed to take no particular note of the new century. Instead, he immersed himself in an intensive study of the works of John Ruskin, England's formidable nineteenth-century art, architecture, and social critic; this in turn directed Proust's attention to France's great cathedrals. That spring, in a kind of Ruskin pilgrimage, Proust visited the cathedral of Amiens, where he sketched in words the appearance of its great façade at different times and in different lights—much as Monet, in his great series, had painted the subtle differences in shadings of the cathedral of Rouen. Amiens' façade, Proust wrote, was "blue in the mist, brilliant in the morning, sunsoaked and sumptuously gilded in the afternoon, rose and already softly nocturnal at sunset."[22]

Yet Proust, whose beloved mother was Jewish, had earlier taken what was for him an unusual degree of interest in the Dreyfus Affair. Although Proust was raised in his father's Catholic faith,[23] he and his brother were active in protesting Dreyfus's conviction, circulating a petition for retrial that quickly received three thousand signatures. Eventually Proust would recall the terrible acrimony of these years, which he depicted in his masterwork *In Search of Lost Time*, especially in its third volume, *The Guermantes Way*. There he would skewer an assorted variety of the *gratin*, or upper crust, of Parisian society as his characters react—with anger, varying degrees of prejudice, and confusion—to this social and political earthquake.[24]

Still, despite his brief fling at activism, by the opening years of the new century Proust was focusing on Ruskin rather than Dreyfus. During these years, despite his asthma, he would visit Venice and keep an active social life. It was now that he became a friend and ardent admirer of Anna de Noailles, the graceful, nerve-ridden, and fascinating young countess who was about to publish her first book of poems, and who already was becoming the toast of literary Paris. Early on, Proust had decided that her ardent pro-Dreyfusism was in her favor, but it was her poetry that won him over. "I was awaiting your poems with the anxious certainty of one who knows he will have new beauty to admire," he wrote her one evening past midnight. "I was as sure of that as the prince in the fairy tale, for whom the bees who worked and made the rose bushes bloom, was sure of having honey and roses."[25]

〜

Honey and roses were the last things on José-Maria Sert's mind when he arrived in Paris just before the turn of the century. This Spanish painter, who unlike Picasso had a fortune at his disposal, soon discovered that his combined assets of wealth, flamboyance, and charm were sure tickets into the colorful and decadent core of the avant-garde. He briefly encountered Misia Godebska Natanson, but he did not realize at the time that this beautiful woman of Polish ancestry would eventually add "Sert" to her list of married names—en route to becoming one of the foremost Parisian patrons of the performing arts.

As 1900 opened, Misia was in fact in the process of shedding one husband and acquiring another, a process that involved far more unpleasantness than she would have preferred. Whether or not she loved Thadée Natanson, her first husband and the editor of the influential *Revue Blanche*, was probably beside the point. He had rescued her from a difficult home life, complete with negligent father and unpleasant stepmother, and he had additionally provided her with a circle of literary and artistic friends over which she enjoyed presiding. Men adored Misia, and although she seems to have been indifferent to sex, she thrived on adoration. Natanson's friends, including the painters Pierre Bonnard and Edouard Vuillard, provided sufficiently worshipful attention, and it was only Natanson's looming bankruptcy that threw a pall over what seems to have been an idyllic life.

It was then that two interrelated events occurred that changed Misia's world: Natanson's money problems and the entrance of Alfred Edwards. Edwards was a boorish and even brutish man of murky background and enormous wealth who was accustomed to getting what he wanted, and Misia was what he wanted. A wife of his own and a husband of hers presented little difficulty, so far as he was concerned, and before long, Natanson's financial difficulties provided exactly the leverage Edwards needed. Soon Natanson had the financial backing he required, and Misia became—at first unwillingly—Edwards's mistress and then, eventually, his wife.

⌒

It was in the exclusive salon of Madame René de Saint-Marceaux, during the autumn or winter of 1900, that Maurice Ravel found himself playing the piano for a young American named Isadora Duncan, who danced with uninhibited grace to his music.

Isadora, who had recently arrived in Paris, was at first enchanted with the city, while the city—especially those artistic circles that gravitated to the most prestigious salons—was enchanted with her. She was young and charmingly innocent, making easy conquests of the sophisticated and the jaded, who found her irresistible.

Raised in a carefree bohemian atmosphere in Oakland, California, Isadora had realized from an early age that she wanted to dance, and to dance in a special way—free from what she passionately believed were the affected and restrictive movements of classical ballet. She brought her close-knit family with her during the trying times of her early career, which included a humiliating stint in vaudeville. Now they were together in Paris, and Isadora was ecstatic. She felt on the brink of discovering the true essence of dance, and in pursuit of this knowledge she raced from one source of cultural enrichment to another, from the Louvre to the Museum of the History of Paris, from the Cluny Museum of the Middle Ages to the Bibliothèque Nationale. She adored the Greek vases in the Louvre, and even the prospect of a visit there sent her dancing en route, through the Luxembourg Gardens. "I burned with apostolic fire for my art," she later wrote.[26]

And yet, despite this cultural banquet, she soon was dissatisfied with Paris. Rodin's sculptures, which she first encountered at his private exhibition on

Place de l'Alma, just outside the entrance to the Paris exposition, convinced her that she had at last encountered a fellow-being whose search for truth was akin to her own. But apart from Rodin, she was disappointed in the Parisians she had met. "I thought I might find some teacher, some help there," she wrote a friend in London, "but it was all stupid, vanity and vexation." As for the dancers at the Paris Opera, she was appalled. "They do not dance for love," she wrote. "They do not dance for the Gods."[27]

⌒

Great throngs had visited the Paris exposition by the time it closed on November 12. Most came for the excitement and the entertainment, although artists young and old, including Picasso, had come with the specific intent of locating their pictures and seeing how well (or how poorly) they were displayed. Monet, who was inundated with work and increasingly beset with eye problems, seems not to have found time to make the trip from Giverny, but Zola came and enjoyed playing the tourist, taking great delight in his camera and photographing the exposition in the kind of detail that he had previously reserved for his books. His daughter, Denise, later recalled that in October, "after dinner at the Eiffel Tower, we attended the electric light show and saw the illuminated fountains of the Château d'Eau."[28] Even the rapidly declining Toulouse-Lautrec attended, enthusing over the moving sidewalk that allowed him to move without the obvious aid of his wheelchair.

For two attendees, at least, the exposition was a revelation. The American historian Henry Adams (of the renowned New England Adams family) was transfixed by the Gallery of Machines. Until the dynamo, he mused, the Virgin "had acted as the greatest force the Western world ever felt." But now there was the magnificent and terrible dynamo, which for him became a symbol of infinity, "a moral force, much as the early Christians felt the Cross."[29]

Young Gabriel Voisin, trained as an architect and hired as a designer and draughtsman for the exposition, had a similar moment of revelation when he encountered a team of workmen setting up the *Avion III*, Clément Ader's flying machine. It was a beautiful creation, built of linen and wood along the lines of an enormous bat, propelled by a four-blade propeller and run by a lightweight steam engine.[30] Voisin, who had never before seen a flying machine, asked if he could sit in the cabin, and one of the workmen let him climb in. "Often I have been moved," Voisin later wrote, "but on that day I was overcome by an enthusiasm which I had never known before. In my hands were the mysterious controls which could give life to this incomparable creation."[31] He now knew what he wanted to do with his life, and his decision would be momentous—for the French aircraft industry, and for the nation as a whole during the Great War.

Yet despite the exposition's undoubted success, its impact on most of those who attended was fleeting. Of the multitudes of buildings erected for the exposition, only the Grand Palais and the Petit Palais would most memorably remain, and even these would never attain iconic status. Despite all the hoop-la and expenditure, it would be Eiffel's grand contribution to the 1889 exposition that would continue to capture the spirit of Paris and the hearts of those who visited it.

Count Harry Kessler, the ultra-sophisticated and peripatetic German aristocrat who was as much at home in Paris as in Berlin, underscored this point. "The general impression of the unfortunate exhibition has become a blur for me," he wrote in his diary, adding how disturbing he found the "disconnected, wild mishmash of the buildings' profiles and ornamentation." By contrast, he found the Eiffel Tower's "calm majesty" reassuring.[32]

As he fondly observed, from a misty nighttime vantage point on the Pont de Grenelle: "From here the picture of the Exhibition is most grandiose, most fantastic, a sea of light on the still river, out of which . . . the Eiffel Tower rises, immeasurably tall and bathed completely in light."[33]

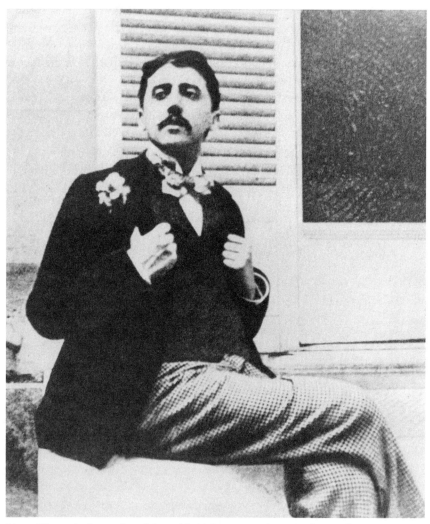

Marcel Proust in the garden of Reynaldo Hahn, 1905. Photo Credit: Snark / Art Resource, NY. © Art Resource, NY.

~

CHAPTER THREE

Death of a Queen

(1901)

On January 22, 1901, Queen Victoria died, ending an era. Monarch of Great Britain for sixty-three years and Empress of India for twenty-five, her extended family of nine children and forty-two grandchildren linked England to virtually all the great royal and noble houses of Europe, most notably those of Germany and Russia.

Claude Monet was present in London at the time of the queen's funeral on February 2 and wrote his wife, Alice, that John Singer Sargent had invited him to view the funeral procession from the balcony of a friend's house. Neither Monet nor Sargent had reckoned on the crowds, which made it nearly impossible to meet up, and so Monet proceeded alone on foot, having decided that it would be impossible to find a cab. Upon reaching his destination, Monet met "a great American writer living in England, who spoke wonderful French and was very kind to me, explaining everything." The name of this gentleman, Monet informed Alice, was Henry James. Sargent let him know that James was "the greatest English writer," but a clearly puzzled Monet asked Alice, "Does Butler [their American son-in-law] know him?"[1]

The house was crowded with people on every floor, and the streets were mobbed, but Monet reported that he was glad he had been there to see it, "for it was a unique sight." He added with his artist's eye that the "weather was superb, a light mist, with a glimpse of sunshine and St. James's Park in the background." Adding to the color, the red-coated cavalry officers stood out against the black of the crowd. Much to his surprise, instead of crepe or black, "every house [was] decorated with mauve fabric, the hearse . . . covered in gold and coloured drapes." Exclaiming over what a feast of color it was, he added, "How wonderful to have been able to do a rapid sketch."[2]

⌒

Picasso returned to Barcelona with Carles Casagemas for Christmas, and then the two departed for a visit to Picasso's birthplace, Málaga. But after a few days, Casagemas's dependence on him was more than Picasso could handle, and he packed his friend off to family in Barcelona and headed for Madrid. This left the unstable and badly depressed Casagemas to return first to Barcelona, then to Paris, without him.

Casagemas had spent his days away from Paris in binge drinking and writing passionate proposals of marriage to Germaine, who already was married and in any case was not interested in marrying or even living with him. During Casagemas's absence their third roommate, Manuel Pallarès, had moved from their studio on Rue Gabrielle to a dingy apartment farther to the west, at 130 Boulevard de Clichy, where he agreed to put up Casagemas when he arrived in Paris in mid-February. Germaine was not in raptures over his arrival, and soon Casagemas announced that he had decided to return to his family in Barcelona. To celebrate his departure, he invited Pallarès and several others, including Germaine, to a dinner at the Hippodrome, a neighborhood hangout on the Boulevard de Clichy. It seemed a good solution to Casagemas's imbroglio with Germaine, and it promised a free meal. Those invited enthusiastically agreed.

Everyone at their table that evening seemed to be having a good time—although Casagemas seemed unusually nervous, giving an edge to the proceedings. Still, all was well until, after rising to give a brief speech, Casagemas suddenly took a pistol from his pocket and aimed it directly at Germaine. She promptly dived under the table and hid behind Pallarès. Casagemas fired, crying "This is for you!" and although Pallarès managed to deflect the gun, Germaine slid motionless to the floor. Thinking that he had killed her, Casagemas then cried, "And this is for me!" and shot himself in the head.

It was ghastly, even though Germaine survived unharmed—either she had played dead to save herself, or the explosion had knocked her to the ground. But Casagemas died later that night at the nearby Hôpital Bichat. Later, his grieving friends buried him in Montmartre Cemetery.

Picasso had not been present for this shocking event, but its impact on him was enormous. He was stunned. And for the next several years the tragic specter of Casagemas would haunt him.

⌒

Another death in Montmartre's artistic community, although not unexpected, caused a great deal of sadness that autumn. Henri de Toulouse-Lautrec, the artist who had produced so many unforgettable images of the theaters, brothels, and dance halls of Montmartre, drank himself to death at the age of thirty-six.

Although from an aristocratic family, Toulouse-Lautrec had sought and found acceptance among the artists and low-life of Montmartre, who took in stride his deformity (child-sized legs on an adult-sized torso) and his addiction to liquor and drugs. As his good friend Thadée Natanson later recalled, "what with his small stature, his sweet disposition, his laugh, his boyishness, his lisp, but especially his height," his favorite prostitutes loved to mother him.[3] In turn, Toulouse-Lautrec recognized the family-like aspects of these brothels, and he painted their inhabitants with humanity, although never with sentimentality.

Yet as the years went by, his addictions and escapades escalated from the merely amusing to the frankly alarming. Stories abounded of Henri setting on fire petrol-soaked wads of rags in his landlady's toilets, or of Henri concocting ever-more-lethal cocktails for his parties—most notably a shattering combination of cognac and absinthe appropriately dubbed "the Earthquake." More disturbing were his hallucinations, his sudden attacks of rage, and his growing paranoia.

The artistic set that revolved around Thadée and Misia Natanson counted themselves among Henri's closest friends and worried extensively about him, especially after he began to experience unmistakable signs of syphilis as well as of advanced alcoholism. His temporary stay in a private asylum (which he referred to as his prison) led to a brief improvement, but once released he immediately reverted to his old ways.

Toulouse-Lautrec had laughed heartily throughout his life, even at the cruel joke that life had played on him. But by the end, as Thadée Natanson recalled, Henri de Toulouse-Lautrec no longer was laughing. By the end, "the old joy [was] no longer there."[4]

〜

After failing to meet Conservatoire requirements by winning a prize in two consecutive fugue competitions, Ravel was expelled from Gabriel Fauré's composition class—despite Fauré's protests that his student was making excellent progress. After this humiliation, Ravel remained on as an auditor in Fauré's class while he worked with Raoul Bardac, Debussy's future stepson, on a transcription of Debussy's Nocturnes for two pianos—"Debussy's wonderful Nocturnes," as he enthusiastically described them to a friend.[5]

Ravel also prepared once again for the Prix de Rome. This time he was considered a serious contender, but the Conservatoire director, Théodore Dubois, was on the jury, and given Dubois' disparagement of Ravel's previous compositions, this did not bode well. Ravel ultimately ended up with third prize, and although he confessed to a friend that his orchestration had been hastily done, he added that "almost everyone here would have given me the first prize. (Massenet himself voted for me every time.)"[6] Saint-Saëns was also on the jury and had been especially impressed with Ravel's cantata: he observed to a friend that "the third prize winner, whose name is Ravel, appears to me to be destined for an important career."[7]

Saint-Saëns would soon change his mind. Eight months after the Prix de Rome competition, Ravel published his extraordinary, and extraordinarily demanding, work for the piano, *Jeux d'eau* (*Fountains*, or *Water Games*), which he dedicated to Fauré. Saint-Saëns took a look at the published music and was not pleased with Ravel's achievement. He promptly declared that *Jeux d'eau* was an unlovely piece of music, completely cacophonous. Given Saint-Saëns's importance in the music world, this was not a good omen for a young composer like Ravel.

⁓

In May, Debussy received the news that every struggling composer longs for—the commitment from a major producer to present his work. In this case the word came from Albert Carré, director of the Opéra-Comique, and the work that Carré promised to produce was Debussy's opera *Pelléas et Mélisande*.

Throughout the long years of the 1890s, Debussy had frequently despaired about *Pelléas*'s future as he endlessly worked on the opera and performed it for friends. Now Carré's approval meant that *Pelléas* would indeed receive a staging with a major Paris opera company.[8]

André Messager was the influential person who had helped bring this miracle about. Messager, who had admired Debussy's music ever since first hearing *La Damoiselle élue* in 1893, was the recently appointed chief conductor and music director of the Opéra-Comique. In 1898, soon after his appointment, he had encouraged Carré to visit Debussy and listen to extracts from *Pelléas*.

Disappointingly, nothing came of Carré's first visit, and Debussy had to wait three more years before Carré committed himself—a difficult time, during which Debussy felt that he was being kept "on a string indefinitely."[9] But in April 1901, Messager encouraged Carré to come again, and this time things clicked. Carré made his offer, and a thrilled Debussy wrote his good friend Pierre Louÿs (the italics are his): "*I have a written guarantee from M. A. Carré that he will put on Pelléas et Mélisande next season.*"[10]

Pelléas et Mélisande, Debussy's operatic adaptation of the popular 1893 Symbolist play by Belgian playwright Maurice Maeterlinck, is a story of forbidden love and doomed lovers. Prince Golaud discovers the lovely but enigmatic Mélisande in the forest and immediately falls in love with and marries her. Then, as is often the case in these stories, she proceeds to fall in love with Golaud's brother, Pelléas. Golaud suspects the lovers and in the end kills Pelléas and wounds Mélisande, who in turn dies.

Unlike the wildly popular Wagnerian operas or the fashionable Italian and French operas of the day, *Pelléas* takes place in a dreamy and eerily tranquil setting, shadowed and draped in gauze, with towers by the sea and the sounds of trickling water. For Maeterlinck and other Symbolists, landscape was a reflection of the human state, mirroring the drama's psychological development. Shrouded in mystery, these characters move in a world of hesitation and dread, "because they know that nothing is certain in the world or in their own hearts."[11]

Debussy, whose literary and artistic preferences leaned decisively toward Symbolism, was quite taken with Maeterlinck's play, which showed the influence of a range of muses that Debussy admired, from the Pre-Raphaelites to Edgar Allan Poe. Debussy especially admired Maeterlinck's belief that "art should explore mystery," and several years earlier had described his ideal poet as "one who states only half of what is to be said, and allows me to graft my dream on to his."[12]

A number of other young Frenchmen entertained dreams of their own at this time, although many—including Louis Renault—held quite different ones from those of Claude Debussy. Renault was still an intrepid auto mechanic, but he was also rapidly evolving into a dashing figure in the daring new sport of auto racing. In the 1901 Paris–Berlin race, he came in first in the light-car class and seventh in overall classification—a significant achievement, proving that his small Renault autos could combine speed with toughness and dependability, especially in cornering and on hills. The orders were picking up, and the Renault brothers had to double the size of their Billancourt factory just to keep up with demand.

Still, there was a distinct downside to these races that was beginning to offset the favorable publicity they bestowed on both the victors and their machines. The number of accidents was increasing, right along with the

automobiles' speed. Not only competitors but also eager onlookers (who typically crowded along the most dangerous curves) were falling victim to this
new craze. In the 1901 Paris–Berlin race, a small boy was knocked down at
a corner and later died, leading newspapers in both Germany and France to
come out forcefully against racing. "At this moment," fulminated *La Petite
Républicaine*, "seventy-one dangerous madmen are driving over open country
at speeds of express trains. These maniacs," it continued, drive at fifty miles
per hour and "knock down . . . anything in their path."[13]

Not surprisingly, the racers themselves were undeterred. "The enthusiasm
of the crowd was terrific," reported one elated driver. He reported that he
and his fellow drivers were "absolutely smothered with flowers thrown by the
villagers in both countries," and champagne, food, and cigars greeted them at
the various control points along the route.[14]

It may have been a heady experience for those who successfully completed
the race, but the specter of danger loomed over the coming year's Paris–Vienna race, which would take the drivers across the difficult and dangerous
Alpine passes of Switzerland and Bavaria.

∽

More placidly, back in Paris, a young man by the name of André Citroën
had recently graduated from Paris's prestigious Ecole Polytechnique and, in
1901, began his required year of military service in an artillery regiment of
the French army. Although demonstrably intelligent, Citroën had yet to
show special flair in any direction. He had never been consumed with a desire to tinker with engines or to race automobiles, like his future rival Louis
Renault. It is not even completely clear exactly when he made his discovery
of double helical gearwheels, whether immediately before or during his army
career. In any case, all agree that this significant event took place in Poland,
when Citroën visited Polish relatives. And all agree that it was a discovery
that would change his life.

André Citroën was born in 1878, the fifth and youngest child of a prosperous diamond merchant. Like Louis Renault, his senior by only one year,
young Citroën was raised in Parisian middle-class comfort. Unlike Renault,
though, Citroën was Jewish—a distinction that still figured large in turn-of-
the-century Paris, where despite the cooling of national passions surrounding
the Dreyfus Affair, anti-Semitism most certainly had not disappeared.

Citroën's father, Levie, the eighth in a family of fourteen, was originally
from Amsterdam, where his forebears had been fruit merchants—thus giving
the family its original patronym: Limoenman, or Lemon-man. Arriving in

Paris in 1871, after the Franco-Prussian War, Levie changed his family name to Citroen—an unusual name, but one that was based on the French word for lemon, *citron*. The family prospered, and André grew up in a large and pleasant apartment on Rue de Châteaudun, in the heart of the ninth arrondissement. There life continued agreeably until André was six, when his father uncharacteristically speculated in a diamond-mining venture that turned out to be a swindle. Faced with financial ruin, Levie Citroen committed suicide.

Told only that their father had left on a journey and would not return for a long time, the children did not discover the truth for many years. In the meantime, although the family had to move to a smaller apartment, André's mother took over her husband's business and managed it well. It was now, at the age of seven, that André began his formal schooling. It was also now, in his school admission records, that his name appeared for the first time as "Citroën"—the *accent tréma* indicating that the two vowels of the last syllable were to be pronounced separately.

Confident, genial, and attractive, André Citroën eventually proceeded in his academic career to the Ecole Polytechnique, and from there into his required service in the army. It may have been following his mother's untimely death in the spring of 1900, or certainly by the end of his army service in 1902, that he visited his mother's relations in Poland. Here, in a foundry belonging to a distant relation, he spotted a set of gearwheels with a design unlike anything he had ever seen before. Instead of having straight, cross-cut teeth, these had an arrangement of V-shaped teeth set around the outer rim of both wheels that could be set to bring the teeth together at an angle. These helical gears were quieter, more efficient, and capable of handling far greater loads and of changing the direction of the power load—an enormous advantage over their traditional counterparts. But this small company had not yet found a way to manufacture these gears with sufficient precision.

It was an exciting discovery, and Citroën was determined to make the most of it. He was not an inventor nor a designer, but he was about to become a pioneer in manufacturing.

〜

In 1901 young Georges Braque also served his required military service, after his parents had looked into ways to reduce his time of service to one year. Having discovered that this was possible if he qualified as an artist or artist-craftsman, they had sent him from their home in Le Havre to Paris (a lengthy trip that he managed by bicycle), where he apprenticed with a decorator.

Born and raised in a reasonably well-to-do family of house-painters, Braque at the age of twelve decided that he wanted to paint something besides houses and had invested in a box of paints. He began attending night classes at Le Havre's Ecole des Beaux-Arts, but he was bored by what he found there. Then, at the age of eighteen, he faced the prospect of military service. Paris, and apprenticeship to a former employee of his father, appeared to be the answer.

Arriving in Paris at about the same time as Picasso, Braque proceeded in quite a different manner, learning to paint imitation marble, mosaics, and rosewood panels, as well as an array of other simulations, all requiring a great deal of skill and impeccable workmanship. Soon he won his artist-craftsman's certificate and served his year of military service, where he was made a noncommissioned officer.

By this time Braque had decided that he was going to be an artist—a real one, not a house-painter and decorator.

～

Madame Zola was unhappy. Her husband, the esteemed author Emile Zola, had previously ended his many years of fidelity and taken a mistress, by whom he fathered two children. Madame Zola was childless, which made the insult even more unbearable—especially when her husband invited his mistress to join him during his exile in England, at the height of the Dreyfus Affair. Madame Zola, who was not issued a similar invitation, began what would become her regular jaunts to Italy, alone. It was there that she found relief from her depression as well as from her asthma.

Zola, meanwhile, finished up the century by starting a new series of novels—having wrapped up his massive and magnificent twenty-volume Rougon-Macquart series and memorably pounded the opposition during the Dreyfus Affair. Churning out his customary thousand words a day, written each and every day following breakfast, he began a series of four novels that he envisioned as four new gospels—a secular epic in which the heroes (or Evangelists) he created would reinvent the world. Dropping his refusal to moralize, he now moralized to the skies. As Zola told his good friend Octave Mirbeau, his justification for this complete change was "the endowment of the new century of progress and universal peace with a faith in moral ideas."[15]

Alarmed by France's declining birthrate, especially in comparison with Germany's bumper crop of babies, Zola turned the first book in this series, Fecundity (1899), into a sermon on the necessity for unrestricted procreation. Having magnified the history of his own family life into universal truths, he now became an avid opponent of birth control and consequently, for the first time in his career, found himself allied with the Catholic Church.

Zola published the second book in his series, *Labor*, in 1901, and then immediately began work on the third, *Truth*, in which he revisited (in minimal disguise) his own celebrated role in the Dreyfus Affair. He did not live to complete his last book, *Justice*.

~

Throughout his long career, Zola had been a proud secularist, one who (with the exception of *Fecundity*, late in his career) was regularly at odds with the Church. By the turn of the century, he was far from alone. French opinion—especially in Paris—strongly supported secularism and anticlericalism, whose roots stretched back to the Revolution.

Early in 1900, Prime Minister Waldeck-Rousseau stage-managed the dissolution of the Assumptionist order, whose newspaper, *La Croix*, had widely spread rabble-rousing anti-Semitic polemics during the Dreyfus Affair. A year later Waldeck-Rousseau introduced legislation aimed at laicizing French education by preventing unauthorized French monastic orders from teaching. The legislation that passed was even more hostile to the religious orders than the bill Waldeck-Rousseau had introduced; subsequently, 120 of these religious communities were closed, and Parliament would staunchly reject requests for further authorization. These measures received widespread popular support, laying the groundwork for the separation of Church and state to come.

"What does it come down to, actually, the life of the Church in France?" mused Abbé Arthur Mugnier, in an August 30, 1901, entry to his journal.[16] Mugnier, who was vicar of the fashionable church of Sainte-Clotilde in the heart of the Faubourg Saint-Germain, had achieved a degree of fame by having most surprisingly converted Joris-Karl Huysmans, author of *A rebours* (*Against Nature*), which in 1884 created a scandal by its daring depiction of homosexuality. Mugnier was a charming cleric—one with a gentle manner but a sharp wit, who harmonized well with the sophisticated and literate members of his parish. They in turn found him a sympathetic confessor and a welcome guest at their dinner parties, which (to their delight) he attended in his shabby garb, his hair always fluttering in a tuft that he took no pains to tame. An open-minded modernist who admitted to a yearning for the Ancien Régime, and an advocate of French control of the French Catholic Church who nonetheless refrained from fervent nationalism, Mugnier admittedly was an unusual mixture. "How to reconcile the disparate forces of my soul?" he had written only a few days earlier.[17]

Yet instead of self-analysis, Mugnier's August 30 entry revealed his deep concern about the French Church and what its religious leaders were—and were not—doing. Their actions, he wrote, amounted to little more than "a series of ineffectual protests against republican annoyances." Beyond that, "these poor bishops" occupy themselves in pilgrimages to Lourdes, to Paray-le-Monial, or to Sacré-Coeur in Paris, in a sad imitation of the Middle Ages. This "abuse of prayer," he wrote, would only end in a loss of all prestige and in self-destruction. "I would like to know," he concluded, "if these perpetual comings and goings produce, in their souls, any more justice, sincerity, goodness, or devotion."[18]

～

Separation of Church and state had been a major battle cry of the left-of-center radical republicans since the beginning of the Third Republic, and Georges Clemenceau had vociferously pushed for this cause since the early days of his career, when he was mayor of Montmartre.[19] During the years that followed, Clemenceau rose in politics to become an eloquent and feared leader in the Chamber of Deputies, where he soon became known as "the Tiger," on account of his ferocity on behalf of the poor and the downtrodden. During the 1890s Clemenceau encountered a tidal wave of conservative forces that booted him out of politics. He then returned to journalism, most memorably during the Dreyfus Affair, when he hammered out a series of remarkable articles on behalf of Dreyfus and helped Zola publish his own earth-shaking pro-Dreyfus denunciation, "J'accuse" (Clemenceau's title) in Clemenceau's newspaper, L'Aurore.

By 1901 Clemenceau had left L'Aurore for Le Bloc, a weekly newspaper of his own that had a small circulation but large influence among political circles. Here he continued to campaign against the combined forces of monarchism and the Church, which he held responsible for exploiting the nationalist and anti-Semitic fervor surrounding the Dreyfus Affair, with the aim of overthrowing the Republic. Soon his political career would rise from the ashes, and his voice would become one of the most prominent in the Third Republic.

French politicians during the first three decades of the Third Republic (1871–1900) had not organized into parties but instead joined in loose coalitions of interests ranging from monarchists and arch-conservative Catholics on the far right to radical republicans on the left, with a variety of moderates in between. Yet both radicals and moderates during these years were republicans, and they shared their staunch belief in and support of the Third Republic.

Clemenceau was a major figure among the radical republicans throughout these years, during which the threat from the monarchist right subsided and the moderates rose in power. Extremists at times threatened, such as the 1880s Boulanger crisis, during which a popular general threatened to overthrow the Republic, and the 1890s Dreyfus Affair, during which the riptides of nationalism, anti-Semitism, right-wing Catholicism, and fervent support of the army almost tore the nation apart. Nevertheless, throughout these difficult years, political moderates managed to maintain their sometimes precarious hold. It was in the interest of moderation and in defense of the tranquility of the Republic that Prime Minister Waldeck-Rousseau in 1899 had so firmly acted to bring the Dreyfus Affair to a peaceful if not satisfactory conclusion.[20]

Yet by the turn of the century, new political voices were clamoring for admission to the ruling coterie. The Waldeck-Rousseau government had famously included a socialist—admittedly one of fairly moderate inclinations, but nevertheless representing a first for the Third Republic.[21] Yet many French socialists condemned rather than praised "Millerandism"—this willingness to participate in a bourgeois government.

Of course the French socialist movement had never been united, and from the outset had splintered largely between revolutionary and reformist aims. Yet by the turn of the century, these diverse forces had begun to coalesce into recognizable parties, even if political participation was not their immediate (or even ultimate) goal. Loosely based on the unification of the proletariat as a class, these disparate organizations held their first French socialist congress in Paris in 1899. The outcome was a composite rather than a merger, and divisiveness remained. Then, at its 1900 congress, the militants walked out, and two years later the split became final. As a result, two separate and very different French socialist parties came into being. By 1902, one had emerged as the Socialist Party of France (PS de F), a party of militants with revolutionary aims and staunch opposition to participation in the bourgeois state. The other, the French Socialist Party (PSF)—also formed in 1902—sought social transformation but embraced defense of the Republic as well as participation in government.

Thus by the early years of the new century, two very different socialist parties had formed in France, with one on record as solidly opposed to the bourgeois state. Still, when the chips were down, both would support the Republic—especially when danger threatened *la patrie*.

⟶

Internal divisiveness could of course present as grave a danger to *la patrie* as external threats—a truth painfully illustrated by the Dreyfus Affair, which had created seismic ruptures within Paris and the entire nation.

The moral problem at the Affair's heart still remained so long as Dreyfus—although pardoned—was not vindicated. Yet Parisians began to put this particularly painful episode behind them once the general amnesty went into effect early in 1901.

That June, Marcel Proust did his own bit to further the healing process. Determined to keep up his glittering social life despite his delicate health, he threw a series of grand dinner parties, including one for an array of sixty guests who had been virtually at knife-point during the recently concluded Dreyfus Affair. Notable among these was Léon Daudet, son of the novelist Alphonse Daudet. A virulent anti-Semite, Léon Daudet had been one of the most strident leaders of the anti-Dreyfus camp. Proust proceeded to seat Daudet next to a beautiful woman whom Daudet did not know and who—much to Daudet's surprise—turned out to be the daughter of a prominent Jewish banker.

Increasing Daudet's astonishment, Proust had arranged the rest of the large party similarly, with ardent Dreyfusards seated next to those who had bitterly attacked the Jewish captain and all who supported him. "Every piece of china was liable to be smashed," Daudet realized, but to his amazement, the dinner party was a success. "The bitterest of enemies ate their *chaud-froid* [meat in aspic] within two yards of each other," he marveled, and even he managed to behave himself for the evening. Only Proust could have pulled off such a feat, Daudet decided, attributing Proust's accomplishment to a keen understanding of others' feelings and to his great charm.[22]

Although Proust was an early and an avid supporter of Dreyfus—much to the dismay of his father, who was not—Proust had characteristically mended parental fences and managed to retain his friendship with even the most vehement anti-Dreyfusards, including Léon Daudet. In the course of time, when Proust wrote *The Guermantes Way* (his third volume of *In Search of Lost Time*), he would depict the impact that the Dreyfus Affair had on Parisian society during those tumultuous years. And he would dedicate this volume to his good friend Léon Daudet.

Yet despite his social triumphs, Proust was nagged by self-doubt. Soon after this triumphant June dinner party, he turned thirty (on July 10), much to his despair. Uncertain in health and unsuccessful at any career, he still lived at home and was dependent on his parents, especially his mother, for everything from financial to emotional support. "Today I'm thirty years old," he told a friend from student days, "and I've achieved nothing!"[23]

~

Proust's daring dinner party had been held in honor of Anna de Noailles, the frail and fabulous poetess whose first volume of poetry, *Le Coeur innombrable* (*The Boundless Heart*), had just appeared in print and was garnering exceptional praise. Delicate in health, plagued by insomnia and a fear of death, she had much in common with Proust, including a preference for sleeping (and working) in bed by day and reigning supreme at the best literary salons by night, where she transfixed those who hovered around her with an endless and impeccable stream of words.

Anna de Noailles may have been emerging as queen of the literary salons, but Isadora Duncan had already made a name for herself with important Parisian hostesses, and now was reserving most of her performances to invited audiences in her own studio.

The Duncans had recently moved from the Rue de la Gaîté in Montparnasse to an apartment on the other side of Paris, on the Avenue de Villiers, north of Parc Monceau. There Isadora performed for select groups and taught an unexpectedly large number of Parisian girls—so many that she had to divide them into three classes. These activities were exhausting, but they helped pay the rent. What inspired her were her efforts to discover what she called the driving principle, or essential theory, of dance. Here she stressed that truth came before technique: "Life is the root," she insisted, "and art is the flower."[24] Bearing some similarity to Method acting, which emerged in Moscow a decade later, her approach rejected the artificiality of classical ballet for movement that deeply and truthfully expressed emotional concepts. She was hovering on the brink of a discovery that would change the history of dance.

She was also about to meet someone who would change her life.

~

Winnaretta Singer, the daughter of Isaac Merritt Singer, inventor of the sewing machine, had inherited a fortune from her American father and a love of music from her French mother. Yet despite these advantages, her early life had been unhappy, clouded by her father's death and her mother's self-absorption as well as by Winnaretta's growing awareness of her own lesbianism. An attempt to escape her unhappy home led her into an even more unhappy marriage, which quickly disintegrated. Then a chance meeting with the elegant and elderly Prince Edmond de Polignac (they met in a bidding war over a Monet painting) led to a happy and companionable marriage of shared interests, while discreetly accommodating the sexual preferences of each.

Winnaretta, now the Princesse Edmond de Polignac, had since childhood displayed a sophisticated interest in the arts in addition to considerable talent as an organist and painter. Her marriage to a connoisseur of the visual as well as the performing arts led her to become a generous patron of the arts and the hostess of one of the foremost salons in Paris. From the Polignacs' marriage in 1893, the Hôtel de Polignac—their lovely mansion on Avenue Georges-Mandel in the fashionable sixteenth arrondissement—became the center for exceptional musical evenings, whether of Bach and the baroque, or Debussy, Ravel, Satie, Fauré, and, eventually, Stravinsky.

It was Prince Edmond who first took a shine to Isadora Duncan. Winnaretta had been somewhat interested in Isadora's performance at the Countess Greffulhe's salon, but the prince had been fascinated. This prompted Winnaretta to arrive on Isadora's doorstep (looking like a Roman emperor, in Isadora's opinion), where she invited her to meet the prince and perform at a studio concert. Isadora readily agreed, and soon she and the prince became close friends.

It was thus a devastating loss for Isadora as well as for Winnaretta when the prince died. He had been in bad health for some time, yet had attempted to keep up his social obligations, including Proust's post–Dreyfus Affair reconciliation dinner in June. This was one of the last times that the prince was seen in public. He died that August, and among the mourners at his funeral was Isadora Duncan. It was then that she met Paris Singer, Winnaretta's handsome, wealthy, and philandering younger brother. On this occasion they seemed to take little notice of one another. But when they met again, years later, sparks would fly.

⌒

It was at about this time that Isadora visited Rodin in his studio. She had seen his private pavilion the year before, just outside the exposition, but this time she came to his studio—presumably his spacious workspace at the state's Dépôt des Marbres on the Rue de l'Université. She noticed that he "murmured the names of his statues" as he worked on them, "ran his hands over them and caressed them." She remembered thinking that "beneath his hands the marble seemed to flow like molten lead."[25]

Rodin seemed to have that effect on women. By this time he had met lovely young Helene von Hindenburg, who became another of his conquests, although a platonic one—her mother usually chaperoned her, which was not a bad idea—and Rodin settled in for a long and companionable friendship. In the meanwhile, Rodin's faithful mistress, Rose Beuret, continued to do the cooking and the housework in their stark and uncomfortable house in Meudon, just outside of Paris.

Rodin built a pavilion on land adjoining the Meudon house, much like the pavilion where he had exhibited during the 1900 exposition, and he took to working and even sleeping there. He spent most of his time in this pavilion or in Paris, while he spent much of his money on his increasingly valuable collection of Egyptian bronzes, Roman marbles, and contemporary paintings.

Meanwhile, Rodin's Meudon residence remained sparsely furnished, with little in the way of decoration or even heat. Rodin now seems to have thought of himself as a gentleman and had became correspondingly dandified, dressing fastidiously—at least in public—and hiring a hairdresser to visit him every morning. Yet in his private life he remained oblivious to discomfort or inconvenience, wearing his overcoat and beret in his chilly house in wintertime, and thinking little of it. All the while, Rose labored on.

$\sim$

It was now, in 1901, that the twentieth-century version of the Sorbonne emerged. The first phase of its reconstruction had been completed in 1889, and at last the final phase was completed. As a result, the very stones of Cardinal Richelieu's seventeenth-century remodeling of the Sorbonne disappeared, with the single exception of his now secularized memorial chapel. During this makeover, the Sorbonne's very entity had been transformed as well. Once the bastion of French Catholic theology, in 1885 it shed its centuries-old Faculty of Theology to become a thoroughly republican and secular institution.

The new Sorbonne's remaining faculties of letters and sciences quickly established their preeminence, and students—now including young women—began to pour in. In fact, the Sorbonne's major challenge in the years to come would be lack of space, making for increasingly crowded classrooms and a sprawling network of outlying annexes for its specialized institutes and research facilities.

La Lorraine, a café in the Rue des Ecoles in the heart of the Latin Quarter, was at this time a favorite gathering place for artists and students. Picasso often met his Catalan friends there, including Jaime Sabartès, a sculptor and writer who had believed in Picasso from the outset, and who would eventually become Picasso's private secretary and biographer. If Picasso arrived at La Lorraine around midday, he and the group would lunch at a Turkish restaurant in the nearby Place de la Sorbonne. If he came later, they would spend the afternoon or evening at La Lorraine.

Picasso had returned to Paris in early June 1901 and promptly moved into the Boulevard de Clichy studio where Casagemas spent his last days. With Casagemas dead and Pallarès back in Spain, Picasso now shared the small premises with his art dealer, Mañach. In addition, Picasso now dumped his former mistress, Odette, for Casagemas's Germaine Gargallo. This enraged Picasso's friend Manolo, who had been sleeping with Germaine ever since Casagemas's death, resulting in a fight that brought in the police.

Despite his frantic social life, Picasso managed to work fast (possibly as many as three pictures a day) for an upcoming exhibit that Mañach had arranged for him at the end of the month. Mañach had done well by Picasso, having lined up the show at Ambroise Vollard's gallery on Rue Laffitte, in the heart of the ninth arrondissement, a street famous for its art galleries. Vollard, a sharp businessman with a good eye for art, specialized in the works of contemporary artists such as Renoir, Cézanne, Gauguin, and van Gogh. He agreed to show around sixty of Picasso's pictures along with some large works from another young Spanish artist. The gallery was small and the pictures were unframed and crammed floor to ceiling or in folders, but the exhibition drew glowing reviews and (despite Vollard's later recollection) was a success. "I really had a lot of money, but it didn't last long," Picasso later recalled.[26] After all, why save if the future looked so bright?

Still, the pictures that Picasso exhibited at Vollard's had celebrated modern French life—colorful, attractive subjects such as can-can dancers, horse racing, and playing children. This phase did not last long; by late summer and early autumn, Picasso had become preoccupied with the dark subjects of death and despair. He was deeply struck by what he saw in a visit to the women's prison of Saint-Lazare, where forlorn women with venereal diseases were identified by white bonnets and isolated from the others. But it was the death of his friend Casagemas that now began to haunt him. Picasso was living in the very quarters where his friend had resided at the time of his death. More than that, Picasso had for a time become Germaine Gargallo's lover.[27]

Moving from bright colors into darker and predominantly blue tones, Picasso began to work single-mindedly on a series of paintings and drawings in which Casagemas's ghostly presence hovered—most especially in *Casagemas in His Coffin* and *The Burial of Casagemas*. It did not matter that Picasso had not been present for the latter event; perhaps this fact even intensified his obsession with the theme.

Collectors were not interested in purchasing such dark and dismal subjects, and Picasso's income dramatically shrank.[28] Winter set in, and his contract with Mañach came to an end, leaving him cold, desolate, and broke. Unlike his triumphant entrance into Paris the year before, he had to wire his father for money for the train fare back to Barcelona.

Picasso was twenty years old, and his Blue Period had begun.

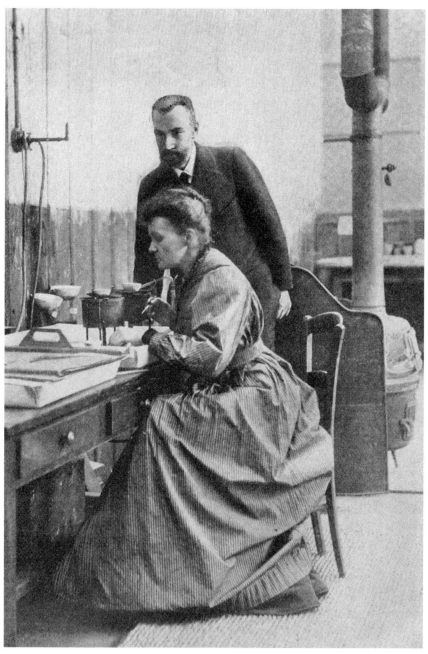

Pierre and Marie Curie in their laboratory, 1904, Paris. Photo Credit: Album / Art Resource, NY. © Art Resource, NY.

CHAPTER FOUR

~

Dreams and Reality
(1902)

Debussy had envisioned a dream world in his opera *Pelléas et Mélisande*, one shrouded in mists and mystery. Unfortunately this dream world quickly collided with the real world when his artistic vision was transferred to the stage. His first major hurdle in bringing *Pelléas* to life turned out to be Maeterlinck's insistence that his mistress, the French soprano Georgette Leblanc, play the part of Mélisande.

Leblanc was well qualified, and she indeed would sing the role in a Boston production in 1912, but Debussy preferred the Scottish American Mary Garden, who was a leading soprano at the Opéra-Comique. This grievously offended Maeterlinck, who stomped off in a rage and claimed that the permission he had granted to set his play to music did not give Debussy the sole right to determine the casting. Maeterlinck would eventually sue Debussy over this dispute, but in the meantime consoled himself by publically hoping that the opera would be "an immediate and resounding flop."[1]

This unexpected flare-up unsettled an already exhausted and nerve-wracked Debussy, who wrote after the last performance that he was "suffering fatigue to the point of neurasthenia, a de luxe illness I never believed in till now."[2] After fifteen intense weeks of rehearsal, his worst fears were realized when, at the all-important dress rehearsal, the audience began to laugh. At first distraught that anyone could or would find *Pelléas* funny, Debussy soon heard that programs were being distributed that gave a wickedly salacious précis of the plot. Later, Mary Garden insisted that Maeterlinck himself was behind this malicious hoax.

Still, opening night on April 30—if not a complete triumph—was far from a disaster. Having heard about the dress rehearsal's fracas, the opera's supporters (including Maurice Ravel) packed the upper galleries, where young music-lovers such as themselves could afford seats, and made their enthusiasm heard. Even though the critics and Debussy's fellow composers were predictably divided between the traditional and the more open-minded, Paris's avant-garde quickly embraced this opera as a masterpiece.

Pelléas did sufficiently well that the Opéra-Comique scheduled a revival for that October and continued to present it during all but two of its subsequent prewar seasons. By January 1913 the Opéra-Comique had performed it one hundred times.

Suddenly Debussy had vaulted into the limelight.

Composer Erik Satie attended *Pelléas*'s opening night and afterward, according to Jean Cocteau, wrote: "Nothing more one can do in that area. . . . I've got to find something else or I've had it."[3]

Satie was favorably astounded, but many others were deeply offended by Debussy's achievement. Predictably, one of *Pelléas*'s severest critics was Camille Saint-Saëns, who claimed that he had not taken his usual holiday so he could stay in Paris and "say nasty things about *Pelléas*."[4] Similarly Théodore Dubois, the arch-conservative director of the Paris Conservatoire, forbade Conservatoire students to attend any *Pelléas* performance—a sure-fire way of guaranteeing that they would, indeed, clamber into those upper gallery seats and applaud and whistle their hearts out.

Ravel attended every one of the fourteen performances of *Pelléas*'s first run, applauding enthusiastically from the upper galleries along with his fellow students. By this time he and Debussy were friends, and although they were not and never would become close, Debussy seems to have appreciated Ravel's deep admiration.

Ravel now was earning a small income by giving private lessons in harmony and composition, after spending the earlier months of the year competing once again for the Prix de Rome. Once again he was a finalist, but this time he failed to take any prize at all.

It was a maddening situation—and challenge—for the young composer, who continued to premiere his works. That April the brilliant young pianist Ricardo Viñes, who in the course of his career would introduce a panoply of contemporary music, including most of the piano works of Debussy and Ravel, premiered Ravel's *Pavane pour une infante défunte* and *Jeux d'eau* at a recital presented by the eminent Société Nationale de Musique.

Camille Saint-Saëns had been a major force in founding the Société in 1871, which he had hoped would help bring young French composers to public attention. It was a worthy ambition, but Saint-Saëns's idea of appropriate music did not include the music of Ravel or Debussy. Vincent d'Indy subsequently took the lead at the Société, and although he embraced conservative musical (as well as political) traditions, he would become an active supporter of contemporary composers such as Debussy, Satie, and Ravel, even if he did not necessarily care for what they wrote.

This recital was an important one for Ravel, and he had placed his music in good hands. Viñes, a good friend whom Ravel had known from the Conservatoire, was a gifted pianist, and the critics enjoyed his performance of Ravel's pleasant and accessible *Pavane*. But they did not like *Jeux d'eau*, which was altogether too challenging for them. Ravel had poured himself into the latter work, which today is considered a landmark in piano composition, but it would be years before his audience would understand what he had achieved.

⌇

Berthe Weill slid almost accidently into selling modern art, first with those three drawings by Picasso that she bought in 1900 from Picasso's dealer Mañach, and then, in early 1902, with a show that included the still-unknown artist Henri Matisse. Nothing by Matisse sold, but a few months later Weill managed to sell one of his still lifes to the avant-garde collector Arthur Huc, who had previously bought Picasso's *Moulin de la Galette*. Already Matisse and Picasso had begun to leapfrog one another in what would become an epic rivalry, although for now neither had an inkling of what was to come.

In June Matisse participated in another Weill show and this time did better, much to his own as well as Weill's pleasure. Although new to the business and facing heavy competition from the likes of Vollard and Durand-Ruel, Weill had good instincts and an even bigger heart. Matisse became one of her "finds," and she championed him, taking delight in the increasing audacity of his painting.

Amélie's hard work in her hat shop was beginning to pay off and promised to help Matisse weather this seemingly interminable period while he was finding himself. It was a major misfortune, then, when a disaster on her side of the family soon removed that reliable prop from their lives. Her parents had for years been the major supporters and right-hand aides of Frédéric and Thérèse Humbert, an influential couple whose progressive politics meshed well with their own but whose massive borrowing, coupled with increasingly irregular financial schemes and influence-peddling, eventually led to disaster. The Humberts' extraordinary access to money and power were based on Thérèse Humbert's elaborately constructed claim to an enormous family inheritance. But when—after many years of high flying—this proved fraudulent, ruin and disgrace quickly followed. In 1902, when the sensational scandal finally broke, the Humberts immediately took to their heels, leaving the faithful and unwitting Parayres ruined and ostracized. Worse yet, the prestige of those elite members of government and society who were caught in the Humberts' web was such that it threatened the very honor and stability of the Republic.

Matisse now used his own previously disregarded legal background to go to his father-in-law's defense, and he succeeded in getting him acquitted of complicity in the Humberts' schemes. Unfortunately Amélie's health had failed, and her hat shop fell victim to the family disaster. With no other options, in early 1903 the Matisses finally left Paris to live with Henri's parents, in the bleak and unforgiving regions of Henri Matisse's birth.

For many months Matisse would produce little. Sleepless and ill, he was about to give up.

~

Unlike Matisse, Georges Braque was filled with hope. In 1902, after successfully serving his one-year term of military service (reduced on account of his artist-craftsman certificate), Braque decided that he wanted to return to Paris to become a real artist.

Unlike the parents of so many other aspiring artists, the Braques did not fuss, and even supplied Georges with a small allowance. Thus fortified, Braque headed off once more to Paris, where he studied painting and rented the proverbial dingy studio in Montmartre. He spent time at museums and at galleries, where he admired the Impressionist paintings of Monet, Renoir, and Sisley. He also found Seurat's pointillism appealing, but in the end it was the work of Vincent van Gogh that moved him to the core.

Van Gogh had sold only one painting during his short lifetime, and although several small exhibits of his work had appeared during the 1890s, it was not until 1901 that a prominent Paris gallery, the Galerie Bernheim-Jeune, held a major retrospective. Seen comprehensively, these van Goghs created a sensation and helped bring together Matisse, Maurice de Vlaminck, and André Derain in what would emerge as the color-drenched Fauve movement. Eventually Georges Braque would join them.

However, this still lay in the future, and none of the principals yet had any idea of what was coming. In the meantime Braque never suffered in the manner of van Gogh or Matisse or so many other artists. He attended classes at a local academy, where the director taught him nothing but at least allowed him to paint as he pleased. Braque then entered a feeder-academy for the Ecole des Beaux-Arts, but found it so stultifying that he left.

It was a great time for learning and for experimentation, and Braque was enjoying himself. Why anguish when one could be happy?

～

They were poor, they were overworked, and they were badly treated by those who should have known better and could have done something about it. Yes, there were occasional grants, but these were unpredictable and never addressed the Curies' basic need for a good laboratory and the regular salaries (and freedom) that professorships would provide. Pierre Curie had a heavy and poorly paid teaching load at the Polytechnic School for Physics and Chemistry (operated by the City of Paris), while his brilliant young wife, Marie Sklodovska Curie—looking for additional ways to make ends meet—had found work at a teacher-training school, the Higher Normal School for Girls at Sèvres, west of Paris. At the same time both Curies were ardently committed to their research work—an ongoing and grueling business that they were carrying out in a rough wooden shed lacking heat or amenities. And they were just as ardently devoted to raising their young daughter, Irène.

Pierre Curie needed a professorship to live on and a laboratory to work in, but he had encountered repeated rebuffs in his attempts to attain either. A quiet and self-effacing man as well as a brilliant physicist, he had neither the ability nor the interest to promote himself. Firmly believing that his work should speak for itself, he repeatedly found that it could not and did not. The same year when he and Marie (with the assistance of Gustave Bémont) discovered polonium and were on the brink of discovering radium, the Sorbonne rejected him for a professorship in physical chemistry. According to his detractors—who turned up their noses at his unconventional, largely home-schooled education—Pierre Curie's many discoveries and publications in crystallography, magnetism, and electricity did not qualify him for the post.

Soon after, based on his pioneering work in crystalline physics, Pierre Curie applied for a Sorbonne professorship in mineralogy and was similarly rejected. After the Academy of Sciences subsequently turned him down for membership, he refused to let his name be included on a list of candidates for the Legion of Honor. He had already wasted too much time in interviews, he said, and in the end he preferred a job and a laboratory over the Legion's coveted red silk ribbon.

"You hardly eat at all, either of you," a concerned friend wrote, as both Pierre and Marie raced between their research, jobs, and family obligations.

"More than once I have seen Mme Curie nibble two slices of sausage and swallow a cup of tea with it," the friend continued. "Do you think even a robust constitution would not suffer from such insufficient nourishment?"[5]

There was no good answer to such a question. Yet despite grinding poverty, Pierre and Marie early on decided against profiting from their discovery of radium and radiation. Instead of patenting the technique that Marie had developed to isolate it, they decided to publish the results of their research, in accord with the scientific spirit. As Marie Curie later wrote, "This was a great benefit to the radium industry, which was enabled to develop in full liberty."[6]

The Curies had decided to forego wealth in the interest of science.

⌒

Emile Zola was old, but he still was thinking expansively. He had recently published *Vérité* (Truth), the third in his projected Evangelical series of novels, and he had told those grouped admiringly around him that "I should be allowed to dream a little in my old age."[7] Conscious of the dangers of war in an increasingly connected world, he saw his next and last book in the Evangelical series as a veritable hymn to international peace. One wonders what his acerbic friend, the late Edmond de Goncourt, would have made of these grand and inevitably self-inflating visions. There had always been an element of pomposity in Zola that Goncourt had been quick to skewer. After all, the great man could be more than a trifle irritating.

Still, Zola was basking in the afterglow of a triumphant career, capped by a political triumph that only an author such as Victor Hugo had previously managed. Zola the novelist had become a hero, and he was proud of it. He was at the head of a general movement of progress, and he had graciously accepted a place among its secular saints.

His home life still had its difficulties, but Zola was beginning to take his illegitimate children to public places, including a performance by Sarah Bernhardt in *L'Aiglon*. As his daughter, Denise, remembered, "He thought it important that we hear her because she had aged and might not, in his view, act much longer."[8] What never occurred to Zola was that he might die before—long before—Bernhardt.

It was in fact an odd and mysterious ending to a remarkable career—one that Zola himself could not have written better. Although a noted hypochondriac, he seemed in reasonably robust health when he retired to bed that chilly night of September 29, 1902, leaving a small coal fire burning and after carefully closing and locking the windows (he had, after all, received numerous death threats). But sometime during the night he became horribly ill and arose, awakening his wife, Alexandrine, who also felt nauseous and dizzy. She saw him reel and fall, but she was unable to pull the cord to summon the sleeping servants. Nor could either of them manage to open a window.

The next morning the servants found them there—Zola stretched out on the floor near the bed and Alexandrine, deadly pale, lying on her pillow. Alexandrine still showed faint signs of life and would survive, but the great novelist was dead.

The verdict was carbon monoxide poisoning. It had affected Zola more than his wife because he had fallen to the floor, where the poisonous gas had most heavily accumulated from what must have been a blocked chimney.

And yet the chimney was not blocked. Nor was there any residual evidence of carbon monoxide. Specialists tried to replicate the fatal incident but could not. They lit fires in the bedroom and shut the windows. They left guinea pigs overnight to test the air, but the little fellows survived. They took apart the flue but found nothing of note there. Despite this mystery, the coroner announced that Zola had died from natural causes and declined to pursue the matter further, ruling only that these reports be kept private.

Many, including Zola's mistress, had their doubts, and whispers of "murder" began to circulate. Years later, a Parisian roofer confessed on his deathbed that he had been working on a nearby roof before that fatal night and, in revenge for Zola's role in the Dreyfus Affair, had sealed his chimney. The following morning he unsealed the chimney before anyone noticed. It sounded plausible, but no one could substantiate the man's claim, and the mystery remains.

The abruptness and the strangeness of Zola's death created enormous shock, and the outpouring of grief was enormous. Flowers and tributes swamped his house on Rue de Bruxelles, arriving from as far away as San Francisco. Zola's efforts on behalf of Dreyfus still resonated with vast numbers of people, great and small, and they wanted to express their grief in tangible ways.

One in particular was Captain Alfred Dreyfus, who quietly stood vigil with the body along with a round-the-clock procession of Zola's closest friends. Although Alexandrine feared that Dreyfus's presence might set off violent protests from the still-simmering ranks of anti-Dreyfusards, he joined the thousands of mourners on October 5 who followed the coffin and its honor guard to Montmartre Cemetery. Much to everyone's relief the huge crowd was well behaved, and only the sound of shuffling footsteps broke the peace and quiet.

At the gravesite Anatole France—once an opponent, but since the Dreyfus Affair a friend and comrade—eulogized Zola as he would have wished to be remembered. "Let us envy him," France concluded, for "he has honored his country and the world through an immense work and through a great action. Envy him his destiny and his heart, which made his lot that of the greatest: he was a moment of the conscience of man!"[9]

⌢

Throughout the Dreyfus Affair, right-wing Catholics' scorching anti-Semitism and appeal to violence, as well as the absence of influential Catholic voices on Dreyfus's behalf, had hardened anticlericalism throughout France and especially in Paris, where anticlericalism formed the basis for a political realignment that increasingly unified the political left. From the Dreyfusards' point of view, the Dreyfus Affair in its largest sense had been a last-ditch attempt by the Catholic Church to overthrow the Republic. Even after passions over Dreyfus himself subsided, strong anticlericalism remained, ready to flair up as the struggle between Church and state intensified.

By the time elections were held in May 1902, the nation had solidly divided into two distinct camps of left versus right, with little between. It was an election marked by passionate polemics and vehement denunciations, whose outcome was a victory for the leftist coalition already in power.[10]

Now firmly in the saddle, the new prime minister, Emile Combes, used his parliamentary majority to take on the religious orders and close a large number of their schools. With the May elections, Georges Clemenceau also reentered politics, this time in the Senate—an institution he had previously condemned as undemocratic and whose abolition he had repeatedly called for. Yet though he now demonstrated a startling new ability to compromise—at least where his career was concerned—Clemenceau still was a tiger on the question of Church and state. In his first Senate speech (on October 30), after distinguishing between the Catholic religion and the Church as an institution, he strongly supported Combes's decision to close so many Catholic schools. Addressing the Church as an institution, he called for an end to its legal privileges, most especially its financing by the state (which had been writ in stone ever since Napoleon's time) and the privileges enjoyed by its religious orders.

Much like Charles de Gaulle's Jesuit school on Rue de Vaugirard, most of France's Catholic schools would find ways of surviving for a while longer. But anticlericalism was ascendant in France, and the fight to assert political supremacy over the Church was rapidly gaining strength.

⌢

During this year of high-decibel elections and growing tension between Church and state, relations between labor and management also became acrimonious. Numerous strikes broke out, prompted by pockets of unemployment and reductions in wages. Miners in particular felt abused and took to the picket lines. Still, France's general prosperity continued, and against this promising background new entrepreneurs such as André Citroën felt sufficiently confident to launch new and cutting-edge enterprises.

It was in 1902, after completing his military service, that Citroën invested everything he had in a small workshop in northern Paris, near the Gare du Nord. Citroën established his firm, André Citroën & Cie (Compagnie, or Company) in the expectation that he could do what others before him had failed to accomplish—figure out a way to manufacture the helical double chevron-shaped gears he had seen in Poland. If successful, the applications for such gears were mind-boggling. Citroën accurately envisioned uses in factories and generating stations as well as in the milling, mining, and metalworking industries. He also anticipated uses in printing and textile machinery—anything where great exactness as well as high operating speed, abrupt speed changes, and sudden reversing were necessary. The future looked bright, if only he could discover a way to manufacture such a complex gear.

The critical element was precision. So far it had proved impossible to manufacture such a gear with the high degree of exactness necessary; such gears could not be successfully cast or molded, as the Polish company had attempted, nor had anyone yet managed to cut such a pattern from a block of steel. Still, Citroën was aware that recent advances in the United States had opened up new possibilities, and within months he developed the machinery he needed, using special cutting tools that he imported from America.

Citroën's discovery came at just the right time, coinciding with the early adoption of electric motors, which required highly efficient and quiet-running gear systems. Yet his business, although state-of-the-art, remained small-scale and customized, which meant that he was constantly in search of new clients. In addition, since his business was small, he had to serve as sales and marketing manager as well as chief engineer and production manager.

Nonetheless, Citroën had made a bold entrance into the world of manufacturing, and his double-chevron logo was already becoming a symbol for success.

⟅

The 1902 Paris–Vienna road race intentionally gave racers and their cars a new challenge by taking them through the Alps. Louis Renault and his brother Marcel were ready for the challenge, convinced that this course gave every advantage to their light automobiles.

The race began at four in the morning of June 28, just outside Paris. By the third day the racers were negotiating the steep and dangerous Arlberg Pass, where one mistake could send an unfortunate driver hurtling into the abyss. Drivers jettisoned extra weight, including doors and seats (which they had to return for, on foot), while Louis Renault's mechanic constantly filled the radiator as its water boiled away. The descent was even more hazardous, since no one had previously put automobile brakes to such a test. Brakes caught fire, and racers hurled themselves out of their seats to keep from following their cars over the edge.

Louis Renault got through this set of adventures unscathed, but then he had the misfortune of crashing into a closed gate at a railroad crossing. After repairing the axle and replacing his wheel spokes with the crossbars from a chair, he set off again, only to be rear-ended by another contestant while stopping for a referee.

Marcel Renault, however, had better luck. After brilliantly negotiating the Arlberg, he decided to push his vehicle to the limit, passing all of his remaining competitors at speeds sometimes reaching nearly seventy miles per hour. He came in first, even ahead of the heavier vehicles, some of which had to rely on horses to pull them to the finish line. Impressively, Marcel had traveled even faster than the famed Arlberg Express, which was then considered the fastest train in Europe.

Word of Marcel's success spread quickly, and sales for Renault autos poured in. From the Renault brothers' point of view, there could be no better form of publicity.

～

Meanwhile, back in Paris, Hector Guimard was running into trouble with his employer, the Compagnie du Chemin de Fer Métropolitain de Paris, or CMP. When he and the CMP collided, he was supervising the placement of his entrances to the Métro's new Line 2, which followed the semicircular path of the old Farmers-General wall around the northern side of Paris.

At first it was a question of money. Looking for a way to reduce its expenses, the CMP had taken steps to work directly with Guimard's suppliers. The CMP had already antagonized Guimard by refusing to pay more than a portion of the percentage in fees that he claimed on materials—a typical practice for contractors, but which in this case amounted to a sizable expense that the CMP was unwilling to pay. Complicating matters were imprecise oral agreements and the fact that the CMP had hired Guimard without the support of Paris's municipal council.

The CMP, acting under an earlier agreement, now claimed that Guimard's projects belonged to it, to be directed as it pleased and by whomever it pleased. Guimard was aghast. How could his style, the "Style Guimard," be implemented by anyone else? How could his project be summarily placed outside his control?

Now, with the question of artistic control as well as cold cash at stake, Guimard took action. Having been paid only half of the money he claimed at the end of 1901, when the final accounts for Line 1 were settled, he took action to block building sites for his entrances to Métro Line 2. This forced a by now thoroughly unhappy CMP to resort to temporary Métro entrances at additional expense. The CMP responded by suing Guimard.

Things were getting nasty.

⌒

Several years after *Pelléas et Mélisande* first appeared, the writer Jacques Rivière recalled his first impressions. He had been a student at the time, and he reminded the reader that for those who were sixteen to twenty when it first appeared, *Pelléas* offered "a miraculous world, a cherished paradise where we could escape from all our troubles."[11]

The element of escapism that drew audiences to Debussy's dreamy *Pelléas et Mélisande* also pulled in audiences for the magical films of pioneering French filmmaker Georges Méliès. Méliès, a Parisian born in 1861, had been fascinated by magic acts since his youth. In 1888 he became the owner and chief creative force behind the Théâtre Robert-Houdin, specializing in dramatic and fantastical illusions. It was but a step to the new field of moving pictures, where the Lumière brothers led the way. Méliès immediately understood the importance of their invention, and after unsuccessfully trying to buy one of their machines (in which their films of less than one minute each were hand cranked through a projector), he bought a similar apparatus from another inventor, which he adapted on his own. Eighteen months later, he began to shoot films under the aegis of his own company, Star Film, located just outside of Paris—the first film company in the world. Soon, notables such as Thomas Edison and the Pathé brothers would visit this remarkable glass-walled and glass-roofed studio, where its technically adept magician wove celluloid magic.

Méliès's films included documentaries, the primitive predecessors of the newsreels that would soon become part of the movie-viewing experience.

But his specialty became inventive special effects, earning him the title of "Sorcerer" or "Magician." He had been making and experimenting with the new medium of film for six years when in 1902 he made film history with his classic *A Trip to the Moon*, in which he rigged up a memorable scene of a spaceship hitting the man in the moon, square in the eye. Running at fourteen minutes and filled with state-of-the-art special effects, this was his most ambitious film to date. *A Trip to the Moon* drew admiring audiences in France and abroad—including Edison and others who unabashedly pirated this and other Méliès films.

⌣

While Méliès was making his mark on popular culture, Rodin was enjoying the fawning popularity that had come to him as he aged. His beautiful young friend Helene von Hindenburg was a favorite correspondent, but it was the young German poet Rainer Maria Rilke who was Rodin's most important visitor that summer of 1902.

At first, Rodin scarcely noticed Rilke, who came to pay tribute and to interview the famous sculptor for a book he was writing. Rilke was searching for guidance in life from a man and artist such as Rodin, and he was thrilled to believe that he had found exactly the person to understand and guide him. Soon after their meeting, the young poet wrote Rodin, "It is not just to write a study that I have come to you, it is to ask you: how should I live?"[12] Rodin rather perfunctorily told him to work hard and finish his book, and Rilke hastened to comply. When the book was published the following year, he sent a copy to Rodin. Because Rodin couldn't read it (it was in German), he promptly set it aside. Rodin may have shrugged off this homage, but subsequently the two did begin an increasingly warm correspondence, and they would meet again. This time Rilke would have a much greater impact on the lauded French sculptor.

In the meantime, as Rodin was beginning what would turn out to be an important friendship with the German poet, across the Atlantic an eminent historian was about to establish Rodin's reputation in America. Although Americans had proved an important and even lifesaving market for the Impressionist painters, especially Monet and Renoir, these artists had never challenged Americans' uneasy relationship to sexuality as Rodin did. For years Rodin had failed to interest American buyers in his work, and as recently as 1893 no American owned a Rodin. That same year a prudish committee removed the sculptures that Rodin loaned Chicago for its Columbian exposition.

Rodin had thus entered American consciousness as a delectable but still forbidden fruit when the distinguished historian Henry Adams encountered his work, probably at the Chicago exposition before the censors removed it. Once Adams saw more Rodin sculptures in Paris, he concluded that although they were unquestionably decadent, he had to have one. "Why can we decadents never take the comfort and satisfaction of our decadence?" he slyly wondered.[13]

Adams never cared for Rodin personally; he described him as "a peasant of genius; grasping, distrustful of himself socially; susceptible to flattery, especially to that of beautiful or fashionable women." Especially distressing to one of Adams's exacting nature, Rodin was "perfectly buzzy about his contracts; keeps no books or memoranda; forgets all he says, and has not the least idea of doing what is promised."[14] Still, Adams became one of Rodin's most important backers. He never did buy a Rodin for himself, but he bought on behalf of friends, especially the wealthy Boston collector Henry Lee Higginson. With Adams's encouragement, in 1902 Higginson became the first American to purchase a group of Rodin sculptures (two marbles and three bronzes).

By this time Rodin's reputation throughout Europe was secure, and he even was gaining a toehold in America, that bastion of puritanism. Yet in his own homeland, matters remained considerably less satisfactory. The year 1902 brought an especially painful series of reminders of this state of affairs. Rodin may have successfully shown his Victor Hugo monument at the 1901 Salon, but when Paris celebrated the centennial of Hugo's birth in 1902, it was another sculptor's monument that went up in Place Victor-Hugo (16th), near the novelist's last home.[15] Even the monument scheduled for Hugo's longtime residence in the Place des Vosges was by a sculptor other than Rodin (the sculptor being Georges Bareau).

When it came time to commemorate Baudelaire in Montparnasse Cemetery, José de Charmoy received the honor. Following Zola's unexpected death, the commission for his monument went to Constantin Meunier. And, topping off the year's round of snubs, Honoré de Balzac's monument at long last was unveiled—not the splendid but controversial monument that Rodin had created, but a vastly inferior one by Alexandre Falguière, which after the latter's death yet another sculptor completed.

Not surprisingly, Rodin found this series of obvious oversights disturbing. Nowhere in Paris but the Musée du Luxembourg was his work on view.

～

While Rodin was brooding on his inability to impress his fellow Frenchmen, Isadora Duncan was reveling in her growing success—which in her case meant leading a wild and crazy life and enjoying it thoroughly. She and her family had virtually adopted the American Mary Desti and her infant, Preston (whom Isadora's mother nursed with spoonfuls of champagne when he became ill). Mary had escaped a bad marriage back in Chicago, and after her introduction to the Duncans, she and Isadora became inseparable. "At this moment," she later wrote, "my heart went out to Isadora, and she still has it with her in eternity."[16]

Isadora had begun to drink pretty heavily—favoring champagne, but not adverse to anything with alcoholic content. According to Desti, it was because Isadora had tipsily spilled whiskey on her sandals that she scandalously danced barefoot at a Paris recital attended by Georges Clemenceau. Clemenceau may or may not have noticed, but others did, and it made such a sensation that Isadora thenceforth made bare feet one of her trademarks.

In 1902 or thereabouts, Desti returned to Chicago with little Preston to marry an old flame, Solomon Sturges, who adopted Preston. Desti would move on to other husbands and lovers, but Preston Sturges would eventually become the famously creative writer and director of madcap films. According to his memoirs, Isadora's and his mother's lives were as screwball as his movies. It was a crazy life, but somehow, he survived.

Isadora did far more than simply survive. During the winter of 1902, she met Loie Fuller, the American dancer who had made a name for herself as a strikingly original dancer at the Folies Bergère. Using electrical lights, colored gels, and billowing silk to summon up visions of fire, butterflies, and huge flowers, Fuller was pushing toward new and more serious horizons, and in the process was exploring some of the same pioneering concepts of modern dance that Isadora was simultaneously making her own.

Fuller, the dancing flower, was also a shrewd businesswoman. Introduced to Isadora, who promptly danced for her and tried to explain what she was doing, Fuller was sufficiently impressed that she invited her to tour Germany with her company. Isadora, thrilled to be asked, accompanied Fuller's troupe through Germany to Vienna, luxuriating in champagne dinners and lavish accommodations along the way. In Vienna, she danced in gauze so thin that the stunned audience at first thought she was naked. Naturally, her fame spread.

Just as naturally, Loie became jealous. As far as she was concerned, Isadora's eccentricity was a pain in the neck, and when Isadora set off on her own for a tour of Hungary, Fuller was astounded. In Fuller's view, she had set Isadora on her feet, and now Isadora was discarding her. It did not make for amiable relations between the two, but this was the last thing on Isadora's mind as she set off for Budapest. It was here, in a run of sold-out performances, that she became a star. And it was here that she met Oszkár Beregi, who became her first lover.

Isadora's evolution from "chaste nymph" to "wild and careless bacchante" was almost complete.[17]

〜

Pablo Picasso returned a third time to Paris in October 1902, during which he unsuccessfully attempted to toss off a few crowd-pleasers, but overall stayed with the themes and somber palette of his Blue Period. It was a dismal winter, during which he first bunked with an impoverished Left Bank sculptor. He then moved to Boulevard Voltaire in the seedy eleventh arrondissement, where he shared a room with the thus-far unsuccessful artist and poet Max Jacob—a friend since Picasso's 1901 Vollard exhibit.

Jacob was knowledgeable in art, literature, and philosophy, and he provided the French viewpoint on many subjects—opening new intellectual horizons for Picasso, who had previously associated almost solely with his Catalan and Spanish friends. Picasso would never speak French without an accent, but it was Jacob who taught him to converse more fluently in French, and it was Jacob who introduced him to the richness of French literature and culture.

Jacob had a wicked sense of fun and would later become the life of raucous Bateau-Lavoir parties, but during this bleak winter in the dingy area between the Place de la République and the Place de la Nation, there were no occasions for the two destitute friends to celebrate. Picasso's later claim that he had to burn his paintings that winter to keep warm probably was an exaggeration. But his misery, and the misery of the subjects he painted, were real.

Gertrude Stein at 27 Rue de Fleurus, Paris. Photo Credit: Heritage / The Image Works. © Jewish Chronicle Ltd / HIP / The Image Works.

CHAPTER FIVE

~

Arrivals and Departures

(1903)

In the autumn of 1903, Matisse and his wife Amélie returned to Paris and to Matisse's fifth-floor Left Bank studio at 19 Quai St-Michel, high above the Seine and Notre-Dame. Their sons remained with their grandparents, but Marguerite—now nine years old—stayed with her father and stepmother, serving as Matisse's frequent model and learning to look after him and their small apartment while her stepmother worked (in an aunt's hat shop) to earn the small income with which they got by.

Matisse was still desperate for work. Friends tried to help, but nothing seemed to go right for him. And then, late in autumn, his three-year-old son Pierre became deathly ill. Amélie traveled to Rouen to nurse him,[1] and when he blessedly survived, brought him back to Paris where she and Marguerite could watch over him. Then, adding to their woes, Amélie's sister Berthe in Rouen grew desperately ill. The upshot was that Berthe, along with Amélie's parents (who had been living with her), moved to the south of France for her health.

In the midst of this unhappy turmoil, Matisse submitted two paintings to the first exhibition of the Salon d'Automne, a new and (at least as envisioned) more forward-looking organization that some of the more liberal among the older artists formed as an alternative to the official Salon and the increasingly stodgy Salon de la Société Nationale. Organized on the fly and under strenuous opposition from the other two salons, it turned out to please neither the traditionalists nor the avant-garde. It certainly did not please Matisse, who in any case was still trying to find himself.

73

It was now, in the darkest days of Paris winter, that Henri Matisse began to dream of moving south to join his wife's family in the Midi.

⌣

For the grand old Impressionist and neo-Impressionist Camille Pissarro, it was the same old story. "I have no luck in exhibitions," he wrote his eldest son, Lucien. "In Berlin . . . the three figure paintings I showed were not sold; at Mâcon . . . nothing was sold; at Dieppe . . . nothing was sold; at Beauvais . . . nothing." Soon after, he reported that he had sold two pictures to the Le Havre Museum (the city's Musée des Beaux-Arts), the first and only paintings purchased by any French museum during Pissarro's lifetime. He sold an additional two paintings to collectors, but reported that he was "hardly besieged by demands!"[2]

Money had always been a pressing problem for Pissarro, who never achieved the same kind of success in his lifetime as had his colleagues Monet and Renoir. In 1903, at the age of seventy-three, he still was supporting his five adult children, including his eldest son, Lucien, who by then was a forty-year-old married father eager for parental help in buying a house.

Pissarro had always been generous with his time as well as with his limited funds, nurturing Cézanne and Gauguin and, more recently, Matisse early in their careers. He was an able and perceptive teacher, who imparted confidence as well as technique. When he encountered Matisse in the late 1890s, Pissarro had told him: "You are gifted. Work, and don't listen to anything anyone tells you."[3] He then took Matisse to visit Caillebotte's magnificent collection of Impressionist paintings at the Musée du Luxembourg, giving him an in-depth tutorial along the way. Subsequently, Matisse took to visiting Pissarro regularly, to talk and to learn—especially about Pissarro's former pupil, Cézanne.

Thus, by his twilight years, Pissarro had formed a link between the then-revolutionary Impressionists, the neo-Impressionists who followed, and the young artists of the new twentieth century who were about to burst on the scene. It was a role he relished, but as he looked back on his life, he also felt a certain degree of melancholy. "I see that we are far from being understood," he told his son Lucien, "even by our friends."[4]

Despite failing eyesight and other physical ailments, Pissarro continued to paint, in particular his cityscapes of Paris, where he enthused about "superb motifs of light." Yet he firmly believed in the necessity of returning to nature—"Renewal is indispensable"—and spent the summer and early autumn of the year in the vicinity of the seaside town of Le Havre. Here he painted his last series, the Jetty at Le Havre.[5]

Soon after his return from Le Havre he became ill, and in November he died peacefully in Paris. With him went the memories of an era.

～

That May, Paul Gauguin died penniless in French Polynesia. Pissarro had provided much-needed guidance when Gauguin (then a stockbroker) moved from collecting Impressionist art to making his own first attempts at painting. Pissarro did not always understand or appreciate the direction in which Gauguin moved, but despite the differences between them, Gauguin (in the year before his death) acknowledged that Pissarro "was one of my masters and I do not deny him."[6]

That July, James McNeill Whistler, the American expatriate artist who lived most of his life abroad, died in far more comfortable circumstances in London. His artistic vision had for years embraced the delicate and dreamy realms which, by the late nineteenth century, the Symbolists made their own. This at last brought him a well-earned measure of fame at the end of a long and productive career.

Auguste Rodin now became Whistler's successor as president of the recently formed International Society of Sculptors, Painters, and Gravers in London, where Rodin felt duly appreciated. In spite of the French establishment's refusal to grant him the recognition he craved, Rodin was finding a gratifying degree of acclaim elsewhere in Europe, and made the most of it. According to one English friend, Rodin's "head was a little turned, he played up to worshippers."[7]

France had earlier (although belatedly) extended the Legion of Honor ribbon to Rodin, and now promoted him to Commander—an honor that thoroughly annoyed his critics, one of whom called for a public investigation of state expenditures on Rodin's works, especially his uncompleted doors, *The Gates of Hell*, which remained unfinished after thirty years. Irritated by Rodin's success in the teeth of traditionalism, and displeased as well by the money Rodin continued to make by selling individual sculptures enlarged from the mass of figures on the uncompleted doors (*The Thinker* being the most popular), his critics in effect called for his head.

In the meantime, Rodin's admirers staged an event to honor Rodin's Legion of Honor promotion. The sculptor Antoine Bourdelle, who for years had served as Rodin's assistant and was beginning to branch out on his own, gave an emotional toast, while Isadora Duncan (back from her European tour) danced in Rodin's honor and then fell in homage at his feet. Rodin, who later regretted that he had never drawn Isadora from life, described her as "sister of the breezes" and praised her ability to "[attain] sculpture and emotion effortlessly." For her part, Isadora simply acknowledged Rodin as a "force of nature" and uncharacteristically concluded that "he is too great for me."[8]

Isadora had already made her debut at Berlin's New Royal Opera House in January, and she accompanied her success with efforts to communicate her vision to Berliners. Addressing the city's press club, she gave what would become her manifesto of modern dance, "The Dance of the Future" (published later that year as a pamphlet). Inspired by Nietzsche's pronouncements on dance ("Only in the dance do I know how to tell the parable of the highest things"), she extolled natural movement, the necessity of being in touch with the elements, and a future of dance in which the body expressed the language of the soul. In case her audience failed to understand what she was saying, she bluntly proceeded to reject traditional ballet's unnatural poses and sterility while ardently praising the potential role of woman, unhindered by men. "The dancer of the future," she promised her audience, "shall dance the freedom of woman."[9]

Isadora was present in Paris to dance for Rodin after deciding (much to her manager's despair) not to tour Germany. She was rich and, as she thought, sufficiently famous to conquer Paris as she had Berlin. In expectation of a repeat hit, she rented the huge Théâtre Sarah Bernhardt. But she had not yet made a sufficient name for herself in Paris outside of artistic circles, and the necessary audiences did not come. At the end of her season, she abruptly left Paris to avoid the debt collectors and returned to touring Germany. After a less-than-idyllic spiritual pilgrimage with her family to Greece, where they camped out, wore tunics and sandals, and tried to build a temple, she returned to Paris, via Vienna and Berlin, late in the year.

In a sage piece of advice, her manager urged her to think less about the ancient Greeks and more about her career.

∿

Gertrude Stein arrived in Paris in October, several months after her brother Leo, and the two took up residence at 27 Rue de Fleurus, a location that at the time had little to recommend it except for its low rents and proximity to the Luxembourg Gardens. Situated unpromisingly between the Latin Quarter and Montparnasse, which itself remained in the artistic shadow of Montmartre, the Steins nevertheless quickly made themselves at home, enjoying the cultural vibrancy of Paris and forming connections throughout its avant-garde artistic milieu.

Gertrude Stein—"Miss Stein," as she preferred to be called—was, like Isadora Duncan, a native of Oakland, California, just across the bay from San Francisco.[10] The pampered youngest of five surviving children, she grew up in the happy assurance that those around her existed to care for and indulge her. As it happened, her supreme confidence and ability to charm usually got her what she wanted. One of the best known of these occasions was the time when, as a Radcliffe student, she got up and left a final exam given by her eminent philosophy professor, William James, after writing at the top of her paper that she did not feel like taking an exam that day. To which James calmly replied (via post card): "Dear Miss Stein, I understand perfectly how you feel. I often feel like that myself," and gave her a top grade for the course. Whether or not this happened as Gertrude Stein later reported, it made for a good story—and certainly helped create the legend that she so consciously fashioned.[11]

Of course James did recognize Gertrude Stein's brilliance, and it was this combination of brilliance, well-directed charm, and expectation that those around her were as eager to please as she was to be pleased, that would enable her to sail through whatever potential difficulties life had in store. Or at least to report it that way.

Gertrude Stein was raised in a reasonably well-off although not wealthy family and spent her earliest years in Vienna and Paris before her father brought his brood to Oakland by way of Baltimore. There young Gertrude read extensively, explored the countryside with her brother Leo, and joined with Leo in rebelling against their father, whom they found overly strict and controlling. The death of their invalid mother was momentarily saddening but came as no surprise, while their father's sudden death merely freed the two from his objectionable ways. Now in their late teens and orphaned, Gertrude and Leo found life much pleasanter under the leadership of their oldest brother Michael, who in his mid-twenties became head of the family.

Michael managed family finances well, along with his job at San Francisco's new Omnibus Cable Company, where his father had been vice president. Michael was fun to be with and indulgent, treating his younger siblings to dinners in fancy restaurants and to plays, including a special outing in 1891 to see Sarah Bernhardt on her third American tour. Gertrude loved it. Unlike other plays, which she had found overly fast-moving and assaultive on both ears and eyes, she enjoyed Bernhardt's voice "being so varied and it all being so French I could rest in it untroubled."[12]

Gertrude Stein did not appreciate being troubled, and after a stimulating stint at Radcliffe College, where she enjoyed a wide range of intellectual challenge—including Professor James's graduate seminar (to which she had been admitted as an undergraduate), as well as formidable philosophy courses from George Santayana and Josiah Royce—she left for Baltimore and Johns Hopkins Medical School. Her aim was to pursue her interest in psychology, but to do this she needed some background in medicine.

After two years of it, she was bored—"frankly openly bored."[13] Summers, she fled to Florence and to Leo, who had given up his studies of history at Harvard and his studies in biology at Johns Hopkins to become a student of aesthetics. Soon enough he would give up on that as well and decide to become an artist. Leo may have flitted from one enthusiasm to another, but Gertrude was devoted to him and to the carefree life he was leading. Certainly she was not devoted to her studies, and when at the end of her final year she flunked a critical examination, she had no intention of making up the work in summer school. Instead, she threw her career in medicine out the window and headed back to Italy.[14]

From Italy she and Leo left for London and Bloomsbury, with pleasant stays in the English countryside. But they found London bleak and depressing, and at length Leo returned to Florence via Paris, where he had dinner with a friend, a young cellist by the name of Pablo Casals. Something about that dinner stirred Leo's inner artist, and that night he began to paint. Inspired by this experience, he decided that he would stay in Paris, and a cousin recommended a vacant apartment at 27 Rue de Fleurus that conveniently combined living quarters with an adjoining studio. Leo was charmed, and soon Gertrude joined him. It was the start of an era.

⌢

In May, the Automobile Club de France organized its great inter-city race, this time between Paris and Madrid. Adding to the danger were the new speeds that some of these vehicles were now capable of reaching—up to ninety miles per hour. Despite the cars' speeds, the roads remained primitive, making auto racing more treacherous than ever.

This only served to heighten the race's appeal, and by the time it began in Versailles early on the morning of May 24, an enormous crowd of spectators had gathered. Motorcars and cyclists had converged on Versailles, while supplementary trains ferried Parisians from the Saint-Lazare and Montparnasse stations. Afterward, newspapers reported that some hundred thousand people had spent the night there, many of them in the open air, waiting for the race to begin.

More than three hundred drivers and their vehicles took part, including the only woman driver, Madame Camille du Gast, a rich widow and concert pianist with a penchant for danger (she also enjoyed ballooning, skiing, and parachute jumping and was reputed to be an excellent shot). Du Gast had participated in the 1901 Paris–Berlin race and the grueling 1902 race from Paris to Vienna. Tightly corseted as the times required, she sat bolt upright in her De Dietrich machine, powering it to eighth position before she stopped to assist a fellow driver who had become pinned in a ditch under his car.

The drivers started at one-minute intervals and headed off in a blaze of dust and exhaust. Crowds surged along the entire route of the first day's race to Bordeaux, with children and cattle straying onto the road, and thrilled onlookers flocking to take photographs of crashed vehicles. Drivers and spectators were courting danger, but few seemed to care.

Louis and Marcel Renault were driving their light Renault vehicles and, from the start, were holding their own. Louis had drawn a better starting number than Marcel, but Marcel had been passing car after car in his race to the front.

And then disaster happened. Marcel attempted to pass in a cloud of dust and did not see the curve ahead. Within moments he had shot across a ditch at eighty miles per hour, his car somersaulting three times before landing on its back. Tragically, Marcel was caught underneath. Taken to a hospital, he did not regain consciousness and died the following morning.

His brother Louis, well ahead, did not learn the news until he arrived at Bordeaux (first in the light category and second overall). It was shattering. Not only had Marcel Renault died, but many others along the route had been injured or killed, some even burned to death. As news of the horrors poured in, the French government ordered that the race be stopped, and stringent measures were taken to prevent any of the competitors from continuing.

But Louis Renault had no intention of carrying on. Stunned by the loss of his brother, he immediately withdrew all the Renault drivers from the race.

Louis Renault would never race again.

～

That August, yet another disaster took place, this time on the Métro's new Line 2, where a fire broke out in one of the train engines. Before it was over, this fire—and the toxic smoke it produced—spread to two other trains in the Ménilmontant station, engulfing passengers caught in the adjacent Couronnes station. In the resulting panic, more than eighty people died—most of them from carbon monoxide poisoning.

Flaws in the equipment were responsible, and failure to fireproof the wood portions of the trains had magnified the disaster—a conclusion that led to shake-ups in upper level management. Hastening to appease the alarmed public, the CMP (Compagnie du Chemin de Fer Métropolitain de Paris) quickly moved to correct these flaws as well as to indemnify the victims' families. As the immediate drama receded from public consciousness, the Métro continued to build its citywide network according to schedule.

Nevertheless, it would continue to do so without the architect Hector Guimard. After a year of acrimony, Guimard and his employer, the CMP, definitively broke in May 1903. According to their agreement, Guimard was paid a favorable sum of twenty-one thousand francs in return for ceding artistic rights to the style that he had developed. As it turned out, his style, the "Style Guimard," could indeed be implemented by someone else, and Guimard's very reliance (much like Gustave Eiffel's before him) on prefabricated modular construction made the hand-off easier.

The CMP finished installing Line 3 that year with Guimard-inspired entrances but without Guimard input or oversight. Since Guimard had only partially overseen the installation of Line 2 entrances, due to disputes with the CMP, Line 1 remained the only line whose entrances bore the stamp of direct Guimard oversight. After 1904, the CMP would turn in an entirely different architectural direction for its entrances, using Marie-Joseph Cassien-Bernard to build the classical entrance for the Paris Opera, a site that had loomed as a major sore point between Guimard and those who feared a Guimard-style entrance in front of this bastion of conservatism. With Guimard gone and Cassien-Bernard in, this battle was over before it even began.

⟍

Within the depths of the Zola household, another battle had ceased. Madame Alexandrine Zola had learned of her husband's death while still in the hospital, and despite her deep jealousy of his mistress, Jeanne Rozerot, had informed Rozerot personally of the terrible news.

It was an unusually thoughtful gesture on Alexandrine's part, all the more so because of the many years of hostility that had preceded it. Even more thoughtfully, Alexandrine began to do what she could to care for Rozerot, to whom Zola had bequeathed little except some income from an insurance policy.

Zola had not left either his wife or his mistress in good financial shape—he had earned grandly over the course of his productive life but had spent even more grandly. In addition, fallout from the Dreyfus Affair had made a significant dent in his bank account. Soon after his death Alexandrine moved to smaller, less expensive quarters and sold many of her husband's most valuable possessions, including nine early paintings by Zola's boyhood friend, Cézanne.

And yet Alexandrine was mindful of her husband's love for Jeanne Rozerot and for the two children that Jeanne had borne him. Jeanne came to rely upon Alexandrine for financial support, but she came to rely upon Alexandrine as a friend as well. Over time Alexandrine would concern herself with the children's health and education, and in 1906 she took steps to legally adopt them, giving them the surname Emile-Zola and making them heirs to her estate.

It was an unexpected and touching denouement to what had been an unhappy family history. Now, as the two women drew together in memory of the man they both had loved, Jeanne could refer to Alexandrine—at least in letters to her children—as B.A., for "bonne amie."

～

In June, Debussy wrote André Messager: "I've been listening to the Prix de Rome competition. You have no idea what goes on in that place . . . and how it breeds distaste for music. . . . Ye gods, what music! And all the artistic sensitivity of a pork butcher."[15]

Ravel had much the same reaction, after having once again tried and failed to win the Prix de Rome. Again stuck with texts that were "so pretentious as to be amusing," he nevertheless had been "required to set them in a serious manner."[16] Afterward, he mused that "[I] now think of the Prix de Rome as a bad dream which I absolutely forbid to happen again."[17]

It had been a difficult year for Ravel. After being expelled two years earlier from Gabriel Fauré's composition class (for failing to win a prize in two consecutive fugue competitions), he had remained, with Fauré's encouragement, as an auditor. In January 1903 he then submitted the first movement of his String Quartet for the composition prize. His String Quartet, which now is a staple in chamber music repertory, did not, however, make the grade at the Conservatoire, and now Ravel left the Conservatoire for good.

He unquestionably had his supporters, including the music critic Jean Marnold—who in 1904 (following the String Quartet's first performance) declared, "One should remember the name of Maurice Ravel. He is one of the masters of tomorrow."[18] Gabriel Fauré also believed in Ravel, and Ravel acknowledged Fauré's courage in declaring "before the entire Institute that the [Prix de Rome] jury's decision was scandalous and obviously prepared in advance." It was especially courageous, Ravel noted, because in so doing, Fauré "permanently excluded himself from the Institute."[19]

While Ravel was engaged in dueling with the musical establishment, Debussy by 1903 had attained sufficient acceptance that he was made a Chevalier of the Legion of Honor. It was a big moment for him, and afterward he went to show his ribbon to his father, who was speechless. Debussy loved to tell this story. "You see," he would say, "in that brief moment I could feel pride at having been good for something."[20]

～

In October, Debussy met Emma Bardac, the mother of his pupil Raoul Bardac and the former mistress of Gabriel Fauré. By this time Debussy was a married man, but not a happily married one. In 1899, after breaking with his longtime mistress Gaby Dupont, he had rather suddenly married a pretty but empty-headed clothing model named Lilly Texier, whom he thought "adorable" and courted passionately, but who soon bored him.

Emma Bardac was quite a different matter. Emma was about Debussy's age (forty-one), the mother of two children, and an accomplished singer. Intelligent and sophisticated, she was everything that Lilly was not. Debussy had a weakness for women who were singers, and Emma—although still married to the father of her children—had an ongoing interest in music and in musical celebrities. Debussy was now a celebrity, and during the course of that autumn, the two were increasingly drawn together.

While Debussy and Emma Bardac were on the brink of shedding their respective spouses, across the Seine, Marie and her beloved husband, Pierre Curie, were hard at work under difficult circumstances in a double act of devotion—to their scientific research and to one another.

In June 1903, Marie Curie finally stood for her doctoral examination in physics. She had begun work on her thesis five years earlier, with the research that led to the discovery of radium. But the intensity of this quest, coupled with her teaching job and the care of her young daughter, had forced her to put off her oral examination. She simply could not find the time to prepare properly.

At last, though, she sent her examiners the text of her thesis: "Researches on Radioactive Substances, by Madame Sklodovska Curie." She was ready.

The examination room was crowded when she appeared, with onlookers eager to see her and hear what she had to say. Her examiners, dressed in formal evening attire, sat behind a long table as they took turns asking questions, to which she answered calmly and quietly. Despite her announcement of the value of radium's atomic weight and its position on the table of elements—a discovery of major importance—there was little overt drama; yet at the end, after her examiners formally conferred upon her the rank of "doctor," one added: "And in the name of the jury, madam, I wish to express to you all our congratulations."[21]

It was a moment to savor. There were other moments that year to savor as well, although the first, the Davy Medal from the Royal Society of London, came when Marie was ill. Pierre represented them both, bringing back a heavy medal on which their names were engraved. Not knowing quite what to do with it, he gave it to their six-year-old daughter, who promptly turned it into a plaything.

And then came the news that the Nobel Prize in Physics for that year would be jointly awarded to Marie and Pierre Curie, for their discoveries in radioactivity, and to Henri Becquerel, who had discovered the spontaneous emissions that the Curies had so successfully researched. Disturbingly, there appears to have been an effort early in the consideration process, on the part of several members of the French Academy of Sciences, to deprive Marie of her part of the prize, by willfully ignoring her contribution to the Curies' discoveries. Fortunately, a prominent member of the Swedish Academy of

Sciences got wind of this and notified Pierre, who insisted on the two being recognized together. In the end, the Swedish Academy of Sciences agreed to recognize the joint discoveries of both Curies.

It was overwhelming news, and apart from the welcome cash that accompanied their half of the prize, more of a problem than a benefit. "We are inundated with letters and with visits from photographers and journalists," Marie wrote her brother, Joseph. "One would like to dig into the ground somewhere to find a little peace."[22]

Nowhere did she mention that this was the first time the Nobel Prize had been awarded to a woman.[23] Or, for that matter, that the Nobel committee came close to omitting her. But the money was needed and could be accepted because, in accord with the Curies' strict principles, it would not be contrary to the scientific spirit to do so. With the money, and the creation of a professorship for him at the Sorbonne, Pierre could at last leave his job at the School for Physics and Chemistry, and the Curies could pay for a laboratory assistant. Marie kept her own teaching position but installed a new bathroom in their rented house and repapered one of the rooms. She also loaned and gave money to family members, Polish students, a childhood friend, laboratory assistants, one of Marie's students in need, and an elderly Frenchwoman residing in Poland who had once taught Marie French, whom Marie invited to come to Paris for a visit, paying for her journey.

Neither Marie nor Pierre attended the ceremony in Stockholm. It was a long and difficult journey to make in winter, and neither could afford to be away for such a length of time. In addition, as Pierre informed the Swedish Academy of Sciences, his wife had been ill that summer and had not yet completely recovered.

It was a sufficiently serious illness that it had also prevented Marie Curie from traveling to London to receive the Davy Medal. The cause, as Marie told her sister Bronya in late August, was that she had suffered a miscarriage. "I am absolutely desperate," she wrote, "and cannot be consoled. Write to me, I beg of you, if you think I should blame this on general fatigue—for I must admit that I have not spared my strength." She had relied on her strength and now regretted this bitterly, "as I have paid dear for it." She had wanted this baby "so badly!"[24]

Marie Curie had been several months pregnant when she stood for her doctoral examination in late June.[25] Despite any satisfaction in having at long last received her doctorate, she was almost immediately plunged into grief and despair—"in such consternation over this accident that I have not the courage to write to anybody."[26]

Marie Curie's illness and depression following her miscarriage cast a shadow over all the year's triumphs.

Portrait of Isadora Duncan dancing, 1904. Photo Credit: Universal Images Group / Art Resource, NY. © Art Resource, NY.

CHAPTER SIX

~

Alliances and Misalliances
(1904)

By June 1904, Debussy's marriage was disintegrating. He and Emma Bardac had become lovers, and in July Debussy dispatched his wife (who remained uninformed of what was going on) to her parents' summer place in Burgundy. He then sent her letters hinting of trouble to come.

The first, addressed to "Petite Lily-Lilo," told her that she "mustn't think I got any pleasure out of putting you so deliberately on the train. It was hard for me! Only, for reasons I'll explain to you later, it had to be done." He signed it, "Yours passionately, tenderly, Claude."[1] Perhaps he should have signed it, "passionately, tenderly, and hypocritically," but in any case, it was enough to send up warning signals.

If this communication was not enough to cause Lilly consternation, Debussy's complete disappearance was. Only his publisher, Jacques Durand, knew his summer address in Jersey (where the composer had gone with Emma), and Debussy instructed Durand to "go on telling *everybody* [Debussy's italics] you don't know my address, including my dear family."[2] By his "dear family," Debussy of course meant Lilly. He never had kept up much with the rest of his relations, and he was not about to begin now.

Debussy had a difficult meeting with Lilly in mid-September, about which he said little except (as he told his friend André Messager) that his life "these last months has been bizarre in the extreme, far more than one might have wished. I'd rather spare you the details, which I find tiresome."[3] When he returned to Paris at the end of September, he moved out of the apartment he had shared with Lilly and into quarters of his own.

Lilly was frantic and threatened suicide. Debussy paid little attention—after all, wasn't this what forsaken lovers did in Belle Epoque Paris? And then, on October 13, Lilly shot herself in the stomach. She survived, but the surgeons were unable to remove the bullet, which remained with her for the rest of her life. Unmoved by this near brush with death (Debussy seems to have regarded Lilly's failed attempt as little more than a bid for his attention and sympathy), Debussy proceeded into an acrimonious divorce.

〜

In January 1904, Misia and Thadée Natanson divorced. The following July, Alfred Edwards and his wife followed suit. Edwards typically had pulled strings and twisted arms to get what he wanted. What he wanted was Misia, and although she had become his mistress, this was not a sufficiently binding arrangement to satisfy him. Edwards bought off Thadée, and soon he would wed Misia. Yet not surprisingly, this marriage—begun in scandal—would not end well.

During these months Rodin, who had never lacked female companionship, entered into a relationship with the English artist Gwen John, who had fallen desperately in love with him. Calling him her master and her god, she told him that her only wish in life was to serve him. Their lovemaking, she assured him, was an act of worship.

Rodin seemed to have taken this in stride and continued work on *The Thinker*, which he was enlarging for the 1904 Louisiana Purchase Exposition in Saint Louis. When a group of his supporters took up a subscription to keep it in France, the state readily accepted the gift, agreeing to place it in front of the Panthéon, where it remained for several years. It now stands in the gardens of the Musée Rodin.

In the meantime, 1904 brought the marriage of Rodin's dear friend Helene von Hindenburg to Count Alfred von Nostitz of Saxony. The marriage, which seems to have been a happy one, did not end Helene's close friendship with Rodin. Letters between them would continue to flow until the outbreak of war in 1914.

〜

Wedding presents for socially prominent Parisian couples during the Belle Epoque were expected to be over-the-top—in large part because the information of who gave what was regularly listed in the newspapers. In 1904, for example, when the Marquis Dadvisard married Geneviève Haincque de Saint-Senoch, their wedding gifts included bags of diamonds, rubies, and sapphires, as well as a diamond-encrusted bodice. Madame Perquer gave the lucky couple a Louis XVI table (carefully reported as "d'époque" rather than a copy), while the Duchesse de Trévise, not to be outdone, presented them with a solid gold vase, and the Marquise de Sers parted with a pear-shaped knot of diamonds and pearls.

Several years earlier, Amélie Parayre had received gifts of jewels from her parents' employers, the high-flying Humberts, when she married Matisse. Yet her treasured emerald ring had long since disappeared, to pay for Cézanne's inspirational *Three Bathers*, and the Matisses' larder had been close to empty for some time. So it was a totally unfamiliar feeling when, following an un-expected visit from a wealthy young entrepreneur named André Level, Henri Matisse found himself counting out franc notes in large denominations.

Level, a previously conventional collector who had taken to modern art, had formed an art-buying syndicate called the Peau de l'Ours, and he was most interested in what he had seen at the Salon d'Automne the previous October. Gamely climbing the five flights to Matisse's Quai St-Michel stu-dio, Level picked out a still life and a landscape, leaving Matisse with four one-hundred-franc bills in exchange.

Dazed by this good fortune, Matisse was at a loss for words when, soon after, a colleague stopped by. Many years later Matisse recalled that the only response he could manage was to place a one-hundred-franc bill on the floor and step back. He then put down another bill and stepped back. Then a third, with an accompanying step, and then the fourth. At that, his friend dubiously asked him, "Have you killed someone?"[4]

That June, Matisse had his first one-man show, courtesy of the promi-nent art dealer Ambroise Vollard. Deciding to play it safe, Matisse selected paintings from his past, ones that were far more conservative than what he currently was creating. Given his financial situation, he felt that he had little choice. When the show was reasonably successful, once again Matisse seemed headed for the kind of acceptance that had appeared to be his all those years ago, before he deliberately threw it away to follow his artistic vision.

Yet once again, Matisse's artistic integrity intervened. When a dealer agreed to pay him handsomely for every conventional still life he could pro-duce, Matisse suddenly realized that he could not do it. This moment of truth struck him as he finished a still life that was reasonably good but very much like the one before it. "There was a temptation to deliver it," he later told the *New Yorker*'s famed Paris correspondent, Janet Flanner, "but I knew that if I yielded it would be my artistic death." On looking back, he realized that it took courage to destroy that picture, but he did it. With relief, he concluded, "I count my emancipation from that day."[5]

Breaking away from that particular hack work may have made all the difference to Matisse the artist, but to Matisse the family man, it was quite a different matter. He had a wife and three children, and the sacrifice they all were making on his behalf was sometimes unbearable. Still, summer in a tiny cottage in St-Tropez opened up a world of light and color for the struggling artist.

In addition, two Americans who would become his staunchest supporters were about to arrive in Paris. Enticed by Gertrude and Leo Stein's letters and prompted by his artistic wife, Sarah, Michael Stein retired from his position with the San Francisco cable car company and, in late 1903 or early 1904, moved with Sarah and his young son, Allan, to Paris.

Although this branch of the Stein family originally intended to stay in France for only a short time, they ultimately ended up remaining for three decades. In the years following their arrival in Paris, their apartment—at 58 Rue Madame, not far from 27 Rue de Fleurus—would become just as much a mecca for the avant-garde as was Leo and Gertrude's.

In the meantime, Leo and Gertrude Stein began to collect. It was soon after Leo's arrival that he bought his first Cézanne from Vollard, but it was not until 1904, following his more in-depth introduction to the artist via Charles Loeser, an extraordinary American collector in Florence, that Leo became a Cézanne enthusiast. As Gertrude recalled, she and Leo told Vollard that "what they wanted was one of those marvelously yellow sunny Aix landscapes of which Loeser had several examples." Vollard, who had been trying to show them everything but landscapes, now came back with "a wonderful small green landscape. It was lovely," Gertrude wrote, "it did not cost much and they bought it."[6] Leo regarded the transaction in far more revolutionary terms: "So now," he recalled, "I was a Columbus setting sail for the world beyond the world."[7]

～

Picasso returned to Barcelona in 1903 as a failure. Gertrude Stein later wrote, "There were things that at that time cut deeply into his spanish pride and the end of his Montmartre life was bitterness and disillusion, and there is nothing more bitter than spanish disillusion."[8]

Gertrude Stein may have been referring to a slightly later period in Picasso's life, but her observation certainly held true for this difficult phase. He returned to his old room in his parents' apartment, dejected and—despite the back of the hand that the City of Light had showed him—longing for Paris.

Yet Picasso immediately took advantage of the security that Barcelona gave him to work through his demons. It was now, after a hiatus of more than a year, that Casagemas's image reappeared—in *La Vie*, the masterpiece of Picasso's Blue period.[9] Here the figure of a suffering Casagemas stands, naked, with a naked Germaine clinging mournfully to him. Facing them is an expressionless robed woman holding an infant.

La Vie has prompted endless debate. Does it represent sacred versus profane love, the cycle of life, or simply a recognition of human misery? No one knows. Perhaps its creator had many ideas in mind, possibly conflicting ones. X-rays have shown that Picasso originally painted himself as the masculine figure, then replaced it with Casagemas. There are also indications that Picasso, always superstitious, was responding to the Tarot readings that Max Jacob had taught him.

Complicating the already complex, Picasso painted La Vie over an earlier work, Last Moments, which he had stored in Barcelona after its showing at the 1900 Paris exposition. Although this offers myriad possibilities for analysis, what Picasso probably was doing was what any impoverished painter would have done in his place—utilizing the canvas from an outmoded painting he no longer valued.

More somber paintings in blue followed, all of pitiful subjects—from a blind beggar to a destitute family standing forlornly on the seashore. Yet by 1904, Picasso had begun to move beyond this somber mode. He had also decided to return to Paris. Although he publicly announced that he and a friend were leaving for an exhibition of their latest works in Paris, there was no such exhibition planned. Instead, Picasso had a more permanent removal to Paris in mind. A friend was moving out of his studio in a ramshackle building called the Bateau-Lavoir on the slope of Montmartre. This studio was Picasso's, if he wanted it.

Indeed, he did.

~

That same spring, Isadora Duncan returned to Paris, where she presented her latest creation, an interpretation of Beethoven's Seventh Symphony. Beethoven's Seventh easily evokes images of dancing, but Duncan's audiences in Munich and Berlin were shocked by her boldness in venturing to interpret the master. Parisians were not so easily shocked, and Duncan performed her interpretation of Beethoven's Seventh Symphony at the Trocadéro before immense and enthusiastic crowds. This, her third visit to Paris, was a triumph. "For the third time a great artist has passed through Paris," wrote Debussy's friend, the critic and musicologist Louis Laloy, "and this time Paris understood."[10]

Never short on daring, Isadora then left for Bayreuth, mecca for Wagner pilgrims. Wagner's widow, the formidable Cosima, had requested her to choreograph and dance in a production of *Tannhäuser* for that summer's Wagner festival. This required Isadora to work with classically trained ballet dancers (whom she openly despised) as well as with Cosima, who did not countenance anyone messing with her beloved husband's legacy. Isadora soon discovered that everything was to remain pretty much as it was, which was hardly the stimulus or latitude for creativity that she required. In the end, her choreography and dancing fought against the strictures of tradition, and her version of *Tannhäuser*'s Bacchanal turned into an unsettling mess.

Isadora's flamboyant lifestyle, which included provocative clothing, costumes, and gentlemen friends, only exacerbated the situation. Not surprisingly, Bayreuth did not invite her back. It hardly mattered, as by this time she was off to other adventures, including the founding of her school in Gruenwald, Germany, an all-important milestone in her life. Of these, the most earth-shaking was her December encounter in Berlin with Gordon Craig.

Craig, son of British actress and national sweetheart Ellen Terry, was a pioneering stage designer who, at the time he first met Isadora, had yet to achieve success. Nonetheless he was drop-dead handsome, sexually magnetic, and keyed to some of the same dramatic ideals as Isadora. He was also monumentally self-absorbed, married, and living with a second woman, his mistress, as well as with a common-law wife. Yet this mattered little to Isadora. She later described their first night together in rhapsodic terms: "Hardly were my eyes ravished by his beauty than I was drawn toward him, entwined, melted. As flame meets flame, we burned in one bright fire."[11] As for Gordon Craig, he announced the beginning of their affair with one single entry in his daybook: "God Almighty."[12]

∿

While Isadora and her lover were busily fanning love's flames, a young Adonis by the name of Jean Cocteau was exploring life and his identity among the sailors in Marseilles. Earlier, as the youngest child in an artistically inclined and well-traveled Parisian family, Cocteau vastly preferred the theater to school. He later remarked that it was during his early teens that he "caught an illness much more serious than scarlet fever or measles—what I call the red-and-gold disease: theatre-itis."[13]

A darker event that he kept well hidden until late in life was his father's suicide, which occurred when young Cocteau was only nine. The details remain vague: "We were a family close to ruin," Cocteau later said. "My father committed suicide in circumstances that would not cause anyone to commit suicide today."[14] His cousin and childhood companion, Marianne Lecomte (later Madame Singer), recalled only that "Jean and I came home from a walk one day and were told that his father was dead. The news made little impression on us at the time—I remember that we were soon laughing and playing as usual. . . . I never heard why he did it."[15]

Despite this single jarring event, it was a protected and pampered childhood, during which Cocteau was treated to concerts, theatrical entertainments, and skating at the famed Champs-Elysées Palais de Glace, the popular skating rink frequented by schoolboys like Cocteau as well as by dandies and their mistresses, the great *cocottes* of the era. Cocteau quickly learned that indulgence came as a reward for being charming and easily manipulated his doting mother; but school was boring, and in 1904, at the age of fifteen—after being expelled from one school and twice failing his baccalaureate at another—he decided that it would be far more romantic to be a sailor. After that, he seems simply to have run away to Marseilles, where he lived in the old quarter, surrounded by brothels, opium-smoking, and crime. By his own account, it was the best time in his life.

This romantic breakaway lasted for about a year, or at least until an exasperated uncle told the police to find him, and two gendarmes subsequently brought him home. As with everything in Cocteau's life, fact is difficult to separate from fiction, but whatever actually occurred, the story of his defiant disappearance and subsequent revolt against any and all attempts to restrain him gave him a glamorous aura of rebellion that would surround him for the rest of his life.

～

The year was 1904, and François Coty was about to engage in his own act of rebellion. Or was it simply a superb marketing tactic? We do not know. What we do know is that on one fateful day, on the ground floor of the Louvre department store, Coty smashed a bottle of perfume on the counter—with momentous results.

Following his decision to learn more about the perfume business, Coty had indeed gone to Grasse, which was the long-established center for cultivating the flowers essential for making perfume. It was also the research center for the entire perfume industry. There, he applied for training at the esteemed Chiris company, which represented the cutting edge of current perfume technology. Fortunately, the head of the firm, now a senator, was a friend of Coty's patron, Senator Arène, which eased Coty's way. Coty then worked diligently for a year to learn all that he could, from flower cultivation to essential oils, spending much of his time in the laboratory. He analyzed, he synthesized, and he learned how to blend.

During his apprenticeship, Coty learned about two new tools that the established perfumers had for the most part neglected in favor of more traditional methods. The first of these was the discovery of extraction by volatile solvents, a technique that made extraction of large quantities of fragrance possible and could even be used with nonfloral substances such as leaves, mosses, and resins. Shortly before the turn of the century, Louis Chiris secured a patent on this technique and set up the first workshop based on solvent extraction. Coty was an early student of this pioneering work.

The second and even more revolutionary discovery was that of synthetic fragrances. Earlier in the nineteenth century, French and German scientists had discovered synthetic fragrance molecules in organic compounds such as coal and petroleum that allowed perfumers to approximate scents that could not otherwise be easily extracted. It was an amazing breakthrough, and a few perfumers experimented briefly with the artificial scents of sweet grass, vanilla (from conifer sap), violet, heliotrope, and musk. A few also explored the possibilities of the first aldehydes, which gave perfumes a far greater strength than ever before. Yet with only a few exceptions, established perfumers in the early 1900s avoided these synthetic molecules.

In studying the successful perfumes of the day, Coty concluded that most were limited in range and old-fashioned, pandering to conservative tastes with heavy, overly complex floral scents that were almost interchangeable. He had educated his nose and learned his trade, and although he never would become a perfumer per se, he had an extraordinary imagination and a gift for using it to explore new realms. It was with this gift, newly honed, that he returned to Paris, and with ten thousand borrowed francs set up a makeshift laboratory in the small apartment where he and his wife lived.

He was willing—even eager—to break with convention, aiming to create a perfume that combined subtlety with simplicity. Even at the beginning, his formulas were simple but brilliant, using synthetics to enhance natural scents. Coty also revolutionized the bottles containing his perfumes. Remembering the beauty of the antique perfume bottles at the 1900 Paris exposition, which made the virtually standardized perfume bottles of the day look boring, Coty unhesitatingly went to the top and hired Baccarat to produce the lovely, slim bottle for La Rose Jacqueminot, his first perfume. As he later remarked, "A perfume needs to attract the eye as much as the nose."[16]

Coty's wife sewed and embroidered the silk pouches with velvet ribbons and satin trim that contained the bottles, and Coty now drew on his sales skills—this time selling his own rather than someone else's product. Much to his dismay, it proved almost impossible to break through the established perfumers' stranglehold on the market. Coty went from rejection to rejection, until one day he lost his composure. He was on the ground floor of the Louvre department store trying to sell La Rose Jacqueminot, and the buyer was about to show him the door. In anger—or in what perhaps was a supreme act of showman-ship—Coty smashed one of the beautiful Baccarat bottles on the counter, and a revolution began. According to legend, women shoppers smelled the perfume and flocked to the source, buying up Coty's entire supply. The buyer took note, became suddenly cooperative, and Coty was on his way.

After the fact, some groused that Coty had staged the entire stunt, includ-ing hiring actresses to play the part of shoppers entranced by his perfume. Yet by this time it didn't matter. Coty had made his first publicity coup, whether or not it was intentional, and he and his perfumes were launched.

～

Throughout France, and especially in Paris, change was bounding along at what seemed a dizzying pace. City and country roads may still have been filled with horses and carriages or horse-pulled wagons, but trains had already brought distant places closer, and in Paris, the Métro's network had by 1904 more than doubled (from thirteen thousand to thirty thousand meters), while its trains had expanded from three to eight carriages apiece to accom-modate the surge in riders.

Bicycles and other horseless vehicles were appearing with more frequency on Paris streets and in nearby rural areas. Young, well-to-do Parisian women had for several years been cycling in the Bois de Boulogne on the trendiest models, the Little Queen or the Steel Fairy, dressed in their *culottes bouffantes*—a dar-ingly short style that allowed them to straddle their bikes while maintaining a certain amount of decorum (although both the style and the activity still aroused disapproval). As for the horseless carriage, by 1901, when the first Sa-lon des Automobiles was held in Paris's Grand Palais, more than two hundred thousand visitors attended. Not all of these, of course, were prospective buyers, but such crowds, along with soaring attendances at French road races, showed that public interest in the motorcar was rapidly growing.

As the new century progressed, motorcars became a more familiar sight. Even in Claude Monet's little Giverny, they had become so much of a nuisance that the municipal council passed a rule limiting all vehicles to a "moderate speed." Monet, a recent convert to the motorcar, was in fact fined in the spring of 1904 for speeding. This by now respectable old gentleman had dared to accelerate through Freneuse, between Giverny and Lavacourt.

As if that were not enough trouble for any one year, Monet now insisted on driving his treasured Panhard automobile all the way from Giverny to Madrid, accompanied by his wife, Alice, and son Michel. Wrapped in dusters, hats, and goggles to ward off the clouds of dust that plagued early automobile travel, they bravely set off, with their Michelin Guide in hand.

Michelin Guides had in fact first appeared only a few years before, as a promotional gimmick for Michelin tires and as an encouragement for auto travel, which the Michelin brothers perceptively understood would benefit their business. The brothers, Edouard and André, came from a family that for years had produced rubber products. The family firm was flagging when the brothers revived it in the late 1880s by specializing in bicycle tires and, soon, automobile tires. In 1891, shortly after the invention of the pneumatic bicycle tire (replacing the solid rubber variety), the Michelins took this discovery one step further by developing pneumatic bicycle tires that were not glued to the rim. By 1895 the Michelins were producing automobile tires, and by 1900, Michelin tires dominated the French tire market, which was the largest in the world until the United States overtook it in 1905.

Bicycle tires may still have represented a far larger market than auto tires in the early 1900s, but the Michelins sensed that the future lay in auto tires and began to specialize in them. This gave them a vested interest in increasing auto sales and auto tourism. André Michelin, the brother in charge of advertising, who was based in Paris (the company itself, run by brother Edouard, was located in Clermont-Ferrand), was adept at marketing. It was in 1900 that André came out with the first Michelin Guide, to make auto travel easier. The 1900 edition ran to thirty-five thousand copies, was free, and contained tips on how to repair tires, where to find hotels and gas stations, and where to find mechanics (there still were precious few).[17] "This Guide was born with the century, and it will last every bit as long," the brothers wrote in the preface to this first Guide. By 1904, when the Monets took off for Madrid, the Michelins had expanded publication to include Belgium, and Spain would eventually follow.

Monet's beloved Panhard made the 800 kilometers from Giverny to Biarritz in four days, but the trip evidently was more wearing on the automobile than on its passengers. After a good deal of trouble, the Monets had to leave the car in Biarritz for repairs while they finished the journey by train. Their stay in Madrid was a success (Monet was moved to tears by the paintings of Veláquez, and was astounded by the El Grecos), and their return journey was blessedly uneventful—although the repaired Panhard seemed dispirited and would not go more than thirty kilometers per hour.

Despite this, soon after returning to Giverny, Monet—who had evidently become an auto enthusiast—set off for the car races at nearby Gaillon. There, amid dust and exhaust fumes, he and his family partook of a leisurely picnic in the grass.

⌒

Picnics in the grass were not among Auguste Escoffier's specialties, although he certainly was interested in making cuisine more accessible and less formidable than the mountainous feasts created or inspired by his legendary predecessor, the celebrated nineteenth-century chef, Marie-Antoine Carême. Escoffier addressed the problem of expanding waistlines and diminishing enthusiasms for the same old grandiose banquets by creating a new approach to cooking and dining, one that cleared away much of the ostentation, the richness, and the sheer overabundance of food. Although neither his recipes nor his menus would appear light or simple to twenty-first-century eyes, they focused on the essentials to a degree not before encountered in Parisian haute cuisine.

Originally, Escoffier had wanted to become a sculptor, but he quickly learned that his family's humble circumstances made this impossible. Both his father and grandfather were blacksmiths, but there was another option: an uncle had a restaurant in nearby Nice, where the family arranged for thirteen-year-old Escoffier to begin his apprenticeship. "Even though this is not the profession I personally would have chosen," he remembered telling himself, "since I am here, let me work to make the grade."[18]

After three grueling years of apprenticeship and several subsequent jobs in Nice, young Escoffier headed for Paris, where he went to work as a lowly kitchen aide at an elegant restaurant in the eighth arrondissement. The Franco-Prussian War landed him in the army as a cook, where his reputation began to build. Once the war (and a brief period of German imprisonment) was over, he returned to Paris—this time as *chef de cuisine*, where he was becoming known for his inventive dishes and menus.

It was in 1874 that he first encountered Sarah Bernhardt, then at the onset of her meteoric career, and created a memorable dish for her—not the *Fraises Sarah Bernhardt* (strawberries, pineapple sorbet, and curaçao-infused citrus ice cream) that he would later present in her honor, but what he termed a "light dish" of calf sweetbreads with fresh noodles served with a purée of foie gras and truffles. He knew that Bernhardt had a passion for calf sweetbreads, and he was right—she adored the dish and asked him to make it for her again and again. Who knew that slim Sarah Bernhardt had such a passion for sweetbreads?

From Paris, Escoffier (now a married man) went to Cannes, then on to a series of better-and-better jobs in Paris, Lucerne, and Monte Carlo, where he met César Ritz, who also was on a phenomenal upward climb. Ritz recognized the importance of a brilliant chef like Escoffier, while Escoffier appreciated Ritz's extraordinary management abilities. "An excellent cuisine,"

Escoffier later wrote, "the best list of French wines, and perfect service made it so that clients never wanted to leave."[19]

Unfortunately Escoffier and Ritz's joint venture at London's Savoy Hotel ended badly, with much finger-pointing all around. But in the meantime Ritz (much to the displeasure of the Savoy's chairman of the board, Richard D'Oyly Carte) was building his own hotel in Paris, the Ritz Hotel, which opened in 1898 with Escoffier in charge of the kitchens. From the outset, the Ritz Hotel was a smashing success, making it possible for Ritz to send Escoffier to yet another new venture, London's Carlton Hotel, whose kitchens Escoffier would direct for twenty years.

It was a breathtaking rise for the boy from a backwater Provençal blacksmith's family, and Escoffier never forgot it. His memoir is larded with the names of the titled, the rich, and the famous, who continued to dazzle him. When speaking of the Carlton Hotel, he remarks that he is "sure that the aroma of the *suprêmes de perdreaux au parfum de truffe* and other such delicacies that I proposed helped to enhance its reputation as a new temple of gastronomy."[20]

Of course he was right, and it was his insistence on perfection, on well-organized kitchens, and on constantly inventing new dishes to vary the menus and satisfy his clients that kept him at the top of his game. By 1903, when he published the first edition of his combined cookbook and textbook, *Le guide culinaire*, he was considered France's greatest chef. He had made his mark on the Belle Epoque and on much of the century thereafter, and this volume of more than five thousand recipes would define French *haute cuisine* for decades to come.

~

Marie Curie never paid much attention to food, and there were long periods when she was either too poor or too preoccupied to eat. Yet as her daughter recalled, on those few occasions when she did entertain, she tried her best, shopping in the Rue Mouffetard or the Rue d'Alésia for fruits and cheeses, and ordering ice cream from the neighborhood patisserie. On a more regular basis, since daughter Irène was a picky eater, Marie made winter trips across Paris in search of suitable apples and bananas for her child to eat.

Yet in the autumn of 1904, Marie Curie craved caviar—just a tiny bit would do, but she longed for it. She was pregnant again, and this pregnancy was difficult, leaving her weak and depressed. The birth itself was long and painful, but on December 6, another daughter was born, whom she and Pierre named Eve.

It would be some time before Marie recovered from this pregnancy and delivery, and her depression often sent her into black and dismal realms.

Eventually, though, the new baby helped bring back her interest in life. Much as with her first daughter, Marie kept track of Eve's developments in a notebook, and as the baby grew, Marie Curie was able to seize life—and her research—again.

In the meantime, following the Curies' Nobel Prize, the Sorbonne had at last found a position for Pierre in physics and (shortly before Eve was born) a position for Marie as chief-of-work in physics. No laboratory had as yet appeared for Pierre, but the two now moved their equipment from the old leaky shed to a new place in Rue Cuvier.

~

Despite their rigorous lives, Pierre and Marie Curie permitted themselves occasional pleasures, including exhibitions of paintings and the occasional concert or play, where they preferred Ibsen to Rostand, and Eleonora Duse to Sarah Bernhardt. Even before their Nobel Prize made them famous, Loie Fuller—the so-called "light fairy"—had come knocking on their door, in the hope of adding a luminous radium dance to her many other stunning showpieces. The Curies were not encouraging—they had already discovered some of radium's dangers—but the friendship remained, leading to other friendships.[21]

Fuller, who was short and stout, had found fame at the Folies Bergère as a dancing flower and other exotics after discovering that long extensions of billowing silk elongated her stage presence and, with dramatic lighting effects, compensated for her otherwise unglamorous face and figure. She was a dynamo, and soon after meeting Rodin (her private theater at the 1900 Paris exposition was located near Rodin's private exhibition), she organized an American exhibition of his work, along with pieces of her own, at the New York National Arts Club, billing it as "Miss Fuller's Collection." These were mostly plasters, although some marble and bronze versions also made the trans-Atlantic trip, and these Rodin sculptures, which included *The Hand of God* and *The Thinker*, gave New York its first up-close look at his work. The show lasted only a week, but Fuller managed to negotiate with the Metropolitan Museum of Art to display some of the works for a year. Much to her surprise and dismay, Rodin refused. As always, the crosscurrent of women in his life had led to backstabbing, and accusations of Fuller's financial interest in the scheme contributed to the abrupt end of this venture.

It was through Fuller, though, that Marie and Pierre Curie met Rodin, and subsequently visited him at his home in Meudon. Meudon had by this time become a kind of mecca for visiting dignitaries, and Count Harry Kessler had already gone to pay his respects. "Today," Count Kessler reported,

Rodin "was particularly talkative," stating that Michelangelo had "freed him from classicism" and "opened his eyes to *nature*." Kessler, who was a perceptive collector, asked how Rodin had discovered (or rediscovered) light and how to incorporate it in his sculptures. Rodin replied that he had hit on it by accident, over the course of fifteen years. "I wanted at first to follow nature as closely as possible," he told Kessler. "But I noticed that it was necessary to exaggerate it a little. . . . Without that, the piece looks thin."[22]

Later, Kessler visited Monet at Giverny, where he found Monet's auto waiting for him at the Vernon train station.[23] Monet, Kessler noted, was somewhat similar in appearance to Rodin, being "short, wide, powerfully built with a large, almost white beard and frank, dark brown eyes." He noted that Monet, however, "lacks entirely the sly glint of Rodin's eyes."[24]

In the course of a marvelous Saturday, including lunch, Kessler asked Monet how it was that he came to use colors for the shadows, and Monet replied: "Ah well, it was by egging each other on, Renoir, [Frédéric] Bazille, and me."[25] And then, after pulling out a number of his London paintings, Monet remarked, "I have always said to English painters, 'How is it possible that you who live here have never done this?'" He then answered his own question: "They make objects but not their atmosphere, that's the problem." When Kessler asked if Monet had ever wanted to paint the Thames at night, Monet replied that indeed he had, "but one is too tired when one has painted all day. And then it would be difficult without imitating Whistler."[26]

Somewhat later, Monet unwillingly relinquished further insights to Paul Durand-Ruel's son, Georges, who asked which colors Monet used. "Is it really as interesting as all that?" Monet testily replied. "The point is to know how to use the colours, the choice of which is, when all's said and done, a matter of habit." And then he added, "Anyway, I use flake white, cadmium yellow, vermilion, deep madder, cobalt blue, emerald green, and that's all."[27]

﹏

Picasso's Catalan friend, Jaime Sabartès, recalled Picasso's own palette from his early Paris days: "As a rule, the palette was on the floor; white, heaped in the center, constituted the basis of that type of mixture which he prepared especially with blue. The other colors brightened the contours." Sabartès did not remember ever seeing Picasso holding the palette in his hand, as with most other artists, but instead, whenever he was composing his colors he was usually "leaning over a table, a chair or the floor."[28]

Picasso had returned to Paris in April 1904, with his friend Sebastià Junyer Vidal (who paid the rent), an assortment of works that Picasso valued, and a dog—a mongrel named Gat (Spanish for "cat"). Two more dogs, Feo and Frika, would follow, as would a mistress named Madeleine, who enigmatically slipped in and out of Picasso's life. Vidal also slipped out, after a few weeks of roughing it in the Bateau-Lavoir, but Picasso was there to stay.

The Bateau-Lavoir was essentially a wooden hillside tenement on Place Ravignan that had been inhabited by anarchists and impoverished bohemians since the late 1880s.[29] It was seedy, but it was cheap, and Picasso gratefully took to it. His old friend Max Jacob may have been responsible for the name, as the ungainly building did faintly resemble a laundry boat; but however dismal the accommodations, its years of glory began when Picasso moved in, attracting a coterie of other artists and writers.

Squalor and camaraderie were mixed in equal parts in the Bateau-Lavoir of the Picasso years. Max Jacob moved there, as would André Derain, Maurice de Vlaminck, Kees van Dongen, and for a brief while, Amedeo Modigliani. Picasso used his slender new mistress, Madeleine, as a model for paintings and sketches as he moved from his Blue to his Rose period, and when Madeleine became pregnant, Picasso readily approved of an abortion. Madeleine no longer figured in his life, for he had just met another young woman, Fernande Olivier, who would become his first great love.

∽

It started with what looked on the surface like a simple state visit. In October 1903, the king of Italy made an official visit to France, and the French president, Emile Loubet, returned the compliment in April 1904. Yet as often happens in foreign affairs, this seemingly simple exchange of visits sent off ripples in many directions, and before long, all hell broke loose.

The key element here was the pope—and the difficult relations between the Vatican and the Kingdom of Italy, which in 1870 had completed Italian unification by capturing Rome. In time, the Church would reluctantly agree to accept the results of 1870 in return for Italy's recognition of the Vatican State, but in 1904 this loss of temporal power (Rome as well as the earlier loss of the Papal States) still rankled mightily in the Vatican, which refused to recognize either the Italian government or its conquest of Rome.

By 1904, other nations had lost interest in the Roman question, especially since far larger issues loomed—most particularly in the east, after the Japanese navy sank the Russian fleet in Port Arthur, leading to the outbreak of war between these two rival empires. For France, this meant that its Russian ally would be preoccupied with Japan and no longer would be able to provide a check on Germany to its west—an arrangement that the French had held dear for more than a decade. This newly opened vulnerability made friendship with Italy of the utmost importance. Loubet went to Italy in April with

The Bateau-Lavoir, Paris. © J. McAuliffe

the near-unanimous support of the Chamber of Deputies and the Senate. Soon after, the papal curia sent a stiff note of protest to Paris.

Unfortunately, the Vatican decided to make this protest public, circulating it to all governments. Soon a copy appeared in the French press, and the French read there a series of insults that few could abide. It would have been difficult to have produced a more provocative communication, and the French promptly recalled their ambassador from the Vatican.

French Catholics witnessed this display of pontifical ire with dismay. It was clear that the pope had given French anticlericals all the ammunition they needed to strike the last blow in the separation of Church and state.

As Abbé Mugnier commented sadly in his journal, "All is going. End of a world!" And then he added, "But this world, has it been truly fruitful?"[30]

⌒

April 1904 turned out to be a busy month for French diplomacy. Not only did President Loubet visit Italy, but the French and the British signed an alliance, the Entente Cordiale, which marked the formal end to almost nine centuries of intermittent conflict and the culmination of almost a full century of peace following the Napoleonic Wars.

Various parts of the agreement settled long-standing disputes, whether in Egypt (where British hegemony was recognized), Morocco (where French hegemony was recognized), or several other portions of each nation's respective empires. The Entente gave France a much-needed ally in addition to Russia, which now was preoccupied with Japan, while it gave previously isolated Britain some protection from the source that worried both nations—a potentially aggressive Germany.

All-in-all, the year seemed to end satisfyingly for France: peace and prosperity, and the prospect for more in the year to come.

Pablo Picasso at Montmartre, Place Ravignan (now Place Emile-Goudeau), Paris, circa 1904. Photo Credit: Adoc-photos / Art Resource, NY. © Art Resource, NY.

CHAPTER SEVEN

~

Wild Beasts

(1905)

Until the autumn of 1905, Henri Matisse was known among his colleagues as "Le Docteur," an artist whose neatly bespectacled appearance was in direct contrast to the passionate artist within. It was at the 1905 Salon d'Automne, held in the eminently respectable Grand Palais, that the Fauvist ("Wild Beast") revolution broke forth, with Matisse as its leader.

What had happened? For years Matisse had battled his conflicting impulses, between commercially viable conservatism and something else, although he had not yet grasped what that something else was. Earlier that year he had helped organize the first official exhibition of Vincent van Gogh's works, as part of the Salon des Indépendants—certainly an influence, for he later gave credit to van Gogh as well as Gauguin for his summer breakthrough. But it was the little fishing village of Collioure that dazzled him with color and light, and drove him to take more risks than ever before. Two summers in the south of France had exposed this northerner to vibrant color, and he responded ardently, even gratefully.

Collioure radiated color and light, but it also exuded an element of savagery, for there was a fierce primitivism in this Catalan town that expressed itself in the explosive colors and contrasts of Fauvism, so unlike the gentler colors of the Impressionists. Embracing Gauguin's insistence that art should primarily communicate emotion, Matisse forged ahead, daring all by rejecting art as representation, and producing works of shattering impact.

The most important painting that he showed at that year's Salon d'Automne was *La Femme au chapeau* (*Woman in a Hat*), a violently colored

103

portrait of his wife that quickly became the most notorious entry in the show. Surrounded by others of similar audacity, including those by his friends Derain and Vlaminck, this explosion of color inspired one critic waspishly to compare these artists and their works to *fauves*, or wild beasts. And among the wild beasts, Matisse was the undisputed king.

This coronation certainly did not make his life any easier; critics and crowds openly jeered these new works. Both his morale and his income had hit rock bottom when, shortly before the Salon closed, an unexpected offer arrived for *Woman in a Hat*. It was for much less than Matisse's asking price, and although he was inclined to accept, his wife was not. They held out, and after several anxious days, the buyer at last came around to their price.

The buyers were Leo and Gertrude Stein. Leo and Gertrude, Michael and Sarah had debated the picture—along with their Baltimore friends, Claribel and Etta Cone, wealthy sisters and close friends of the Steins who were, like the Steins, about to become major collectors of modern French art.[1] Gertrude later insisted that it was she who spotted Matisse's *Woman in a Hat*, but Sarah remembered that Leo first called it to her attention, and that she too was attracted to it. After the four considered buying it jointly, Leo put in a low bid, which (to the Steins' surprise) Matisse rejected. Eventually Sarah and Michael would buy it from Gertrude, but it first went to Leo. It was "a thing brilliant and powerful," Leo later recalled, "but the nastiest smear of paint I had ever seen. It was what I was unknowingly waiting for."[2]

～

Picasso did not participate in any of the official salons in Paris, and never would do so. Instead, he relied on his principal dealers (soon to become Ambroise Vollard, then Daniel-Henry Kahnweiler) and on the exhibitions they arranged for him in other major cities. In addition, he relied on a growing group of collectors. As he later observed, even though most of the poets and women in his life at this time were French, most of the people who kept him alive were from other places.

This included the Russian collector Sergei Shchukin; the German collector Wilhelm Uhde; and the American Steins—Leo and Gertrude, Michael and Sarah. Leo Stein had bought Matisse's *Woman in a Hat* shortly before he purchased his first Picasso, *Harlequin's Family with an Ape*. Leo followed this with Picasso's *Girl with a Basket of Flowers*, which Leo bought over Gertrude's strong objections (something about the legs and feet repelled her).

Despite their argument over this painting, Leo and Gertrude soon found their way to Picasso's studio in the Bateau-Lavoir, where Leo was overwhelmed as much by Picasso's intense gaze as by his art. As Leo later recalled, "When Picasso had looked at a drawing or print, I was surprised that anything was left on the paper, so absorbing was his gaze."[3] Gertrude later described Picasso as "thin dark, alive with big pools of eyes and a violent but not rough way."[4] Clearly fascinated, Leo added, "He seemed more real than most people while doing nothing about it."[5] Both Gertrude and Leo were sufficiently impressed with the young Spaniard that soon after their first introduction, Picasso and his latest love, Fernande Olivier, dined with the Steins at 27 Rue de Fleurus—the first of many such visits to come.

Picasso was as fascinated with Gertrude Stein as she was with him, and soon after this first dinner he asked to paint her portrait. What followed was an enormous number of sittings (Gertrude claims some ninety of them), for which she regularly crossed Paris by horse-drawn omnibus to Place Blanche and the Moulin Rouge, where she got off and climbed up steep Rue Lepic to Place Ravignan (now Place Emile-Goudeau) and the Bateau-Lavoir. There, in what would soon become (in Max Jacob's words) "the Acropolis of cubism," she sat in a broken chair by a red-hot stove while Picasso perched on a kitchen chair and leaned close to his easel while he painted from a very small palette of "a uniform brown grey color."[6]

Picasso painted intently, ignoring comings and goings, cooking, distractions, and much disorder, while Fernande graciously offered to read La Fontaine's stories aloud to amuse them while Gertrude posed. By this time Picasso would have seen Matisse's extraordinary *Woman in a Hat*—probably at the Salon d'Automne and certainly at 27 Rue de Fleurus—and, keenly aware that his portrait of Gertrude Stein would hang in the same room as Matisse's own glorious breakthrough, every competitive bone in his body would have compelled him to come up with a portrait that would overshadow Matisse's. And so, at the end of the afternoon, when Leo and others came to look at what Picasso had done and exclaim at its beauty, Picasso shook his head and said, non, it would not do.[7]

Afterward, Gertrude would walk home (about two miles, much of it downhill), accompanied on Saturdays by Picasso and Fernande, who stayed to dinner. And that, as Gertrude Stein later explained, was the beginning of the Steins' celebrated Saturday evenings.

〜

Picasso regularly carried a gun, a Browning revolver that had once belonged to the legendary poet and playwright Alfred Jarry, the bizarre and outrageous creator of the bizarre and outrageous *Ubu Roi*. Picasso and Jarry seem never to have met—Jarry was dying at the time Picasso was reestablishing himself in Paris. But they shared many friends, and Picasso biographer John

Richardson hypothesizes that either Max Jacob or Apollinaire nabbed the revolver or arranged for it as a gift at the end of Jarry's life.[8] However it came into his possession, Picasso regularly carried this rusty old revolver. He claimed (in Jarryesque fashion) to use it to ward off bores and morons as well as anyone who spoke ill of Cézanne, and is credited with having fired off several shots at the Lapin Agile in exasperation with several Germans intent on extracting aesthetic theories from him.

Despite the bucolic memories of former residents, a revolver could be a useful accessory in Montmartre, especially by night. Artists generally did not encounter trouble, largely because they were too poor to attract attention. Yet even Picasso's favored cabaret, the Lapin Agile, encountered occasional violence—especially one memorable night, when a thug shot the owner's son-in-law.

Before meeting the Steins, Picasso had already established a routine for nighttime revels, which included weekly jaunts to the Closerie des Lilas (clear across town, at the northern edge of Montparnasse). These revelries also included more frequent outings at the Circus Médrano or Circus Bostock (both located just a few blocks south of the Bateau-Lavoir) as well as the Lapin Agile cabaret (nestled just over the top of the Butte). Circuses had long fascinated Picasso, and the circus inspired his *Saltimbanques*, which he completed during the summer of 1905. Earlier in the year he painted *Au Lapin Agile*, to pay his bar tab by decorating one of that tavern's dingy walls.

The Lapin Agile had been around for a couple of decades before Picasso and his gang gravitated to it, acquiring its name when the illustrator André Gill designed its sign of a nimble-looking rabbit jumping out of a pot. The place subsequently took the punning name of the Lapin à Gill, or Lapin Agile. During earlier stays in Paris, Picasso and his friends had been too broke even to drink at the Lapin Agile and had instead frequented a sordid little tavern on Place Ravignan called Le Zut, which attracted a lowlife clientele and specialized in cheap beer. Finding it unbearably filthy, Picasso and company cleaned up a back room for themselves, whitewashing and decorating it with murals. Picasso's was *The Temptations of St. Anthony*.

Le Zut's owner was Frédé Gérard, an itinerant fish seller, who in 1903 left Le Zut to its fate and moved to the Lapin Agile. Picasso and his friends followed, contributing to the place's glory years, from about 1905 to 1912, when Picasso left Montmartre. It was an attractive enough place in the summer, shaded by acacias, and Picasso seems to have brought his dogs along to enjoy it. Yet the picture he painted, *Au Lapin Agile*, was a somber one, featuring himself as Harlequin with Germaine Gargallo as Columbine by his side. Both look straight ahead rather than at one another, in eerie solitude.

Picasso painted *The Death of Harlequin* after this, in late 1905, but the Harlequin image would continue to haunt his work.

～

In September, Marcel Proust's mother died, leaving him a considerable fortune. She also left him in complete anguish. His father's death in 1903 had grieved him, but his mother's death left him desolate. "She takes away my life with her," he wrote, "as Papa had taken away hers."[9]

He now kept his promise to his mother and checked into a clinic for nervous disorders, located just outside Paris in Boulogne-sur-Seine, where he languished. "My life has now forever lost its only purpose," he wrote Count Robert de Montesquiou, "its only sweetness, its only love, its only consolation."[10] After less than two months he left the clinic, no better than when he arrived.

Much like Proust, Louise Michel never fully recovered from her mother's death, which had occurred fully twenty years earlier. Michel was a dedicated activist and had been at the forefront of virtually every Parisian effort on behalf of the poor since the bloody Commune uprising of 1871. By the time of her death in early 1905, she was widely revered and beloved by those she sought to help, as well as by those who sympathized with them—including Georges Clemenceau, who as mayor of Montmartre had assisted Michel during the horrors of the 1870–1871 German siege of Paris and who remained her friend.

Although an unapologetic anarchist, Michel never embraced violence. When gunned down by an assassin, she characteristically forgave the man and defended him in court (she survived, although the bullet remained in her head until her death, many years later). Never a Marxist or a theoretician, her anarchism was based on a deep identification with the poor and the suffering. She could not bear to see anyone or anything suffer, human or animal, and her pain was the keenest if this suffering was the result of cruelty or injustice. Although more of an irritant than a threat to France's establishment, her politics and her protests had for years made her unwelcome in her native land. After exile in New Caledonia (which she spiritedly survived) and a five-year self-imposed exile in London, she returned to France to brave the authorities while, despite deteriorating health, she kept up an ambitious schedule of talks and lectures.

She died in Marseilles in January 1905, prompting an enormous turnout of mourners along the funeral route to the cemetery. Memorial services subsequently took place throughout France and other countries, and when her body was disinterred and taken to be buried with her mother in Levallois-Perret, just outside of Paris, another crowd formed, which the newspapers reported as being the largest since the massive turnout for Victor Hugo's funeral twenty years earlier.

The funeral route wound its way through the heart of Communard territory: from the Gare de Lyon in the twelfth arrondissement, where the casket arrived from Marseilles, through the Place de la Nation and past Père-Lachaise cemetery, where government troops had gunned down the last of the Communards in 1871—a date still raw in the memories of many of the people paying tribute that day. The hearse, preceded by a wagon laden high with wreaths, continued through militant Belleville, where much of the male population of a certain age was missing, martyred to the Communard cause. It slowly continued past Sacré-Coeur, where someone cried out, "Down with the priests!" And finally, it reached its destination in Levallois-Perret. Anticipating trouble, the government had stationed dozens of infantrymen and cavalry around the Gare de Lyon and along the entire route across Paris to the cemetery.

There was no trouble in Paris, but in a remarkable coincidence, the day of Louise Michel's funeral coincided with the Bloody Sunday massacre in St. Petersburg, when an unarmed and peaceful crowd of Russian workers and their families attempted to deliver a petition to their czar and were gunned down as they approached the Winter Palace. As many as one thousand were killed or wounded, leading to widespread strikes, mutinies, and general unrest throughout the Russian Empire. By 1907 this first Russian Revolution would be brutally suppressed, but the stark misery that created it remained. For those who listened, it was either a call to arms or an alarm bell in the night.

There were other events in 1905 that set off alarms in France, in particular Kaiser Wilhelm II's landing in Tangier. The poet and essayist Charles Péguy presciently noted that Germany's action opened "a new epoch in the history of my life, in the history of this country, and undoubtedly in the history of the world."[11]

The Tangier Crisis, or Moroccan Crisis, erupted when the German Kaiser used his presence in Tangier to assert Germany's support of Moroccan independence—testing France and Britain's recently signed Entente Cordiale, which had placed Morocco under France's imperial colors. Pushing the issue further, Germany now sought a multinational conference to call France to account. When the French refused to back down, Germany threatened war.

After considerable altercation, the French agreed to attend a conference in the Spanish city of Algeciras in 1906. Despite German pressure, France would retain its effective protectorate over Morocco, and the British-French alliance would remain firm. Yet this would not be the last of German provocations, nor of the steady ratcheting-up of diplomatic confrontations between the imperial powers in the years to come.

An altercation that year on the domestic front marred an otherwise pleasant family gathering at one of Sarah Bernhardt's Sunday lunches. Marcel Proust may have been able to navigate the difficult shoals that still surrounded the Dreyfus Affair, but Sarah Bernhardt had neither the patience nor the inclination to do so. When one of her luncheon guests, an ardent opponent of Dreyfus, made a disparaging crack about the Jewish captain, another guest took offense, leading to general disruption. Salad was spilled, guests began to yell at one another, and Sarah—a fervent supporter of Dreyfus—took umbrage at her anti-Dreyfusard son, Maurice, and furiously broke her plate in two. When Maurice (deeply offended) tried to pull his wife away from the table, Sarah broke another plate on the arm of the guest who had first denigrated Dreyfus. The Sunday afternoon bonhomie now irrevocably shattered, the party withdrew in general disarray.[12]

According to Jean Cocteau, Sarah Bernhardt "presented the phenomenon of living at the extremity of her person in life *and* on the boards."[13] Yet she was not about to put up with any nonsense from young upstarts like sixteen-year-old Cocteau, who in 1905 made his entrance at a ball given at the Théâtre des Arts dressed as the decadent young Roman emperor Heliogabalus, complete with "russet curls, a crippling tiara, a train embroidered in pearls, rings on my toes, and painted nails." Even though accompanied by the legendary actor Edouard de Max, who was dressed just as outrageously, Cocteau quickly learned that he had overstepped the line when Sarah Bernhardt sent him a note (via her maid) saying, "If I were your mother, I'd send you to bed."[14]

Sarah Bernhardt was passionate, but she was a hard-headed businesswoman and a thorough professional who never confused self-promotion with mere self-indulgence. She also never let illness or pain get in the way of ticket sales or a performance. That same year she began a long tour of the Americas, even though her right knee was giving her trouble. In Buenos Aires, she had to have the knee operated on, and all seemed well for a time. Then in Rio de Janeiro, she leaped from a stage parapet down onto bare boards where thick mattresses were supposed to be. It was the death scene from *La Tosca*, and it about did her in.

Still she went on. And on. From New York she went to Chicago, Montreal, and Quebec, where the archbishop denounced her play, *La Sorcière*, as blasphemy, and indignant members of his flock pelted her and other members of the cast with rotten eggs. In Kansas, her private (and luxurious) train jumped the tracks, while in Dallas she had to perform in a tent, thanks to the war between her management (the young Shubert brothers) and the powerful Klaw and Erlanger theatrical syndicate. In San Antonio, she performed in a music-hall saloon, while in Houston, she did her best in a skating rink. In San Francisco, she arrived shortly after the great earthquake and performed (according to her account) in the only theater left standing.

Few people knew that in addition to severe knee pain, Sarah Bernhardt suffered from terrible stage fright. Her granddaughter, who accompanied her on a later American tour, recalled Sarah going all clammy-handed an hour before each first night, exclaiming, "My God, my God! If only the theatre would burn down!"[15] Yet Sarah never regarded this as a liability, and in fact thought it made her a better actress. And she unquestionably made money from her American tours—lots of it—as well as stockpiling enough stories about her American adventures to last the rest of her long life. She would tour three more times in America, each time a "farewell tour."

⟶

By March, Debussy's lover, Emma Bardac, was two months pregnant, and Debussy's divorce proceedings were under way, even though an anguished Lilly insisted that she still wanted to live with him. Debussy wrote in his notebook that Lilly exercised "a daily tyranny over my thoughts and dealings" and accused her of lying to their friends.[16] "I'm being hounded by the press campaign Madame Debussy has been kind enough to launch against me," he complained to his publisher, Jacques Durand. "It seems I'm not allowed to get divorced like anybody else."[17] Certainly it was true that most of his friends now left him. "I've had to look on as desertions take place all round me," he wrote the music critic Louis Laloy.[18] Maurice Ravel and Debussy's longtime friend Pierre Louÿs even contributed to a fund for Lilly. Only Jacques Durand, Louis Laloy, and the composer Erik Satie remained loyal to him.[19]

"So, after a year, the nightmare is finally over," Debussy wrote Durand in August, shortly after the divorce was finalized.[20] Debussy and Emma now moved into a rented house in a small cul-de-sac that opened onto the elegant Avenue du Bois de Boulogne (now Avenue Foch). There, at the end of October, their daughter, Claude-Emma, was born. Chouchou, as they affectionately called her, delighted her parents, although Debussy at forty-three was not about to sacrifice any of his musical priorities for parenthood.

Certainly by October, Debussy was in the midst of a professional as well as personal whirlwind, for in the midst of publishing his first set of *Images*, he had also completed the score of *La Mer* and now was anxiously hovering over rehearsals for an October 15 first performance. As always with Debussy's music, the critics were divided about *La Mer*, but among those who understood that Debussy had succeeded in creating something entirely new, one wrote: "One has the impression that M. Debussy . . . has here considerably condensed and clarified the mass of his discoveries," and that his music was on its way to achieving the "hallmark of masterpieces."[21]

One of *La Mer*'s movements is titled, "From dawn to midday on the sea." Erik Satie, who enjoyed a well-deserved reputation for sly humor, told Debussy, "Ah, my dear friend, there's one particular moment between half past ten and a quarter to eleven that I found stunning!"[22]

Satie, whom Ravel as well as Debussy had befriended during Satie's years as a piano player in Montmartre cabarets, was about to return to school. Oddly enough, given Satie's predilection for remarkably original and avant-garde compositions—including his three *Gymnopédies* for piano (of which Debussy set the first and third to orchestra) and a piano duet that he mysteriously titled *Three Pieces in the Shape of a Pear*—Satie chose to attend the rigorously conservative Schola Cantorum, headed by the prominent traditionalist composer Vincent d'Indy.

Debussy warned Satie, "At your age one does not change one's skin,"[23] but Satie (now almost forty) had decided that the rigors of counterpoint and theory were exactly what he needed at this stage in his development. D'Indy was open to backing contemporary composers, even if he was not enthusiastic about what they wrote, and he accepted the modest but unpredictable Satie as a pupil.

~

Ravel's position in the spring of 1905 was unusually frustrating. On the one hand, he was a rising young composer, the well-known and highly regarded author of works such as *Jeux d'eau*, the String Quartet, and *Shéhérazade*. On the other hand, he had unbelievably failed once again in his attempt at the Prix de Rome. At the age of thirty, he had reached the age limit for the prize; there would be no further attempts, even had he been willing to undergo the humiliation. This time the judges eliminated him in the first round, having decided that Maurice Ravel lacked the technical proficiency to be considered as a finalist.

This infuriating decision did not go unnoticed, and soon the affaire Ravel not only roused music critics to battle but became front-page news. As the eminent author Romain Rolland lamented: "I can not comprehend why one should persist in keeping a school in Rome if it is to close its doors to those rare artists who have some originality—to a man like Ravel, who has established himself . . . through works far more important than those required for an examination."[24]

The scandal escalated when news leaked that all six of the finalists were pupils of the same professor of composition at the Conservatoire, who most damningly was also a member of the jury. Charges and countercharges filled the air, with the Prix de Rome judges and the Conservatoire itself under attack. As one critic charged, the Conservatoire had become "little more than a stronghold of time-worn conventions and blind prejudices." Even Ravel's persistent critic Pierre Lalo joined in complaining that the Conservatoire taught little more than stultifying rules and formulas.[25]

Among the casualties of this uproar was Ravel's longtime adversary Théodore Dubois, who resigned as Conservatoire director. Several others of the most hidebound faculty members left with him. It was now that Ravel's esteemed former composition teacher, Gabriel Fauré, unexpectedly vaulted into power as the Conservatoire's new director, bringing the promise of reform with him. As Debussy noted, in a congratulatory letter to Fauré: "If they're going to put 'the right man for the job' in charge of the Conservatoire, who knows what will happen? And how much dust of old traditions there is to shake off!"[26] As hoped for, Fauré immediately launched a series of much-needed curriculum reforms, giving new life to the place. At Fauré's request, Ravel would now participate in various juries, including the piano jury and, in a final triumph, the jury for the Prix de Rome itself.

In the midst of this furor, Ravel received a lifeline to peace and quiet when he accepted an invitation from Misia Natanson Edwards to join her and her second husband, Alfred, on their yacht for a summer cruise through Belgium, Holland, and Germany. Ravel had met Misia through her brother and sister-in-law, Cipa and Ida Godebski, who would become two of his closest friends. Indeed, the Godebskis would become a second family to Ravel, including their two children, whom Ravel adored.

Misia had been irate about the Prix de Rome jury's treatment of Ravel, and she prodded her new husband to publicize the scandal in his newspaper, *Le Matin*—contributing to the widespread press interest in the story. She also decided that Ravel needed a respite from the mess, and during his much-needed vacation on Misia's yacht, the *Aimée*, Ravel indeed relaxed and enjoyed himself. "I'm not doing a thing," he wrote his friend Maurice Delage, "but I am storing things up, and I believe that a lot will come out of this trip."[27]

They visited museums and saw the birthplaces of Goethe and Luther, but one of the sights that truly mesmerized Ravel was a nighttime view of a huge foundry on the Rhine. "How can I tell you about these smelting castles, these incandescent cathedrals, and the wonderful symphony of traveling belts, whistles, and terrific hammerblows which envelop you?" he wrote Delage. "How much music there is in all of this!—and I certainly intend to use it."[28]

He was about to embark on many years of great creativity, which would last until the outbreak of war. He also was about to receive regular and substantial remuneration, since he now began a professional relationship with Auguste and Jacques Durand of Durand and Company, who agreed to publish his works in return for a twelve-thousand-franc annuity. All in all, as Ravel told another friend, "I have never been so happy to be alive, and I firmly believe that joy is far more fertile than suffering."[29]

〜

Unlike Ravel, by the summer of 1905, the poet Rainer Maria Rilke was in poor health, broke, and drifting. Yet he continued to regard Rodin as the lodestar of his life, and from Germany wrote him: "What moves me, Master, is the need to see you again and feed for a brief while on the glowing vitality of your beautiful works."[30] Rodin was flattered and sent a letter expressing his affection and admiration. Reassured by this vote of confidence, Rilke decided to return to Paris.

The upshot was a happy one—at least at first. Rodin effusively welcomed Rilke and invited him to stay at Meudon as his secretary, an offer that Rilke enthusiastically accepted. After all, as Rilke wrote his wife, "He is so alone and there are hundreds and hundreds of things that take up his time, and he never finds the right secretary to take care of the correspondence."[31]

At first Rodin treated Rilke like a son—unlike Auguste Beuret, Rodin's despised illegitimate son by Rose Beuret, whom the sculptor refused to acknowledge. The autumn months of 1905 were rich and relaxed, filled with walks, talks, and expeditions. Yet Rodin was accustomed to tyrannizing those who served him, and soon gentle Rilke would discover "what it was like to live at close quarters with a moody and autocratic giant."[32]

In the meantime, Isadora Duncan was beginning to learn what it was like to live with her own moody and autocratic giant. In late 1904 she had gone to St. Petersburg, where she upended the dancing world and made an indelible impression on devotees and dancers alike—including the impresario Sergei Diaghilev and a young dancer by the name of Michel Fokine.[33] She took a brief time-out to open her school in Gruenwald, but then returned to St. Petersburg in February 1905, soon after the Bloody Sunday massacre. Gordon Craig, who accompanied her, seems not to have noticed the aftermath of this tragedy, but Isadora—who would become a passionate supporter of the pre-Stalin Soviet regime, and who eventually dedicated one of her dances to the victims of Bloody Sunday—recalled the deep impression made on her by one of the funeral processions on the dawn of her arrival.[34]

This tour was not as successful as her first Russian tour; traditionalists had anticipated her return and rallied to criticize her dancing and her use of concert music to dance to. In addition, Isadora's relationship with Gordon Craig was beginning to fray. By now, she was fully paying for everything, including his support, for which he seemed quite pleased with himself. "I'm not making a penny but living like a Duke," he bragged to his friend, the composer and musicologist Martin Shaw.[35] Worse, in March Isadora discovered that Craig's English mistress (Elena Meo) had given birth to a son (Edward A. Craig, who already had two sisters by Craig, one of whom had died). Isadora may not have known at the time that Craig was sending Elena money—Isadora's money—and had promised to return to Elena as soon as he was financially able to do so. Yet the shock of this baby was great enough on its own, especially since Craig had talked of marriage with Isadora, and she so desperately wanted a baby of her own.

Despite this, Isadora remained hopelessly in love with Gordon Craig. She adored him, she believed in him, and after she erupted in anger upon learning of his deception, she abjectly apologized. "Dear," she wrote him, "I feel awfully ashamed—ashamed is not the word. I feel dust & ashes—it was an awful kind of rage that took possession of me—let my pain atone for it."[36]

Confronted with his perfidy, Craig played the puzzled innocent,[37] a role at which he was especially adept, despite his three children by Elena and five other offspring by his wife, May Gibson, and his common-law wife, Jess Dorynne. It is unclear whether Isadora yet knew of Craig's marriage or his common-law wife, or even the number of children he had fathered. The new baby was enough, and she was desolate.

∽

By 1905, Paul Poiret had prospered. His atelier on Rue Auber, well located by the Paris Opera, had become too small for his growing business, and he was about to move again, this time to a private house on Rue Pasquier (8th). There he would elegantly refrain from shop signs or window displays. He needed neither, having already established a loyal clientele by challenging the established dressmaking conventions of the day.

He already had jettisoned the corset—"this abominated apparatus," as he called it, that divided its wearer into two masses, with the bust stuck prominently out in front and the behind projecting just as prominently to the rear, "so that the lady looked as if she were hauling a trailer."[38] Dispensing with this unforgiving and uncomfortable understructure made new concepts in draped designs possible, starting with Poiret's famous kimono that had so shocked a Russian princess at the House of Worth that it prompted his original decision to strike out on his own. From then on the kimono, in various versions, would be a Poiret staple.

Poiret was not the only denizen of the Belle Epoque attuned to Greek and Far Eastern influences, as Isadora Duncan and the Spanish designer Mariano Fortuny clearly showed, but Poiret would also revolutionize fashion's color palette. It probably was no coincidence that at this time he was living near the Fauvist painters Maurice de Vlaminck and André Derain in Chatou, a former Impressionist haunt just west of Paris. Poiret later wrote that when he began to do what he wanted to do in dress-designing, the only colors being used were "washed-out and insipid." Given to metaphorical bomb-throwing, he "threw into this sheepcote a few rough wolves; reds, greens, violets, royal blues, that made all the rest sing aloud."[39]

Dramatic to the core, this wild beast of fashion would soon find his inspiration in some of the most striking theatrical events of the Belle Epoque.

∼

André Citroën's company had expanded and prospered so much by 1905 that he decided to move to larger premises in a new industrial area on the Seine's left bank, beyond the Eiffel Tower, on what now is the Quai André-Citroën. It was at this time that Citroën first became involved with the fledgling automobile industry, producing five hundred engines for the Paris-based Sizaire-Naudin auto manufacturers. An old friend, Jacques Hinstin, headed the Sizaire-Naudin firm, and Citroën would soon be seeing a lot of him.

François Coty was also doing well in new quarters, which he had shrewdly taken in an affluent part of town, just north of the Champs-Elysées. Space there was limited, but the address (on Rue La Boétie) was a good one and worth the effort to cram showroom, shop, laboratory, and packaging department under one small roof. Much as Coty expected and desired, his perfume business continued to surge. The year 1905 was a big one for him, during which he presented two new hits: Ambre Antique and, especially, L'Origan, which according to perfume aficionados was an exceptionally daring blend, suitable for those daring Fauvist times.

It was while Coty was launching his seductive new perfumes that an ambitious young woman by the name of Helena Rubinstein was studying dermatology in Paris. Born in Krakow's Jewish ghetto, by her late teens she had fled to an aunt and uncle in Vienna to escape an arranged marriage. From Vienna she then decamped for Australia, where she began to make and sell face cream—Crème Valaze, as she called it, billed as containing herbs imported from the Carpathian Mountains but largely composed of sheep lanolin, one of Australia's most accessible but least glamorous products. Rubinstein found a backer, sold pots of the stuff at steep prices, and soon could afford to open a salon in Melbourne that melded the beauty-care business with the trappings of scientific and medical techniques, diagnosing the patron's skin and prescribing proper treatment.

Rubinstein's 1905 stay in Paris was little more than a way-stop (spent with one of her sisters, who resided there) as she burnished her reputation by studying skin treatment with specialists throughout Europe. She soon returned to Australia and to her booming business; but given the nature of that business, Paris would inevitably beckon again.

⟋

Paris had long held the crown in culture, fashion, and style, but staunch French Catholics still prayed for a reversal of the materialism and secularism that so blatantly flourished around them. In 1905, as work began on its bell tower, the basilica of Sacré-Coeur rose white and shining from its pinnacle on the Butte of Montmartre, holding the light of morality and spirituality high above the benighted masses below. Despite the efforts of anticlerical republicans, who saw Sacré-Coeur as a flagrant symbol of the superiority of Church over state, and despite the fury of former Communards, who resented Sacré-Coeur's most certainly intentional placement on the very spot where the 1871 Commune uprising had burst forth, the basilica had overcome a host of physical as well as political obstacles and by now was a permanent if still incomplete presence overlooking Paris.[40]

Simmering for years behind the pristine whiteness of Sacré-Coeur was the rumble of anticlerical discontent with the Church's power, its invasiveness in political affairs, and its dominance in education. Still, for years all but the political far left were wary of attacking the Church head-on, and since the 1880s anticlericals had chipped away at secularizing French life only in those areas most likely to receive public support, mainly in the realm of education. Education meant the Jesuits, who had long dominated French secondary education (the *collèges*) and who for just as long had stirred up suspicion, hatred, and suppression in several nations, including France, which had abolished them even before a pope formally dissolved the order in 1773. Following the revival of the French monarchy, another pope reestablished the order, and the Jesuits staged a sturdy comeback in France until, in the 1880s, the Third Republic removed the clergy from the schools and once again dissolved the order in France. Despite this setback, the Jesuits managed to return to their roles as schoolmasters through legal loopholes and the staunch support of conservative Catholics like the de Gaulles, who comprised a sufficiently vocal and prickly minority that they were for the moment allowed their way.

Relations between Church and state in France had a long and tangled history, complicated during the opening years of the twentieth century by the agreement struck a century before between Napoleon Bonaparte and the Church—the agreement known as the Concordat. This defined Roman Catholicism as the religion of the majority of the French people, and stated that the state would henceforth pay the clergy and nominate bishops. In return, the Church agreed to renounce its claims to the extensive property it had lost during the Revolution. The Concordat lasted for more than a century, but its life now looked in peril. In 1902, a commission was established to examine propositions regarding the separation of Church and state and the elimination of the Concordat, and by 1905 the combination of a strongly anticlerical prime minister (Combes, followed by his successor, Maurice Rouvier), backed by the Assembly and goaded by Clemenceau, brought the long-simmering problem to a head.

To separate Church and state would be "as foolish an act as to release wild beasts from their cages in the Place de la Concorde to pounce on pedestrians," one fervent Catholic warned,[41] but by December 1905 both Senate and Assembly had accepted the law ending the Concordat and promulgating the separation of Church and state during the year to come.

Standing apart from the fray, Abbé Mugnier quietly declared—in the privacy of his journal—that this frantic concern about religious associations and organizations completely missed the point of what religion should be about. "What about justice," he asked, "and charity, and resignation, and courage, and everything which makes the human soul to live!" Religion, he continued, "is a spirit, a movement of the heart. You make of it a power, a society, an exterior force, something which struggles with other powers and other societies. To love God and one's fellow man, is it necessary to have so much materiality?"[42]

Yet Abbé Mugnier was a rarity among the clergy. In a year that had begun with the rebellion of the Fauvist "wild beasts," the break-up of Church and state seemed, to the apprehensive faithful, to signal the end of the world as they knew it and a tide of revolutionary secularism to come.

Maurice Ravel at the piano. Bibliothèque des Arts Décoratifs, Paris, France. Photo Credit: Gianni Dagli Orti / The Art Archive at Art Resource, NY. © Art Resource, NY.

CHAPTER EIGHT

~

La Valse

(1906)

Early in 1906 Maurice Ravel began work on a grand waltz, which he called "a sort of homage to the memory of the great Strauss." Not Richard Strauss, he clarified, but "the other one, Johann." Writing to his friend, the music critic Jean Marnold, he added: "You know of my deep sympathy for these wonderful rhythms, and that I value the joie de vivre expressed by the dance."[1]

At first Ravel simply called the work "Vienna," and several months later he wrote Misia Edwards: "Perhaps I'll make up my mind to undertake 'Vienna,' which is intended for you, as you know."[2] Yet Ravel put his waltz aside and would not complete it until after the war, by which time it had taken on far darker tones. No longer "Vienna," it became simply *La Valse*, and instead of expressing the joie de vivre of the dance, it summoned up memories of a vanished world spinning out of control.

Ravel would indeed dedicate the work to Misia in 1920, after it emerged as *La Valse*. He had valued Misia's support during the Prix de Rome and was grateful for the much-needed summer respite she had given him on her yacht, the *Aimée*. There was little that he could give her in return except for this dedication; her new husband, the wealthy Alfred Edwards, gave her everything she wanted, and much more. She had piles of jewels, a yacht of her own, and a husband who seemed desperate to please her. And then, quite suddenly, all of this changed.

Not surprisingly, this total reversal occurred because of another woman. Edwards had recently renovated his Théâtre de Paris for Bernhardt's great rival, Réjane, and he and Misia presided over the opening gala. It was the same theater where Misia had first caught Edwards's eye, but on this occasion a beautiful and ambitious young actress and demimondaine by the name of Geneviève Lantelme caught Edwards's eye. Quite abruptly he forgot Misia and set off in pursuit of Geneviève.

From Edwards's point of view, Geneviève's lurid reputation only enhanced her desirability, and he deluged her with jewels and flowers. Much as Misia had done, Geneviève first ignored him. Then Edwards wrote a play for her and cast her in the leading role. Soon they became lovers, and Misia discovered, too late, that she was jealous. Worse, Edwards now was beginning to treat Misia as he had treated his former wife. It was unbearable.

Edwards installed Geneviève in an expensive town house on Rue Fortuny, just north of Parc Monceau. As it happened, Geneviève was cheating on Edwards with a handsome operetta star, and one day Edwards's detective caught them *in flagrante*. Yet instead of cooling Edwards's ardor, this offense merely intensified it. Edwards wanted most what he could not get, and Geneviève was playing hard to get. Misia had been hard to get, too, but she had not been playing at it. Now, she discovered that for the first time in her life she was lowering herself to chase a man she had already lost.

Despairing, she escaped for the fashionable Grand Hôtel, Cabourg, in Normandy. Unfortunately there was no escape from her social set, which traveled to all the same places she did. In the Grand Hôtel's dining room, Marcel Proust was amused to see Misia in the center of what he described as a stage set for the third act of a farce. Near the unfortunate Misia were her husband, Edwards, and his beloved, la belle Lantelme. Nearby was Edwards's former brother-in-law ("first husband of the last Mme Edwards," Proust slyly explained, and "the fourth of the species because before the present one he had already married two Americans, a Frenchwoman and a Greek"). Worse yet, Misia's first husband, Thadée Natanson, was among this jolly throng. Proust, who witnessed and thoroughly enjoyed the scene, wrote to his friend and former lover, Reynaldo Hahn, that "yesterday evening there was a rumor circulating that Mme Edwards (Natanson) had killed Edwards (the Englishman who is in fact a Turk), but there was nothing in it, nothing happened at all."[3]

⌒

While Ravel was starting on his waltz, which would eventually summon up images of a world whirling dangerously near the edge, Misia Natanson Edwards's world was about to fall apart, while Isadora Duncan's was entering a daunting new phase. Isadora was pregnant, and although deliriously happy about it, she fully realized the financial sacrifice that this would involve. She would have to stop dancing before and after the baby's arrival, and to make up for this, she took on a frantic schedule during the first part of 1906, taking on as many engagements as she could despite the physical challenges of her pregnancy. During these months, Craig's friend Martin Shaw, who had agreed to serve as Isadora's conductor, was impressed with Isadora's endurance as well as her calm ("Her serenity made me think of a still, deep lake over which no breeze made the faintest ripple"). Isadora, as usual, danced the entire program: "This in itself is remarkable," he wrote. "I doubt whether any other dancer has ever been able to carry through a whole evening's entertainment unaided."[4] Discreetly unmentioned was the fact that she was doing this during her early months of pregnancy.

The baby was due in late August, and the doctor had told her that she could dance until the end of May, which she managed for a while without overt comment from dance critics or audience (this at a time when strictures against unwed mothers were harsh). Yet despite the flowing robes in which she danced, it became impossible to disguise the obvious. Word of her pregnancy spread, creating a scandal. No longer an image of purity, Isadora became the embodiment of a woman with loose morals. All the while, despite the arduous physical challenge, she danced and danced, earning enough money to support her dependent family, her school, and her lover. "Often, in spite of myself," she later wrote, "I felt very miserable and defeated. This game with the giant Life was too much."[5] As for Craig, he showed no interest in the baby and little in Isadora, while he continued to indulge his expensive tastes.

In Germany, Isadora's friends tried to convince her to abort the baby or give it up for adoption, leading her to consider getting away and spending the summer near Lake Como, until she began to fear that Italy might be even more oppressive. Craig was usually somewhere else, and at times Isadora did not even know where to find him. "You might ring me on the telephone now & then & say Hello," she wrote him from Germany, followed by, "Dearest Love—Where are you?—No letter since a century."[6] By this time it was clear that Isadora would have the full responsibility for rearing the child, a baby girl, who was born in late September after a long and grueling labor.[7]

For Isadora's last months of pregnancy, and for the delivery itself, she chose to hide out in a cottage on the coast of the North Sea, near Leiden, with only a cook for company until Isadora's young niece, Temple Duncan, and Isadora's friend, the sculptress Kathleen Bruce, arrived. Despite Isadora's determined cheerfulness in writing to Craig, Kathleen was appalled to find her friend "pitiful, helpless, . . . nothing more than a frightened girl." According to Bruce, Isadora even contemplated suicide, walking one night into the waves. "So loudly and arrogantly had I proclaimed that complete indepen-dence for a lass was fraught with no dangers whatever, given character and intelligence to back it," Bruce later wrote. "I was very young."[8]

During these difficult months, Isadora begged Craig to visit and even offered to share her abode with one of Craig's women, if that would make him happy ("If there is anyone you care for very much who feels unhappy and wants to come with you she can have half my little house with *all my heart*. It will give me joy—and Love is enough for all").[9] He appeared once during the long wait and was treated (as Bruce later said) "as the Messiah."[10] Surprisingly, he was briefly present for the birth, although he rapidly took off again after telling Isadora that she could call the baby "anything you damn please—Sophocles, if you like."[11] Eventually, Isadora would name her daugh-ter Deirdre, or "Beloved of Ireland."

⁓

"I have already been living here with Pablo for six months," Fernande Olivier wrote in her journal in February/March 1906. When she first began living with him, the Bateau-Lavoir had been brutally hot inside; now, in midwin-ter, it was "so cold that if we leave a little tea in the bottom of our cups it's frozen by morning." This did not stop Picasso from working through the night—his preferred time to work, free from disturbance. "We have no coal, no fire, no money," Fernande wrote, "but I'm happy in spite of this." She added, with a burst of enthusiasm, "I don't know how I could have resisted Pablo for so long. I love him so much now!"[12]

Fernande Olivier, by her own account an unwanted illegitimate child brought up by a family who never accepted her, had married young, run away from her brutal husband, and spent the years before she met Picasso as an art-ist's model. She was beautiful and had lived with a series of artists—including the sculptor with whom she currently was living at the Bateau-Lavoir when she first met Picasso. "He [the Spanish painter] looks at me with his huge deep eyes," she told her journal in August 1904. "I don't find him particularly attractive, but his strangely intense gaze forces me to look at him in return." One memorable late summer afternoon, as a thunderstorm broke, she dashed for shelter and found Picasso laughingly blocking her way and holding out a kitten to her. "He seemed to give off a radiance, an inner fire," and suddenly she "couldn't resist this magnetism."[13] She went with him to his studio, and their on-again-off-again affair began.

"Picasso is sweet, intelligent, very dedicated to his art, and he drops every-thing for me," she wrote a short while later. "He's asking me to come and live with him, and I don't know what I should do." For a while she managed to cheat on her sculptor lover, but she had a problem with Picasso: "He's jealous, he has no money at all, and he doesn't want me to work. It's ridiculous! And besides, I don't want to live in that miserable studio." At the root of her indecision was her fear of yet another botched love affair. "You see, I'm not in love with him—it's another mistake."[14]

Other men were pursuing her and even proposing marriage, but she disliked them—and anyway, she couldn't marry without finding her husband and asking for a divorce, "and nothing in the world would persuade me to confront my husband again."[15] And so she ricocheted from one man to another, resisting Picasso's pleas to move in with him, loving his attention and fearing his jealousy. And then, on a Sunday in early September 1905, after a heady seduction enhanced by opium, she moved in with him.[16]

They managed on fifty francs a month, with Picasso sweeping out the studio and doing the shopping while Fernande did the cooking—and a great deal of reading. They ate out only at places like the Lapin Agile, where they could eat for a pittance, or places where they could eat on credit. By springtime, Fernande happily recorded in her journal that although they had fights, "our love for one another has not diminished in any way. On the contrary, the ties between us seem to be getting stronger and stronger."[17]

Still, Picasso was jealous. He would not let Fernande leave the studio without him, and he even took the key whenever he left her there alone. That spring they had a bad fight at the Lapin Agile, when Picasso accused her of flirting with one of the other diners, and she retorted that he had been behaving overly familiarly with one of the women there. She ran out, he chased after her, and before it was over she had blurted out that she was wasting the best years of her life in abject poverty with a man whose jealousy was set off by "the slightest involuntary gesture." She told him that he was forgetting that she was entitled to a more comfortable way of life. He said nothing, but when she woke up the next morning he had disappeared, only to return with a few banknotes and a small parcel of perfume. She fairly melted.

By this time Leo and Gertrude Stein had arrived in their lives, and Fernande noted that "they're rich and intelligent enough not to worry about looking ridiculous and are so self-assured they wouldn't care what other people think anyway."[18] Picasso was in the midst of painting Gertrude Stein's portrait when the art dealer Ambroise Vollard bought twenty paintings from him for a windfall of two thousand francs. It was then that Picasso decided to return for the summer to Barcelona, taking Fernande with him.

∽

A certain amount of tension was beginning to enter the relationship between Ravel and Debussy, largely—as others later pointed out—because of efforts by music critics to stir up trouble between them. Although Ravel's musical setting of five animal sketches from Jules Renard's *Histoires naturelles* would be jeered in early 1907, his *Miroirs*, Sonatine, and *Noël des jouets* (1906) were all well received. Ravel had become the music scene's latest enthusiasm.

Yet with that, he now found himself being held in comparison with Debussy—sometimes, he felt, unfairly. Following the introduction of *Miroirs* (played by Ricardo Viñes at the Société Nationale), the influential music critic Pierre Lalo complimented Ravel for being "one of the most finely gifted [musicians] of his generation"—praise immediately diminished by the qualification, "despite [his] several very apparent and rather annoying faults." The most salient of these faults, wrote Lalo, was "the strange resemblance of [Ravel's] music to that of M. Claude Debussy"—a resemblance that was both "extreme" and "striking."[19] Ravel, deeply stung, immediately pointed out that his *Jeux d'eau* "was published at the beginning of 1902, when nothing more than Debussy's three pieces, *Pour le piano*, were extant." Despite Ravel's avowed admiration for these Debussy pieces, "from a purely pianistic point of view, they contained nothing new."[20]

While Ravel and Lalo would spar for the next three decades, critics such as Jean Marnold were unstinting in their praise of Ravel, terming the entire suite of *Miroirs* as "exquisite" and two pieces in particular ("Oiseaux tristes" and "Une Barque sur l'océan") as "absolute masterpieces."[21] Ravel hastened to tell Marnold how much his review had consoled him in the wake of Lalo's criticism, but Ravel's new prominence—especially after all the Prix de Rome coverage the year before—put him in the limelight, with its attendant discomforts. Jules Renard, author of the *Histoires naturelles* that Ravel set to music, wrote in his journal that Thadée Natanson had initiated the contact between them by describing Ravel as "an avant-garde musician who is dependable, and for whom Debussy is already an old fogey."[22] Somehow the remark became public and made the rounds, despite the fact that Ravel never would have considered Debussy as such. But the rumor stuck and spread.

Following the premiere of Ravel's *Histoires naturelles*, Debussy wrote his friend Louis Laloy (who had written an enthusiastic review) that he agreed "in acknowledging that Ravel is exceptionally gifted." Still, Debussy was irritated by Ravel's "posture as a 'trickster,' or better yet, as an enchanting fakir, who can make flowers spring up around a chair." Unfortunately, Debussy added, a trick "can astonish only once!"[23]

Adding to the tension, Ravel's antagonist Pierre Lalo published an article in *Le Temps* in late March 1907 in which he attributed to certain "young musicians" the view that they owe Debussy nothing, and that "it is completely erroneous and unjust to claim that they resemble M. Debussy; one could just as well say that M. Debussy resembles them."[24] Ravel immediately wrote a response, published in *Le Temps* shortly after Lalo's article appeared, in which he noted that although Lalo had not specifically named him, "as my name is cited rather often in the article, a regrettable confusion might occur, and some uninformed readers might believe that I am one of the musicians in question." Given this, Ravel stated that he would "like to issue a formal denial to M. Lalo, and challenge him to produce one single witness who has heard me utter such absurdities."[25] To this, Lalo merely replied that Ravel had defended himself "without having been accused."[26]

Louis Laloy, who was friendly with both composers, later wrote that he did "everything possible to prevent a misunderstanding between Debussy and Ravel, but too many thoughtless meddlers seemed to take pleasure in making it inevitable." Laloy firmly believed that "their esteem was mutual," and he just as firmly believed that "they both regretted this rupture."[27]

Ravel continued to maintain his independence from Debussy, but he remained a stout supporter of Debussy's work. In 1913, he would write a ringing defense of Debussy and a vigorous attack on Pierre Lalo and Lalo's brother-in-arms, Gaston Carraud, who "tried to turn [young musicians] against their revered master [Debussy], and he against them." These critics, Ravel predicted, will continue to close "their eyes before the rising sun, while loudly proclaiming that night is falling."[28]

⌒

In the meantime, Debussy was having a quiet year, working on two operas based on tales by Edgar Allan Poe (*Le Diable dans le beffroi* and *La Chute de la maison Usher*), whose writings he had long admired, as well as several other projects. Ricardo Viñes's premiere performance of the first set of *Images* for piano seems to have pleased him, but baby Claude's health worried him ("One has so little idea of what's going on inside such a tiny frame").[29] Debussy seemed in a thoughtful mode when he wrote his stepson, Raoul Bardac: "Collect impressions. Don't be in a hurry to write them down. Because that's something music can do better than painting: it can centralize variations of colour and light within a single picture."[30]

Elsewhere, when a bust of Paul Cézanne's childhood friend, Emile Zola, was installed in Aix-en-Provence in May, Cézanne attended the ceremony— a magnanimous gesture, given the split that had occurred between them, for which Zola bore much of the blame.[31] Already ill and frail, Cézanne died that October, after being caught in a storm while painting.

By this time Madame Zola had already sold the Cézanne paintings in her husband's collection. Whether or not the split between the former friends figured into her consideration, financial reasons certainly played a large part: Zola had not provided for her sufficiently, and she needed to raise money. Yet despite the challenges facing her after her husband's dramatic death, Madame Zola continued to retain her hard-won tranquility, reaching out to her husband's mistress and, in late 1906, taking the initial steps to officially adopt Zola's illegitimate children. Denise and Jacques Rozerot would henceforth be known as Denise and Jacques Emile-Zola.

~

France as a whole was anything but tranquil during this unsettling year, when steps began for actually implementing the separation of Church and state. It was one thing to close the schools run by religious orders and to expel religious orders such as the Carthusians; it was quite another to take property from the Church that it had legally acquired since the Concordat went into effect, or to withdraw state subsidies of the clergy. French bishops discouraged violence, as did the February papal encyclical *Vehementer nos*— although the vehemence of the encyclical's condemnation of the Law of Separation significantly deepened disgruntlement among French Catholics. Yet even before *Vehementer nos*, riots had broken out in Paris and Lille as well as in rural districts throughout the country. It was the arrival of government officials charged with inventorying Church property that set off the worst violence. Church bells rang and people barricaded themselves in their churches, piling up chairs behind doors and singing hymns while the men armed themselves with sticks, stones, pitchforks, and iron-tipped lances. In the Pyrenees, Basques even brought their bears.

In Paris, at least, the rioting was in large part provoked by the far Right, especially by a new and small coalition, the Ligue d'Action Française, which combined royalist and nationalist extremists in a particularly lethal mix. The group had originally formed because it regarded the right-wing nationalist and anti-Dreyfus Ligue de la Patrie Française as "too soft." Action Française's extremists, led by Charles Maurras and largely funded by the Daudet family, thrived on memories of the Dreyfus Affair and on Edouard Drumont's brand of vitriolic anti-Semitism. Yet instead of pushing the Republic toward the kind of nationalism that the Ligue de la Patrie Française envisioned, this group of young militants fervently believed that a restored monarchy—and an unfettered Church—was the answer.

Abbé Mugnier witnessed firsthand the results of this militant protest. On February 1, a government revenue agent attempted to enter Mugnier's church, Sainte-Clotilde, but was manhandled and blocked by a mob of young men—"our so-called friends," Mugnier said scathingly, calling them "Catholic loud-mouths" and "pious thugs." The scene was chaotic, with the tocsin insistently ringing while guardsmen, on foot and on horseback, surrounded the church. Finally, firemen were able to open the door by force, and a second vicar received the revenue agent. The majority of Mugnier's flock strongly supported the resistance, and he blamed this on the fiery incitements of both press and clergy; but at root, he believed, were the machinations of those who wanted to sweep away the Republic and restore the monarchy.[32]

Faced with riots at church doors and cries (from the Right) of government persecution, the anticlerical but relatively moderate government of Maurice Rouvier began to back off. For his part, Clemenceau continued to press Rouvier hard on continuing the separation. A number of centrist deputies now made a political miscalculation by deciding to cast their lot against Rouvier, resulting in the caretaker government of Ferdinand Sarrien, who appointed the grand old radical Clemenceau as minister of the interior. After thirty years in politics, Georges Clemenceau now took his place in office.

The new government, formed only a few weeks before the general elections, faced critical situations in two areas other than Church-state tensions: foreign affairs, where negotiations over the Tangier Crisis had reached a crucial point, and widespread strikes and social unrest prompted by a catastrophe in a northern coal mine, where an explosion killed more than one thousand men. In the absence of a strong prime minister, Clemenceau virtually took over, stiffening French resolve at the Algeciras conference (a role that he would again play during the Great War) but showing a surprising willingness to back off on the religious question, allowing the inventory-taking to cease until emotions had quieted.

It was on the social front that Clemenceau took the most surprising turn. The strikes, which had erupted spontaneously, quickly surged out of control and became violent. Clemenceau sent in troops to quell the unrest, and suddenly this defender of the workingman gained a new reputation as a defender of law and order—"France's Premier Cop"—a reputation reinforced by his actions in confronting and defusing the radical trade union movement, the Confédération Générale du Travail (CGT), in its attempt to launch a general strike on May 1. There were rumors of revolution, and panic spread among Paris's middle classes. Clemenceau, who was determined to put a stop to the kind of disorder that might swing votes to the Right in the upcoming elections, arrested the CGT's secretary and several other militants on grounds that there was evidence of a plot linking the extreme Left with the monarchist Right. No revolution occurred (Abbé Mugnier reported that his street was even quieter than usual) and no evidence of a plot ever surfaced, but the electorate in the May 1906 general elections gratefully proceeded to vote Clemenceau and the republican Left into power.

The republican Left had benefited from Clemenceau's handling of the strike scare and the resulting influx of votes from the Right. But this influx would have a definite impact on the republican Left's political future—especially given the breakup of the left-wing Parliamentary bloc, which now began to disintegrate as the anticlerical fight as well as the Dreyfus Affair disappeared as political issues.

Indeed, by midsummer, the intense emotions stirred by the Law of Separation were quieting, and the Dreyfus Affair was finally coming to a close. That July, the High Court of Appeal at long last completely exonerated Alfred Dreyfus. The minister of war now proposed to confer upon Dreyfus the rank of squadron chief (the equivalent of commandant, or major) and award him the Cross of the Legion of Honor. Only a few were opposed, including the fervent nationalist and anti-Dreyfusard Maurice Barrès, and on July 21, the ceremony took place making Dreyfus a Knight (Chevalier) of the Legion of Honor. In response to cries of "Long live Dreyfus!" he movingly responded, "Long live the Republic! Long live truth!"[33]

Dreyfus and his supporters were indeed grateful for his exoneration,[34] but despite the relief it brought, it did not bring him a rank commensurate with his full term of service, including those lost years on Devil's Island, which would have made him a lieutenant-colonel or colonel. The following year, with his career virtually ended, Dreyfus opted for retirement and was placed in the reserves. At the same time as Dreyfus's exoneration, a particular hero of the Dreyfus Affair, Georges Picquart, was reintegrated into the army with the rank of brigadier general. When Prime Minister Sarrien retired in October (on grounds of ill health) and Clemenceau became prime minister in his place, Clemenceau appointed Picquart as his minister of war.

Benefiting from the same winds of change that brought justice to Picquart and (at least in part) to Dreyfus, Emile Zola now received the attention of the Chamber of Deputies, which overwhelmingly voted to transfer his remains to the Panthéon. Maurice Barrès objected strenuously, but the socialist leader, Jean Jaurès, carried the day.

Perhaps oddly, Madame Zola was more shocked than gratified by the news of another resting place for her husband. She insisted on maintaining his tomb at Montmartre Cemetery, where it remains to this day—although she eventually resigned herself to the Panthéon honor. The actual ceremony would not take place until 1908; unfortunately it would be accompanied by the high drama that characterized the latter years of Zola's life, as well as his death itself.

⁓

Rodin was nervous. His sculpture *The Thinker* was due to be placed in front of the Panthéon soon after Easter. There was as usual an ongoing current of establishment opposition, and Rodin would not feel secure about this all-important event until it had actually taken place.

It was during this difficult time that George Bernard Shaw and his wife arrived at Meudon for Rodin to do Shaw's portrait bust. Shaw did not speak French well, and Rodin refused to venture into English, making an enormous mental as well as conversational gap between the two egocentric geniuses. While Shaw was intent on communicating to Rodin that he was an intellectual and should be portrayed as such, Rodin did not seem to have grasped this point—or at least refused to acknowledge it: "M. Shaw does not speak French well," Rodin tartly commented, "but he expresses himself with such violence that he makes an impression."[35]

Rilke, who had remained on at Meudon as Rodin's devoted secretary, fully appreciated Shaw and was in awe of him—an attitude that Rodin did understand and evidently resented. Two days after the final sitting and Shaw's departure for London, Rodin fired Rilke. Rodin had discovered that Rilke had written to some of Rodin's friends, which implied a familiarity that Rodin found unacceptable. Whether or not this was the real reason for the dismissal, the damage was done. Rilke was hurt and appalled. After clearing out, he wrote Rodin that he had always thought that Rodin meant for him to consider these as mutual friends. "Here I am," he wrote, "dismissed like a thieving servant."[36]

In the meantime, *The Thinker* was indeed installed at the Panthéon's entrance, fulfilling Rodin's dearest wish of being prominently recognized in his own city.[37] At the same time, his affair with the Welsh artist Gwen John was probably at its height. Still, following the inauguration of *The Thinker*, Rodin entered a long period of depression. As he wrote his dear friend Helene von Hindenburg-Nostitz, "the tiredness which I drag about me is terrible."[38]

It would be more than three years before he pulled himself out of the abyss.

⁓

Gertrude and Leo Stein brought Matisse and Picasso together for the first time in March 1906. Gertrude had been posing regularly for Picasso for many months when she and Leo took Matisse and his daughter, Marguerite (then eleven years old), to visit Picasso's squalid Bateau-Lavoir studio. (According to Marguerite's reminiscences, Sarah Stein also accompanied them.)[39]

Matisse had already set the bar high with his *Woman in a Hat*, shown at the 1905 Salon d'Automne, where Leo and Gertrude acquired it and then displayed it prominently at their much-visited Rue de Fleurus studio. Matisse created similar shock waves (and derision) with his *The Joy of Life* (*Le Bonheur de vivre*), which Leo and Gertrude also acquired after he exhibited it at the 1906 Salon des Indépendants. Just prior to the Salon des Indépendants, Matisse gave his second one-man show, this time at the gallery of Eugène Druet, a former barkeeper with an instinctive liking for the works of those painters who once frequented his establishment. Druet was beginning to carve out a place for himself as a dealer in contemporary art, and he now bought a number of Matisse's latest paintings, motivating Ambroise Vollard to do the same. Matisse's work had begun to stir up interest outside of France, in Brussels and Munich; it had also attracted the attention of the Russian collector Sergei Shchukin, as well as Gertrude, Leo, Sarah, and Michael Stein. Sarah Stein, after all, had been influential in encouraging Leo and Gertrude to buy *Woman in a Hat*; in time, it would be Shchukin and Sarah Stein who would provide the backbone of support for Matisse, as Matisse's prices rose and Leo and Gertrude's interest faded.

But for now, Leo and Gertrude had performed an important function with their pioneering purchases of *Woman in a Hat* and *Joy of Life*. And they had brought together Picasso and Matisse, two giants of their age, or any age. Picasso seems to have said little during this encounter; he still spoke little French, and as he later told Leo, "Matisse talks and talks. I can't talk, so I just said *oui oui oui*. But it's damned nonsense all the same."[40] Although Matisse would be generous in sharing good fortune with Picasso and other artists (he would in fact bring Shchukin to see Picasso's *Les Demoiselles d'Avignon* at the Bateau-Lavoir), the two seem to have been aware early on of the competition that each represented to the other. As Gertrude Stein noted, "They had . . . to be enthusiastic about each other, but not to like each other very well."[41] Despite—or perhaps because of—their rivalry, Picasso's famous observation from his later years is especially trenchant: "No one," he said, "has ever looked at Matisse's painting more carefully than I; and no one has looked at mine more carefully than he."[42]

∽

Soon after this meeting, Picasso took Fernande with him to Barcelona, and then spent the summer high in the mountains at Gósol, where a twelfth-century church Madonna with widely staring eyes riveted his attention and subsequently found its way into his work.

Matisse summered once again in Collioure, but his recent interest in African tribal masks and primitive art impelled him first to journey to North Africa. Through Gustave Fayet, Gauguin's first and most important collector, Matisse already was familiar with Gauguin's "Maori" carvings, made during a visit to Auckland—even though these had not yet been publicly exhibited. Yet it was in Biskra that he first saw boldly patterned carpets for sale, each merchant with a bowl of goldfish beside him. Matisse returned to Collioure with the determination to learn how to paint North Africa's blinding light, but it was memories of the textiles and the carpets that would especially stay with him.

When Matisse returned to Paris in the autumn, he found that for the first time in his career, collectors—and dealers—were competing for his work. Cézanne's stock had risen as well, although unfortunately too late for Cézanne to enjoy it. "At the Salon d'Automne of 1905 people laughed themselves into hysterics before [Cézanne's] pictures," Leo Stein wrote, but "in 1906 they were respectful, and in 1907 they were reverent."[43]

During that autumn, Matisse bought a little Congolese figurine from a shop specializing in curios, and brought it to the Steins, where he showed his find to Picasso. Picasso became completely engrossed with the figurine and subsequently drew it compulsively. It was around this time that he also completed Gertrude Stein's portrait, whose face he had blanked out after all those sittings, saying irritably, "I can't see you any longer when I look." Now he quickly painted her face, this time with masklike features perhaps inspired by that medieval Madonna and perhaps by Matisse's African figurine. Under these influences, Picasso captured Stein's essence, and even her appearance as she aged. "When she saw it he and she were content," Gertrude Stein wrote afterward.[44]

By late 1906, both Matisse and Picasso had thus absorbed primitivism and African art, although they were about to express this influence in very different ways. As Gertrude Stein put it, "Matisse through it was affected more in his imagination than in his vision. Picasso more in his vision than in his imagination."[45]

Gertrude Stein was not personally interested in African sculpture, noting that "as an American she liked primitive things to be more savage."[46] Influenced instead by Flaubert's *Trois contes* (*Three Tales*, which she had just finished translating into English) and by Cézanne's portrait of his wife that she and Leo had bought, she began the stories that became *Three Lives*—a bold and unconventional approach to reality in which she jettisoned the traditional elements of fiction-writing, including narrative and plot. "I think it a noble combination of Swift and Matisse," she wrote Mabel Weeks, who thoroughly approved, calling it big, earthy, and rich.[47] And to Gertrude's evident pleasure, a French critic observed, "By exactitude, austerity, absence of variety in light and shade, by refusal of the use of the subconscious Gertrude Stein achieves a symmetry which has a close analogy to the symmetry of the musical fugue of Bach."[48]

Gertrude Stein wrote *Three Lives* with pencil on scraps of paper, which she despaired of turning into typewritten copy—at least until she corralled Etta Cone (then in Paris) into doing the typing. Next came the work of finding a publisher, which was not proceeding very well by the time she and Leo left Paris that summer for Florence. There, she began to write *The Making of Americans.*

⁓

At the end of the 1906 academic year, Charles de Gaulle's school on the Rue de Vaugirard closed for good, the victim of the Law of Separation. By this time Charles, almost sixteen years old, had quite suddenly emerged as a good student, having decided that he wanted to qualify for entrance to the French military academy of Saint-Cyr. His parents now sent him to a Jesuit-run school in Belgium, which met their strict standards. There, young de Gaulle buckled down, in preparation for a military career. His sister later recalled that "suddenly he became another boy." At about the same time, de Gaulle—evidently envisioning the kind of future he had in mind—wrote that "a summit is not a crowded place."[49]

Even as de Gaulle was dreaming of a military career, developments were taking place both in America and in France that would forever change the look of warfare. Travel by hot air balloon and by airship had begun in France, but it was the American Wright brothers who in December 1903 first achieved powered flight with a heavier-than-air airplane.[50] From the outset, the Wright brothers understood their airplane's military possibilities, but after the U.S. Army rejected their initial offer (on the grounds that their airplane was not yet practical), the Wrights began to look abroad.

Until Wilbur Wright's demonstrations at Le Mans in 1908, many Europeans did not believe the Wrights' claims, but the French military paid attention, especially during the first Moroccan Crisis, when tensions between the European powers reached the boiling point. Octave Chanute, the French-born American aviation pioneer, was quick to promote the Wrights, and the French military responded. The Wrights, however, requested a sizable sum of money (one million francs), in return for which the French demanded long-term exclusive rights in addition to requiring that the Wrights develop their airplanes to reach an altitude of three hundred meters by August 1, 1906. Not surprisingly, negotiations quickly broke down.

In the meantime, the Moroccan Crisis abated, while in Europe, the Brazilian Alberto Santos-Dumont was creating a stir with his own biplane. In November 1906, Santos-Dumont managed a brief (722 feet) but successful flight—the first officially verified heavier-than-air flight in Europe (although as Gabriel Voisin was quick to point out, Santos-Dumont crashed on landing). During the same year, Gabriel and Charles Voisin established one of the first aircraft manufacturing companies (Appareils d'Aviation Les Frères Voisin), near the Renault automobile works in Billancourt, just outside of Paris. The French were eager to get into the competition.

⌒

It was in 1906, at a ballet performed at the Paris mansion of the Comtesse de Béarn, that Mariano Fortuny's lighting and textile creations first made their debut. Fortuny, a Spaniard from a wealthy and artistic family, had been raised in Paris and Venice. By 1906 he was ensconced in a Venetian palazzo, but his fashions would soon have an enormous impact on the most artistically inclined of the fashionable world, from Paris to London and New York. These included Proust's narrator in *The Captive*, who expensively and exactingly dresses Albertine in Fortuny gowns. Their exotic beauty pleases her and evokes for him the Venice that he longs to see.[51]

Fortuny's 1906 debut featured long scarves of stamped silk inspired by the art of long-vanished Aegean cultures. These scarves would soon become known as "Knossos scarves" and were wound gracefully around the body in ways that were meant to allow freedom of expression—quite the opposite of what the rigidly corseted women of Paris were accustomed to.

Soon Fortuny would develop the Delphos robe, a garment simply cut of shimmering pleated silk, which hung loosely from the shoulders. The well-dressed (and well-to-do) woman who wore Fortuny soon learned to wrap her Knossos scarf gracefully and creatively around her Delphos robe. Over the coming years, the basic model would remain pretty much the same; unlike the great fashion *couturiers* of Paris, Fortuny was not interested in yearly changes of "look" or of ornament and trim. Nevertheless, his constant work on painting and stamping his silks and velvets meant that his fabrics would always be extraordinary.

Not surprisingly, Isadora Duncan—who had adopted the flowing silks and chiffons reminiscent of ancient Greece—would become an avid fan of Fortuny. But in late 1906, when she began to dance again, she had little interest in anything but sheer survival. Having left her baby and its nurse with her mother in Italy, she traveled to Warsaw, where, as she wrote in her memoirs, she was "not in the least prepared for the ordeal of a tour." She had not yet recovered from giving birth, and the baby had been abruptly—too abruptly, as it turned out—removed from breast-feeding. The theaters were sold out, but what she remembered was that "when I danced, the milk overflowed, running down my tunic."[52]

She could not eat and was exhausted, but theater managers warned her that postponements would mean big losses, and so she soldiered on. "This is all *too much suffering*," she wrote Craig on December 19. Craig was in Berlin, staging a production for Eleonora Duse, having just staged a successful production for Duse in Florence. Usually Isadora did her best to conceal any woes from him, but now she was completely drained and unable to conceal it. "It seems as if the Gods were piling everything on my head just now to prove how much I can stand!"[53] At one point in this nightmare of a tour, she collapsed on stage and had to be carried back to her hotel.

Later, on looking back at this time, she could only exclaim, "How difficult it is for a woman to have a career!"[54]

〜

Marie Curie could well have joined in Isadora Duncan's lament. She was the recent mother of a second child and was continuing her teaching at Sèvres, in addition to her ongoing work in the laboratory. Yet despite her exhaustion, she could take satisfaction in her eldest daughter's improving health: after a summer holiday at the beach, Irène was healthier than she had been in a long while, and Pierre's health also seemed to be improving. He had long complained of pain in his fingers and tired easily, but Marie ascribed this to rheumatism and prescribed special diets for him. What he and she did not see, or perhaps refused to see, was the impact that their newfound substance, radium, had on them.

Although already being hailed for its possibilities in treating cancer, radium had other, dangerous properties that the Curies had by now noted, most especially the burns it caused in contact with the skin. Any substance that could bring freezing water to a boil within a short time (as the Curies had found) must be hazardous, and in his Nobel address (which he delivered in his and Marie's name in 1905), Pierre concluded "that in criminal hands radium could become very dangerous, and here one can ask if humanity is at an advantage in knowing nature's secrets, if it is mature enough to make use of them or if this knowledge might not be harmful to it."[55]

Pierre had anticipated the debates over atomic energy and atomic weapons, but more immediately, his own health was at issue. Whether or not his long exposure to radium was to blame for what happened that afternoon of April 19, it was clear that Pierre Curie was not sufficiently quick-witted or sure-footed as he approached the Pont Neuf and Rue Dauphine at the Quai des Grands-Augustins, a busy and dangerous intersection, especially in the rain. Pierre had his umbrella up and may not have seen the rapid convergence of a heavy wagon, a tram, and a horse and carriage. Crossing the street in the midst of this bedlam, Pierre collided with one of the wagon horses and fell under the wagon's wheels. He died instantly.

Marie Curie's first reaction to the news was stunned shock and disbelief: "Pierre is dead," she desolately wrote in her journal, "he who I expected to press in my arms this evening. . . . He is gone forever, leaving me nothing but desolation and despair."[56]

Marie had once written her sister Bronya, "I have the best husband one could dream of; I could never have imagined finding one like him. He is a true gift of heaven, and the more we live together the more we love each other."[57] Years later, looking back on that terrible day, she wrote, "I lost my beloved Pierre, and with him all hope and all support for the rest of my life."[58] Yet despite her devastation, she would somehow go on, raising her two daughters and throwing herself into her teaching and research, carrying the flame for them both.

Portrait of Serge Dyaghilev [Sergei Diaghilev] with Jean Cocteau. Jerome Robbins Dance Division, The New York Public Library, New York, NY, U.S.A. Photo Credit: The New York Public Library / Art Resource, NY. © The New York Public Library / Art Resource, NY.

CHAPTER NINE

~

Winds of Change

(1907)

The winds of change that swirled through Paris in 1907 first came from the east. Although since the time of Peter the Great, imperial Russia had looked to Western Europe, especially France, for inspiration and guidance in matters of culture and taste, a young man by the name of Sergei Diaghilev was about to bring a new artistic sensibility from Russia to Paris's avant-garde.

Diaghilev had been raised in wealth (from a family-owned distillery) and was nurtured in the arts by an artistic stepmother. Unfortunately his free-spending family spent its way into a hole, with the result that his father declared bankruptcy while Diaghilev was in his teens. To repair family fortunes, Sergei was groomed to enter the civil service by first studying law, but he had little interest in either law or the civil service. Instead, he dreamed of a career in music, and he entered the St. Petersburg Conservatory, where he acquired a network of friends and acquaints in musical and artistic circles. His dreams fizzled when the venerable Rimsky-Korsakov took one look at Diaghilev's compositions and derisively declared that the young man had no musical talent whatever.

Recovering from this major setback and looking for ways to remain in the artistic world, Diaghilev founded a progressive art journal. From that springboard, he used connections and charm (reputedly sufficient to "revive a corpse")[1] to snag the position of special assistant to the director of Russia's imperial theaters, where he became responsible for a handful of venturesome musical and theatrical productions. Here, despite his charm, many found Diaghilev's forceful personality irritating. Along with his ever more open homosexuality and avant-garde artistic tastes, he soon managed to antagonize even his erstwhile supporters and was fired.

Overwhelmed by his dismissal, Diaghilev wrote his stepmother that he was "frightened of everything: frightened of life, frightened of death, frightened of fame, frightened of scorn, frightened of faith, frightened of the lack of faith."[2] Still, beneath this terror Diaghilev ultimately believed in himself. As he had written several years earlier, "I'll be successful as the promoter of great ideas, followers will gather round me, and success will be my lot."[3] It was now that he began to build on his talent as an impresario. He had already organized and mounted exhibits of contemporary Russian and Scandinavian artists, and in 1905 he pulled together an extraordinary exhibition of Russian historical portraits, which he showed to great acclaim (and national pride) in St. Petersburg, even as Japan was battering the Russian fleet in the Far East and revolution was spreading throughout the land. "I closed the exhibition almost without any scenes," he wrote his friend and future collaborator Alexandre Benois, who had fled to Paris, "but I am not sure that the pictures will get back to their rightful owners!"[4]

Diaghilev celebrated with his friends when the czar authorized the creation of a legislative body, the Duma. Yet it soon became clear that the Duma would be toothless, and that any hope for meaningful political and social reform in czarist Russia was doomed. Even the arts were affected: when Rimsky-Korsakov publicly went to the defense of students from the St. Petersburg Conservatory who demanded a greater say in decision making and an end to corporal punishment, he was fired and the czarist government forbade future performances of his works.

It was in the midst of this explosive situation that Diaghilev looked westward, as many of his compatriots had already done and would continue to do in the years to come. In 1906 he brought a large exhibition of Russian art, ranging from historic icons to the most progressive contemporary works, to Paris's Salon d'Automne, piquing the interest of sophisticated Parisians, who had been largely ignorant of what was going on artistically in the land of the Cossacks.

While in Paris, Diaghilev made allies of the wealthy arts patroness Countess Greffulhe and her cousin Count Robert de Montesquiou, who provided him with financial backing and contacts for yet another endeavor, this time in music. After joining forces with the French impresario Gabriel Astruc, Diaghilev presented a series of five major Russian concerts in May 1907 at the Paris Opera, featuring the great Russian bass Feodor Chaliapin; Sergei Rachmaninoff, who played his own Second Piano Concerto; Josef Hofmann, who played Alexander Scriabin's piano concerto; and Rimsky-Korsakov, who conducted his own *Scheherazade*. Rimsky-Korsakov was the most reluctant participant, but after being exposed to Diaghilev's relentless insistence, he left the impresario his visiting card, on which he had written: "'If one has to go, one has to go!' cried the sparrow as the cat dragged him downstairs."[5] Despite his reluctance, Rimsky-Korsakov went.

The concerts were an artistic triumph, if not a complete financial success, but Diaghilev was already on the move to organize another season for the following year. He also was about to meet a seventeen-year-old dancer by the name of Vaslav Nijinsky.

~

The first foreign production of Debussy's *Pelléas et Mélisande* took place in Brussels in January 1907. From there Debussy would go to Frankfurt, followed by 1908 productions of *Pelléas* in New York and Milan, the latter at La Scala, under the baton of Arturo Toscanini. As always, Debussy took an active part in rehearsals, which he typically denigrated in private even while he profusely thanked the conductors and musicians in public. Shortly before he expressed his deep appreciation to the Belgian conductor Sylvain Dupuis, he irritably wrote his publisher, Jacques Durand, that there was a bell that "ought to give a G and which, out of a spirit of Belgian contradiction, gives a C! . . . It sounds rather as if it's dinner time in the castle." In exasperation, he wrote Louis Laloy: "I had to spend a fortnight re-educating an orchestra whose Flemishness is about as flexible as a 100 kg. weight." To his surprise (as he wrote Durand), "it seems I'm the most demanding composer they've ever come across."[6]

In October, Debussy negotiated a hefty fee to conduct some of his orchestral works in London, and thus entered a demanding six-year period during which he would conduct and play extensively throughout a number of countries. He may have enjoyed the fame, but he distinctly did not enjoy the time it took from his composing. Nor did he like the travel, especially as his health deteriorated. Yet the concerts, and the travel, were necessary. He had always spent more than he earned, but by early 1907 his financial difficulties had become critical, following the death of Emma's uncle, a wealthy financier from whom she expected a substantial legacy. Unfortunately for Emma and her husband, the uncle did not approve of Emma's relationship with Debussy, nor of Debussy's failure to generate sufficient income for a family of three, and he unexpectedly left the bulk of his fortune to assorted charities.

Debussy now began the peripatetic life of the professional musician, even while some at home were questioning whether he was past his prime or even had met his match in a younger rival, Ravel. Debussy privately commented on Ravel's gifts—and what he saw as his limitations.[7] Yet perhaps Debussy's strongest response to this kind of criticism and engineered rivalry was his second book of piano *Images*, which appeared in October 1907. Without question, this particular master was not about to step aside.

⁓

In late 1906, Marcel Proust moved into an apartment at 102 Boulevard Haussmann. It was a necessary move, given the size and expense of the old apartment, but the new one was a bizarre choice, given Proust's extreme sensitivity to dust and noise. Boulevard Haussmann, although a fashionable location, was a main thoroughfare plagued by dirt and incessant racket, especially from the streetcars and horse-drawn vehicles that clattered over its cobblestones. In addition, the building itself was, as Proust readily admitted, an ugly one. In the end, he was drawn to it because of associations with his mother, whose recently deceased brother had owned it.

Proust never did anything without bouts of indecision and a multitude of complications, and this was no exception. Still, the furnishings for his bedroom, where he would spend the bulk of his time, were quickly decided. To avoid dust, there would be no wall tapestries, and the carpets and rugs would be removable so they could be frequently taken up and beaten. Proust also decided against portraits in the room, but he agreed to place portraits of his mother and father in the nearby drawing room, where he could see them often—but not so much as to cause pain. As for his bedroom furnishings, he would use those from his beloved mother's blue room.

It would not be until 1910 that Proust would famously line his bedroom with cork, to deaden the outside din. By this time, despite invalidism, he would be launched on his masterwork. Already, he was pondering some of its central ideas, as when he told Lucien Daudet, "You are wrong to think of yourself always inside time. The part of ourselves that matters, when it matters, is outside time."[8] And in an article on Anna de Noailles' latest book of poetry, he wrote: "She knows that a profound idea which has time and space enclosed within it is no longer subject to their tyranny, and becomes infinite."[9]

⁓

In early February, Claude Monet sent a message to his longtime friend Georges Clemenceau to remind him of an outstanding obligation. Back in 1889, Monet had realized that Edouard Manet's seminal painting *Olympia* did not yet reside in any museum or collection. In fact, Manet's widow still owned it, and Monet decided that in order to prevent it from eventually leaving France in the hands of American collectors, the best course would be to pool enough money from Manet's friends and admirers to purchase the painting and donate it to the state—with the important caveat that it hang in the Louvre.

Monet collected the money, but the Louvre strenuously resisted the bequest. In the end, he had to settle for the Musée du Luxembourg, which several years later would also receive the controversial Caillebotte bequest of Impressionist art. Monet was not satisfied with this solution, and shortly after Clemenceau became prime minister in late 1906, Monet decided to give him a nudge. As Monet told their mutual friend, art critic Gustave Geffroy: "When in Paris the other day it occurred to me that I should track Clemenceau down and tell him that it was incumbent upon him to arrange it [the transfer to the Louvre]. He got the message and within three days . . . it was done, and how glad I am."[10]

By the early years of the twentieth century, Claude Monet was riding high among collectors, and his income showed it. In 1900, he recorded an income of 213,000 francs, making him one of the wealthiest individuals in France.[11] Yet within the roiling world of early twentieth-century painters, he already was passé. In 1905 a number of French artists, including Kees van Dongen, Raoul Dufy, Jean Puy, and Paul Signac, responded to a questionnaire sent them by the influential critic Charles Morice, who concluded from their answers that Impressionism's day was over and that art was transitioning into something quite different from what it had been in the past. Artists, Morice noted, were now taking the revolutionary step of drawing upon their feelings and ideas rather than striving for literal representation of objects from nature.[12]

Within this radically new artistic viewpoint, Cézanne and Gauguin ranked high, and indeed, the Cézanne retrospective at the 1905 Salon d'Automne had an enormous influence on many of the newly emerging French painters, especially the Fauvists. Pissarro once told Matisse of the difference between Cézanne and an Impressionist: "A Cézanne is a moment of the artist," he told Matisse, "while a Sisley is a moment of nature."[13] Even during his difficult early years, Matisse had stretched himself to the limit to acquire Cézanne's *Three Bathers*, as well as a Gauguin painting and two drawings by van Gogh.

Yet if Monet was out-of-date, Manet was not. The Manet retrospective at the 1905 Salon d'Automne had enthralled Picasso, who throughout his own career would refer to Manet's paintings, especially *Le Déjeuner sur l'herbe*. Picasso would return to this in a series of works over many years—an exploration via variations on Manet's theme. For Picasso, Manet was the first modern artist, and an enticingly subversive one.

Still, it was Gauguin, rather than Cézanne or even Manet, who inspired Picasso to take the next dramatic step in his artistic development. Picasso had seen the Gauguin retrospective at the 1903 Salon d'Automne, but it was the exhibit of Gauguin's Tahitian-inspired sculptures in the 1906 Salon d'Automne that truly gripped his imagination. By 1907, this, along with African tribal art and early Iberian sculpture, was pulling Picasso toward an entirely new artistic vision.

He began work on *Les Demoiselles d'Aviginon* (originally *Le Bordel d'Avignon*)[14] in late 1906, driven by the need to create this particular painting, which he fervently believed would challenge the centuries-long traditions of European art and place him at the forefront of the modern art movement. He and Matisse had continued to joust for supremacy, making regular visits to each other's studios, meeting most Saturday evenings at the Steins, and even exchanging paintings, but always with the care of rivals circling around one another. Not only had Matisse startled the art world in 1906 with his *Joy of Life*, but early in 1907 he showed yet another shattering masterpiece, *Blue Nude*, at the Salon des Indépendants. And in the meantime, Picasso worked on.

He increasingly worked in seclusion. The Steins had provided money for a second studio in the Bateau-Lavoir, where he could paint without interference—especially from Fernande or the thirteen-year-old girl, Ramonde, whom Fernande and Picasso adopted for a brief time in the spring of 1907, in a futile attempt by Fernande to establish a kind of family unit with Picasso.

Picasso insulated himself as well from the reactions of his closest friends—the poets Guillaume Apollinaire and André Salmon, along with the poet and painter Max Jacob—who seemed nonplussed by *Demoiselles* and resorted to strained praise or virtual silence. As for Fernande, she made no mention of the painting in either of her memoirs. It was during these months, when Picasso was wrestling with *Demoiselles*, that his relationship with Fernande deteriorated. His total preoccupation with *Demoiselles*, if not the only cause for their increasingly troubled love affair, seems to have been sufficiently painful that Fernande did not want to speak of it.

By late spring, Picasso had progressed sufficiently far with *Demoiselles* that he invited Leo and Gertrude Stein to see it. They were shocked by his five confrontational and distorted prostitutes, two with what looked like tribal masks instead of faces, and the whole depicted on a radically flat, two-dimensional plane. Picasso had expected shock, but he did not expect Leo's response. Leo burst into laughter and called it "a horrible mess."[15] Other painters who visited Picasso's studio to see what all the rumpus was about had similar reactions. Braque was reported to have said that it made him feel as if Picasso was "trying to make us drink petrol to spit fire,"[16] while Derain predicted an unhappy end for the painting's unfortunate creator. The novice twenty-three-year-old art dealer, Daniel-Henry Kahnweiler, was alone in being dazzled by *Demoiselles*, feeling that something "admirable, extraordinary, inconceivable had occurred."[17] Not surprisingly, he and Picasso began a firm friendship, and the appreciative Kahnweiler would become Picasso's art dealer.

Matisse was especially repelled by *Demoiselles*; its brutality and insolence struck him as a blatant perversion of everything he had tried to accomplish. Still, the following year, Matisse would bring the Russian collector Sergei Shchukin to see the painting, and after an initial negative reaction, Shchukin would become a regular collector of Picasso's works.[18] Yet Shchukin, who continued to collect Matisses, was unusual in supporting both artists. Sarah and Michael Stein would collect Matisse to the exclusion of Picasso, while Leo and Gertrude Stein's purchase of *Blue Nude* would be their last Matisse. From then on, Gertrude, at least, would be a strong Picasso supporter. Derain would also transfer his allegiance from Matisse to Picasso, and soon Braque, a newcomer to Fauvism (whose work strongly appealed to Kahnweiler), would abandon the Fauvist movement and gravitate into Picasso's orbit, beginning a competitive partnership as the two developed Cubism together.

Picasso would not show *Les Demoiselles* until 1916, and it would remain in his studio until 1924, when he sold it to the fashion designer Jacques Doucet. Yet its influence had already begun.

~

In the meantime, Michael and Sarah Stein returned from San Francisco, where they had gone following the 1906 earthquake to see what remained of the family's rental properties. They returned with the good news that their financial base was safe—which meant that all four Paris-residing members of the Stein family could continue buying pictures. At last Gertrude and

Leo were able to pay Matisse for *Le Bonheur de vivre*, which Leo had bought shortly before he learned of the San Francisco disaster. "The Steins may well find themselves almost ruined," Matisse had written a friend soon after hearing about the earthquake, but agreed that the painting should go to the Rue de Fleurus, even if the Steins could not pay for it.[19] Now they could pay, and did, and continued their purchases from other artists, while Sarah and Michael bought increasingly from Matisse.

In addition to bringing good news, Sarah and Michael prompted the arrival of two women who longed to escape San Francisco and visit Paris: the journalist Harriet Levy and Levy's friend, Alice B. (for Babette) Toklas. Harriet and Alice arrived in the autumn of 1907 and took up residence in a small apartment on Rue Notre-Dame-des-Champs, not far from the two Stein residences. Eventually, Alice would move in with Gertrude.

Alice, a small, dark woman with an unobtrusive and refined manner, was the unmarried daughter of a well-to-do Jewish family that had settled in California a half-century earlier. The Toklas family being friends of the Steins, it was natural for Alice to be among those who greeted Michael and Sarah upon their return to San Francisco, and to hear of all the wonders of Paris. With limited personal prospects, Alice began to dream of visiting the City of Light. After inheriting a small legacy from her grandfather and persuading her father that a Paris trip would be beneficial, she and Levy joined the Steins in Paris. Once established there, she joined Gertrude and Leo on their many excursions, whether to galleries or to concerts and the theater, and soon she became an accepted presence among Gertrude's extensive circle of friends. In time, she became an essential part of Gertrude's life.

Within months, Alice became Gertrude's secretary. Gertrude had finally worked through the problem of getting *Three Lives* published by agreeing to pay for publication with a New York publisher. Etta Cone had originally typed the manuscript from Gertrude's scattered notes, but it now fell to Alice to correct the proofs—which arrived after awkward inquiries from the publisher, who was under the impression that the author's knowledge of English was limited, or alternately, "that perhaps you have not had much experience in writing." Gertrude retorted that "everything that is written in the manuscript is written with the intention of its being so written and all he has to do is print it and I will take the responsibility."[20]

So the proofs arrived, and Alice had the job of correcting them. She also began to type up Gertrude's burgeoning manuscript, *The Making of Americans*, which Gertrude described as "a history of a family," which by this time "was getting to be a history of all human beings, all who ever were or are or could be living."[21] Etta Cone previously held this typing responsibility, as well as what probably was an intimate relationship with Gertrude, but Etta eventually begged off due to illness and left Paris—much to Gertrude's annoyance, although their friendship continued. Alice soon took Etta's place at the typewriter. She also took a primary place in Gertrude's affections, to the evident discomfort of Etta, who plainly did not like Alice.

Yet other rivalries beside this were developing *chez* Stein. Gertrude was less and less interested in what Matisse was painting and had some personal bones to pick with him, especially with his rising prices. Propelling Gertrude's disaffection was an increasing rivalry with her sister-in-law. Sarah and Michael held their own salon on Rue Madame, not far from Gertrude and Leo's on Rue de Fleurus, and many preferred Sarah and Michael's salon, finding it warmer and less daunting than Gertrude and Leo's. Sarah was devoted to Matisse, who later described her as the "really intelligently sensitive member of the family."[22]

Gertrude now had plenty of reasons to favor Picasso, especially since he and Matisse had become serious rivals bent on very different goals. "What I dream of is an art of balance, of purity, and serenity," Matisse wrote in 1908, in his "Notes of a Painter."[23] Picasso, for his part, wanted to burn the house down.

⌒

While Picasso was hard at work in the Bateau-Lavoir, yet another promising young artist appeared in Montmartre—the Italian Amedeo Modigliani. It had been a rather good year for him: he had managed to get seven of his works into that year's Salon d'Automne, although admittedly none of them sold. Still, he could console himself with the fact that his works had hung in close proximity to those of the most well-known avant-garde artists of the day, including a large memorial exhibition of Cézannes.

The youngest child of a poor but cultured Italian Jewish family, twenty-two-year-old Modigliani had arrived in Paris in 1906, determined to make a name for himself. He was a survivor, having already successfully battled several life-threatening illnesses, and he would continue to struggle with tuberculosis throughout the rest of his short life. Yet during his early years in Paris, his tuberculosis was in remission, and the biggest obstacle he had to face was indifference to his art and the grinding poverty that resulted.

He moved to Montmartre, where he lived in a shanty-like structure, rented a tumble-down studio, and frequented the Lapin Agile. Despite his poverty, Modigliani dressed with bohemian flair, and his good looks and

charm soon drew him into the center of Montmartre's social life, including Picasso's gang (which Gertrude Stein described as "the little bullfighter
followed by his squadron of four"—Derain and Braque, Salmon and Apollinaire, all of them large).[24]

In 1907, after being evicted from his shanty, Modigliani moved his studio
to a derelict house at the foot of Montmartre that was due for demolition but
saved by a certain Dr. Paul Alexandre, who made it a shelter cum clubhouse
for impoverished artists. It was a ruin, but its inhabitants were grateful for a
roof, however leaky, and the meals and companionship that Dr. Alexandre
provided. Dr. Alexandre was a dermatologist but, much like Georges Clemenceau a generation earlier, operated a general clinic for the impoverished
residents of his Montmartre neighborhood. Only a few years Modigliani's
senior, he was enchanted with avant-garde art, and immediately took note of
Modigliani's work. Soon he became Modigliani's staunch friend and patron.

By this time Modigliani had also become friends with the Romanian
sculptor Constantin Brancusi, a man of great artistic gifts but little education
and fewer means, who had walked most of the way from Bucharest to Paris
in order to reach this center of the arts, the home of his hero, Rodin. Not
surprisingly, Brancusi's early work showed Rodin's influence, but by 1907,
when he met Modigliani, Brancusi had become interested in abstract forms.
As a result of Brancusi's explorations as well as Modigliani's own discovery of
the African art that had already influenced Matisse and Picasso, Modigliani
would reconceive his own ideas about sculpture.

Brancusi had a studio in the Cité Falguière, a ramshackle group of artists'
studios in Montparnasse near the workshops of the sculptor Antoine Bourdelle. For years Bourdelle had worked for Rodin as his assistant, or *praticien*,
helping carve Rodin's enormous output into marble.[25] It was a love-hate
relationship; Bourdelle idolized Rodin even as he strove mightily to break
free of his influence and establish his own artistic identity. As the Lithuanian
sculptor Jacques Lipchitz noted: "Modigliani, like some others at the time,
was very taken with the notion that sculpture was sick, that it had become
very sick with Rodin and his influence."[26] Although Lipchitz did not agree
that sculpture was sick, he and Modigliani, Bourdelle, and Brancusi were
determined to find their own way—one that did not follow in anyone's footsteps, least of all Rodin's.

⌒

Several years later, in fulfilling a commission to provide decorative friezes
for the new Théâtre des Champs-Elysées, Antoine Bourdelle would portray

an imaginary dance between Isadora Duncan and Nijinsky—something that never happened, but certainly was worth dreaming about.

In 1907, though, Isadora Duncan's life was more of a nightmare than a dream. In February, she collapsed during a performance in Amsterdam, suffering from severe menstrual pain and fatigue. By May she was somewhat recovered, but her summer schedule, in which she danced continuously throughout Germany, left her "tired to tatters."[27]

She longed to see her baby, but the doctor warned that bringing the still-unnamed child (called Snowdrop) from Italy to a colder climate might be fatal. "O darling I am so sad & distracted," Isadora wrote Craig in January, "but will try & be brave. . . . *Too much Too much*."[28] Adding immeasurably to her unhappiness was Craig's response, a nasty mix of reproaches, evasions, and lies. "Visions of Craig . . . in the arms of other women haunted me at night, until I could no longer sleep," she wrote in her memoirs.[29]

The break came that autumn in Florence. Isadora, who was in Venice, wrote Craig (in Florence): "If at the end of the week you don't come I will & see you—*if* you want me. Do you?"[30] She had underlined the "if" fourteen times. On an earlier request, he had penned in the note, "No,"[31] and he meant it. When Isadora subsequently visited him in Florence, Craig completely turned from her. Within twenty-four hours she left, in tears.

Isadora now began her series of affairs with a long string of lovers, accompanied by epic drinking and partying. It was not a happy life. "I have been en fête perpetual here [Warsaw]," she wrote Craig in November. "Champagne & dancing—it was the only alternative to suicide."[32]

～

In the days and weeks following Pierre Curie's death, Marie battled severe depression and thoughts of suicide. "In the street," she wrote in the journal she kept after his death, "I walk as though hypnotized, without care about anything. I will not kill myself, . . . [but] among all these carriages, isn't there one which will make me share the fate of my beloved?"[33]

Worsening her depression was self-condemnation. Uncharacteristically, she and Pierre had quarreled during what turned out to be their last moments together. He had reproached their maid, who wanted a raise, for not keeping up the house sufficiently. "I was taking care of the children," Marie recalled in her journal. "You left, asking me from below if I was coming to the laboratory. I answered you that I had no idea and begged you not to torment me. And that is when you left, and the last sentence that I spoke to you was not a sentence of love and tenderness." She could scarcely bear the thought of it: "Nothing has troubled my tranquility more."[34]

In the end it was her children, and her responsibility to them, that pulled her through, as did her laboratory work[35]—although at first she could not bear to visit the premises where she and Pierre had worked so closely together, or touch the instruments that Pierre had handled. Pierre's chair at the Sorbonne now was vacant, and the question arose: How to deal with this? The chair had been created specifically for him, and the obvious answer was to appoint Marie to the position; after all, she and he had worked jointly together on their discoveries, and her qualifications were unquestioned. What was in question was her suitability as a woman; no woman had previously been appointed to teach, let alone hold a chair, at the Sorbonne, and the idea was much too radical for the old guard to stomach.

Instead, the Faculty of Sciences finally proposed that the chair be left vacant, but that Marie take on Pierre's responsibilities in teaching and research. After a long internal deliberation, during which she sometimes despaired of ever being able to work without him, Marie finally agreed to accept. She added, "There are some imbeciles who have actually congratulated me."[36]

She gave her inaugural lecture on November 5, taking up at the exact point where Pierre had left off. She also moved with her two daughters and father-in-law to Sceaux, just outside of Paris, where her daughters would be raised with a garden and fresh air. It meant extra commuting time for Marie, but she could not bear to remain in the house where she and Pierre had lived together. Pierre's father, Dr. Curie, continued to reside with them, devoting himself to supporting her and his granddaughters.

In 1908, Marie Curie published a volume of the *Works of Pierre Curie*—a work of six hundred pages that she had collected and edited, prefaced by her own introduction. "A new period of his life was about to open," she wrote. "Fate did not wish it thus, and we are obliged to bow before its incomprehensible decision."[37]

⌢

In March 1907, the huge Savoy bell, named Françoise-Marguerite-Marie du Sacré-Coeur, took its place in Sacré-Coeur's new bell tower, high above the cupola of the chapel of the Virgin Mary.

Yet while Sacré-Coeur rose white and shining above Paris, life in the city below had—at least for the privileged—become ever more madly materialistic and self-indulgent. Abbé Mugnier, who was no prude, nonetheless reported with evident discomfort that the young girls of high society "are now smoking in front of their mothers." On a recent evening he had even witnessed one particular mother and daughter smoking together.[38]

The previous year, André Citroën's brother, Bernard, opened Sans Souci, a trendy café-bar near the Opéra. Sans Souci was the first in Paris to feature the new fad of tea-dancing *à l'anglaise*, and its opening was a grand event, attracting celebrities from high society and show business. It was, as its name suggested, a place of sophisticated assignation, and when Isadora Duncan returned to Paris, she was rumored to be a regular.

Bernard's brother, André, was also a regular, joining Bernard and his amusing friends in a round of parties and entertainments. André Citroën, who now had money to spend, may have worked hard during the day, but he was known for playing in high style at night. His lifestyle contrasted dramatically with that of his future rival, Louis Renault, who did not play at all, period.

A hard worker who wore the same kind of overalls as his employees and labored right beside them, Louis Renault was respected but not beloved. "Hard, he is," his employees agreed, "a real slave-driver. But you can't refuse him anything. Because he works harder than you do." Renault rarely slept more than five hours a night, regularly working until 11 p.m. and returning to work by 6 a.m., having already bathed, breakfasted, and exercised. He was an intense and ubiquitous presence on the factory floor. "Working for him," one of his employees commented, "was like being with a volcano." Outside the factory, he had a reputation for boorishness. "The rudest man I've ever known," one acquaintance recalled.[39]

In 1904, when France led the world in automobile construction (producing more than thirty thousand vehicles annually), Renault still was a small player. Yet unlike Panhard, the French maker of luxury automobiles, Renault continued to focus on lighter and less expensive vehicles. When Panhard turned down the opportunity to build a fleet of inexpensive taxis for the city of Paris, Renault jumped at the chance. By 1906 he had supplied the city with fifteen hundred such taxis, and by 1907 his taxis had spread to London. Also, by this time Renault's first bus was on the streets of Paris, and Renault delivery trucks and milk vans were appearing throughout France.[40]

In addition, Renault was learning to use his growing financial power to his own advantage, suing those firms who dared to infringe on his patents. Proceeding carefully at first, he took on a small entrepreneur who was illegally using the Renault direct-drive. Renault's legal adviser pointed out that suing this individual would bring Renault little in the way of recompense, and that the man would probably go bankrupt. "Exactly!" replied Renault. "Sue him."[41] Sue him they did, and the man indeed went bankrupt. But Renault had now established his patent in the courts, and the larger firms (in

Germany, England, and America, as well as in France) who had infringed on his patent suddenly turned tail and settled out of court. For his part, Renault was perfectly willing to infringe on others' patents, provided the inventor was unlikely to have sufficient funds to press a case against him. In other instances, Renault simply negotiated for the lowest price.

As for expanding his plant in Billancourt, Renault typically offered a low price for the desired land, and then—if the owner refused to sell—had Renault vehicles drive up and down outside the person's house, day and night, revving up continuously, until the owner capitulated. When Renault began to make airplane engines in 1907, their piercing noise was even more effective in persuading landowners to evacuate.

Louis Renault was similarly tough with his brother, Fernand, who was his sole surviving partner. Taking due note of his brother's declining health, Louis threatened and blandished him into relinquishing his share of the firm at a low price. Despite the fact that Fernand had children to inherit, he eventually capitulated. "Louis was *hard*, hard with me," Fernand later told his wife. "You know what he is like when he wants something."[42] With Fernand's death in 1908, Louis Renault at last had complete control over the automobile firm that would soon be the largest in France.

～

There were other ruthless and volcanic entrepreneurs hard at work in and around Paris at this time. Young Eugène Schueller was one of them. Raised in poverty by hardworking parents in the heart of Montparnasse, young Eugène—the only surviving child of five sons—was given a good education, despite the expense. Unlike his schoolmates, he was accustomed to working long hours in his parents' pastry shop as well as working hard at school.

His scientific ability emerged early, and until his family faced financial ruin, it looked like he was headed for the elite Ecole Polytechnique. Overcoming adversity after adversity, he eventually entered the Institute for Applied Chemistry, paying his way by working nights as a pastry cook. Graduating at the top of his class, he became an instructor at the Sorbonne. After a life of hard work, he found his days there boring and left for a job at the Pharmacie Centrale de France, the major French manufacturer of chemical products. There he quickly became head of research and eventually head of chemical service.

Not one to rest easily in success, Schueller now decided, at the age of twenty-six, to branch out on his own. He had already become interested in a project to invent a safe and natural-looking hair dye. Until then, hair dyes were jarring in color and definitely unsafe, for customers and hair-dressers alike. No one had bothered to explore this problem before, largely because it was of little interest to male chemists. Still, a fortune awaited in the beauty business, and Schueller spotted it. He worked at a hairdresser's salon from the crack of dawn until his day job started, and then from eight to eleven o'clock at night, sandwiching his work at the Pharmacie Centrale in between. Sensing that he was on the right track, he quit his job at both places (to the utter disbelief of his employer at Pharmacie Centrale, who was paying him well) and lived on next to nothing while sleeping on a little camp bed next to his laboratory equipment and cooking on the Bunsen burner he used for his experiments. By 1907, he had discovered the formula he was looking for.

Shy by nature, Schueller found it devastatingly difficult to go out and sell his revolutionary new hair dye, but he did it. He had an excellent product, and soon he was selling to the top fifty hairdressers in Paris. By night he made his hair dyes; by day he took orders and made deliveries. He first gave his product the brand name of L'Auréole, after a hairstyle popular when he began his research. Soon the name would evolve into L'Oréal.

∿

Women's fashions as well as beauty aids were changing rapidly as the new century progressed. As Jean Cocteau later noted, a high-speed film of the fashion changes during these years would be truly gripping, with hems rising and "sleeves inflating, deflating, and reflating; hats plunging and rearing, peaking and flattening, sprouting feathers and moulting; chests swelling and shrinking, enticing and shaming."[43]

By 1907, a new fashion "look" had emerged, with Poiret and Fortuny in the lead. Fortuny may have viewed himself as an artist rather than as a *couturier*, but Poiret gladly embraced his role as a leader ("the" leader, in his own view) in the emergence of modern fashion. This fashion rejected the corseted shape of the nineteenth century for a more natural and uncorseted silhouette—a movement toward freedom in clothing and activity that was part of a larger movement to free women from their traditionally restrictive roles. "I waged war upon it," Poiret later boasted about his hostility toward the corset.[44] A flowing Delphos robe by Fortuny or a softly draped tunic dress by Poiret marked a revolution in comfort as well as style for the well-dressed Parisian woman.

Women's perfume, as an important fashion accessory, was evolving just as quickly as was clothing. In 1905, François Coty introduced L'Origan; within a week, L'Origan was on virtually every dressing table of well-to-do Parisian women, and at subsequent opening nights of the Opéra, one could smell its characteristic mix of carnation and jasmine everywhere. It was daring, vivid, and an immediate success—reminiscent, some said, of the intensity and audacity of the Fauves. By 1907, Coty had hired seven sales representatives to support his rapidly expanding business throughout France. He also set up a new laboratory in Neuilly, just over the Paris city limits. By 1908, he would have to expand again.

That November, Count Kessler immersed himself briefly in the world of women's fashion and observed the Paris fashion shows. He was fascinated by what he saw, noting in particular the "Byzantine orchid-like quality of the current evening fashions" and the contrasting "abrupt, short, smart street clothes" for daytime. This "*contrast*," he added, "between an esotericism verging on the perverse and a plain, but elegant, utility appears to be the character of today's fashion and perhaps of the age itself." What he found especially significant was neither the refinement nor the practicality in and of themselves, but the "simultaneous saying 'yes' and 'no' to modern reality."[45]

～

It was still early days for the European aircraft industry, but the Voisin brothers were in the vanguard. "We worked day and night," Gabriel Voisin recalled. "Working hours were fantastic. My team [of two workers] slept when I slept and ate little."[46]

It was a matter of constant problem-solving at every level. Even finding a place to test their machines was a challenge. The Voisins tested their flying machines in the Parc de Bagatelle, near Billancourt, until the police banned them. The next best alternative was the Bois de Vincennes, but this was clear across town, which raised a transport problem. Using creative know-how, Gabriel solved this particular difficulty by attaching old parts from Serpollet steam cars to a Stanley steam car, minus boiler, that he had earlier bought "for a song" at a sale of bankrupt stock. Then he fitted a towing attachment, becoming the first to use car trailers with towing bars.

In the spring of 1907, Charles and Gabriel Voisin built a pusher biplane for the early aviation pioneer, Léon Delagrange. Soon after, the Voisins built an almost identical biplane for the former racing car driver, Henri Farman. Within a few months, Farman would use this Voisin biplane to become the first European to complete a one-kilometer closed-circuit flight, an event that took place just outside of Le Mans.

By this time, Henri Juliot had designed and built for Lebaudy Frères the dirigible *Patrie*, which they tested throughout the summer and early autumn of 1907 before handing it over to the French army for military service. In July, Count Kessler noted in his diary that the dirigible *Patrie* had that morning "rushed over our heads like a giant, yellow whale." It is possible that the dirigible he saw was *Patrie*'s predecessor, *Le Jaune*, which was painted yellow. Yet whichever one of the huge airships he saw, it had an unsettling impact on him.

"A strange feeling of a new era," Kessler recalled feeling as he looked up at the sky.[47]

Louis Blériot flying his airplane, circa 1909. French Photographer / Private Collection / Archives Charmet / The Bridgeman Art Library. © The Bridgeman Art Library.

CHAPTER TEN

~

Unfinished Business

(1908)

Early on the evening of June 3, 1908, a hearse slowly entered Montmartre Cemetery and approached the tomb of Emile Zola. There it began the momentous job of transferring the great novelist's remains to the Panthéon. Eternal rest in the Panthéon was the highest honor that the nation could bestow, and now that those who had supported Zola during the Dreyfus years had attained political power, amends would be made for the abysmal treatment the novelist had suffered during those difficult years.

Clemenceau and Jaurès led the movement that brought about this honor, but they and the rest of Zola's supporters faced a residue of royalists, nationalists, and anti-Semites, whose hatred of Zola—and Dreyfus—remained white-hot. Shortly before the ceremony, the royalist journal *Action Française* published a manifesto by Léon Daudet that ended with the lines: "Get Zola's corpse out of the tomb! Bring Dreyfus to the execution block! Re-establish the Monarchy!"[1] Daudet may not have had the intention of literally carrying out all of these words, but there were those among his readers who took him seriously. And so, on the evening of June 3, some thirty of Zola's defenders took the precaution of escorting the hearse on a secret course across the city, to avoid the possibility of violence.

All was well until the hearse and its escort crossed to the Left Bank and approached the Panthéon. There they encountered hundreds of rowdy nationalists who menacingly blocked Rue Soufflot and the other main approaches. Taking a detour up narrow streets to the rear, the cortège almost reached the Panthéon when a mob descended. Only the timely intervention of a squadron of horse guard and a company of foot soldiers, plus some well-armed police, held off the bully boys and managed to escort the bier into the Panthéon, where it was placed on an enormous catafalque beneath the dome. While police continued to patrol outside, Madame Zola sat vigil throughout the night.

The ceremony took place the next morning, with the Zola family as well as Alfred Dreyfus in attendance. It was at the close of the eulogy, after the minister of fine arts praised Zola for the courage he had shown during the Dreyfus Affair, that a shot suddenly rang out, then another. Maurice Le Blond, who would soon marry Zola's daughter, was standing directly behind Alfred Dreyfus when he heard the first ominous click and wheeled about. Fortunately, Dreyfus heard this sound at the same time and threw up his arms, protecting himself from the bullets that followed. Le Blond tackled the would-be assassin, a military journalist who later claimed that he had not wished to kill Dreyfus, but only to wound him, to protest against his rehabilitation and the glorification of that arch-fiend, Zola.[2]

Dreyfus suffered a flesh wound to his forearm, but otherwise was unhurt. The ceremony proceeded, and Zola was at last peacefully interred in the Panthéon's crypt, next to his boyhood idol, Victor Hugo. Yet the vestiges of hatred that had bubbled up during this solemn ceremony remained.

～

Early in 1908, Debussy at long last married Emma Bardac, whom Debussy had referred to as "Madame Debussy" since at least 1906.[3] Emma and her first husband had divorced in 1905, shortly before she gave birth to Debussy's daughter Chouchou; yet for almost three years she and Debussy did not wed.

We know virtually nothing about the actual event. What is known about Debussy's life at that time is that on two successive Sundays in January he conducted La Mer with the Colonne Orchestra in Paris, the first time he had ever conducted. "It was not without a furiously beating heart I climbed the rostrum yesterday morning for the first rehearsal," he wrote his friend, the doctor and all-around Renaissance man Victor Segalen. "It's the first time in my life I've tried my hand at orchestral conducting and certainly I bring to the task a candid inexperience which ought to disarm those curious beasts called 'orchestral musicians.'"[4] Debussy conducted La Mer on January 19 and 26; on January 20, he married Emma—whether with or without a furiously beating heart, we do not know.

Why marry Emma on that particular date, and why so suddenly after all this time? Debussy leaves us no clue, but one biographer speculates that

Debussy's upcoming conducting engagement (on February 1) at the Queen's Hall in London was sufficiently high profile that it may have provided the impetus to regularize his and Emma's relationship. We do not know. His thoughts seem to have been primarily on his conducting adventures, as when, two days after his marriage, he wrote his friend, the poet and novelist Paul-Jean Toulet: "It's interesting while you're using the little stick to obtain the colour you want, but . . . the reception of your success isn't very different, I feel, from that of a conjuror or an acrobat bringing off a successful leap."[5]

While Debussy was making forays into the world of conducting, Ravel was trying to complete the orchestration of his *Rapsodie espagnole* for the same Colonne Orchestra, where it was due for performance on March 15. On March 3, Ravel wrote the young English composer Ralph Vaughan Williams: "My *Rapsodie espagnole* is supposed to be performed at a Colonne concert on March 15, and only the 4th movement is orchestrated!"[6]

Ravel and Vaughan Williams had met the previous winter, after Vaughan Williams requested lessons in composition and orchestration. These lessons took place over the course of three months and consisted largely of orchestrating piano works by Ravel or by some of the Russian composers whom Ravel especially admired. Vaughan Williams later recalled that Ravel showed him "how to orchestrate in points of color rather than in lines," adding that "it was an invigorating experience to find all artistic problems looked at from what was to me an entirely new angle."[7] It was the beginning of a close friendship, during which Vaughan Williams and his wife would welcome Ravel almost as a member of their family during his future visits to England.

Ravel did indeed complete the orchestration of *Rapsodie espagnole* in time for the March 15 performance, although (as he wrote Ida Godebska on March 9), he was "exhausted. No time to sleep." The program was long, so much so that its conductor, Edouard Colonne, decided to leave out one number, a *Scherzo* by Edouard Lalo—father of the critic Pierre Lalo, who so deeply disliked Ravel's and Debussy's music. Ravel feigned some concern on this account, telling Ida in a sly aside not to "say anything to the son of the lamented master."[8]

Ravel's group of avant-garde friends swarmed into the cheap balcony seats for the concert, where they loudly supported their man. Following some hissing after the *Rapsodie*'s second movement, one of Ravel's cadre called out in a booming voice, "Once more, for the public downstairs, which didn't understand!" When the conductor complied, the same voice rang out, "Tell them it's Wagner and they will find it very good."[9]

Even without this kind of assistance, the *Rapsodie espagnole* received generally favorable reviews, although Pierre Lalo predictably panned it. "He's consistent," Ravel drily remarked to Cipa Godebski, and then quickly moved on to other things.[10] There were soirées and dinners to attend, plus proofs and scores to correct, and work on multiple new projects. In the months to come, Ravel would complete *Gaspard de la nuit* and begin to compose *Ma Mère l'Oye*, his Mother Goose suite, written for and dedicated to the Godebski children, Mimi and Jean. (Coincidentally, during these same months, Debussy was completing the *Children's Corner* suite for his daughter Chouchou.)

Yet occupying a large part of Ravel's thoughts at this time was his father's long illness. Two years before, Ravel had brought his father to Switzerland, in the hope that a stay with the family's Swiss relatives might strengthen him. Sadly, neither this nor a subsequent stay did much lasting good, and Joseph Ravel died in October 1908. The Ravels were a close-knit family, and following Joseph's death the two sons and their mother moved from Levallois-Perret to a more centrally located and certainly more fashionable address, on the seventeenth-arrondissement side of the Place de l'Etoile (now Place Charles de Gaulle). There, the three would continue to live together.

～

Both Ravel and Debussy deeply admired the Russian composer Modest Mussorgsky, which added to the growing competitiveness between them. The year before, Debussy criticized his friend Louis Laloy for favorably comparing Ravel's *Histoires naturelles* with a particular Mussorgsky song cycle, while in late spring 1908, Ravel expressed amazement that Debussy had actually told a person who was going to a performance of Mussorgsky's *Boris Godunov*: "Go see it, all of *Pelléas* is found in it!"[11]

The occasion for Debussy's remark—and Ravel's irritation—was yet another spectacular event brought to Paris by Sergei Diaghilev. Diaghilev's 1907 season in Paris had featured concerts that had included opera excerpts, but no fully staged operas. Diaghilev corrected this omission in a grand way for his 1908 season, presenting what many considered to be Russia's greatest opera, Mussorgsky's *Boris Godunov*, featuring the renowned Feodor Chaliapin in the title role. The costumes and sets were magnificent, the music was sublime, and the audience was enraptured. Despite preproduction chaos, during which French and Russians worked and clashed in a plethora of multicultural dramas, the end result was a triumph.

Misia Natanson Edwards was so enthralled that she attended every one of the seven performances and bought all the unsold tickets, urging them on her friends. Soon she would wangle an introduction to Diaghilev, which in turn would lead to a magnificent role for her as a patron of the arts.

Yet Misia did not need to look to the stage for drama, as those who knew her fully appreciated. Born in St. Petersburg following her mother's wild dash from Brussels during the height of winter, Misia entered the world as dramatically as any Bernhardt could wish. Her mother, then in her last weeks of pregnancy, had embarked on her bone-shattering midwinter journey in the attempt to break up a torrid love affair by Misia's father in that far-off city. The two-thousand-mile journey proved fatal; soon after her arrival she collapsed and died—but not before giving birth to her child.

Misia, whose father was Polish, was first raised by her maternal grandmother, the Russian widow of a renowned Belgian cellist, and as a child Misia showed great talent as a pianist. She continued piano lessons (from none other than Gabriel Fauré) after she moved to Paris to live with her uncaring father, the sculptor Cyprien Godebski, and the second of Godebski's three wives. Misia's adolescence was unhappy and rebellious, and she repeatedly ran away from home. As punishment, she was sent for several miserable years to the strict convent school of Sacré-Coeur, or the Sacred Heart.

Her feistiness and beauty attracted attention, especially that of her first stepmother's nephew, Thadée Natanson, who proposed marriage. Misia accepted and soon found herself at the center of a life filled with artists, writers, and musicians—friends from Thadée's world, in which she thrived. When Thadée's finances collapsed, and their marriage with it, marriage to Alfred Edwards brought unimaginable riches but, in the end, rejection and misery. In 1908, after Edwards had left Misia for Geneviève Lantelme, the Spanish painter José-Maria Sert reappeared in Misia's life. Physically unattractive, but rich, romantic, and for the moment satisfyingly attentive, Sert was exactly the sort of man she was looking for. Although still married to Edwards, Misia did not hesitate to leave Paris with Sert for a passionate and fantasy-infused escapade in Rome.

Upon their return to Paris, she and Sert attended Diaghilev's production of *Boris Godunov*—*the* event of that spring's season. Sert had already met Diaghilev, so it was not difficult to arrange an introduction. Misia was overcome, and she poured out her feelings about the music and the performance with a clear comprehension of what she was talking about. Diaghilev, who was no fool, undoubtedly understood the importance of such a wealthy connection. Still, it was their commonalities, including their Slavic backgrounds, rather than simply Misia's money that made for their long-lasting if tempestuous friendship.

∼

Early in 1908, Henri Matisse moved his studio to the Hôtel Biron, the dilapidated mansion that had been the convent and school of Sacré-Coeur—the very school that Misia had unwillingly endured for so many years. Following the separation of Church and state, neither the school nor the convent survived, and the mansion and its extensive grounds came under the charge of the government, which offered portions of it for rent at attractively low prices.

Matisse by now was familiar with the way this sort of thing worked. Two years earlier, he had moved his studio from its cramped quarters on the Quai St-Michel to another former convent, on the Rue de Sèvres. It was here, encouraged by Sarah Stein, that he began to teach. Sarah had started to paint, and she was serious about it. She was just as serious about getting Matisse to help her, and by the year's end she had persuaded him to take a small class on a regular basis. It was at this time that he became famous for advising his pupils that "you must be able to walk firmly on the ground before you start walking a tightrope!"[12] He consequently began with drawing techniques and did not let his students paint for several months.

By late 1907, Matisse received notice that he had to move from the Rue de Sèvres, and soon after, he and his family made the move to the Hôtel Biron. For fifteen years the Matisse family, minus one or more of the children, had lived in one apartment or another at 19 Quai St-Michel, overlooking the Seine and Notre-Dame. Now, Matisse found ample work and living space in the Hôtel Biron, where he turned the former convent's huge refectory into a studio, and installed his family on the ground floor of another building on the mansion's extensive grounds. For the first time his oldest son, Jean, could move in with them, and Amélie enjoyed the luxury of entertaining guests in an extensive parlor once used by the nuns of Sacré-Coeur.

∼

Within a short time, Rodin would also find his way to the Hôtel Biron, with important consequences, but during 1908 the great sculptor was in the throes of a difficult love affair. Two affairs, actually, as he was winding down one affair with the British artist Gwen John while embarking on yet another. The new woman in his life, Claire de Choiseul, was an American of French descent who had married the Marquis de Choiseul-Beaupré. As often happened in such marriages, the Frenchman had gladly bestowed his title in return for an influx of funds from his American wife, in his case to pay off gambling debts. Her money helped, yet because of their lavish lifestyle, Claire de Choiseul and her husband soon found themselves in considerable financial difficulty. It was the marquis' query to Rodin about the possibility of selling him a family heirloom that led to introductions all around and, soon after, to a torrid relationship between Rodin and the marquis' strong-willed wife.

Claire de Choiseul was determined to latch onto Rodin, and by 1907, she was writing Rodin as "Mon Amour adoré" and signing herself as "your little wife." She wrote him daily whenever she did not see him on a daily basis, and did not hesitate to order him about, mixing commands with not-so-subtle flattery. Her evident goal was to cut him off from his friends and relations, especially Rose Beuret, but also from former and ongoing lovers such as Gwen John. Claire de Choiseul evidently enjoyed being the lover of a famous man such as Rodin, but there was money at stake as well. The Choiseuls' financial needs were great, and Rodin had never married Rose nor acknowledged his illegitimate son by her. Rodin's friends were frankly appalled at the situation and resented Choiseul's domination of the aging sculptor, who—as one friend put it—was "as clay in her hands."[13] So far as they were concerned, Choiseul's behavior easily canceled out whatever title she had managed to snag.

However indebted the marquis may have been to his wife financially, he was embarrassed by her flaunted liaison and sent Rodin a telegram asking him to stop encouraging Claire's daily visits. In July 1908, the marquis finally wrote Rose Beuret. "It is unendurable," he told her, "that you tolerate the state of things which I can no longer abide." Caught between Rose, Gwen John, and Claire de Choiseul, Rodin went into seclusion, hiding out in La Goulette, a small property that he owned in Meudon. While he was there, both Gwen and Claire tried desperately to see him, the latter imperiously: "I *beg* you to send me a word tomorrow morning," she wrote. Shattered, Rodin told Gwen John, "I am like a broken vase: if someone touches me, I'll fall to pieces."[14]

Rodin finally relented to see Claire that Christmas, but only after her maid wrote him that Madame was not eating and was in a terrible state. He and a presumably triumphant Claire then spent Christmas together at the marquis' country house in Dijon. The marquis spent Christmas elsewhere.

∽

Sometime between 1908 and 1909, Marcel Proust began to work on *Swann's Way*—the first volume of what would become his chef-d'oeuvre *In Search of Lost Time*.[15] For years he had alternately hoped for and despaired of a breakthrough as a novelist, and in late 1902 had written a close friend: "A thousand characters for novels, a thousand ideas urge me to give them body, like the shades in the *Odyssey* who plead with Ulysses to give them a little blood to drink to bring them back to life."[16]

Anna de Noailles had early sensed Proust's capabilities for greatness, praising his "precious and marvelous soul" and encouraging him to work to "satisfy those who are here and those who are no longer here." Yet Proust floundered, continuing with his painstaking translation of Ruskin until, by 1904, he wrote Marie Nordlinger (his colleague in the grueling translation process): "This old man is beginning to bore me."[17]

Proust's translation of Ruskin's *Bible of Amiens* appeared in early 1904, to considerable acclaim, and Maurice Barrès even suggested that Proust continue his career as a translator. Proust dismissed this idea, partly because he still had more Ruskin translations to do, "and after that I shall try to translate my own poor soul, if it doesn't die in the meantime."[18]

Yet even while translating Ruskin, Proust was finding his own literary voice, one that his former history professor, Albert Sorel, described (in a review of *La Bible d'Amiens*) as "flexible, floating, enveloping, opening on to infinite vistas or colors and tones, but always translucent."[19] This voice first appeared in Proust's preface to *La Bible d'Amiens*, but Proust initially distrusted this style as an effective vehicle for a work of fiction. What would his story be? And could he possibly write it before his life slipped irretrievably past?

The answer would lie within the realm of memory, in the web of subtly linked past impressions that remained in his imagination. Yet several more anxious years passed before Proust was able to begin *Swann's Way*—years in which he continued to suffer invalidism and the effects of a mounting ingestion of drugs, as well as what he was beginning to perceive as the dangers of society: "All these compliments, all those greetings," he wrote, "[that] we call deference, gratitude, devotion, and in which we mingle so many lies, are sterile and tiresome," the "sterilizer of inspiration."[20]

His mother's death in 1905 left him in a state of near collapse, but it also weaned him from her anxious hovering and over-indulgence, which he had grown accustomed to manipulating. It is this intricate interplay of longing and manipulation that Proust's narrator portrays in *Swann's Way*, where he recalls his childhood yearning for his mother's good-night kiss. The strands of this story, and the setting of the narrator's childhood home in Combray—the lightly fictionalized town of Proust's father's birth—interweave with the story of Charles Swann, the narrator's elegant Jewish neighbor, and Swann's desire for and marriage to the unsuitable and manipulative Odette. This in turn is woven into the story of the narrator's own adolescent attraction to Swann's daughter, the equally manipulative Gilberte.

All of these are memories, involuntary memories, linked by a narrator who summons them up irrespective of time, at least in a linear sense. For Proust creates a world where personal time is not made up of fixed moments in chronological order, but consists rather of intertwined memories and experiences, in which a character can be pulled out of the present simply by sensory associations, such as the taste of the famous madeleine that the narrator dips into his lime-leaf tea (*infusion tilleul*). Adding to the complexity, Proust's narrator exists on at least three different levels: the book-loving child who longs to become a writer; the grown man telling of his quest for artistic identity; and the author, who is keenly observant and comments extensively throughout.

Proust was fracturing traditional literary perception, but he was not alone in smashing long-established ways of understanding. As he began to write *Swann's Way*, Picasso (whom Proust did not yet know) had begun to shatter conventional visual perception,[21] while new conceptions of time and space had begun to radically—and often uncomfortably—shift people's views of the world around them. Ever more rapid movement across greater distances had already required the establishment of a profoundly new concept, that of standardized time.[22] But it was Albert Einstein's theory of relativity, first published in 1905, that upended the world as people had hitherto known it, posing space and time as relative and changing rather than as constants in a clockwork Newtonian universe.

The impact of Einstein's discovery was at first greatest on physicists and astronomers, but its challenge reached deep into conventional beliefs. Whether or not Proust knew about Einstein at this early date (and it is doubtful that he did), by the end of his life he was pleased with the comparison. A 1922 article, "Proust et Einstein," delighted the author by noting that, among other similarities, Proust and Einstein "have the sense, the intuition, the comprehension of the great natural laws." Proust, well pleased, saw this comparison as "the most immense honor and the keenest pleasure one could grant me."[23]

∽

Automobiles, trains, and especially airplanes were at the heart of the revolution in speed and its related conception of time that was beginning to define the new century, and first encounters with any of these wonders, especially airplanes, could be boggling. Witnessing his first airplane in flight, Proust's narrator was moved "as might a Greek have been setting eyes for the first time on a demigod." For a moment, the narrator "felt there to lie open . . . every course through space, or through life." The pilot glided on for a moment and then, "with a slight movement of his golden wings, he headed straight up into the sky."[24]

Proust's narrator (and Proust himself)[25] was not the only one transfixed by his first sight of manned flight. Wilbur Wright's demonstration flights near Le Mans in August 1908 riveted the French, many of whom had never quite believed what they heard of the Wrights' accomplishments.[26] "For me," Count Kessler wrote in his diary following his observation of the great event, "the strongest impression . . . were the majestic and graceful turns. It looks as if flying were completely safe."[27]

Even as Wilbur Wright was astonishing French crowds by maneuvering his biplane into sharp angles and figure eights, the French aeronautical pioneers were rapidly catching up with the Americans. Henri Farman had already won the Grand Prix de l'Aviation for the first closed-circuit flight of more than a kilometer, which until Wright's demonstration flights was seen as a major breakthrough. In subsequent months, Farman and Léon Delagrange would leapfrog one another in breaking records, and by the time of Wilbur Wright's demonstration flights, a Voisin plane had already made a flight of more than twelve miles—and bested the Wrights by leaving the ground solely under its own power. In the following years—prompted by military necessity as well as by engineering derring-do—the Europeans would emerge as the dominant force in aviation.

Meanwhile, on the ground, automobiles were becoming increasingly common, prompting the ever-alert Michelin brothers to create their first travel office in 1908. Called the Bureau of Itineraries, it was located in the old Michelin offices on Boulevard Pereire, in northwest Paris. As the Michelin brothers shrewdly recognized, their dominance of the French pneumatic tire market meant that any increase in sales would have to come from an increase in auto travel. This innovative service, which provided motorists with travel itineraries free of charge, proved a success with travelers and the Michelin brothers alike. By 1910, Michelin road maps would further enhance the driving experience, as would the road signals and directional signs that were beginning to appear, thanks to the Michelins' encouragement.

At about the same time as the Michelins' new marketing venture, André Citroën dipped his toe into the turbulent waters of the fledgling automobile industry by becoming a consultant to the Mors auto makers, whose luxury sedans and expensive racing cars no longer dominated the market. Mors in fact was in deep trouble, and it was only after Citroën spotted a quiet and smooth (but expensive) engine, designed by the American Charles Knight, and installed it in a new range of Mors cars that he was able to revive sales and revitalize the foundering company. In time, Citroën would produce his own automobiles and would absorb Mors, but that still lay in the future.

In the meantime, Line 4 of the Paris Métro was encountering difficulties. To begin with, it was the first to run beneath the Seine. Further complicating an already-challenging situation, the most direct route for the line passed directly beneath the Institut de France—a plan that greatly upset certain individuals, especially the *Immortels* of the Académie Française, who argued that the construction would damage the Institut's structure. As a result, the line's route had to be substantially modified to its present irregular course, taking a considerable jog around the Institut (it now crosses the Seine between Boulevard Saint-Michel and the Place du Châtelet). In their bid for support, the detour's advocates argued that this would substantially improve service to the fifth arrondissement.

We do not know what Hector Guimard's reaction was to these challenges besetting the Métro's builders, but then again, he had little reason to care. Having wed an American heiress, he now was free from financial worries. He and his wife would live for many years in Guimard's very own Hôtel Guimard on Avenue Mozart (16th), until moving to New York shortly before the outbreak of World War II.

⁓

It was now that Helena Rubinstein, who had already established herself in London, learned of an herbal skin-products business that was for sale on Paris's chic Rue St-Honoré. Rubinstein had never been slow to act, and—recognizing the importance of a prime Paris location—she promptly acquired it and its stock, soon transforming it into her up-and-coming Paris salon. Concurrently, Eugène Schueller was on his way to fame and fortune with his L'Oréal hair dye, while François Coty now opened a shop in the exclusive Place Vendôme and expanded his laboratory to nearby Suresnes. By catering to women's anxieties about their appearance and their fear of aging, each of these entrepreneurs in the early years of the twentieth century had tapped into a huge and relatively unexploited market. Yet it was Coty who most clearly understood the importance of his product's appearance, and it was Coty who memorably reached out to an artist to handle this end of the business—the remarkable jeweler René Lalique.

Coty's new shop at 23 Place Vendôme was situated right next door to Lalique's jewelry store. Lalique, who already was a recipient of the Legion of Honor, was by then famous for his Art Nouveau designs, which were snapped up by his devoted (and wealthy) customers, including Sarah Bernhardt. He had even been granted an entire pavilion to himself at the 1900 exposition. Coty immediately spotted Lalique as the man he wanted to design his perfume bottles, and he was surprised when Lalique at first turned him down. Still, Lalique was fascinated by glass and had even built a furnace in his garden in which to experiment with it. Coty was persistent, and eventually he convinced Lalique that "a perfume needs to attract the eye as much as the nose."[28]

Lalique's first design for Coty, in 1908, was a small rectangular plaque depicting a woman languidly emerging from the petals of a flower—a design that he then incorporated into a bottle. Mass-production still was not within his reach, but by autumn he had rented a glassworks at Combs-la-Ville on the Seine, and within a few months he would patent a new casting method "applied to the production of all bottles, carafes, and vases with openings narrower than their interior space." Three years later he would apply for a second patent: "a production process for glass objects and vessels using casting, and simultaneously applying pressure and blowing."[29] These techniques amounted to a significant technological advance, but perhaps Lalique's greatest discovery was of a semi-crystal that was lighter, cheaper, more pliable, and more transparent than the material traditionally used by crystalmakers such as Baccarat.

Lalique's casting was not a cheapening method, but one that he combined with other processes, especially his acid frosting and felt-wheel polishing, to create true works of art. He did not even overlook the bottle stoppers, which appeared in an amazing array of shapes and sizes, including balls topped with flowers in bloom or with large bees. By 1909, Lalique had created his famous Dragonfly bottle designed for Coty's perfume *Cyclamen*, and a long and remarkable partnership had begun.

～

It was sometime during the autumn of 1908 that Picasso purchased a naive but arresting portrait by the gentle and somewhat strange little painter, Henri Rousseau, also known (from his former job as a customs agent) as Le Douanier. Picasso bought it dirt-cheap for its canvas, which he meant to paint over—at least until he took a good look at it. Or so the story goes. It never has been clear whether Picasso was making cruel fun of Rousseau or truly praising him when, following a series of rather scrambled events, he decided to give a party in Rousseau's honor.

As usual for this gang, things went wildly wrong. The caterer never showed up, but no one minded. Everyone had come for the booze and a good time, and by early evening, as they set out from their café rendezvous for the Bateau-Lavoir, a spirit of drunken good cheer had developed. Gertrude Stein had to push the painter Marie Laurencin all the way up Rue Ravignan, steadying her as she swayed. When Fernande Olivier (who had never liked Marie) demanded that she leave, Gertrude—feeling aggrieved—was adamant that she stay. No one opposed Gertrude, especially when adamant, and so Marie stayed, but the disasters and the good times continued. There were fights, toasts, dancing, and songs (including a rousing rendition of the University of California fight song, graciously contributed by Alice B. Toklas's friend, Harriet Levy). Rousseau sat on an improvised throne of packing cases, where he seemed to be enjoying himself, even though hot wax regularly dripped from a Chinese lantern onto his head. Perhaps the climax came when a very drunk guest ate the huge yellow flower off of Alice B. Toklas's new hat.

It was the stuff of legends, and thanks to Gertrude Stein's celebration of it in *The Autobiography of Alice B. Toklas*, the story of the Rousseau banquet has made the rounds for years. Yet despite its over-familiarity, this rowdy affair did have its importance, by capturing the feeling of an era in Montmartre—one that already was beginning to vanish.

～

Artists in Montmartre and Montparnasse may have been impoverished, but theirs was not the poverty of despair that had set off the Commune uprising in 1871 and in fact continued throughout the Belle Epoque, which hardly was a golden age for Paris's poor. In 1908, as a reminder of 1871's tragic events, the present simple plaque was placed on the Mur des Fédérés in Père-Lachaise cemetery, in memory of the 147 Communards shot against this wall at the culmination of the last ferocious battle of the Commune uprising. In the days following this massacre, many more bodies were collected and added to what became a communal grave and a natural memorial for those who wished to pay tribute.

Over the years, political gatherings gravitated here, which the Third Republic began to tolerate. By the 1880s the municipal council granted the land around this communal grave to the families of the dead. This led to dis-

Mur des Fédérés, mass gravesite at Père-Lachaise cemetery. © I. McAuliffe

cussion—and argument—over what kind of monument would be most suitable. Some wanted a dramatic rendition of the martyrs, but others thought this would be "too bourgeois." At last, in 1908, they settled on the dramatically simple plaque, letting those few words evoke the story.

Life remained difficult for the poor of Paris. By the first decade of the twentieth century, most of Paris's working poor were located on the city's outskirts—in the outer arrondissements and in the industrial suburbs that lay just outside the city's borders. They had fled there following Baron Haussmann's mid-nineteenth-century renovation of central Paris, which created a more attractive and salubrious city, but in the process destroyed the tenements and the dark and narrow streets that held their homes. Within a few decades, the population of these outer arrondissements and industrial suburbs doubled, to more than one and a quarter million residents. Most of these individuals no longer worked in handicraft production but in the factories that increasingly dominated the city's rim. This in turn left the center of Paris as a residence largely of the bourgeoisie and the workers who directly served it.

Although for the most part invisible, at least to those bourgeois Parisians and visitors with a disinclination to notice, the service portion of Paris's population was sizable, including some thirty thousand coachmen, cabbies, and delivery men; ten thousand railroad and tramway workers; nine thousand butchers' assistants; twelve thousand café waiters, and many others. An important segment were the sixty thousand cooks and workers who labored in restaurant kitchens, in addition to the thousands who worked in private homes—an unenviable way to eke out a living, given the typically abysmal working conditions.

Turn-of-the-century Paris kitchens usually were located in cramped and poorly ventilated basement quarters, and those who labored in these hellholes had to endure suffocating heat, poisonous gas fumes, and odors from the filth that typically collected there. Fourteen-hour days in such surroundings took their toll; at the turn of the century, cooks and kitchen workers suffered from more occupational diseases than did miners, resulting from long hours of standing, heavy loads, and putrid air, as well as from undernourishment—a particularly ironic fate for kitchen workers. And of course there was the constant danger from fire and accidents. Not surprisingly, many cooks and kitchen workers turned to drink to get them through their days and nights. Life expectancy was low, and few cooks lived beyond their early forties.

One who did live well beyond his forties was Escoffier, who had worked his way out of an appalling apprenticeship and up through the ranks with admirable dispatch. By the 1890s, when he became *chef de cuisine* at the Savoy Hotel in London, he did his best to correct the worst abominations of kitchen life by insisting on clean and light kitchens, large and dirt-free staff quarters (including the luxury of bathrooms), and ample staff meals. He would continue these requirements throughout the rest of his career, and in 1910 he published a pamphlet proposing a society to provide financial assistance to the poor, including cooks. In addition, he supported several charities aimed at helping those in the profession who were in need.

Unfortunately, there were many in need. Despite the increase in wealth in Paris by the early years of the century, along with a corresponding rise in living standards,[30] poverty remained widespread, with the majority of working-class Parisians living at or close to the edge. Unemployment and underemployment were the chief culprits, and even highly skilled laborers faced steep variations in the demand for their work. Boilermakers faced seasonal layoffs; workers in the clothing trades earned half their yearly income during four months of the year (of sixteen-hour days); and skilled cabinetmakers had to resort to ordinary piece work, at less pay, during slack times.

For unskilled workers, conditions were worse. Employment at factories fluctuated widely, and layoffs frequently left workers unemployed for months at a time, especially during times of recession—such as the one that hit the Paris area in 1908. Hardest hit were households headed by women, whose wages were lower than those of their male counterparts, although the elderly of both sexes also suffered disproportionally: well before old age, workers' wages generally declined. With the working poor relying extensively on bread and other cheap carbohydrates for sustenance, the creation of school lunch programs during the late nineteenth century provided some welcome additional calories. Even though the nutritional value of these lunches was questionable, at least they staved off immediate hunger.

Still, despite these ongoing conditions, certain elements of life had improved, even for the poor. Cleaner water now was more widely available, and Paris's new sewer system helped remove much of the filth that had previously threatened public health. The very fact that many bakers no longer used contaminated water to bake their bread had a significant impact on their customers' health. Yet, as with every other aspect of life, the purest water and the best sewage facilities went to those who could afford them. The poor, as always, had to settle for what they could get.

⌇

Despite Baron Haussmann's pioneering efforts in providing cleaner water and better sanitation, as well as his massive construction of roads and parks throughout Paris, the City of Light faced a new wave of urban problems by the opening years of the twentieth century—something that the urban plan-ner, Eugène Hénard, proposed to rectify.[31]

Between 1872 and 1911, metropolitan Paris had burgeoned from just under two million to almost three million inhabitants. Not only were there far more people crowding in, but automobiles had proliferated—from around two thousand in 1903 to fifty-four thousand in 1910 (although these fig-ures are for all of France, most of France's autos at that time were in Paris). Congestion had become a problem, and it required a new way of looking at things.

Hénard, the son of a professor of architecture at Paris's Ecole des Beaux-Arts, studied in his father's atelier before snagging an appointment at the office in charge of the city's architecture, where he would remain throughout his career. At first he merely designed school buildings, but soon he became involved in planning the expositions of 1889 and 1900 (earning him a gold medal and the accolades of the Legion of Honor, which made him a Che-valier). With the opening of the new century, Hénard began to study city problems in Paris, making an analysis of pedestrian and vehicular movement as well as a post-exposition proposal for the preservation of the Champ de Mars. More than anything, Hénard wanted to put in place a long-term mas-ter plan to improve open space, housing, traffic circulation, and development in the entire Paris region.

This included preservation of the best of the past, and under Hénard the most important of Paris's historical areas were catalogued, described, and ranked in order of urgency for preservation. As a result of his work, entire perspectives have been preserved, including the banks of the Seine as well as the tip of the Ile de la Cité at the Pont Neuf. But Hénard looked with par-ticular urgency to the future, where (despite the construction of the Métro) he correctly anticipated an enormous growth in automobile traffic. And so he began to analyze Paris's road network.

Drawing on plans from other major cities, he concluded that a major north-south transversal was needed, as well as more bridges across the Seine. He also proposed counterclockwise circular traffic flow at major intersections such as the multi-branched intersection at the Arc de Triomphe, and he correspondingly designed what may have been the first underpass to protect pedestrians at this same intimidating spot.

Hénard also concerned himself with parks, which despite Haussmann's additions had declined significantly during the previous century, even as population burgeoned. The city government viewed any open space as a source of revenue and, in the opening years of the new century, had already sold off one-third of the Esplanade des Invalides for development. It also was considering the sale of part or all of the Champ de Mars as well as the extensive zone along the city's outer borders surrounding Paris's last remaining wall, the Thiers fortifications—the single largest land reserve left in Paris.

In 1909, Hénard proposed replacing the outmoded Thiers fortifications with nine new landscaped parks in areas where they were badly needed, linked by a new kind of road that Hénard called a stepped boulevard. This in turn incorporated gardens and courtyards in the uneven spaces between buildings and the street. The alternative, he feared, would be haphazard and unattractive development and the loss of open space. Yet, faced with strong opposition from the city government and real estate interests, his plan was defeated, and after the war the City of Paris tore down the fortifications and sold nearly all the land to private developers. Hodge-podge development and the much-maligned ring road, the Périphérique, soon followed.

As for the Champ de Mars, Hénard envisioned converting a portion into the first in-city airfield in the world, with the Eiffel Tower as its signal tower and a sprinkling of cafés, sports facilities, and gardens throughout. The idea of an airfield never was popular, but Hénard's proposal to keep the Champ de Mars as an open space gained many adherents. Yet here, too, real estate interests prevailed, and by 1910, ninety-meter strips along each side of the Champ de Mars had been sold and filled with houses.

Hénard did not live to see his dream of a master plan for Paris and its surrounding regions put into effect. But in 1934, such a plan, authored by one of his assistants, was at last accepted. With subsequent modifications, it remains in effect today.

⁓

Late in 1908, Abbé Mugnier showed his age by despairing over the younger generation. He had already noticed that young women of high birth were increasingly seen smoking in public;[32] now, in the privacy of his journal, he unleashed a few choice words about the self-centeredness of the young, whose favorite word was "amusing." They live to amuse themselves, he wrote, and they prefer to sit rather than play tennis or outdoor games. Rather than dance, they prefer to flirt. "When a young couple sets up house, they are more concerned with a 'garage' than with quarters for children. 'No children, two autos,'" he added acidly.[33]

Seventeen-year-old Charles de Gaulle was not of this sort. That summer of 1908, prior to entering Paris's Collège Stanislas, he traveled in Germany. There, going from Baden to the Black Forest, he read the newspapers and observed that they "are quite hostile to us." And then he added: "Something has changed in Europe these last three years, and as I observe it I think of the unrest that comes before a great war."[34]

Young de Gaulle was rigorously preparing for a military career, and already he sniffed the coming conflagration.

The Hôtel Biron, now the Musée Rodin. © M. McAuliffe

CHAPTER ELEVEN

Idyll

(1909)

It was autumn when Jean Cocteau wandered into the huge courtyard of a decaying mansion at the corner of Rue de Varenne and the Boulevard des Invalides.[1] The mansion was the Hôtel Biron, and until the separation of Church and state it had been the convent and school of Sacré-Coeur, or Sacred Heart.

Neither the school nor the convent any longer existed, and the property now was under the custody of a liquidator of government property. But the concierge told Cocteau that the sculptor Auguste Rodin lived in the central part, and that if Cocteau wanted one of the remaining rooms, he should make an offer to the liquidator. Cocteau immediately found his way to the man in charge, and by that afternoon had become the proud tenant, at a nominal fee, of the nuns' former dance and music classroom.

The Hôtel Biron had a noble past, having been designed—at least in part—by Jacques-Ange Gabriel, the architect of the Petit Trianon and the palatial residences flanking the northern entrance to the Place de la Concorde. The mansion acquired its name from an early owner, the Duc de Biron, who was responsible for its extensive gardens. Unfortunately the sisters of Sacré-Coeur had banished all signs of luxury, including hot water and heat, and sold off the mansion's paneling, its huge wall mirrors, and its painted decorations.[2] The sisters also built a chapel and a boarding school, and let the grounds go wild.

Rainer Maria Rilke discovered the property through his wife, the sculptor Clara Rilke, and took up residence there after his wife returned to Germany.

Rilke told Rodin about the property—a generous gesture, considering Rodin's treatment of him—and this act prompted a reconciliation. After one look at the romantically run-down mansion, Rodin immediately rented the large ground-floor rooms facing the garden. He never lived there, but it was his favorite studio, where he loved to work and to receive visitors. It was a "realm from a Perrault fairy tale," Cocteau wrote, bordered by romantically tangled gardens that were perfect for fêtes and poetry readings. Brambles and bushes overran "a little virgin forest, an impenetrable vegetable chaos." Even the tall windows to Cocteau's room were impeded by a thick carpet of forget-me-nots; once opened, they revealed "a veritable tunnel of greenery, leading to the unknown"[3]—much like the magic wood that would appear in Cocteau's 1946 classic film, *La Belle et la Bête*.

Of course young Cocteau had no way of knowing that fame as a poet, novelist, and filmmaker lay ahead. Indeed, only several months earlier, Cocteau had begun his public career with a poetry recital at the Théâtre Femina, a fashionable little playhouse on the Champs-Elysées. This event was entirely underwritten and promoted by the actor Edouard de Max, whose over-the-top antics had gotten Cocteau in trouble with Sarah Bernhardt not so long before.[4] In contrast with Cocteau's previous outing, his verses on this occasion (which would be printed as *La lampe d'Aladin*) were fashionably delicate—a youthful product that Cocteau would later denigrate as "stupid."

Yet Cocteau's idyll at the Hôtel Biron was anything but stupid, a dream world that abruptly ended when his usually permissive mother accidentally discovered her son's secret bachelor pad. At the time, and apparently until her death several decades later, she supported him with a regular allowance, which seems to have been his most reliable source of income. In addition, Cocteau was accustomed to living rent-free at home. It may have been about the time of his residence at the Hôtel Biron that his mother "made a very serious and painful scene on the subject of my 'excessive freedom, that I put to such bad use,' the 'appalling people I see,' my idleness, not earning my living, etc. etc."[5] As always with family relations, there may well have been more to the story than that, but the outcome was clear enough: Cocteau left behind his idyllic garden at the Hôtel Biron.

⌢

Rodin may never have lived at the Hôtel Biron, but it became his treasured hideaway, where he worked and welcomed visitors in the company of his determined companion Claire de Choiseul, who referred to it as "our enchanted abode."[6] Rodin bought a phonograph, on which he played everything from Gregorian chants to folk dances and music-hall ditties. During these retreats, Choiseul was ever by his side—a presence that annoyed Rodin's friends, including Count Kessler, who described her as a "no longer young, chubby lady with very red-painted lips." When Choiseul had the temerity to thank Kessler for "all that I have done for the master," he merely noted to himself how astonishing it was that "that old man has the stamina for all these Americans."[7]

Yet it was Rilke who was the most disturbed by Choiseul's influence over Rodin. Rilke shared his concerns with Kessler, telling him that originally Rodin had "seemed to me to be a living example for how an artist growing old could be beautiful." But then, "it suddenly turned out that growing old is something terrible for him, exactly as terrible as for your average person." Not only was Rodin afraid, Rilke told Kessler, but he was bored and susceptible to women, "as one would expect from any other old Frenchman." It was disconcerting for Rilke that Rodin seemed to need Choiseul to entertain and distract him, to keep his "naked fear of death" at bay.[8]

～

In addition to Rilke, another of Kessler's and Rodin's mutual friends was the Basque sculptor Aristide Maillol. Maillol, who was born in a village on the French Mediterranean coast near the Spanish border, had struggled to become a sculptor after a bout with rheumatic inflammation and blindness forced him to abandon painting and tapestry design. By 1905, his sculpture *La Méditerranée*—exhibited in that year's Salon d'Automne—seemed to many to embody the same revolutionary spirit as Matisse's *Woman in a Hat*.

Kessler may have first encountered Maillol's work at a 1902 Vollard exhibition, but it was not until 1904 that he first visited Maillol's studio, located in his small, primitive house in Marly, to the west of Paris. Maillol, who by then was in his forties, "with a long untrimmed black beard [and] very expressive, luminescent blue eyes," did not bother to introduce himself or learn his visitors' names, but simply led them into his studio.[9] Kessler immediately purchased a small model.

Thus began a patronage that would last for more than thirty years, interspersed with frequent visits to their mutual friend, Rodin. Along the way, the two had many good conversations. Why did Maillol always sculpt female figures, Kessler wanted to know. "Eh," Maillol replied, "because I don't have a model. Rodin, he can pay for as many models as he wants, but us other artists, we must typically make use of our wives." As for a proposal to illustrate Virgil's *Eclogues* for Kessler, Maillol was enthusiastic: "I read Virgil all the time," he assured Kessler.[10] Maillol's greatest treasure, Kessler noted, was his collection of woodcuts by Gauguin.

Despite a trip together to Greece in 1908, during which Maillol's peasant manners and narrow-mindedness got on Kessler's nerves, their friendship, and the patronage, continued.

⌢

It was autumn of 1909 when Picasso moved from the Bateau-Lavoir to a remarkably bourgeois apartment on the top floor of 11 Boulevard de Clichy, complete with a maid. Although the top floor location would not have signified what it would now (ground floor apartments then commanded the highest prices, especially in a walk-up), this clean and comfortable apartment at the foot of Montmartre was a clear sign of Picasso's growing success. Yet despite the Bateau-Lavoir's bohemian squalor, Picasso departed with reluctance.

It was during this same autumn that Henri Matisse made his escape from the Hôtel Biron and Paris to the southwestern suburb of Issy-les-Moulineaux, where he rented a house for himself and his family. His academy had quickly burgeoned, thanks to his reputation as well as to his reluctance to charge fees. But his students had taken far too much of his time and energy, and a move to what then was the countryside (but still within reach of Paris) represented a safe haven, where he could work relatively free from interruption.

Substantial purchases and commissions from the Russian collector Sergei Shchukin had for the first time put Matisse on a somewhat easier financial footing, and now the Matisse family could afford an entire house and garden in which to live and breathe freely. This was especially important for Matisse's daughter, Marguerite, who that spring had endured yet another tracheotomy (her first, several years earlier, had left her with a damaged windpipe that she regularly covered with a ribbon). The government's decision in the summer of 1909 to put the Hôtel Biron up for sale provided the final push. The Matisse family moved to Issy that autumn, after another summer on the Mediterranean coast.

Although Shchukin had become Matisse's foremost patron, Sarah and Michael Stein continued to be devoted collectors, and by now Matisse was beginning to be appreciated and collected by Germans and Scandinavians as well as by Americans and Russians. The French did not share in this enthusiasm for one of their own, and when not avidly hostile to his work, they were at best complacent about the fact that the best of it was leaving France.

When Matisse published his "Notes of a Painter" in 1908,[11] French critics reacted with particular vehemence to one particular statement: "What I dream of is an art of balance, of purity and serenity, devoid of troubling or depressing subject matter, an art that could be . . . a soothing, calming influence on the mind, something like a good armchair that provides relaxation from fatigue."[12] This set up a howl from those who saw Matisse's work as anything but serene or soothing. At the same time, it gave Matisse's rivals within the avant-garde—especially Picasso and his adherents—considerable ammunition with which to attack him for being a lightweight, little more than an entertainer or decorator.

In fact, with this essay, Matisse was drawing a line between his artistic vision and Picasso's, which (although he never named the artist) he viewed as overly abstract and theoretical, guided by the brain rather than by emotion, intuition, and the senses. Although Picasso would never give voice to, let alone write, an explanation of Cubism, those who viewed his work and that of his colleague, Braque, believed that their general goal "seemed to be the representation of the three-dimensional and its position in space on a two-dimensional surface."[13] A more recent specialist in Cubism has noted that "what makes Les Demoiselles a truly revolutionary work of art is that in it Picasso broke away from the two central characteristics of European painting since the Renaissance: the classical norm for the human figure, and the spatial illusionism of one-point perspective."[14] Whatever the definition, Matissse completely rejected the end product.[15]

Yet by now it mattered little what Matisse thought or wrote; within the avant-garde, Cubism already was in ascendance. Picasso and his band openly derided Matisse, while others, envious of Matisse's commissions and what they wrongly presumed was his opulent country lifestyle, claimed that he was charging (and receiving) obscenely high prices and that he and his household were living in splendor. A telephone, a bathroom, and central heating may have counted as luxuries in France at the time, but the house was a relatively modest one, and the Matisses still had financial problems, alleviated somewhat by the lucrative contract that he signed that September with the prestigious Paris gallery Bernheim-Jeune. This was unusual in that it allowed him to accept outside commissions, providing he gave a share of the profits to the gallery. Word of this, too, quickly made the rounds in exaggerated form, adding to the malice.

Matisse had only one response to the invective: "I rolled myself into a ball in my corner as an observer," he wrote, "and waited to see what would happen."[16]

⁓

Picasso, not surprisingly, viewed matters quite differently. "When we invented cubism," he later remarked, "we had no intention whatever of inventing cubism. We simply wanted to express what was in us."[17]

Despite Matisse's claim to "expression" and "expressionism," dating from his 1908 "Notes of a Painter" and his 1907 *The Red Madras Headdress* (also titled *Tête d'expression* and submitted to that year's Salon d'Automne), Picasso was not about to give ground here. Theoretical? Absolutely not. Picasso flatly rejected formulas and theories; from his standpoint, there was nothing cerebral about him or his artistic output. Physicality and potency, that was the key, along with radical daring and a new view of realism that rejected the three-dimensional simulations of the past.

Matisses's problem, as Picasso viewed it, was Matisse. After all, it was he who had laughed at *Demoiselles* and rejected Braque's submissions to the 1908 Salon d'Automne. Or so they thought. This may not have been the case—or at least not entirely the case. Janet Flanner, the *New Yorker*'s Paris correspondent, later wrote that although Braque had gagged at his first sight of *Demoiselles*, he quickly found his way to his own early vision of Cubism—although with Cézanne rather than Picasso as his guide. Inspired by Cézanne's words, that "you must see in nature the cylinder, the sphere and the cone," Braque began to paint the scenery of the French Midi village of L'Estaque in a burst of cones, cylinders, spheres—and cubes.[18] Triumphantly, he submitted six (some say seven) of these breakthrough paintings to the 1908 Salon d'Automne and was astounded when the jury refused every one. Following this total rejection, two jurors each voted to save one of his pictures (every juror had this right), but Braque, deeply angered, withdrew them all.

Matisse was one of the members of this jury, which Braque regarded as a betrayal and a massacre. After all, Matisse was the leading Fauvist—a group that Braque had briefly joined—and, until now, a friend. Matisse, by his own account, had voted to include one of Braque's paintings in the exhibition, having (as Flanner put it) "an eclectic's interest in any new formula."[19] Yet he was not one of the two who voted to save two of the Braque pictures for exhibition, and despite whatever Matisse offered in his own defense, Braque regarded Matisse as the one who had engineered his rejection.[20]

This was not all. In addition to Matisse's real or imagined role in the 1908 Salon d'Automne affair, it was Matisse who famously described Braque's pictures as having been composed "*avec les petits cubes*"—a phrase that the French art critic Louis Vauxcelles promptly picked up and published, with the result that the term "Cubism" caught on. Both Picasso and Braque detested this description (which Vauxcelles had originally intended as an epithet), although they quickly found that they had to use it. But it amounted to yet one more grievance against Matisse.

It was a touchy situation, made more so by Braque's desertion of one camp for the other. Matisse felt abandoned, and Braque felt ill-used. Picasso resented Matisse's teaching academy and his printed pronouncements on art, which Picasso regarded as self-serving and pretentious. And of course, underlying the whole were deep reserves of rivalry, envy, and misunderstanding, exacerbated by the artists' dramatically different personalities and lifestyles.

Picasso—the younger by more than a decade—was Spanish to the core, with a corresponding *machismo* that Gertrude Stein deftly summed up in her description of him as "the little bullfighter, followed by his squadron of four" (Derain, Braque, Apollinaire, and Salmon); she also hit the mark with her description of him as "Napoleon followed by his four enormous grenadiers."[21] Picasso needed to be at the center of an exclusive coterie, as its ringleader and star, and achieved this dominant position easily. He rarely went anywhere alone, and references to the "Picasso crowd," "Picasso court," or "*la bande à Picasso,*" abound throughout the Bateau-Lavoir years. Men and women gravitated to him, although women (with the possible exception of Gertrude Stein) held a distinctly inferior position in his life. He acquired, dominated, and shed women easily, and although Fernande would stay with him for the better part of seven years, she, too, would eventually be cast aside.

Matisse, despite his renegade youth, was by this time a conservatively dressed family man who felt his family responsibilities keenly. Although he had friends and saw some of them on a fairly regular basis, the core of his life was his family and his studio, where he preferred to work alone. It was the interruptions from friends, students, potential clients, and a variety of others that drove him to Issy-les-Moulineaux. Privacy and peace were essential to him, and despite the catcalls from his detractors, he sought in his art a serenity and stillness that was completely alien to Picasso.

In seeking this stillness, Matisse was willing to endure self-sacrifice, including sexual abstinence, which he had attempted to put into practice ever since 1905, believing that this would conserve his creative energies. Picasso would have found such renunciation laughable, as would Rodin, who gloried in the female body in both his art and his life, and viewed sexual energy as the source of his inspiration and creativity. Believing Victor Hugo to have been similarly inspired, Rodin symbolized this in his first (and unaccepted) rendition of a Victor Hugo memorial by placing a crotch-revealing sculpture of the goddess Iris directly above Hugo's head. That Hugo in old age was regarded by those who knew him as a sadly salacious old man, and that Rodin was rapidly acquiring the same reputation, did not seem to occur to the sculptor.

～

That spring and summer, Rodin supervised the site in the Palais Royal gardens for his monument to Victor Hugo, which was unveiled in September.[22] By this time, although he may not have realized it, public interest in such monuments was declining, and trends in art had significantly shifted from his focus on drama-infused naturalism.

Simultaneously, it was this summer that Rodin's depression—which had first appeared three years before—became significantly worse. He anguished that he was "always worn out by a senseless life," and that he was "totally out of touch with [his] energy."[23] Evidently exacerbating the situation was the death of Claire de Choiseul's sister and the resulting bequest to Claire's husband, the marquis. Rodin paid for the marquis' trip to America to sort things out, and by the year's end, the marquis—quite on his own volition—had upgraded his title in the social register to "Duc de Choiseul." Correspondingly, Claire de Choiseul began to refer to herself as "Duchess." Perhaps this was what Rodin had in mind when he said he found life especially senseless.

Nonetheless, Claire de Choiseul continued to play an intimate role in Rodin's life, and by the year's end, he seemed happier. Perhaps his refuge in the Hôtel Biron was responsible for this change in mood. He certainly seemed content there, and it was only the prospect of its disappearance that created a new set of clouds on his horizon.

⌒

It was during this time that Isadora Duncan also found her way to the Hôtel Biron. After touring extensively throughout Europe and America, she returned to Paris early in 1909, where she rented apartments for herself and her daughter, Deirdre, and for the students she had brought from her disbanded school in Germany. She also rented a long gallery in the Hôtel Biron that she used for dance rehearsals. She and her pupils made their debut in late January at the large Gaité-Lyrique theater, accompanied by the prestigious Colonne Orchestra. Tickets sold out within hours, and they played to full houses for the entire run.

Isadora and her young dancers quickly became a great hit, and it was during the early days of her success at the Gaité-Lyrique that a new man unexpectedly entered her life: Paris Singer, brother of Winnaretta Singer (the Princesse Edmond de Polignac), and as unlike Winnaretta as possible except for his inherited wealth. Handsome, charming, and a notorious playboy, he did everything he could to sweep Isadora off her feet. They had met once before, briefly, at the funeral of Winnaretta's elderly husband, Prince Edmond de Polignac. At that time Isadora had barely taken note of him; but now, she understood completely what his appearance meant in her life. She had already turned to telepathy, using the positive thinking system of Emile Coué to ask repeatedly for a millionaire to pay for her enormous expenses, including her school. Now, when Singer entered her dressing room, her first thought was, "Here is my millionaire!"[24]

They soon became lovers, although they quarreled constantly. Singer dispensed largesse without limit but (as Duncan later wrote) "had the psychology of a spoilt child." He was domineering, and Isadora was not one to be dominated. Making matters worse, he had no particular interest in or appreciation of her dancing. Repeatedly, they left one another, only to make up and start over. Still, Isadora admitted to loving him, and undeniably, all that money made for some good times and a life of luxury, such as sailing for Italy on Singer's yacht, and dining at the best restaurants in Paris. Singer paid for everything, including Isadora's clothing binges at the salon of Paul Poiret, who (according to Isadora) "could dress a woman in such a way as also to create a work of art." And although Isadora insisted that she paid for her glamorous new studio in Neuilly before she even met Singer, it probably was his money that paid for the lavish decoration, done by none other than Paul Poiret.[25]

It was in Venice that autumn, without Singer, that Isadora learned that once again she was pregnant. Torn, she considered an abortion, "filled with revolt that such a deformation should again come to my body, which was the instrument of my Art." Yet she simultaneously was "tortured by the call, the hope, the vision" of the baby to come. In the end, she decided to keep the baby, and then left for a second tour of America. There, she danced continuously and with great success, managing to hide her pregnancy until one day in January, when a woman came to her and exclaimed, "But, my dear Miss Duncan, it's plainly visible from the front row." At which point Isadora decided that it probably was best to stop the tour and return to Europe.[26]

⌇

During this time Paris Singer's sister, Winnaretta, the Princesse de Polignac, had been quietly conducting her own love affairs, including one with the young American artist Romaine Brooks. Brooks, who idolized and pursued Winnaretta, had not yet met Natalie Clifford Barney, the American writer who would become the great love of her life. Indeed, after Winnaretta, Brooks would spend several years with the celebrated Russian dancer, Ida Rubinstein. In any case, it was not Romaine Brooks but Olga, the lovely Baroness de Meyer who, from 1909 until the coming of war, became Winnaretta's love interest.

Typically, Winnaretta was drawn to individuals who shared her love of the arts. A talented musician as well as painter in her own right, she had for many years—first with her husband, then by herself—presided over one of the foremost salons in Paris, where avant-garde composers and musicians could perform their latest works. It was as a major patron of the arts that she first encountered Sergei Diaghilev in 1906, at the home of Grand Duke Paul of Russia (who by then lived in Paris, having dared to marry a commoner). Diaghilev needed private patrons for his productions—especially in the spring of 1909, after the czar unexpectedly withdrew his financial support. When Diaghilev and Gabriel Astruc drew up a list of possible supporters, the Princesse de Polignac, along with Misia Edwards, was at the top. By the time Diaghilev arrived in Paris to launch his 1909 season, both Winnaretta and Misia had become major patrons, and they would continue in this role throughout the twenty years until his death.

Diaghilev's 1909 program was huge and daring. In addition to Rimsky-Korsakov's opera *Ivan the Terrible* (originally titled *Maid of Pskov*), starring Feodor Chaliapin, Diaghilev decided to bring Russian ballet to Paris—not the famed Russian imperial ballet, but a new company, the Ballets Russes. This would be the ballet of a new era, uniting the talents of Michel Fokine, Anna Pavlova, and Vaslav Nijinsky, the most progressive dancers and choreographers in the land.

For more than a decade, Diaghilev and his colleagues had grown increasingly dismayed and bored with the tradition-entrenched Russian imperial ballet, and Isadora Duncan's 1904 performances in St. Petersburg made a deep impression on them. "We do not deny that Duncan is a kindred spirit," Diaghilev wrote some years later. "Indeed, we carry the torch that she lit."[27]

Almost undone by the czar's abrupt withdrawal of support, as well as by the temporary desertion of Anna Pavlova, the intended star of the ballet program (fearing the collapse of the entire season, she had gone off on her own tour), Diaghilev salvaged what turned out to be a magnificent season. In addition to *Ivan the Terrible*, he presented five ballets by Fokine: *Le Pavillon d'Armide*, *Les Danses Polovtsians* (from Borodin's *Prince Igor*), *Le Festin*, *Les Sylphides*, and *Cléopâtre*. As the first non-narrative ballet, *Les Sylphides* (originally *Chopiniana*, and danced to music by Chopin) paid tribute to Isadora's innovations in dance.

It should be noted that young Igor Stravinsky's first contributions to the Ballets Russes were a couple of Chopin orchestrations for the 1909 production of *Les Sylphides*. It was after hearing complaints about the conservatism of the program's music in an otherwise brilliant evening (the critic Louis Laloy, for example, panned the score for *Le Pavillon d'Armide* as "insignificant music," whose "only extenuating circumstance . . . is that after five minutes one no longer hears it"),[28] Diaghilev set about commissioning several new ballet scores, including one from this young composer—a work titled *The Firebird.*

Yet that still lay in the future. Opening night in May 1909, featuring three of the ballets, justified everything that Diaghilev had risked and dared. Dazzled audience members endlessly enthused about the Ballets Russes as "a sudden glory" and a "phenomenon."[29] Proust, who had made it from his sickbed to the theater, was enchanted by the Russians' "charming invasion."[30] As it turned out, Pavlova's temporary absence[31] boosted the careers not only of her substitute, Tamara Karsavina, but also that of young Vaslav Nijinsky, on whom the spotlight shone especially brightly. On subsequent nights the spotlight would also gravitate toward the star of *Cléopâtre*, Ida Rubinstein, an expressive dancer with great grace although fewer classical skills, who had already drawn attention for her scandalous St. Petersburg performance of the Dance of the Seven Veils from Oscar Wilde's *Salomé*. During the dance's climax, she had dared to cast aside even the last of her veils to appear completely naked before her stunned audience. News of this event traveled rapidly (possibly alienating the czar en route), and by the time she reached Paris, Rubinstein was a celebrity, if not an outright star.

Despite Diaghilev's huge expenses (250 dancers, singers, and technicians, plus an 80-piece orchestra), he had undertaken the complete renovation of the Théâtre du Châtelet, including recarpeting, technical improvements, and the construction of a new stage. He even had pipes installed beneath the stage to carry water from the Seine to spout from the fountains in the final act of *Le Pavillon d'Armide*. Leaving nothing to chance, Diaghilev and his dancer/choreographer, Michel Fokine, along with his set and costume designers, Léon Bakst and Alexandre Benois, undertook to create a sense of total theater. Their Parisian audiences, aware that they were in the presence of something exciting and even revolutionary, were ecstatic.

Offstage, Diaghilev had even more reason for happiness. Nijinsky, who previously was under the protection of a wealthy Russian prince, had gravitated into Diaghilev's orbit, and the two now embarked on a passionate affair. That summer, following the Ballets Russes season, they traveled to Venice, where Isadora Duncan was staying. Seated next to Nijinsky at one of Diaghilev's parties, Isadora (according to the recollection of Nijinsky's sister, Bronya) proposed that he and she should marry. "Think what wonderful children we would have. . . . They would be prodigies. . . . Our children would dance like Duncan and Nijinsky." According to Bronya's recollection,

Nijinsky replied "that he didn't want his children to dance like Duncan—and that, besides, he was too young to get married."[32]

⌒

Misia and her second husband, Alfred Edwards, were divorced in February 1909, allowing Edwards and his volatile mistress, Lantelme, to marry several months later. By this time Misia had become Sert's mistress and was like a sister to Diaghilev. Although she and Winnaretta would both become great patrons of Diaghilev and the Ballets Russes, it would be Misia who would be Diaghilev's closest friend, in an often stormy—and totally platonic—relationship.

It was now that Jean Cocteau began to enter this world across the footlights, through Misia's salon. There he charmed everyone. According to one frequent observer, Cocteau "was the most entertaining talker conceivable. . . . In a word, he was irresistible."[33] Using charm and brilliant conversation, the twenty-year-old propelled himself into the world of ballet—Diaghilev's world and the world of Nijinsky. Cocteau courted Diaghilev, all the while hovering yearningly near Nijinsky. He marveled at the dichotomy between the onstage airborne performer and the backstage athlete, on the verge of collapse. He did not see (or did not choose to see) the muscular oaf whom Misia called "an idiot of genius."[34] Although Cocteau's persistent backstage hovering did not lead him to Nijinsky, it soon led him into work as a painter and draughtsman for the company, under the tutelage of Léon Bakst. It even led him into writing publicity for the impresario Gabriel Astruc. Not a bad beginning for what would become a brilliantly diverse and unconventional career.

⌒

While Jean Cocteau was making his way into the sparkling world of high society and the theater, in a quieter corner of Paris two prodigiously talented young sisters had dreams of taking the musical world by storm. Born into a musical Parisian family in 1887 and 1893, respectively, Nadia and Lili Boulanger were raised in a home filled with fine music and prominent musicians. Nadia studied piano with one of the leading teachers in Paris and entered the Paris Conservatoire at the age of nine, having audited classes from the age of seven. Deciding to mop up as many prizes possible in the shortest amount of time, she soon embarked on an impressive collection of awards. In 1904, she began studying composition with Gabriel Fauré—indicating her serious interest in original composition—and won first prizes in organ, fugue, and piano accompaniment, having won first prize in harmony the year before.

At the same time, Nadia's younger sister, Lili, was (if possible) even more precocious, making her public debut on the violin at a tender age, after having already becoming accomplished at the piano, voice, and harp. Unfortunately Lili had been severely ill as a youngster and remained sickly. Unable to follow a regular course of study, she accompanied Nadia to classes and learned from her older sister, who felt responsible for the fragile younger one.

While Lili battled chronic weakness and illness, Nadia forged ahead. After leaving the Conservatoire while still in her teens, she began to teach privately at her family's apartment on Rue Ballu, in the northwest corner of Paris's ninth arrondissement. She also began to perform publicly on the piano and organ, to substantial acclaim. Yet despite her many successes, there remained one more prize to grasp: the Prix de Rome. No woman had ever won it, but her father, Ernest Boulanger, had attained it in 1836, and she was determined to follow in his footsteps.[35]

In 1907, Nadia Boulanger reached the final round of the Prix de Rome, but the following year she created a scandal when she submitted an instrumental rather than the required vocal fugue. According to Lili's diary, "[Camille] Saint-Saëns didn't want Nadia's work to be heard, but the jury overruled him and allowed it to go forward."[36] Saint-Saëns of course was the renowned but by now crotchety and conservative composer who so severely disapproved of Debussy's and Ravel's works; it was unlikely that any change to the Prix de Rome, especially by a woman—even one with Nadia Boulanger's connections and credentials—would meet with his approval. In the end, Nadia won second Grand Prize for her cantata, "La Sirène," but the first prize eluded her—whether because she had challenged the hidebound traditions of the Prix de Rome and its most conservative members or, as some thought, because she was a woman.

In 1909, Nadia once again tried and failed to receive the Prix de Rome. It was then that Lili—unschooled but hugely talented in everything musical—announced that she was going to become a composer and win the Prix de Rome herself.

～

Soon after the close of Diaghilev's triumphant 1909 Ballets Russes season, he concluded that, to remain in the limelight, he would have to mount world premieres rather than merely perform repertory. He also decided that these world premieres should include works by non-Russian—preferably French—composers. He could have looked to long-established French composers such as Saint-Saëns, d'Indy, or Dukas, but he preferred those who were more cutting-edge and exciting. In this category, two names stood out: Debussy and Ravel.

By now Debussy was regarded, at least in the most forward-looking circles, as the leading French composer of his generation, and Diaghilev went to some pains to persuade him to write a ballet. At first Debussy was reluctant, telling his publisher, Jacques Durand, that he couldn't suggest a ballet sub-ject "at the drop of a hat" and that Diaghilev was proposing something that would take place in eighteenth-century Venice—"which, for Russian danc-ers, strikes me as a bit contradictory." Yet the idea was sufficiently intriguing that Debussy began to work on a libretto for *Masques et bergamasques*. "I intend to enjoy myself writing this ballet," he wrote Louis Laloy. "I have no intention of asking Nijinsky to describe symbols with his legs or Karsavina to explain Kant's philosophy with her smile."[37]

But then something happened, and the entire project disappeared. Possi-bly it was a misunderstanding; possibly it was something more. Diaghilev had more than merely one ballet and one composer in mind, including concepts that would become *The Firebird* and *Scheherazade*, as well as a ballet from Ravel. Whatever actually happened, Debussy clearly was angry when he wrote Laloy in August that "the Russian whom we both know imagines that the best way to deal with his fellow men is first of all to lie to them."[38] It was not a good way to end their first venture together, but Diaghilev seems not to have understood the extent of Debussy's ire and would later approach him on further ideas for ballets. Debussy would continue to work with Diaghilev, but the episode left a lingering blot on their relationship.

By this time Diaghilev had turned to Ravel, and in late June the com-poser was already in the throes of preparing a ballet libretto for *Daphnis et Chloé*, due for performance during the Ballet Russes's upcoming 1910 season. The libretto, based on an ancient Greek romance, was Fokine's idea, which meant that Ravel had to work with him, despite distinct linguistic difficul-ties. Writing Madame René de Saint-Marceaux in late June, Ravel told her that he had just had an insane week: "Almost every night, I was working until 3 a.m. What complicates things is that Fokine doesn't know a word of French, and I only know how to swear in Russian."[39]

As it turned out, language barriers would not be the only problem, and *Daphnis et Chloé* would not be performed by the Ballets Russes until 1912.

⌒

In January, Ravel's brilliant and demonically difficult *Gaspard de la nuit*, a suite for solo piano, received its premiere at a Société Nationale recital by Ricardo Viñes, where it was well received. As it happened, Ravel was about to break with the Société, where he served on the steering committee; to his mind, the organization had become too staid and conservative, despite its original intent. As he put it, the Société was turning down works that "didn't offer those solid qualities of incoherence and boredom, which the Schola Cantorum [of d'Indy] baptizes as structure and profundity."[40]

In its place, he was forming a new society, the Société Musicale Indépendante (SMI), with Gabriel Fauré as president. This organization would be active for almost three decades, attracting the interest and support of Winnaretta, Princesse de Polignac, as well as her husband's niece, the Princesse Armande de Polignac, and would provide useful competition to the Société Nationale.

In the meantime, Debussy's *Pelléas et Mélisande* was enjoying continued success, with two more foreign premieres, in Rome and in London. Its continued popularity from then until the outbreak of war seems to have been at least in part related to the escapism it offered. As Jacques Rivière (editor of the *Nouvelle Revue Française*) noted, *Pelléas* created a dream world, a paradise where audience members could forget their cares.[41]

Yet Debussy found the theatrical experience far from idyllic. He attended rehearsals for the London premiere but did not attend the premiere itself: "The theater atmosphere makes me ill," he wrote, noting that he "rarely had such a strong desire to kill anybody" as one of the producers. Nevertheless, after the premiere, he wrote his parents that "the singers were recalled a dozen times and for a quarter of an hour there were calls for the composer, who was settled peacefully in his hotel." He added, with considerable pride, that "received opinion states that such [exuberance] is extremely rare in England." And then he concluded, with unaccustomed fervor: "So long live France! Long live French music!"[42]

Still, Debussy with his feet up in a London hotel room was not as carefree as he would have liked to convey. He was suffering from depression (as he would tell a friend, "I'm in the sort of mood where I'd rather be a sponge at the bottom of the sea or a vase on the mantelpiece, anything rather than a man of intellect; such a fragile kind of machine").[43] In addition, as he would eventually realize, the weakness and pain he already was experiencing would not be going away.[44]

～

In July, Louis Blériot crossed the English Channel in his tiny monoplane—a first, marking a major turning point in aviation history. Blériot's flight was a daring one, during which he managed to gauge his direction from the destroyer *Escopette*, which accompanied him. After he overtook the destroyer, he had to make his lonely way through fog and clouds until the wind rose, improving visibility.

Blériot then gauged his course from boat traffic along the Channel, and he kept moving northward at approximately a ninety-degree angle from the boats below until he spotted the rugged cliffs of Dover. Once within range, he followed the coastline until he saw a prearranged sign, a friend waving a huge Tricolor at the landing place—a low point in the cliffs near Dover Castle. Blériot landed amid gusty winds, and although portions of his plane were damaged, he was unhurt. Excited members of the press soon radioed the news back to France that Blériot had landed and was safe. He had successfully flown the Channel in thirty-six minutes and thirty seconds.

Blériot's success had real financial benefits: not only did he win a handsome monetary prize, but orders now poured in for copies of the aircraft he had flown across the Channel. It also served as a wake-up call to the English, who no longer could be assured of protection from invasion solely by their fleet. By the same token, Blériot's flight proved the airplane's military significance.

In October of that same year, at Châlons, Raymonde de Laroche piloted her small airplane into the air for some three hundred meters, thus becoming the first woman to fly a heavier-than-air machine alone. A tall, elegant brunette who was the daughter of a Parisian plumber, Laroche had already made her mark as a model, actor, and race car driver. By the time she was twenty, she changed her name from Elise Deroche to Raymonde de Laroche, and she soon earned the informal title of Baroness, in tribute to her commanding presence, fashionable clothes, and easy entry to the worlds of fashion and the arts. Along the way she had an illegitimate son, André, reputedly fathered by another early star of French aviation, Léon Delagrange.

Speed and danger attracted her, and she quickly graduated from bicycles to motorcycles and then to automobiles before switching to airplanes. Early in 1910, she suffered severe injuries when she crashed her plane, but soon she was back in the cockpit. The Baroness de Laroche was determined to be the first woman to receive her pilot's license—which she did in March 1910. The risks never bothered her. "In any case," she said with a shrug, "what is to happen will happen."[45]

⌢

That same year, another daring woman—albeit with an entirely different purpose and personality—received recognition. Joan of Arc, who had fearlessly led French troops against English invaders five centuries earlier, was beatified in Notre-Dame de Paris, leading to her eventual canonization as a saint in 1920.

Joan of Arc has always been held in especial reverence by the Catholic Right, and by the nation as a whole during times of great duress. Throughout the Great War, French troops would carry her image into battle with them, and during World War II, General de Gaulle was reputed to have identified himself with the Maid of Orléans ("I am Joan of Arc," he is supposed to have told President Roosevelt, although the story may well be apocryphal).[46]

Now, as Franco-German relations were deteriorating and armaments were piling up in the nations of the Triple Alliance (Germany, Austria-Hungary, and Italy), some among the French were developing a fervent nationalism that bordered on the religious. It was around this time that a professor at the Ecole Militaire declared that the nation should place its faith in the French 75 mm gun, which was—as he put it—"the Father, the Son, and the Holy Ghost."[47]

It was during the summer of 1909 that Georges Clemenceau was ousted from office, following a difficult winter and spring when tensions between European nations overshadowed domestic affairs. He had spent much of his three years as prime minister in an attempt to cobble together a coalition of the moderate Left while fending off attacks both from the Right and from the socialists, especially from socialist leader Jean Jaurès, who regularly accused Clemenceau of having become reactionary—fighting words for someone of Clemenceau's left-wing history. By 1908, Clemenceau had managed to attain the nationalization of a major railway, and the Chamber had passed a hard-fought income tax reform, making it possible to tax the interest payment on the French government debt. (A law making a weekly rest day compulsory had already been passed in 1906.)

Yet despite his long record of championing reforms, which reached back to the 1870s, Clemenceau in office had committed himself to suppressing disorder, and now he was better known for repression than for reform. Violent strikes in 1906 and 1908 had brought him into direct conflict with the trade union movement, but it was foreign rather than domestic affairs that provided the main elements of tension in Clemenceau's ministry during 1908 and 1909, especially after Austria annexed Bosnia in the autumn of 1908. Russia's acceptance of the annexation during early 1909 helped defuse the situation, although Bosnia continued to contribute to deteriorating relations between Russia and the Triple Alliance right up to the outbreak of war in 1914.

By midsummer of 1909, Clemenceau's government seemed out of danger. It was an unexpected turn of events, then, when Clemenceau brought about his own downfall through some imprudent (although probably accurate) language involving a report on the inadequate state of France's navy. Clemenceau was a master tactician, but he could erupt in anger, especially when prompted by personal grudges. This was a prime example, and although he was effective in his attack, suddenly all the pent-up opposition of three years rose up in a groundswell of opposition to him and his government. Quite suddenly the "dictator," the "red beast," and "the emperor of the informers" was gone.[48]

⁓

By comparison with the tumultuous world of politics and national affairs, the world of Abbé Mugnier was satisfyingly tranquil. Or at least it would have been, had the gentle and forgiving Abbé not entangled himself in a terrible mess.

The problem was the Abbé's willingness to forgive. This, according to Church doctrine, was quite appropriate for a priest. However, there were certain things that, according to the Church, were not forgivable; one of these was the denial of papal infallibility, and another was the marriage of priests. Abbé Mugnier, despite his conservative position on many issues, was surprising tolerant on others, including the decidedly toxic Père Hyacinthe Loyson. Loyson was an eloquent preacher, but along the way had evolved a sort of deistic religion of his own, including the denial of papal infallibility. "The Pope is not the master of the Church and of souls," he had written, "but their servant."[49] This promptly led to his excommunication. Worsening the situation, Loyson married an American heiress and moved back to Paris, where he established his own church, L'Eglise Gallicane.

Mugnier longed to return Loyson to the fold—much as he had so successfully done with the notorious novelist Joris-Karl Huysmans. In addition, Mugnier may have harbored a secret admiration for Loyson's independence and for the courage with which he had defied the laws of the Church and the disapproval of the world. In 1907, Mugnier even invited Loyson and his wife to luncheon; Loyson's wife wisely stayed away, but Mugnier continued the friendship, exchanging visits and letters. In one, of June 1909, Mugnier went so far as to state: "I have admired and revered you for a long time."[50] He was frank that he could not follow Loyson in the ecclesiastical paths that he advocated, but he expressed the desire to maintain his friendship with him.

Before long, the Abbé agreed to come to the defense of another married and defrocked priest, Charles Perraud, who had died several years earlier. News of this was published in the Catholic journal L'Univers Religieux, edited by Louis Veuillot—a bad-tempered monarchist and defender of the pope's temporal authority, who delighted in violent polemics. Mugnier was no match for him. Mugnier wrote explanatory letters; he wrote apologetic letters; he visited *L'Univers Religieux*; he was called on the carpet by the archbishop. "Mon Dieu," he confided to his journal, "how bored I would be were I the Archbishop of Paris!"[51]

In October, Mugnier received the archbishop's decision. He was to take a leave of absence, following which he would depart from his beloved church, Sainte-Clotilde, and receive another appointment. "Perhaps," Mugnier mused sadly, "it is time for me to retire."[52]

Having been told to resign as vicar of Sainte-Clotilde, he left his nearby apartment, stored his furniture, and departed for Greece. He had longed to see it since his youth, but as he prepared to leave—just before the November 2 *fête des morts* (a day of remembrance for the dead)—he wrote bitterly: "Tomorrow is the Day of the Dead. I am one of them."[53]

～

Since the summer of 1909, Rodin's idyllic Hôtel Biron had been up for sale, with the sale date set for late December. The Hôtel's overgrown but glorious grounds were to be divided into forty-five lots, with a price tag of more than five million francs.

It was more than Rodin could bear. After contemplating his alternatives, he contacted a deputy in the National Assembly to propose that he give all of his sculptures and drawings, as well as his by now extensive and valuable collection of antiquities, to the state. In return for this bequest, the state would keep the Hôtel as a Rodin museum and allow him to reside there for the rest of his life.

One senator did intervene to postpone the sale, but no one jumped to accept Rodin's offer. Unfortunately, Rodin's stay in this paradise looked like it was coming to a close.

People in boats during the flood of Paris, 1910. Repro Photo: Hervé Lewandowski. Musée d'Orsay, Paris, France. © RMN-Grand Palais / Art Resource, NY.

~

CHAPTER TWELVE

Deep Waters

(1910)

The Seine always rose in January. Parisians were used to it, and so the city's residents were not alarmed when, by the third week of the new year, the river had climbed to well above its usual level.

Devastating floods had once regularly inundated Paris; the worst, in 1658, swelled the river to twenty feet above normal. Yet in 1910, Parisians were not worried. After all, quay walls along the river's edge had long since been enlarged and raised, while the Seine's tributaries—the Oise, the Yonne, and the Marne—had been channeled and dammed. New bridges across these arteries boasted larger arch openings, and Baron Haussmann's modernization of the city's water and sewage system provided assurance of further protection. If the Seine rose too high, the sewers would simply carry the excess away. Flooding would of course continue to occur, but not to catastrophic levels. Or so Parisians believed.[1]

Thus when the water began to rise from its usual level (more than thirty feet below the street-level quays), few paid much attention. Temperatures were unusually warm for winter, and prospects for the New Year appeared bright. Yet northern France had already been drenched by an unusually wet summer and weeks of heavy winter rain, leaving the soil saturated. The warm weather melted snow, and by the second week of January, the Seine and its tributaries upriver were beginning to overflow, creating havoc along their paths.

Still, Parisians were not concerned. Their informal water level gauges, the statues on the Pont de l'Alma, still stood well above the river. These were twenty-foot sculptures of four soldiers erected on stone foundations attached to the bridge, one of which—the most beloved—was a Zouave, a colonial soldier in full dress and cape.[2] By January 21, the water had reached his ankles—meaning that it was about six feet above its normal level. Nevertheless, the quay walls reached well above the Zouave's head, and so few were worried.

But by now the water was moving swiftly, carrying a large amount of debris—everything from tree trunks to barrels and furniture—which crashed into bridge supports all along the Seine's course through Paris. City engineers were beginning to sandbag the most vulnerable neighborhoods. And more ominous yet, water had entered the unfinished construction of the Nord-Sud Métro Line (Line 12), whose tunnel crossed beneath the Seine at the point between the National Assembly and the Place de la Concorde.

By January 21, even the most complacent Parisians were starting to realize that things were beginning to go badly wrong. First, the clocks stopped, as water submerged the plant that pumped the compressed air that ran elevators, factory motors, the postal service's message delivery system, and many of the city's clocks. The Seine had risen four feet in a single day, to ten feet above its normal level, reaching the Zouave's knees. "Who would have ever imagined that Paris could be inundated," Ravel's aunt wrote in alarm from Geneva, "and that the Seine could overflow its elevated banks?"[3]

Yet overflow was only the beginning. Despite increasingly desperate sandbagging and construction of emergency retaining walls, the water began to invade from beneath, through the unfinished Métro line and the sewers, which began to back up. Runoff from the streets pushed beneath the city, erupting into basements and collapsing streets and sidewalks. Soon electrical power plants short circuited, putting most of the Métro out of service. Instead of affording relief, the city's infrastructure was working against it, providing conduits for the mounting flood, which now infiltrated areas even a good distance from the Seine. Astonishingly, water swamped Gare Saint-Lazare and its surroundings—including Boulevard Haussmann, which turned into a rapid river streaming past and into Marcel Proust's apartment building.[4] And the heavy rains continued.

During the days that followed, as the water dramatically rose, rescuers evacuated stranded Parisians by boat from their houses, while others, including the army, helped construct wooden walkways, or *passerelles*, across deeply flooded streets. Life became increasingly strange and daunting. Gas street lamps—normally lit and extinguished daily by hand—went dark, and much of the city with them. Suddenly Paris was a threatening place, full of darkness and danger.

The fast-moving icy water continued to climb. Food became scarce, and prices rose. Factories stopped, electricity and gas went out, telegraph communication failed, and subscribers to the new telephone service found themselves cut off. Shops closed; people evacuated if they could or stayed huddled up at home if they could not. Train stations became emergency shelters, while charitable organizations frantically did their best to distribute food and clothing to a growing horde of refugees (according to one newspaper account, the Red Cross distributed a hundred thousand loaves of bread a day during the height of the devastation). Garbage-processing plants shut down, making it impossible to burn the tons of waste that Paris produced daily, and rats emerged in droves as garbage was now dumped into the Seine. Older residents recalled the worst days of the siege of Paris, back in 1870–1871, but others thought grimly of Dante's Inferno.

By January 28, when the now putrid and dirty yellow Seine crested, it had reached the Zouave's neck—almost twenty feet above its normal level. Could Paris possibly survive a disaster of this magnitude?

Ill and discouraged, Octave Mirbeau wrote his good friend Claude Monet that he found the mud-filled ruin of Paris a spectacle "of desolation and of terror." The water would recede and rise again several times before its final departure in mid-March, but in mid-February, as water once again began to rise, Mirbeau wrote: "It will never be over. I am beginning to believe it is the end of the world."[5]

In the midst of this ongoing disaster, Ravel—located on relatively high ground near Etoile—managed to complete the piano version of *Daphnis et Chloé*, despite the floods "bringing life to a virtual standstill," as he graphically put it.[6] But Matisse, newly located just outside the city at Issy-les-Moulineaux, was mentally and emotionally immobilized by the onslaught. The six-foot-deep flooding in Issy was bad enough; in addition, the fast-moving flood waters swirled chemicals in a local factory into a flammable mixture, whose explosion rocked neighborhoods as far away as central Paris. This, plus the driving rain and rising water, almost paralyzed Matisse, who would remember this experience with horror.

Nearby, in Billancourt, six-and-a-half feet of water flooded the Renault plant, destroying six hundred chassis and a large amount of machinery, while at the Voisin aircraft plant, flood waters covered the machinery in mud and lifted the flooring, crushing aircraft under construction. In Giverny, to the northwest of Paris, the Seine's floods covered most of Monet's garden and all but the top of the Japanese bridge, leading him to fear that all his plantings would be destroyed. He and Alice endured isolation for days, with much of the lower road into Giverny and the nearby railway impassable. When the water at last receded, Monet acknowledged that despite the loss of many plants, "it will probably be less calamitous than I'd feared. But what a disaster all the same!"[7]

Despite anxiety for his garden, Monet's greatest concern was for Alice, who was seriously ill. By April, her decline occupied all of his thoughts. "A glimmer of hope remains," he told Durand-Ruel, "but it is a hope."[8]

～

Abbé Mugnier, who was abroad at the time, escaped the Seine's flood waters, but in personal terms, he was facing deep waters of his own. He had long wished to see Greece, but his trip was permeated with melancholy; he felt more an exile than a tourist, and upon his return to France after ten months of travel, he had no position to fill or even a place to stay. During his absence his friends, including the Countess Greffulhe, had faithfully attempted to plead on his behalf, but to no avail. The archbishop informed him that there was no question of his staying at Sainte-Clotilde. Instead, after being rebuffed by a series of parish priests who refused to accept such a controversial figure into their midst, the archbishop decided to place him as chaplain for the Sisters of Saint-Joseph de Cluny, located in a working-class neighborhood in the fourteenth arrondissement. The position was admittedly "little engrossing,"[9] as the archbishop put it, but with no other choice, Abbé Mugnier left for his new home, where he would spend the rest of his life.

It was "a solitary and sad quarter," Mugnier noted despairingly in his journal. "I am truly buried there. I will live soberly, solitarily. I am finished!"[10]

～

Was it possible? Could Marie Curie, the grieving widow and self-effacing scientist, be having an affair? Not only was it possible, but it was in fact the case. By midsummer of 1910, Marie Curie and Paul Langevin had become lovers. On July 15 they even rented an apartment together near the Sorbonne, a small place where they could be alone with one another. In their letters to each other they called it *chez nous*, or "our home."

Paul Langevin was a prominent French physicist five years Marie Curie's junior who had been a student and close friend of Marie's beloved husband, Pierre. He also was a badgered husband and devoted father, who had endured physical as well as mental abuse from his wife, her mother, and his wife's sister. His wife, Jeanne, appears to have been mentally unstable, but the root cause of her anger seems to have been Paul's devotion to scientific research and his refusal to sacrifice it in order to take a more lucrative position with private industry.

Marie Curie had suffered yet another loss that February, when Pierre's father died. A beloved and essential member of their small family unit, Dr. Curie had played a large role as grandfather to the two girls following Pierre Curie's death. Now Dr. Curie was gone, and Marie seemed more than ever in danger of following him. But then, quite suddenly, she revived. What, her friends wondered, had happened?

She had known Paul Langevin for years; after all, he had studied under Pierre at the City of Paris's Ecole de Physique et de Chimie Industrielle (Polytechnic School for Physics and Chemistry) and then assumed Pierre's job there when Pierre left for the Sorbonne. Paul also taught with Marie at Sèvres and took her job there after her appointment to Pierre's Sorbonne post. A gentle man, a brilliant researcher, and an outstanding teacher, Paul was a devoted friend of Pierre Curie and shared many qualities and basic beliefs with him. Like Curie, a republican and a critic of tradition, Paul Langevin would devote his life to causes, especially those involving human rights.

The Curies and the Langevins had been close and even vacationed together, but Marie did not realize what was going on in the Langevin household until sometime during the spring of 1910. Then, learning of the violence (Jeanne had broken a bottle over Paul's head), she was all sympathy. Soon sympathy turned to love. "Isn't it natural enough that, many years after Pierre Curie's death, this friendship, reinforced by mutual admiration, be transformed, little by little, into a passion and a liaison?" wrote Langevin's son, years afterward.[11]

Not surprisingly, Jeanne began to be suspicious, and things quickly turned nasty. Jeanne told Paul that she was "going to get rid of this obstacle"— meaning Marie. According to a friend who visited regularly at this time, Jeanne was highly agitated and "shouted threats for everyone to hear, that if Madame Curie didn't leave in eight days she would kill her." Jeanne and her sister also accosted Marie in the street and threatened her, telling her to leave France. Terrified, Marie did not even dare to go home but sought refuge with friends.[12]

Finally, friends arranged a truce: in return for Marie and Paul breaking off their liaison, Jeanne Langevin would stop her threats of physical violence and public scandal. Yet Jeanne's threats continued, while Marie allowed herself to dream of a life together with Paul Langevin—something that seemed less and less likely as the weeks and months passed. Paul responded to Marie's lengthy letter weighing all aspects of a divorce with a harried-sounding protest about the extreme difficulties of his existence, and how shattering a divorce would be for his four young children.

Despite his suffering, Paul Langevin did not have the will to make the break.

～

Langevin's marriage was not the only one in trouble. By now, Debussy's marriage to Emma was showing severe strains, with Emma even writing a lawyer about a possible separation. In his own defense, Debussy explained to his friend and publisher, Jacques Durand, that "those around me resolutely refuse to understand that I've never been able to live in a world of real things and real people. . . . After all, an artist is by definition a man accustomed to dreams and living among apparitions."[13]

Debussy then reverted to a familiar theme: "It's pointless expecting this same man to follow strictly all the observances of daily life, the laws and all the other barriers erected by a cowardly, hypocritical world."[14] When life and his own needs conflicted, Debussy preferred to place the blame on the constrictions and hypocrisies of others.

Yet despite illness and dissatisfaction with his personal life, Debussy's professional life was blooming, demanding his ever-reluctant presence in far-off places. These engagements paid well, and, as always, he needed the money. From Vienna, he wrote Chouchou humorous postcards ("which would make a goldfish weep"),[15] and from Budapest he informed Jacques Durand that he was not cut out for that sort of life. "It needs the heroism of a commercial traveller and a willingness to compromise which I find decidedly repugnant."[16]

～

Igor Stravinsky, on the cusp of fame, was hardly of the same mind. He was only twenty-seven when he first saw Paris—in spring, from the arrival platform of the Gare du Nord. His colorful fellow Russian, Sergei Diaghilev, had personally commissioned the ballet *The Firebird* from him for the 1910 Ballets Russes season, and Stravinsky made the long trip westward with every confidence of success.

Life had not always been so filled with promise. The third of four sons born to a respectable St. Petersburg family with connections to minor nobility, Stravinsky later described his childhood as unbearable. His father seems to have been bad tempered, and his parents clearly preferred their taller and more handsome eldest son. Yet young Igor's life was not one of deprivation or hardship; he was not even denied music. His father, a well-known opera singer, acquainted him with the world of music, and his parents gave him piano lessons. Still, Stravinsky felt unappreciated and misunderstood—by his parents and by virtually everyone else in St. Petersburg, with the exception of the great composer Rimsky-Korsakov, who privately tutored him, and a quiet and perceptive first cousin, Katya, whom Stravinsky eventually married. Recognition would first come in Paris, where Diaghilev had decided to take a chance on the young unknown.

Filled with dreams of glory, Stravinsky immediately joined in rehearsals, which already were under way at the Paris Opera. There, he discovered that the casting was not what he had expected (Tamara Karsavina rather than Anna Pavlova would dance the part of the Firebird), and the entire production, including the musicians and the choreography, was to his mind dismayingly crude. "The choreography of this ballet always seemed to me to be complicated and overburdened with plastic detail," he later wrote, "so that the artists felt . . . great difficulty in coordinating their steps and gestures with the music."[17]

Especially disconcerting was the conductor's curt dismissal of Stravinsky as an inexperienced youth. In his autobiography, Stravinsky would warmly compliment Gabriel Pierné for "the mastery with which [he] conducted my work,"[18] but at the time Stravinsky was displeased that his directives for the score were not regarded as sacred. In fact, to his surprise and dismay, Pierné on one occasion flatly disagreed with him in front of the entire orchestra. Stravinsky had written *non crescendo* in several places, regarding this as a "sensible precaution," but Pierné irritably told him, "Young man, if you do not want a *crescendo*, do not write anything."[19]

Happily, opening night made up for any indignities that Stravinsky had suffered along the way. It was a glittering affair, with everyone who was anyone in attendance: Misia Sert, the Princesse de Polignac, and the Countess Greffulhe—Diaghilev's primary financial backers—as well as Count Kessler, who seemed to show up whenever anything of note was going on. Kessler reported that the painter Pierre Bonnard commented afterward, "After having been to see the Russians (Russian Ballet), you see harmonies everywhere."[20] Sets and costumes were sufficiently sumptuous to set off a new craze for Orientalism in fashion (where Paul Poiret astutely led the way). More important, Diaghilev had the satisfaction of having brought his Ballets Russes into the world of the avant-garde, both in music and in dance.

Without question, this was a triumph for Stravinsky, who suddenly was a celebrity. Diaghilev had already announced to the company, "Take a good look at him—he's about to be famous,"[21] and his prediction (admittedly helped by the buzz that he carefully crafted around his young discovery) proved correct. "I sat in Diaghilev's loge," Stravinsky later recalled of this dazzling opening night, "where, at intermissions, a path of celebrities, artists, dowagers, . . . writers, balletomanes, appeared. I met for the first time Proust, [Jean] Giraudoux, Paul Morand, St John Perse, [Paul] Claudel. . . . I was also introduced to Sarah Bernhardt, who sat in a wheelchair in her private box, thickly veiled."[22]

The audience received *The Firebird's* score enthusiastically, and composers such as Ravel and Debussy quickly made their way backstage to meet the young celebrity. Ravel (according to Stravinsky) "liked *Firebird*" and noted that "the Parisian audience wanted a taste [but only a taste!] of the avant-garde, and . . . *Firebird* satisfied this perfectly." Stravinsky agreed (he later wrote that *The Firebird* "belongs to the style of its time" and that it "is also not very original"), and he and Ravel soon became good friends.[23]

Debussy, too, "spoke kindly about the music" when he joined Stravinsky backstage, and soon after, he wrote Jacques Durand that *The Firebird* was "not perfect, but, in certain respects, it's an excellent piece of work none the less because the music is not the docile slave of the dance. . . . And every now and then there are some extremely unusual combinations of rhythms!" Late in 1911 Debussy would write Robert Godet about "a young Russian composer: Igor Stravinsky, who has an instinctive genius for colour and rhythm."[24]

Although Stravinsky's friendship with Ravel would remain relatively free of rivalry, his relationship with Debussy proved pricklier. Later, when asked by Stravinsky for his real feelings about *The Firebird*, Debussy replied, "Oh well, you had to start somewhere."[25] Stravinsky returned the favor: "I thought *Pelléas* a great bore on the whole," he wrote, "in spite of many wonderful pages."[26]

⌒

In October, Sarah Bernhardt—now sixty-six and a great-grandmother—left for yet another "farewell tour" of the United States, bringing her handsome twenty-seven-year-old lover with her. Everyone was shocked, but for three years, both on tour and in Paris, Lou Tellegen would perform the principal men's parts in all of Bernhardt's productions.

When Sarah returned, her youngest granddaughter, fifteen-year-old Lysiane, moved in with her after her own mother's death. Lysiane adored Sarah, who for years had entertained both of her granddaughters at weekly luncheons, after which they were allowed to roam in the "precious glory-hole" of her studio and romp with Sarah's menagerie of dogs and parrots (by this time Sarah had given up her pumas, which she decided were too dangerous, and the monkeys, which she thought were too exhibitionist).[27] As the grandchildren grew older, they and their friends were invited to matinees at the Théâtre Sarah Bernhardt, followed by over-the-top teas in Sarah's backstage apartment, where the youngsters gleefully ate themselves sick on sandwiches, mocha cakes, babas, and brioches.

While the youngsters gorged on cakes, businessmen throughout Paris were finding new and better ways for making money. François Coty, who regarded Paris as a mere stepping-stone to the rest of the world, opened his first foreign store that year in Moscow, following Louis Cartier and other prestigious retailers in the hunt for the profits to be had from the Russian upper classes and the imperial court. That same year, "Boy" Capel financed Coco Chanel's first independent millinery shop, Chanel Modes, on fashionable Rue Cambon, while filmmaker Georges Méliès—who between 1895 and 1910 had produced around 685 reels of film, at far longer lengths and complexity than those of his competitors[28]—agreed to give Charles Pathé and Pathé Frères control over the editing and distribution of his films, in return for what looked like a lucrative financial deal.

Meanwhile, Ravel took a tough negotiating stance with Diaghilev over anticipated royalties from his upcoming *Daphnis et Chloé* (Ravel argued that under no circumstance would he accept less than 50 percent). While negotiating, Ravel continued to work on orchestrating the ballet: "Which other instrument, played in the orchestra by an E clarinet, might a shepherd be holding?" he asked a friend. While thus preoccupied, he consoled himself by playing Debussy's *Preludes*. "They are wonderful masterpieces," he enthused. "Do you know them?"[29]

That year, Marcel Proust lined his bedroom with cork as he continued to write his masterpiece,[30] and Thomas Fortune Ryan, a self-made American millionaire, purchased two works from Rodin, which he gave to the Metropolitan Museum of Art in New York as a first step toward establishing a Rodin gallery there. Characteristically, Rodin's by-now entrenched companion, Claire de Choiseul, was quick to take all the credit for this development, but with Ryan's money, Choiseul's push, and the less vaunted but essential efforts of others, the Metropolitan Museum's Rodin Gallery would open in 1912 with forty sculptures plus numerous drawings and watercolors.

By 1910 it was clear that Gertrude Stein's first book, *Three Lives*, was not going to be a financial success: of the one thousand copies (five hundred of them bound) that the Grafton Press had printed at her expense, few sold. Still, *Three Lives* garnered a satisfying array of compliments from friends, including her former professor, William James, who called it "a fine new kind of realism." She now sent it to a list of celebrities she thought might help promote it (most of whom, including George Bernard Shaw, John Galsworthy, and Booker T. Washington, never replied). Yet her audience had always been the avant-garde, and *Three Lives* brought her a welcome degree of notoriety among this milieu. Although she had vividly built the portraits of her characters through a rich and innovative layering of dialogue, her style was not for the faint of heart, as her publisher was painfully aware. When learning that Gertrude Stein was embarked on yet another novel, *The Making of Americans*, he is said to have groaned, "Tell her I'm dead!"[31]

While Gertrude Stein continued to write her way into a new style and voice, Isadora Duncan retired temporarily from dancing to give birth to a son, after spending the winter sailing up the Nile with Singer. "For those who can afford it," she later wrote, "a trip up the Nile in a well-appointed *dahabeah* is the best rest cure in the world."[32] Fortunately, this birth was far easier than her first, and once again she found herself "lying by the sea with a baby in my arms."[33] Without hesitation, she refused Singer's offer of marriage, and only her name, not Singer's, appeared on the birth certificate. "I was against marriage," she later wrote, "with every intelligent force of my being. I believed it then, and still believe it to be an absurd and enslaving institution."[34]

～

By summer of 1910, Cubism was emerging full-blown from Braque's and Picasso's canvases, and other artists—including Fernand Léger, André Derain, André Lhote, Francis Picabia, Marie Laurencin, Alexander Archipenko, and the three Duchamp brothers (Marcel, Raymond Duchamp-Villon, and Gaston, known as Jacques Villon)—had begun to embrace it. Picasso was tutoring his shy Bateau-Lavoir neighbor, Juan Gris, in the form, and Gris would soon become (after Braque and Picasso) a major figure, if not a pioneer, in the Cubist movement. As Janet Flanner noted, Cubism was becoming so pervasive among the avant-garde that "subject matter was fully recognizable almost for the last time."[35]

Yet Matisse continued on his own road,[36] completing his huge panels, *Dance* (*La Danse*) and *Music* (*La Musique*), in time for the 1910 Salon d'Automne, after months of intensive work and rework. He may not have expected unmitigated praise, but the reception these extraordinary panels received was unexpectedly brutal, spanning the breadth of tastes and generations from the young avant-garde to deeply entrenched conservatives. This major slap in the face came only months after Matisse's one-man exhibition at Bernheim-Jeune aroused similar vituperation. And so it came as a particular shock when Sergei Shchukin, who had commissioned *Dance* and *Music* for the stairwell of his palatial Moscow residence, unexpectedly refused both on grounds of propriety—Shchukin was squeamish about hanging these large panels of nudes on the staircase of his home. In time, Shchukin would retreat from his prudishness, but for the moment Matisse was so shattered by this as well as by the hostility he was encountering in Paris that he left for Spain, only returning to France in early 1911.

For his part, Picasso was making a bumpy transition from bohemianism and poverty to comfort and its attendant problems. He would never again need to worry about money, but he would find that a starring role in Paris's avant-garde brought more than its share of tedium and irritation. Social conventions annoyed him, yet he was stuck in an endless round of dinners, at-homes, and other occasions that combined marketing and schmoozing, which he hated. Even the old gang was splintering, as its members became increasingly well known and prosperous. Fernande noted the underlying tensions of envy and resentment that were creating fissures "between these artists who had once been so united, which they now tried in vain to disguise."[37] She, too, was increasingly unhappy, as Picasso's boredom and indifference to her grew.

〜

In April, nineteen-year-old Private Charles de Gaulle was promoted to corporal in the 33rd Infantry Regiment. A new law—the expression of post-Dreyfus efforts to assert political control over the army—required him to serve for a year in the ranks before entering the officer corps via the military academy of Saint-Cyr. De Gaulle had passed his entrance exam to Saint-Cyr the previous autumn, and so in compliance with the law, he promptly headed for the regiment's barracks in Arras.

He did not like the experience but made the most of it, including any opportunities for impressing his superior officers. He and his comrades were marched with "very like the full load" through the rain and mud of the January floods, but rather than complain, de Gaulle wrote his father that it was "good training for the trial-marches."[38] By April 1910, he had been promoted to corporal, and he seems to have pressed for immediate further promotion. To this, his superior officer replied, "Why do you think I should make a sergeant of a young fellow who would not feel he had had his due unless he were made Constable?"[39]

De Gaulle continued on this path after entering Saint-Cyr in October. Easily noticed for his height (six foot five inches), which earned him the mocking nickname of the "Great Asparagus," he quickly established himself as an earnest student and a "grind." He just as quickly earned a reputation for arguing with and even besting his instructors—an irritating trait that landed him in the school's magazine with a cartoon captioned, "The Saint-Syrien de Gaulle undergoing an oral in history: the examiner is in a tight corner."[40]

Raised with a rigorous devotion to Church and country, de Gaulle later wrote that he had never doubted that "France would have to go through enormous trials, [and] that the whole point of life consisted of one day rendering her some conspicuous service."[41] Despite footsore marches through the mud and the heckling of his schoolmates, he seems never to have forgotten this goal—nor his conviction that someday he would have the opportunity to render this service.

∽

By 1910, the disrepute into which nationalism and patriotism—and indeed the military itself—had fallen following the Dreyfus Affair was beginning to fade, and a groundswell of patriotism (known as the réveil national, or national wake-up) was gathering strength. A series of crises, especially in Morocco, stoked hostility to Germany, especially among the ardent supporters of Léon Daudet's Ligue d'Action Française, who remained a small but vociferous and potentially influential minority.

It was against this background of heightened Franco-German tensions that Debussy decided not to attend a festival of French music in Munich that September. He made this decision based on the conviction "that nothing will be achieved by performances of our works in Germany. It will be suggested, of course," he continued, "that a closer understanding will result from these performances. The answer to this is that music is not written for such purposes. And the time is badly chosen."[42]

Fauré also declined to attend the Munich festival. But two composers, Camille Saint-Saëns and Richard Strauss, attempted to bridge the growing Franco-German divide by giving an informal concert of light-hearted waltzes there, including waltzes that Strauss had only recently completed for his upcoming opera The Rosenkavalier.[43]

∽

Late in the year, Abbé Mugnier noted that the flooding was beginning again and that the Seine was rising rapidly—a spectacle he had not witnessed the previous winter, having been away from Paris. This time, as the rain beat down and the wind blew, he agreed to meet with Countess Anna de Noailles, who wished to make his acquaintance.

Not many months before, Charles Demange—a young nephew of Maurice Barrès who had fallen desperately in love with the countess—killed himself when she did not return his love. The countess had already conducted a long and fervent but unconsummated relationship with Barrès, which ended several years earlier ("they did in their heads what others do with their bodies," the Abbé wryly observed).[44] Following Demange's suicide, his friends launched a campaign against the countess, insinuating that she had broken the nephew's heart in vengeance for the uncle's betrayal. It was a sticky situation, and one that the Abbé might be forgiven for wishing to avoid. Now, as the rain poured and the wind blew, Mugnier considered what he would say to the countess about Demange.

Undogmatic when it came to theology, and with the soul of a poet, the Abbé was a little leery of Anna de Noailles, who to his way of thinking had gone Saint Francis of Assisi one better by saying to the melon, "You are my brother," and to the raspberry, "You are my sister!"[45] In time, the Abbé would successfully mediate between the warring parties in the Demange affair, but on this first meeting with Anna de Noailles, little seems to have been said about Demange. Instead, she regaled the Abbé with her views on everything, especially herself and her genius, and fairly drowned him in words.

In person, Mugnier (like so many others) found Anna de Noailles overwhelming. Yet he greatly admired her poetry, which he described as lyrical, melancholy, pagan, and thoroughly Parisian. "No one," he acknowledged in his journal, "has given me, as she has, the perception of the infinite."[46]

La Ruche, Paris. © J. McAuliffe

∼

CHAPTER THIRTEEN

Between Heaven and Hell

(1911)

Early in the year, Proust wrote Lucien Daudet that he was living "suspended between caffeine, aspirin, asthma, angina pectoris, and in . . . six days out of seven," between "life and death." He continued to work on his book, but "God knows if I shall ever finish it."[1]

In July, Alfred Edwards's latest wife, twenty-four-year-old Geneviève Lantelme, drowned in the Rhine—after having fallen from Misia's beloved yacht, the *Aimée*. Lantelme's death was ruled accidental, but the yellow press screamed that Edwards had murdered her to buy his freedom. Edwards sued, and the trial went on for months before he was awarded damages of one franc.

Debussy, in the meantime, had spent months composing music for Gabriele d'Annunzio's verse-play, *The Martyrdom of Saint Sebastian*. After working almost unceasingly on it from January until its premiere at the Théâtre du Châtelet in May, Debussy was exhausted. According to stories, Léon Bakst, who designed the sets, argued long and hard with him over the appearance of Paradise in Act 5. "You've been to Paradise then, have you?" Bakst demanded. To which Debussy replied, "Yes, but I never discuss it with strangers."[2]

∼

Early in 1910, when the cross of chevalier in the Legion of Honor was offered to Marie Curie, she followed Pierre's example and refused it. Then late in the year, she unexpectedly decided to place her name in nomination for membership in the French Academy of Sciences, where a member had recently died, leaving his position open. It was a momentous decision, since the Academy of Sciences exercised enormous power, and French scientists avidly sought membership.

Having already won a Nobel Prize and recently published a massive nine-hundred-page *Treatise on Radioactivity*, Marie Curie was not only a logical choice but, in the minds of some, a necessary one. As the Academy's permanent secretary, Gaston Darboux, put it: "Where would the Academy find a scientist with greater authority than Madame Curie to give it an opinion on these works about radioactivity, whose number is growing so rapidly?"[3]

Her only serious challenger was Edouard Branly, the physicist who invented the radio receiver that made Marconi's transmission of wireless signals possible. As a teacher at the Catholic Institute of Paris, Branly had widespread support from clerics and nationalists, who were upset that Marconi had won the Nobel Prize in 1909 without any mention whatever of Branly. One of Marie Curie's supporters told her that "the struggle between you and M. Branly will arise most strongly on the clerical issue" and added that "his work has little in it to compare to your qualifications."[4]

Marie Curie's supporters either overlooked or chose to play down the factor that turned her candidacy into a front-page circus: if elected, she would be the first woman to become a member in the long history of the Institut de France.[5] Instead of a tussle between Catholics and secularists, the struggle became primarily one over the admission of a woman to the Academy. "Women cannot be part of the Institute of France," one member pronounced indignantly,[6] and the press trumpeted the dangers of admitting a woman, underscoring Madame Curie's threat to the Belle Epoque feminine ideal. Intensifying her opponents' ire, Marie Curie had not renounced husband and children for her career but had, in the face of daunting obstacles, managed to do it all.

In the end, she lost to Branly—by one vote. Of course the Academy had rejected Pierre in his first attempt at membership, and once a member, he never particularly enjoyed the experience. But still, rejection was rejection—especially under such circumstances and for such reasons. The only thing that could have been worse was what did in fact follow, when Paul Langevin's wife, Jeanne, took steps to exact her own personal revenge.

It was not long after the Academy affair that someone (evidently hired by Jeanne Langevin) broke into the small apartment that Marie and Paul had shared and stole letters that they unfortunately had saved. Soon after, Madame Langevin's brother-in-law, a newspaper editor, informed Marie Curie that Madame Langevin had the letters and was prepared to expose Marie as Paul Langevin's mistress.

Having a mistress certainly was no crime in Belle Epoque Paris; if anything, it was expected. Yet the typical mistress was anonymous and remained in the background, allowing the wife to take her place publicly by her husband's side. Marie Curie was hardly anonymous, and after the vilification she had received at the time of her Academy nomination, any further scandal promised to be especially nasty.

Months of hell followed for both Paul and Marie, with threats and possibly blackmail from the scheming wife and her brother-in-law until, in November, the scandal hit the front pages. Interviewed, Madame Langevin assumed the role of the injured and grieving wife, swamped in tears, with small children at her knee. Her tale of woe was ugly, malicious, and shot through with lies. Still, there was enough substance to the liaison itself to give credit to the whole web of falsehood and to Jeanne Langevin's pose as everything a Frenchwoman and wife should be. With release of the letters, the press swung into attack mode, vilifying the foreigner Marie Curie, who was destroying a French home. It was, as one tabloid editor put it, the Dreyfus Affair all over again, showing "France in the grip of the bunch of dirty foreigners, who pillage it, soil it and dishonor it."[7]

In the midst of this, the Swedish Academy awarded Marie Curie an unprecedented second Nobel Prize, this time in chemistry. The French press, caught up in denigrating the recipient, barely acknowledged the news. Then, as a final insult, the Swedish Academy informed her that had it been forewarned of the scandal, it probably would not have awarded her the prize. Further, the Academy suggested that she put off accepting her prize until she demonstrated that the accusations against her were baseless.

Marie Curie was down but not out. "I believe that there is no connection between my scientific work and the facts of private life," she wrote the Swedish Academy, adding that she planned on being in Stockholm for the ceremonies. Despite fatigue and illness, she indeed did attend, accompanied by her sister Bronya and her daughter Irène. There were no awkward moments, and Madame Curie carried off her part of the occasion with great dignity, for the first time underscoring the role that she had played in discovering and isolating radium, and proving her hypothesis that "radioactivity is an atomic property of matter and can provide a method for finding new elements." In effect she was saying that, contrary to the beliefs and assertions of others, she had not ridden to glory on the coattails of her husband or male colleagues.[8]

Upon her return, she was rushed to the hospital. For two years, she would be incapacitated, and throughout the rest of her life she would suffer from ill health. In the meantime, Paul and Jeanne Langevin came to an out-of-court settlement that awarded Jeanne a substantial cash settlement and custody over the children until the sons reached the age of fifteen.[9]

Three years later, Paul and Jeanne Langevin were back together. With his wife's acquiescence, Langevin had found another mistress—this one, a secretary.

∽

In July, war once again seemed imminent.

The 1911 Moroccan crisis began when France entered Fez, in violation of the 1906 Algeciras agreement, leading the German gunboat *Panther* to enter Agadir to protect German interests. Britain's late entry into the confrontation threatened to blow the incident into war, but calmer heads finally prevailed, and by October, France and Germany had come to an agreement by which Germany ceded control to France in Morocco in return for part of the French Congo.

Prompted by France's gains in Morocco, Italy hastily annexed Tripoli, leading to war with Turkey, which refused to recognize Italy's acquisition. Despite ongoing efforts to mediate, the war continued for a year, during which Russia invaded northern Persia, Germany bulked up its navy, and Bulgaria and Serbia took advantage of Turkey's preoccupation with Italy to join the attack on the Turks over the question of autonomy for Macedonia. Montenegro soon joined what became known as the first Balkan War.

It was during this highly volatile situation that Italy became the first nation to use airplanes for military purposes. France's military was carefully watching. The previous year it had purchased thirty planes and ordered sixty more, and in November, the French held their first military air show, in which a monoplane achieved an average speed of seventy miles per hour. Along with the impressive performance that year by French aviators in French air games, this served as a wake-up call to the German General Staff, which previously had focused almost entirely on airships. Although (in contrast to the French) the German War Ministry issued few contracts for aircraft until 1913, Germany definitely was in the race.

It was about this time that Count Kessler noted a remark made at lunch by the Belgian poet Emile Verhaeren, a deeply committed pacifist, who talked with concern about the mounting chauvinism in France. "It's the airplane that has made it explode," he told Kessler and the others.[10]

∿

During the Dreyfus Affair of the 1890s, French nationalism had clearly belonged to the political Right, which combined a drum-beating patriotism with diatribes against Jews, foreigners, socialists (deemed "dangerous ideologues," "pacifists," and "internationalists"), and those opposed to French imperial expansion. But ever since the first Moroccan crisis (1905), nationalism in France had expanded its base to include a strong anti-German strain.

In 1911, as yet another Moroccan crisis raised the international temperature, anti-German sentiment in France swelled—aided by memories of France's ignominious defeat to Germany in the Franco-Prussian War, only four decades before. By now, French republicans and anticlericals had joined with monarchists and right-wing Catholics in the rising nationalist fervor. They did not like one another, but their tolerance for each other was growing. Nationalism and patriotism, disseminated by sources such as Léon Daudet's well-funded daily, *Action Française*, now were gathering sufficient steam to make an impression on national thought and, most important, on foreign policy.

Beneath the Belle Epoque's brilliance, wealth, and tranquility, there were troubling signs, wrote French historian Jules Bertaut, signs that appeared "most clearly in the disposition of the younger generation. Perhaps the most notable of these [was] the steady resurrection . . . of the patriotic idea."[11] In September, Count Kessler noted in his journal that war within the next decade was a certainty, partly because "the younger generation in France wants a war," and partly because "the French are persuading themselves ever more of their superiority (aviation, 'culture latine')." He also noted the push from England's financial circles, and added, from the German perspective, that "we have had it with being constantly threatened on our western front." All of these factors pointed to war, he concluded, "which will break out as soon as the mass of Frenchmen are convinced of the French advantage, and the Russian government believes it has finally crushed the revolution."[12]

It was in this atmosphere that Charles de Gaulle, at the end of his first year at Saint-Cyr, decided to choose a career in the infantry rather than in the more elite cavalry, for which he was eligible. Despite a future of "foot-slogging," he chose the less glamorous option because, as he later put it, "it is more military!"[13]

∿

One day in 1911, Juan Gris was arrested and dragged to the Montmartre police station, having been mistaken for the "redoubtable Garnier" of the dread Bonnet gang. Gris, a large man who was sufficiently formidable-looking for the role, owed his deliverance to André Derain, who lived near the police station and swore to his identity.

Violence continued to permeate life on Montmartre. The Bateau-Lavoir crowd was generally too impoverished to attract cutthroats, but Frédé Gérard was engaged in an ongoing war with the hooligans he repeatedly kicked out of the Lapin Agile—one of whom returned one night to shoot Frédé's son-in-law. Even more shocking, though, was the arrest of Picasso's good friend Apollinaire for the theft of the *Mona Lisa* from the Louvre.

Apollinaire, born Guillaume Albert Wladimir Alexandre Apollinaire de Kostrowitzky, was the illegitimate son of a young Polish beauty and a dashing Italian soldier of sufficient prominence that his identity as Apollinaire's father remained hidden for years. After splitting with her soldier lover, Apollinaire's mother raised her two sons on the Côte d'Azur, where she found protectors among its glittering demimonde. Fleeing bill collectors, the family eventually made its way to Paris, where Apollinaire set to work on his much-desired literary career. It was slow going, but in 1902 he signed his first published story with the name Guillaume Apollinaire.

Soon after, he founded a small (and short-lived) literary review with André Salmon and became friends with Maurice de Vlaminck, André Derain, and Picasso. Surrounded by painters such as these, Apollinaire now emerged as an art critic, poet, editor, and figure to reckon with among the younger members of the avant-garde. He was handsome, witty, widely traveled, and—given his shadowy roots—infused with a certain exotic mystery. Accompanied by his lover, the painter Marie Laurencin, he could be found in the thick of whatever was going on, which generally meant staying close to Picasso.

By 1911 Apollinaire had published a volume of collected stories and was writing a column for a leading literary review, the *Mercure de France*, as well as serving as art critic for another important review, *L'Intransigeant*, where he strongly championed Cubism. Then, in September, disaster struck. The *Mona Lisa* went missing from her sanctuary in the Louvre's Salon Carré, and the police arrested Apollinaire as their prime suspect.

It was an audacious theft—so much so that for a full day no one even realized the *Mona Lisa* was missing. "Oh, the photographers have it," a guard replied when a visiting artist inquired. The artist's persistent inquiries at last led the authorities to put the Louvre into lockdown and send dozens of policemen to scour the premises' forty-nine acres from top to bottom. It was fruitless; all they discovered were the sad remains of the *Mona Lisa*'s frame, stashed in an inner staircase.

The work of a maniac, some thought, or a discontented Louvre employee, angling for a ransom. Yet no leads or ransom notes appeared, and in the days that followed, disconsolate Parisians lined the Salon Carré to stare at the empty space on the wall where the *Mona Lisa* had once hung.

With a dying trail and no leads, an increasingly frantic Sûreté and Prefecture of Police at last lit on a couple of suspects: Guillaume Apollinaire and his good friend, Pablo Picasso. The basis for this extraordinary accusation lay in events dating from 1907, when Picasso was working on *Les Demoiselles d'Avignon*. At that time Apollinaire had a Belgian friend, Géry Pieret, whom he passed off as his secretary, but who seems to have been little more than a self-aggrandizing con man devoted to risk-taking and theft. Picasso and Fernande found Pieret amusing, and it was at a dinner with him and Apollinaire early in 1907 that Picasso seems to have expressed an interest in certain of the Louvre's primitive Iberian sculptures.

Soon after, Pieret headed for the Louvre, after asking Apollinaire's mistress, Marie Laurencin, if there was anything she needed (she assumed that he was going shopping at the department store, the Magasin du Louvre). Although Pieret later claimed that he had never planned in advance to steal the sculptures, he managed to lift exactly the ones that Picasso coveted, and he quickly made a sale. Their influence can readily be seen in the *Demoiselles'* two central figures, who have extraordinary ears, much like those of the sculptures Pieret sold to Picasso.

Picasso and Pieret seemed to regard the matter as a joke, but Apollinaire was alarmed and tried to persuade Picasso to give the statues back, with no luck. Then, after having left Paris for several years, Pieret once again turned up—just as the *Mona Lisa* disappeared. Pieret could not resist confessing his Louvre thefts in a letter to the *Paris Journal*, leading the police to conclude that there was a connection between the two events, and they soon decided that Apollinaire was the leader of an organized gang. Pieret skipped town, and a panicked Apollinaire and Picasso tried to return the sculptures but couldn't figure out how to do it. At length, Apollinaire turned them over to the *Paris Journal*. And then the police arrested Apollinaire.

Picasso, according to Fernande, was "practically out of his mind with terror"[14] when a plainclothes detective appeared on his doorstep to take him before the examining magistrate. It was there that he first saw Apollinaire, who had already spent two days in the notorious La Santé prison, where he had been stripped, searched, put in solitary, and subjected to long interrogations. In the end, Apollinaire implicated Picasso, while Picasso denied having any part in the affair or even knowing Apollinaire. They remained friends afterward, but the affair—and the humiliation as well as the nastiness of the experience—had a lasting impact on Apollinaire, who spent several miserable days and nights in prison before being released for lack of conclusive evidence. Picasso, on the other hand, managed to escape all charges.

〜

Picasso's departure from the Bateau-Lavoir signaled the beginning of the end for that establishment's position as center of the avant-garde universe, and Montmartre with it. It was around this time that a new center began to emerge in Montparnasse, focused around an odd building on Passage Dantzig called La Ruche.

La Ruche dated from 1900, when a successful society sculptor and committed philanthropist by the name of Alfred Boucher bought land at the southern edge of Paris, just inside the Thiers fortifications, where he created an artists' colony. Cleverly recycling the octagonal wine rotunda from the recently closed Paris exposition, he divided it into numerous small trapezoidal studios, each with its own source of natural light, and opened these to a passel of struggling artists. Boucher charged next to nothing for these accommodations (thirty-seven francs per quarter, when he even bothered to request it), which was about what the traffic could bear. Grandly inaugurated as the Villa Médicis, the place quickly became known as La Ruche, or the Beehive.

Buzzing with activity (as well as with the usual array of vermin), La Ruche became home to the most starving of starving artists, many of whom (including Marc Chagall, Ossip Zadkine, Chaim Soutine, Alexander Archipenko, and Jacques Lipchitz) had made their way to Paris from Eastern Europe. Many years later, the painter Pinchus Krémègne recalled that when he first arrived at Paris's Gare de l'Est, he spoke no French and had only three rubles to his name. The only phrase he knew in French was, "Passage Dantzig," which fortunately was enough to get him there.

The building looked fine enough from the outside, with its imposing doorway splendidly flanked by carved female figures, or caryatids, but the interior studios were cramped, squalid, and without heat. Worse yet, Boucher's land was located downwind of a major slaughterhouse and surrounded by a notorious wasteland known as La Zone. Freezing in winter, broiling in summer, it required grit simply to survive there. It was a very cold January when Gabriel Voisin arrived, early in his and La Ruche's career, at a time when he had just about used up his savings in the effort to develop a heavier-than-air aircraft. He froze until February, when he could afford to put in a stove to heat the place, to tide him over "to the first of the better days," which indeed came.[15] As Marc Chagall later recalled of La Ruche, "You either snuffed it or departed famous."[16]

Chagall, who arrived in Paris from Vitebsk in early 1911,[17] would of course become famous, but that was far from evident during the early years. Although he breathed more freely in Paris than in his native Russia, this scion of an impoverished Jewish family was at first desperately homesick. It was only the great distance between Paris and Vitebsk that prevented him from leaving, and—in the end—the exhibitions, the gallery windows, and the museums of Paris that convinced him to stay. He wandered through Rue Laffitte, gazing at the Renoirs, Pissarros, and Monets at Durand-Ruel's, and the Cézannes at Vollard's. At Bernheim's, he found van Goghs, Gauguins, and works by Matisse. Yet it was at the Louvre where he "felt most at home." There, "Rembrandt captivated me and more than once I stopped before Chardin, Fouquet, Gericault."[18]

After a period in the Montparnasse warren of studios shared with Antoine Bourdelle, Chagall made his way to La Ruche, where he holed up in one of the tiny rooms on the second floor. "While in the Russian ateliers," he later wrote, "an offended model sobbed; from the Italians' came the sound of songs and the twanging of a guitar, and from the Jews debates and arguments, I sat alone in my studio before my kerosene lamp." Nearby, amid the breaking dawn, "they are slaughtering cattle, the cows low and I paint them. . . . My lamp burned, and I with it."[19]

～

In time, Chagall met Apollinaire, "that gentle Zeus [who] . . . blazed a trail for all of us." One day while eating lunch together, Chagall asked why Apollinaire didn't introduce him to Picasso.

"Picasso?" Apollinaire responded quickly, smiling as always. "Do you want to commit suicide? That's the way all his friends end."[20]

Yet during the first months after his arrival in Paris, Chagall was thinking not so much of Picasso as of his acquaintances from St. Petersburg, especially Léon Bakst, the much-lauded set and costume designer for Diaghilev's Ballets Russes, who was his former art teacher. Chagall managed to attend that Ballets Russes season, where he saw Nijinsky in Le Spectre de la rose, a new ballet and showpiece for the breathtaking young dancer. Le Spectre was a tremendous success and became a regular on Ballets Russes programs, but Chagall was not impressed. Everything new in it, he objected, was "polished to reach society in a piquant and sophisticated style." As for him, he was the son of workers, "and often, in a drawing room, . . . I feel inclined to dirty the shining floor."[21]

Backstage, he spotted Bakst, who had earlier advised him not to come to Paris, telling him that he would probably die of hunger—hardly a vote of confidence. Yet now, to Chagall's surprise, Bakst offered to come by and see what he was doing. Eventually he came, and his appraisal was a favorable one: "Now," he told Chagall, "your colors sing."[22]

~

Despite the favorable splash made by Nijinsky in *Le Spectre de la rose*, the big news of this Ballets Russes season was Igor Stravinsky's *Petrushka*.

Unlike *Firebird*, the story for *Petrushka* was Stravinsky's, and he had written much of the music even before the story was fully developed. From the outset, Stravinsky had in mind the equivalent of Punch and traditional puppet theater as well as Punch's forerunners in the Commedia dell'Arte. "I had in mind," he later wrote, "a distinct picture of a puppet, suddenly endowed with life, exasperating the patience of the orchestra with diabolical cascades of arpeggios." Soon afterward, during Diaghilev's visit to Stravinsky in Switzerland, he persuaded Stravinsky "to develop the theme of the puppet's sufferings and make it into a whole ballet."[23]

Stravinsky finished the score in Rome, where the company was giving performances during an international exhibition, and it was there that rehearsals for *Petrushka* began. It was not long before the choreographer, Michel Fokine, found himself overwhelmed by the complexity of Stravinsky's rhythms. Fokine later wrote that "it was necessary to explain the musical counts to the dancers. At times it was especially difficult to remember the rapid changes of the counts."[24]

From Rome, the company went to Paris and the Théâtre du Châtelet, where the musicians were so overwhelmed by the score that they burst out laughing when they first saw it. Nothing was right with the sets or the lighting, and chaos threatened to destroy the dress rehearsal. Even on opening night there was a delay in raising the curtain while Misia Edwards raced home for the cash to give Diaghilev to pay the costumier.

Yet the production—starring Nijinsky and Karsavina, and conducted by young Pierre Monteux—was an overwhelming success. This success, according to Stravinsky "was exactly what I needed in that it gave me the absolute conviction of my ear as I was about to begin *The Rite of Spring*."[25]

~   —

Soon after *Petrushka*'s premiere, Stravinsky met Erik Satie at a luncheon at Debussy's, and they became friends. In 1915 Stravinsky would dedicate his "ice-cream wagon Valse" in *Eight Easy Pieces* in homage to Satie, and the following year Satie in turn dedicated his song "Le Chapelier" to Stravinsky. "He was certainly the oddest person I have ever known," Stravinsky later wrote, "but the most rare and consistently witty person, too."[26]

Debussy and Ravel had been friends of Satie's since his Montmartre days, and Satie's bold innovations, especially his harmonic inventiveness, had an impact on both composers, which Ravel in particular was quick to acknowledge. In a score of *Ma Mère l'Oye*, for example, Ravel wrote: "For Erik Satie, grandpapa of 'The Conversations of Beauty and the Beast,' and others. Affectionate homage from a disciple."[27] Debussy expressed his admiration by orchestrating two of Satie's three *Gymnopédies*. And in January 1911, Ravel and other musicians decided to introduce some of Satie's works to the public through their newly formed Société Musicale Indépendante (SMI).

At this concert, Ravel played several of Satie's works and certainly approved (and may well have written) the program note, which saluted Satie as "a forerunner of genius," whose works "anticipated the modernist vocabulary" with "the almost prophetic character of certain harmonic inventions which they contain." M. Maurice Ravel, the program note went on, "bears witness to the esteem which is felt by the most 'advanced' composers for the creator who a quarter of a century ago was already speaking the daring musical 'jargon' of tomorrow."[28]

Suddenly Satie was a celebrity, bathed in laudatory public recognition. Publishers sought out his early works, and he began to acquire a significant following among young musicians. The only downside to this happy state of affairs was Debussy's absence from the January concert and apparent annoyance that Ravel was responsible for presenting the works of Debussy's longtime friend to the public. Still, only a few months after the SMI concert, Debussy included his orchestral versions of Satie's two *Gymnopédies* in a Paris concert that he conducted of his own works (an inclusion that Satie gratefully interpreted as prompted by Ravel's earlier concert).[29] Unfortunately, on this occasion it was Debussy's orchestrations that caught the critics' attention, prompting Satie to comment sadly, "Why won't he allow me just a little corner of his shade? . . . I don't want to take any of his sun."[30]

⌒

Ravel, for his part, continued to be free in his praise of Debussy. In March, he told an interviewer that "there is more musical substance in Debussy's *Après-midi d'un faune* . . . than in the wonderfully immense Ninth Symphony of Beethoven." Contemporary French composers, he added, "work on small canvases but each stroke of the brush is of vital importance."[31]

Ravel also told the interviewer that "I am happy that I am alive today. . . . I love our modern life; the life of the city, of the factories as well as the life among the mountains and at the sea-shore."[32] In direct contrast, Debussy that year was ill, exhausted, and miserable. He was overworked, his wife was interminably sick with liver complaint, and he was overwhelmed with bills. "July bristles with bills, landlords and a whole collection of domestic worries which repeat themselves every year with a distressing regularity," he wrote his publisher. "I always end up 3,000 francs short, and even by selling my soul to the devil I don't know where I shall find them."[33]

In addition, there was the rocky state of Debussy's marriage. After a seaside holiday, he wrote Jacques Durand that "the truth is that at the end of this holiday we have to admit we don't know why we came."[34] Emma's staunch opposition prevented Debussy from traveling to Boston that autumn to see a production of *Pelléas* conducted by his good friend André Caplet, then assistant director of Paris's Colonne Orchestra. Debussy wrote Caplet of the "continual arguments and battles,"[35] and added that "I have not . . . told anybody what it cost me to give up my journey to America."[36] "Sometimes," he confided to Robert Godet in December, "I'm so miserable and lonely . . . though there's no way round it and it's not the first time. Chouchou's smile helps me through some of the darker moments."[37]

By now, Isadora Duncan had begun to explore themes of darkness, hopelessness, and despair. Her audiences, and especially the critics, found her depiction of the Furies in *Orpheus* especially unsettling. Her life had become unsettling as well. She wrapped up her stay at Singer's English country house, where she had been thoroughly bored, by having a brief but intense affair with Debussy's friend André Caplet, whom she had hired to play the piano to accompany her in this remote spot. Early in 1911 she then departed for New York and another tour of American cities with Walter Damrosch and the New York Symphony, which did not go well. She was drinking too much and putting on weight. Anna Pavlova—who had by now quit Diaghilev's company and was touring the United States on her own—easily provided a ravishing contrast. For the first time in memory, Isadora faced half-empty houses.

That November, Isadora danced with some of her better pupils at the Théâtre du Châtelet, where a shoulder strap on her tunic broke in the middle of the performance, exposing her breasts. As a result of this scandal, she was investigated for "public indecency," and police were subsequently posted

in the theater to make sure that she experienced no further wardrobe mal-
functions. She was outraged. "If they annoy me about this," she informed a
journalist, "I will dance in a forest naked, naked, naked . . . with the song of
birds and elemental noises for an orchestra."[38]

Singer, for his part, decided that he had better provide Isadora with a
theater of her own.

~

Paul Poiret was inherently dramatic, and so it was no surprise when the 1910
Ballets Russes production of Rimsky-Korsakov's *Scheherazade* provided the
inspiration for him to launch an array of exotic Oriental fashions, including
his 1911 harem pantaloons and, soon after, his so-called lampshade tunics.
The photographer Edward Steichen was enchanted with these novelties and
published photos of them in the April 1911 issue of *Art et Décoration*, making Poiret and Steichen the originators of what quite possibly was the first
modern fashion shoot.

Poiret from the outset of his career had created his most fantastical costumes for the stage, and the rest of his output had always exuded a theatrical
quality. This, of course, especially appealed to women like Isadora Duncan,
Ida Rubinstein, and the dance hall queen Mistinguett. Still, Poiret never
limited himself when it came to potential customers. It was now that he
decided to expand the merchandise he offered to include furniture, room
decoration, and perfume. He had transformed one particular apartment in
Isadora Duncan's studio into a lushly dangerous retreat, whose windows
were sealed and whose doors "were strange, Etruscan tomb-like apertures."
According to Duncan, "sable black velvet curtains were reflected on the
walls in golden mirrors," and "a black carpet and a divan with cushions of
Oriental textures" added to the heightened sense of drama.[39] Now, much
like Isadora Duncan, the wealthy could nest in dreamy abodes swathed in
lush Paul Poiret decor.

Not surprisingly, Poiret accompanied the launching of each piece of his
growing empire with appropriate splash and glamour, and so in 1911 his new
fragrance company, Parfums de Rosine, received a memorable outing at an
over-the-top costume ball themed as the Thousand and Second Night, for
which Poiret commanded his three hundred guests to dress in Oriental garb.
Those who failed to do so were politely asked to help themselves to appropriate costumes that Poiret had provided or (gasp) leave.

Of course no one could resist the enticements he offered, including a
harem (starring a luxuriating Madame Poiret) enchained in an immense

Sorbet evening ensemble by Paul Poiret, 1912. Silk chiffon and satin, embroidered with glass beads and trimmed with fur. From Mme Poiret's collection. Victoria and Albert Museum, London, Great Britain. Photo Credit: V & A Images, London / Art Resource, NY. © ARS.

golden cage; the unquestionably dramatic actor Edouard de Max perched on a mountain of cushions, where he told stories from the *Thousand and One Nights*; pink ibises that stalked among gushing fountains in the darkened garden; and a hidden orchestra that played softly in the background, while monkeys, parrots, and parakeets chirped and swung. Dancers danced, a monkey merchant provided comic relief, and the bar did enormous business with drinks color-coordinated to match the setting. At the evening's climax, flames unexpectedly rose from the ground and then "spread out like glass flowers." Suddenly "the air resounded with a rending thunder," followed by a "luminous rain," alternately silver and gold, which "left behind phosphorescent insects hanging to the branches and suspended everywhere in mid-air."[40]

"Naturally," Poiret commented long afterward, "there have been people who have said that I have these fêtes as an item of advertisement, but I want to destroy this insinuation." In fact, he added, "I have never believed in the virtue of advertisement."[41] Such protests brought knowing smiles to those who witnessed these grand displays. "He was a patron of the arts, and he dressed an époque," wrote André Salmon, giving Poiret his due. "All the same, he was something of a Barnum."[42]

Matisse finished off the previous year in Spain, having experienced an almost complete physical and emotional breakdown. His father had recently died; Shchukin had rejected the *Dance* and *Music* panels for which Matisse had (in his words) moved heaven and earth for more than two years;[43] and the critics had been brutal, both at the Salon d'Automne and the subsequent London Post-Impressionist show. Shchukin soon changed his mind and sent for Matisse's panels, but Matisse fled south in hope of unwinding his unbearably taut nerves. By the time he reached Seville, he had not slept for more than a week and was in a state of virtual collapse. A friend helped nurse him back to health, and Matisse at last invited the abandoned and furious Amélie—who in turn had fled to her sister and father—to join him in Seville. As it turned out, money for her ticket was scarce, and so Amélie returned on her own to Paris, where the two eventually met and made up.

That spring of 1911, Matisse talked with Count Kessler in Paris about the mockery that greeted the new in art, which Matisse admitted caused him much suffering. "Often," Kessler recorded in his journal, "he wakes up in the middle of the night and tosses about sleepless, thinking of the malicious critique of some unknown journalist."[44] Still, Matisse had embarked on another project, or series of projects, for Shchukin, and soon he and the entire family would leave once again for a summer of work and play in their beloved Collioure.

That autumn, Matisse traveled to Moscow with Shchukin, to inspect the space where Shchukin proposed to hang *La Danse* and *La Musique*. Not only had Shchukin reconciled himself to the audacity of his newly acquired panels, but he wanted to commission eleven additional decorative paintings, all of them large. Shchukin's goal was clear. As he told Matisse, "I want the Russian people to understand that you are a great painter."[45]

⁓

Gertrude Stein completed *The Making of Americans* in the autumn of 1911. Friends already were reading portions of the enormous manuscript and trying to find a publisher, which proved difficult; the manuscript would go unpublished for years.[46] On occasion she uncharacteristically admitted discouragement, but then immediately propped herself up with the comforting knowledge, "I am a rare one. I have very much wisdom."[47]

She was buoyed by the conviction that she was paralleling Picasso in her unconventional approach to literature, without the usual narrative line, much as Picasso and his fellow Cubists were challenging traditional painterly usages of images and space. Afterward, she wrote: "I was alone at this time in understanding [Picasso], perhaps because I was expressing the same thing in literature."[48] More specifically, she explained that in writing *The Making of Americans*, she was trying to "escape from inevitably feeling that anything that everything had meaning as beginning and middle and ending."[49] In the process, she believed she was becoming closer to Picasso than to her own brother.

Certainly, she and Leo were growing farther apart, and the presence of Alice B. Toklas in the household only drove the wedge deeper between them. Alice had moved in with Gertrude in 1910, after Sarah and Michael Stein hurried back to San Francisco to be with Sarah's dying father, bringing Harriet Levy with them. Harriet's departure left Alice with Gertrude in Italy, which suited Gertrude just fine. Did Alice want to stay on alone at the Rue Notre-Dame-des-Champs flat she had shared with Harriet? Of course not. Alice preferred to be with Gertrude. And so, late in the summer of 1910, their life together officially began.

Gertrude and Alice soon departed for Venice, where they had themselves photographed together and sent photos to friends as postcards. Leo was informed of Alice's imminent arrival at Rue de Fleurus. He responded by continuing his fasting and reading, and then left for London. It did not augur well for relations between the previously close brother and sister.

∼

It was during the spring of 1911 that Claude Monet's beloved Alice died. Her death was not unexpected—she had been seriously ill for quite some time—and yet it still came as a shock. "I can't tell you what I've been going through," Monet wrote Paul Durand-Ruel. "My strength and courage are giving out."[50]

Edgar Degas, now an old man and almost blind, stood in the front row at the funeral, to pay his respects. He and Monet had never been close (Degas had always turned up his nose at landscape art); but then again, there were few who had ever been close to the crotchety and difficult Degas. It was a touching tribute, all the same—a clear expression of sympathy from an elderly and frail artist for a companion of long ago.

∼

That October, despite efforts by Rodin's friends to lobby politicians and prepare petitions, the government ordered everyone, including Rodin, to leave the Hôtel Biron. Those in charge had decided that the state would keep the building, and although it was not yet clear for what purpose, it would not (much to Rodin's disappointment) become a Rodin museum. Rodin stayed on in his beloved studio, but his position there, as he acknowledged to a friend, was extremely insecure.

Earlier that year, the Paris Conservatoire moved from its decaying structure on Rue Bergère, in the ninth arrondissement, to Rue de Madrid in the eighth.[51] Everyone agreed that the old Conservatoire was derelict, and yet some, like Camille Saint-Saëns, profoundly missed "that Conservatoire . . . which I cherished so dearly." Saint-Saëns had by now reached his mid-seventies—an age when nostalgia came easily, especially in a world where music was becoming, to his ears at least, rude and cacophonous. "I cherished [the old Conservatoire's] decrepitude," he wrote, "its total absence of modernism, and its air of *olden times*."[52]

About the same time, Jean Cocteau moved with his mother into an apartment on Rue d'Anjou, just off the fashionable Rue du Faubourg St-Honoré. Cocteau had by now begun to work his way into Diaghilev's Ballets Russes, painting the poster of Nijinsky as well as one of Karsavina for the 1911 season and contributing publicity text as well. Soon Diaghilev would commission him to write the libretto for a ballet for the 1912 season, *Le Dieu bleu*.

Cocteau was adept at making contacts, and among his most important during this period was Countess Anna de Noailles, by now the author of several acclaimed books of poetry and the undisputed star of the literary salons.[53] Cocteau had just published his own second book of poetry, Le Prince frivole, and his friend Maurice Rostand (son of the playwright Edmond Rostand) later wrote that "we thought of ourselves as really the gods of the moment. Cocteau and I were setting out to make a conquest of life."[54] Cocteau quickly became Anna de Noailles' devoted attendant and companion, mirroring her to an extraordinary degree—especially in his endless conversation and monologues, which echoed the brilliant torrent of words that were her trademark. Later, Anna's son remarked that "each was the only one voluble enough to make the other keep quiet and listen."[55]

While Cocteau was eagerly providing Anna de Noailles with the sensitive soul that vibrated in accord with her own, his friend (and by now lover) Lucien Daudet,[56] youngest son of the novelist Alphonse Daudet, was devoting much of his life to the former Empress Eugénie. Having escaped France for England in 1870, following her husband's capture by the Prussians and the fall of the Second Empire, the eighty-five-year-old widow now spent much of her time in her villa at Cap Martin on the Mediterranean. Yet she sometimes returned to Paris where, strangely enough, she chose to stay at the Hôtel Continental, overlooking the Tuileries gardens. From her well-appointed rooms there, she could hardly avoid seeing the vast empty space where her palace, the Palais des Tuileries, once dominated the gardens' eastern end.

Given this particular hotel's unfortunate location, her devoted retinue feared that the view would call up unhappy memories, even though the palace itself had disappeared—burned and gutted during the Commune uprising of 1871 and swept away by the Third Republic, which wanted no imperial memories to contend with. Yet the former Empress, when Cocteau met her, was not at all inclined to dwell on unhappy memories. Rather than a faded romantic, she turned out to be an energetic and crusty old lady, with no frailty, no delicate wistfulness, and none of the dreamy crinolines, pantalets, or parasols that had been her trademark all those years ago. Instead, tiny and acerbic, she dressed in simple black and questioned Cocteau sharply about Isadora Duncan and the Ballets Russes. She sometimes cackled with laughter, especially when baiting her companions about the follies of their pasts, from absurd fashions to forgotten eccentricities and scandals.

"What remains of the past that could still affect this woman, several times dead?" Cocteau speculated, remembering her deceased husband, their lost empire, and the unexpected death of their only son.[57] He concluded that she had returned to that location merely out of habit. It was neither heaven nor hell for her. The Tuileries, quite simply, was a neighborhood she knew well.

Portrait of Igor Stravinsky and Claude Debussy, Paris, 1912–1913, by Erik Satie. Erik Satie / Private Collection / Photo © Christie's Images / The Bridgeman Art Library.

~

CHAPTER FOURTEEN

Dancing on the Edge

(1912)

The 1912 social season in Paris set a new standard for reckless extravagance, with Paul Poiret leading the pack. The central motif for his glittering June ball, held in the forest of Versailles, was *Les Festes de Bacchus*, a resurrected Lully ballet from the court of the Sun King. In tribute to this theme, his three hundred guests (costumed as nymphs and gods) consumed several hundred gallons of champagne while watching dancers from the Paris Opera, accompanied by forty musicians, perform Lully's opulent celebration of Dionysus. After partaking of a "grandiose buffet" beneath "tunneled trellises," the guests then wandered off into the decorated forest until the first rays of dawn, when lobster, melon, foie gras, and ices were served.

Poiret later protested that "the scene was so beautiful and the spirit of the fête so elevated that no scandal, no unpleasantness occurred," but the entire affair was an outsized tribute to decadence, complete with rumors of orgies (Poiret himself described transporting back to Paris "the half-unclothed nymphs and their slightly rumpled gods" after the party was over).[1] By now, opium and cocaine circulated openly at the most exclusive Paris parties, and sexual scandal had become an essential element of life in the fast lane. Life for this brilliant set had become intensely theatrical, and it was no surprise that the worlds of theater and society overlapped ever more closely.

It was in this overheated environment that Diaghilev presented a ballet of *Après-midi d'un faune* set to Debussy's music. The choreographer was Diaghilev's protégé, the astonishing Nijinsky, who danced the role of the Faun—easily the most scandalous of the season. His costume, complete with a bunch of grapes over the genitals, was by itself sufficiently suggestive; but it was the ballet's ending, with the Faun having graphically depicted sex with the veil of one of the departing Nymphs, that set off an uproar. The audience was stunned, and critical reaction soon split into two diametrically opposed camps. Among the detractors was Debussy, who had only reluctantly given permission to use his music, and who detested the choreography, criticizing the "atrocious 'dissonance'" between it and the music.[2]

Debussy did not, however, get involved in the subsequent uproar, which featured Gaston Calmette, editor-in-chief of Le Figaro, and Auguste Rodin, whom Diaghilev had lined up in advance to defend the ballet if needed. Calmette (who had angrily substituted his own review for that of his critic) wrote, "No decent public could ever accept such animal realism . . . as those vile movements of erotic bestiality."[3] Rodin responded, citing his admiration for Loie Fuller, Isadora Duncan, and "the last in this line, Nijinsky, [who] has the added advantage of physical perfection and . . . also the extraordinary capacity to give expression to a wide range of feelings." Continuing in his praise, Rodin enthused that "no role has shown Nijinsky in such an extraordinary light as his last creation, L'Après-midi d'un faune." In particular, Rodin singled out for praise the ballet's most controversial part: "One can imagine nothing more arresting," he wrote, "than his impulsive gesture at the conclusion of the ballet when he again stretches himself out . . . on the stolen veil which he now embraces and grasps with voluptuous fervor."[4]

"Voluptuous fervor" was exactly what Calmette found objectionable, and he immediately turned on Rodin, lambasting the aging sculptor for exhibiting a series of deeply objectionable drawings in the former chapel and rooms of the nuns of Sacré-Coeur. Calmette then expressed his amazement that the French state and the French taxpayers were currently subsidizing "our richest sculptor" by allowing him to stay in the Hôtel Biron. Suddenly the fracas had turned into something nasty. At a time when Rodin was doing everything in his power to assure his lifetime tenure at the Hôtel Biron, his letter in defense of Nijinsky's choreography threatened to undermine his cause.

As it turned out, Rodin had not even written the letter to which he signed his name. He really had slight idea of what he was talking about, having had little previous exposure to ballet—although in recent years he had expressed some interest in dance. Yet he had the necessary credentials for Diaghilev's purposes, as a superstar who had long shown a predilection for eroticism in art. Unfortunately, Rodin also was aging, and the journalist (Roger Marx of Le Matin) sent to collect supportive statements from him quickly discovered that he had slim pickings. The outcome was a rebuttal to Calmette signed by Rodin but written by Marx.[5]

Fortunately for Rodin, this melee did not derail his prospects. In July, the Council of Ministers finally agreed to let him remain at the Hôtel Biron for life, with the prospect of a Rodin museum on the premises after his death.[6] Widespread support from Rodin's friends helped secure this decision, but an undoubtedly important factor was a political one: Rodin's longtime friend and admirer, Raymond Poincaré, had recently become prime minister of France.

⌒

While Rodin was fending off attacks in the public sphere, his private life was also undergoing severe strain. The actual events of this episode remain murky, but they seem to have involved the disappearance of some of his drawings, for which Claire de Choiseul blamed Rodin's current secretary. Instead, Rodin's friends as well as the secretary blamed Choiseul, and feared she was robbing Rodin. The matter was so grave, they insisted, that it required police intervention.

The situation may have involved more than simple theft: according to one close friend, Claire de Choiseul had persuaded—or was attempting to persuade—Rodin to bequeath to her and her husband the rights of reproduction for the works Rodin intended to leave to the state. Although there is no written evidence to support this accusation, unquestionably Choiseul had no interest in Rodin's dream of a Musée Rodin. Something of the magnitude of the future ownership of his work seems to have been operating here, to bring their relationship to such an abrupt end.

Whatever the exact details of the rupture, Rodin left it to others to tell Choiseul of his decision and to take back her key to the Hôtel Biron. Then, in a characteristic move, he left Paris. He agreed to send Choiseul monthly payments in support, but the break was final. It evidently was a wrenching decision for him: "I am like a man who walks in a woods overcome by darkness," he wrote a friend several months later.[7] Choiseul was distraught and for years unsuccessfully attempted to reestablish their former relationship, but Rodin's friends were greatly relieved.

⌒

That June, Debussy had a stark vision of the future, and it shocked him. He joined Stravinsky in a remarkable play-through of the piano four-hand version of the completed parts of Stravinsky's *The Rite of Spring* (*Le Sacre du printemps*). Stravinsky played the treble and Debussy the bass, and Louis Laloy (at whose country house this event took place) later recalled that those present "were speechless, crushed as if by a hurricane from the depths of the ages, come to seize our lives by the roots."[8] As for Debussy, he later wrote

Stravinsky that this performance "haunts me like a beautiful nightmare and I try in vain to recall the terrifying impression it made." He promised to anticipate its performance "like a greedy child who's been promised some jam,"[9] but it was clear that the experience had unsettled him. From then on, as one biographer notes, "he had in his mind the unpleasant premonition of a musical world that might be not only *post* Debussy but *sine* Debussy."[10]

Stravinsky's own impression of Debussy was that he was "not especially interested in new developments in music," and "in fact my own appearance on the musical scene must have been a shock to him."[11] A major event in Stravinsky's own musical life that year was the performance of Arnold Schoenberg's *Pierrot lunaire*, which he heard Schoenberg conduct in Berlin. (*Pierrot lunaire* would not be performed in Paris until 1922, when it started a riot.) This work, which is atonal and performed in *Sprechstimme* or spoken singing, was unquestionably challenging, but Ravel was enthusiastic. Debussy, on the other hand, responded to Stravinsky's description of the new work simply by staring at Stravinsky and saying nothing.

⌒

Soon after the Ballets Russes premiered *L'Après-midi d'un faune*, Diaghilev presented Ravel's *Daphnis et Chloé* to Paris. Ravel was disappointed in the outcome, especially since he regarded *Daphnis et Chloé* as his "most important work."[12] Fokine was the choreographer, and the growing conflict between him and Nijinsky exacerbated an already difficult situation.[13] The many rehearsals that *Faune* required left little time to rehearse *Daphnis et Chloé*; in addition, Diaghilev had pushed *Daphnis et Chloé* to the end of the Ballets Russes season, which meant that it received only two performances.

Most critics were favorably impressed with Ravel's score, but Ravel did not like Léon Bakst's sets and costumes or Fokine's libretto. As he told Jacques Rouché (who then was director of the Théâtre des Arts): "The precedent of *Daphnis et Chloé* . . . has made me extremely reluctant to undertake a similar experience again."[14]

Debussy had been similarly burned by his experience with *Après-midi d'un faune*, but—beset by bills—in late June he signed a contract with Diaghilev to write the ballet that would eventually have the title *Jeux* (Games). "At lunchtime one has to eat," Debussy would tell *Le Matin* upon the occasion of *Jeux*'s 1913 opening, and "one day I happened to lunch with Serge Diaghilev, a terrifying but irresistible man able to instill the spirit of the dance into lifeless stones."[15] Stravinsky preferred the title *Le Parc*, but Debussy assured him that *Jeux* was better. "For one thing it's shorter," he wrote Stravinsky. "For another it's a convenient way of expressing the 'horrors' that take place between the three participants."[16]

In August Debussy wrote Jacques Durand that recently he had received a visit from Nijinsky and his nanny (meaning Diaghilev), who were in a great hurry to have the music for *Jeux*. Nijinsky wanted to work on it during his upcoming stay in Venice ("apparently the peaceful air of the lagoons will inspire his choreographic reveries"). Debussy refused to play for them what he had already written, "not wanting Barbarians sticking their noses" into his still-developing work, although he had every intention of completing the score shortly. "May God, the Tsar and my country stand by me in my hour of need," he added.[17]

He finished it quickly, and in late August was able to write André Caplet that he was amazed that he was able to "forget the troubles of this world and write music which is almost cheerful, and . . . [containing] that orchestral colour which seems to be lit from behind."[18] Nevertheless, the troubles of this world continued to plague him: a sick wife, an unhappy marriage, and insufficient income, in addition to the harsh criticism that continued to come his way, despite his hard-won eminence as a composer.

That April, Ravel came to Debussy's defense in a review in which he lambasted the press and the ignoramuses in it who insisted on writing about the arts. Debussy, he concluded, "remains the most important and profoundly musical composer living today."[19] Yet at year's end, after *Pelléas et Mélisande* was performed for the one hundredth time at the Opéra-Comique, Debussy's promotion from Chevalier to Officer in the Legion of Honor—which should have been a shoo-in—did not happen. Instead, in what appeared to be a deliberate snub, the honors went to that bastion of musical conservatism, Vincent d'Indy, and a light opera composer whose name no one remembers.

～

Jean Cocteau's first big assignment for Diaghilev, writing the libretto for *Le Dieu bleu*, fell flat. The ballet—an Oriental fantasy, whose score, by Reynaldo Hahn, was no more interesting than Cocteau's libretto—was not a success and soon disappeared from the Ballets Russes repertory. It was around this time that Diaghilev, walking home with Cocteau and Nijinsky after a performance, famously told Cocteau: "Astound me! I'll wait for you to astound me."[20]

It would be fully five years before Cocteau would in fact astound Diaghilev, but Cocteau later attributed his abrupt break with frivolity to this command. "I was quick to realize that one doesn't astound a Diaghilev in a week or two," he later wrote. "From that moment I decided to die and be born again. The labor was long and agonizing."[21]

In the meantime, Anna de Noailles was mentoring Cocteau, and his third volume of verse, *La Danse de Sophocle*, published in 1912, showed signs of her influence, both in its subject matter and its newfound seriousness of tone. It was this volume that received a review in the September issue of the *Nouvelle Revue Française*, which already was emerging as an influential literary review under the leadership of Jean Schlumberger, Jacques Copeau, and future Nobel Prize winner for literature, André Gide.[22]

Cocteau had earnestly sought this review, having contacted Gide (whom he had not yet met) following a spring trip to North Africa with Lucien Daudet. Gide's connections to North Africa were well known, given his 1902 publication of *L'Immoraliste*, whose depiction of a young man's self-discovery in the company of Arab boys in Tunis shocked even the blasé French reading public. Cocteau poured on the flattery ("Your light beckons to me"), and sent a copy of *La Danse de Sophocle* to Gide soon after it was published, but no review appeared. Cocteau then wrote Gide again: "So you loathe my book so much you don't speak?"[23]

In September, the longed-for review at last appeared, written by Henri Ghéon, although Gide may well have had a hand in it. Although outwardly favorable, it contained some barely disguised slurs that made it clear that the author viewed Cocteau as little more than a frivolous addition to the Paris literary scene. Soon after, Cocteau and Gide met for the first time, but it was not a cordial encounter. Gide clearly had no use for Cocteau, and he would have more to say on this subject in the years ahead.

Soon Proust would have his own difficulties with Gide. In September he completed *Swann's Way*, the huge first volume of *In Search of Lost Time*, but could not find a publisher. Fasquelle turned it down, based on the report of one reader—a poet and playwright whom Proust had earlier parodied and who now strongly condemned the manuscript. Proust's preferred alternative was to publish with the *Nouvelle Revue Française*, but here André Gide gave a firm thumbs down. Convinced that Proust was merely a dilettante with literary pretensions, Gide read only two passages before sending the manuscript back.[24]

Proust, who had "put the best of myself, my thought, my very life" into this work,[25] now prepared to publish the manuscript at his own expense.

⁓

Proust worried endlessly about details—the right kind of hat for one character, the precise cries of Paris street vendors for the background of a scene, or the exact details from statuary in Notre-Dame de Paris for his description of the church at Balbec.[26] Despite illness and weakness, he even made a trip to the countryside to study the colors of hawthorns and apple trees in bloom—carefully keeping a closed car window between him and the cut branches he admired, to prevent them from bringing on an asthma attack. When he met Helena Rubinstein, soon after her relocation from London to Paris, he made use of the opportunity to quiz her about makeup. Would a duchess use rouge?

he wanted to know, or did demimondaines put kohl on their eyes? "How should I know?" Madame Rubinstein retorted. She thought Proust was "nebbishy looking" and noted that he "smelt of moth-balls [and] wore a fur-lined coat to the ground." Given such an unpromising appearance, "how could I have known he was going to be so famous?"[27]

There were others on the Paris scene whose success would be every bit as surprising. Few, for example, would have predicted that Coco Chanel, the self-described country bumpkin and innocent, would soon emerge as a fashion powerhouse. Paul Poiret later remarked: "We ought to have been on guard against that boyish head. It was going to give us every kind of shock, and produce, out of its little conjuror's hat, gowns and coiffures and jewels and boutiques."[28] Having done well in selling her sleek and attention-getting hats, Chanel began to sell women's clothes as well, many inspired by menswear, and all modeled on the simplicity of design that suited her and (in her own estimation) enhanced the youthfulness of the wearer. By 1912 she was earning enough to operate without Boy Capel's, or anyone's, financial support. This freed her from anyone else's control—much as her corset-free fashions freed their wearers.

While Chanel was making fashion waves, François Coty continued to expand his perfume empire, opening a subsidiary in London and commissioning Lalique to design a unique set of windows for the façade of Coty's Fifth Avenue store in New York.[29] Not to be outdone, in 1912 Jacques Guerlain, of the third generation of the House of Guerlain, created L'Heure Bleue, one of the great perfumes of all time. Similarly, Eugène Schueller continued to prosper, expanding sales of his L'Oréal hair dyes to Austria, Holland, and Italy.

That year, both André Citroën and Louis Renault made their way to Dearborn, Michigan, to meet Henry Ford and observe Ford's production-line methods that were creating, at rock-bottom prices, the Model T—the world's first standardized, mass-produced vehicle. Both came away impressed with what they saw and convinced that it was necessary to adapt to this revolutionary way of production, inspired by the scientific management ideas of Frederick Winslow Taylor. Citroën made improvements to his gear factory, but his automobile company (Mors) produced only luxury cars, and so the lessons of modernization and the Model T had a more immediate impact on Renault, who already had captured one-fifth of the French market (10,000 of the 50,000 vehicles sold in France that year) and had expanded his sales to Japan, New Zealand, India, and Russia.[30]

Renault was no fool and had noted the decreasing competitiveness of Renault automobiles in America. Realizing the importance of Ford's methods in maintaining his competitive edge, he attempted to put these methods into practice following his trip to Michigan. Yet Renault had not anticipated the strength of his employees' resistance to this new way of doing things. They were craftsmen, they informed him, not machine-minders, and were proud of it. They also held out for their long-established perquisites, including time-devouring hourly cigarette breaks.

Renault did not back down. As a book he admired put it: "It is indeed fortunate for the progress of civilization that the power of the masses was born only after the great discoveries in science and industry had been made."[31] It was only the intervention of the prominent labor leader, Albert Thomas, who helped bring Renault's workers around by telling them that they were hurting themselves as much as Renault; without these new methods they would soon be out of jobs, because America would dominate the market. Renault's promise to pay more if output increased provided the clinching argument, and a threatened strike was called off.

Yet working conditions, whether at Renault's factory or another's, remained harsh: the normal factory workday for French men at that time was twelve hours, six days a week. A weekly "rest day" had been put into law in 1906, but there still was no paid annual holiday. Women and children worked nine-hour days (marginally improved by a cut from ten hours in 1909). When Citroën's workers at Mors went on strike, demanding a five-day week and the right to join a trade union, Citroën immediately opened negotiations that led to major improvements in their conditions. But Citroën was unusually progressive for the times, and already his presence in the French auto industry was drawing attention—and disfavor—from other owners, especially from Louis Renault.

∽

It was a year marked by tragedy, most memorably by the sinking of the luxury liner the *Titanic*, in which more than fifteen hundred lives were lost. On a far smaller scale, but no less devastating for the survivors, was the death that September of thirty-year-old Charles Voisin in an automobile accident. The Baroness de Laroche, who was with him, was severely injured. Gabriel Voisin had broken with his brother two years earlier, in large part over the wild life he was leading with the baroness. Despite hopes to mend the breach, Charles died before they ever saw one another again.

After the accident, Gabriel Voisin continued the expansion of his Boulogne-Billancourt factory, now without his brother's name. Despite Voisin's personal tragedy, it was a good time to be in the aviation business, especially as interest in air warfare was heating up. By now air shows were featuring demonstrations of aerial bombing, and in 1912 the tire manufacturers André and Edouard Michelin (with the French War Ministry's blessing) introduced a prize to encourage French aviation development. The Prix Michelin established various feats for aspiring aviators to accomplish, including artillery spotting and dropping mock bombs on target—all with a large cash prize as a reward. In the meantime, the Michelins had taken to heart the ideas of Henry Ford and Frederick Winslow Taylor and had modernized their own company's tire production. They also published millions of brochures advocating these "American" ideas to the French, with the aim of improving their nation's competitiveness with the rising American behemoth. As Etienne Rey's *The Renaissance of French Pride* (published in 1912) put it: "The martial spirit, that inheritance from our past, which we have for so long thought to be dead, has suddenly burst into flower by a magic germination."[32]

France had just suffered defeat at the 1912 Olympics, held in Stockholm (the United States won the most gold medals, while Sweden won the most overall; France came in fifth in gold medals and, most maddeningly, behind Germany in overall medals). In response, with the nation in agitation over how France could improve its prospects for the 1916 Olympics, the Marquis de Polignac founded an athletic training college in Pommery Park, near Reims. It was an immediate hit, attracting all ages, but especially drawing the younger generation, who by now were "mad on physical development."[33] The grounds contained race tracks and courses, facilities for all kinds of games, and the latest equipment for it all. Pommery Park became a favored destination, where those intent on improving their physiques camped in the open, performed Swedish exercises "with utmost vigour and regularity," and did what was necessary to pound themselves into shape.

It was in this environment of escalating competitiveness and militarism that Charles de Gaulle graduated from Saint-Cyr in September 1912 with the rank of second lieutenant. "A very highly gifted cadet," his captain reported. "Will make an excellent officer."[34]

With his choice already made for the infantry, de Gaulle could have gone into the rifle regiments, the Foreign Legion, or any of the glamorous overseas units then in Morocco. Instead he chose to return to the 33rd Infantry Regiment in Arras where he had served as an enlisted man, despite the fact that he had not liked it. Quite possibly a determining factor was the new commanding officer, Philippe Pétain—reputed to be an outstanding instructor—who held the strong conviction that what mattered in modern warfare was which side had the greatest concentration of firepower. Pétain firmly believed that the offensive should only advance with the line of fire—a view that ran directly counter to the received wisdom of his high command, which preferred to put its faith in taking the offensive, complete with successive dashes and the determined use of the bayonet. Cantankerous and contemptuous of military conventions, Pétain was hardly beloved by his superiors—which explained his posting to the backwater regiment in Arras.

Yet he would quickly earn the respect of young second lieutenant Charles de Gaulle, despite de Gaulle's own personal preference for taking and maintaining the offensive. De Gaulle always admired a nonconformist.

⌢

Nonconformists? Paris was full of them. On the political front there was Georges Clemenceau, who refused easy categorization and in early 1912 was once again making his presence known after a two-and-a-half-year hiatus. It was now that he asserted himself in characteristic fashion by helping to overthrow yet another government (by this time he had brought down several) and bringing in that of Rodin's friend and supporter, Raymond Poincaré.

In her own quiet way, Marie Curie had been among the boldest of the nonconformists, both in her career and in her personal life, and she had paid the price for it. Those who knew her best believed that her collapse in late 1911 was due in part to overwork, but mostly to emotional exhaustion following the excruciating public airing of her affair with Paul Langevin, not to mention the aftershocks from her rejection by the Academy of Sciences. It would take a long while for her to recover, and during 1912 and 1913 she traveled under assumed names from one retreat to another, looking for a cure. At each place she worried that her location would be discovered, and she begged her friends to keep her address a secret.

One of her stays was with a friend in England, Hertha Ayrton, who was not only a scientist but also a political activist who ardently supported Irish independence and women's suffrage. Marie Curie had always kept her distance from causes, but when Ayrton in mid-1912 asked her to sign a petition to protest the imprisonment of the leaders of the English suffrage movement, Curie readily agreed. "I was very touched by all that you told me of the struggle of English women for their rights," Curie wrote Ayrton. "I admire them very much, and I wish for their success."[35]

⌢

Claude Monet remained depressed for months following Alice's death, despite the attempts of friends to distract him. Renoir, Mirbeau, and Clemenceau were chief among these, and Clemenceau (who was in poor health himself, and about to undergo a prostate operation) encouraged Monet to remember "the old Rembrandt whom you know from the Louvre. . . . He clings on to his palette, determined to battle through to the end despite his terrible ordeal. There is your example."[36]

Still Monet remained discouraged and dejected. After a few attempts to finish several paintings, he wrote Paul Durand-Ruel that he was "completely fed up with painting and I am going to pack up my brushes and colours for good."[37] In April 1912, he wrote his other major dealers, Josse and Gaston Bernheim-Jeune, that he had "enough good sense in me to know whether what I'm doing is good or bad, and it's utterly bad." Shortly after, he wrote Paul Durand-Ruel, that "now, more than ever, I realize just how illusory my undeserved success has been." The following month he wrote his friend, the art critic Gustave Geffroy, "No, I am not a great painter." Geffroy had just written two complimentary articles about him, but Monet was adamant: "I only know that I do what I can to convey what I experience before nature and that most often, in order to succeed in conveying what I feel, I totally forget the most elementary rules of painting, if they exist that is." This will never change, he added, "and this is what makes me despair."[38]

Adding to Monet's despair was his own health and that of his eldest son, Jean. Jean was seriously ill, and although he had recovered somewhat by late summer, Monet's own eyesight had by then become a major problem. He could only see clearly through one eye, and a specialist recommended an operation. What Monet feared was not the operation itself but the possibility that it would totally alter his sight. Impelled by this fear, he once again began to paint, yet continued to express discouragement about the final product. Overall, despite overwhelming critical and financial success (several prominent exhibitions and a grand total of 369,000 francs for 1912 alone), this was a difficult time for Monet.

That year, Lili Boulanger took a huge step toward her own dearest goal when she was accepted to the Paris Conservatoire. Despite years of invalidism, she had never given up on her dream to enter the Conservatoire and compete for the Prix de Rome. Her sister, Nadia, helped every step of the way, teaching and encouraging her. Lili also received extensive private lessons from instructors at the Conservatoire, and she audited classes there whenever she was able.

In the meantime, she embarked on an ambitious reading program and began to learn several languages, in the attempt to become as well-versed in culture, history, and languages as the rest of her family and its cultivated milieu (her mother spoke Russian, French, and German fluently). Lili unquestionably received much assistance along the way, but in the end it was her own brilliance that won her acceptance to the Conservatoire at the advanced age of eighteen. Her teachers soon reported that she was "very gifted." Yet as one onlooker noted that summer, "it was evident even then that the flame of Lili's talent was likely to overtax her meager physical resources."[39]

Despite illness that spring, Lili continued to prepare for the Prix de Rome and insisted on entering the competition for that year. Unfortunately she became ill midway and had to withdraw; but no one was able to step into what she regarded as her place since, as it turned out, no Grand Prix de Rome was awarded that year.

After recovering sufficiently, Lili went to work again—this time preparing for the 1913 competition. Yet health problems constantly interfered, and it was a question of whether she could even continue her classwork at the Conservatoire. By year's end, she was undergoing physical therapy on the remote northern coast of Normandy, near Calais. There, separated from her friends and family, and surrounded by other invalids, she endured bad weather and gloom. It was a thoroughly depressing end to the year.

⌒

Leo Stein did not like Alice B. Toklas, and Gertrude Stein did not like Leo's recently acquired love interest, Eugénie Auzias, otherwise known as Nina of Montparnasse (as she was called throughout the quarter). Nina, the daughter of a provincial professor of mathematics, had originally come to Paris to study singing, but she ended up singing on the streets to support herself. She sang, she modeled, and she slept around. The men in the neighborhood all knew and loved her, calling her the soul of the quarter. Leo came to love her as well, which was a happy outcome for Nina, who had loved him from afar ever since first glimpsing him several years earlier.

By 1910, when Gertrude and Alice officially became a couple, Leo and Nina had become lovers—his first romance, as he told her. Gertrude did not approve of Nina, whom she considered an opportunist and a woman of the streets. Still, Gertrude was somewhat sympathetic to Leo's romance—at least at the beginning. It was when it became apparent that this was no passing fancy that Gertrude's disapproval grew. By 1911, Leo was quite thoroughly enamored of Nina, who kept up a virtual stable of men friends but seemed to love Leo quite honestly in return. On the other hand, Leo was finding Alice's constant presence at 27 Rue de Fleurus unpleasant. Alice, as Ernest Hemingway would later note, could be frightening.[40]

By 1912, the return of Sarah and Michael Stein to Paris added more friction to the mix. Gertrude feared that Sarah and Leo would make common cause, especially about Gertrude's work, and she was right. Sarah did not manage the proper enthusiasm about Gertrude's writing or Picasso's painting, and she did not seem to take to Alice. At the same time, Sarah and Leo easily renewed their friendship with one another. Gertrude began to study the two and their relationship, which turned into a new book, at first titled "Two," or "Leo and Sally," to help explain what had happened to these two family members who had once been close to her.[41]

Gertrude and Leo disagreed strongly over Picasso and Cubism, but it was Leo's criticism of her writing that stung Gertrude the most. "No artist needs criticism," she later said; "he only needs appreciation." Yet Gertrude's word portrait of her new friend, the American heiress Mabel Dodge, aroused so much derision in Leo that he could no longer retain a veneer of politeness. "Damned nonsense," he called it, and told their friend Mabel Weeks that "Gertrude . . . hungers and thirsts for gloire and it was of course a serious thing for her that I can't abide her stuff and think it abominable." According to Leo, Gertrude once had had something to say, but in order to give her writing more edginess, had twisted and abused syntax and words. Gertrude later commented that Leo's response to her writing "destroyed him for me and it destroyed me for him."[42]

Their friends thought that far more was at stake here than a quarrel about writing, or even about Cubism. Some thought that Leo's liaison with Nina had provided the final blow. Most, though, blamed Alice. "Alice didn't really want them to be as close as they had been," Virgil Thomson later noted,[43] and many others agreed.

⁓

"Things were not in those days going any too well between them," Gertrude Stein later wrote of Picasso and Fernande, when they were leaving the Bateau-Lavoir to live on the Boulevard de Clichy.[44] Once there, things rapidly went downhill. Fernande, by her own account, was not happy, and Picasso was bored and irritated by what he called her "little ways."

By this time Cubism had begun to evolve under Picasso and Braque into what later was called synthetic Cubism, as differentiated from their earlier analytic style. They worked together in a remarkable dialogue as their paintings evolved to include printed words, lettering, and a variety of small café trivia such as playing cards, scraps of music scores, and cigarette packaging. Braque, who loved music, introduced musical instruments to the mix, most notably in his 1910 masterpiece, *Violin and Pitcher*. Picasso, who was quite taken with guitars, soon followed.

By summer of 1912, the two friends (who had escaped to the Provençal village of Sorgues) began to paint imitations of objects, whether stenciled letters or simulations of wood and marble. Committed as both were to representation in painting, neither artist stepped over the line into total abstraction—although Braque would come closer to this than would Picasso.

In the meantime, the two pathfinders had more followers than they would have preferred, who flooded that year's Salon d'Automne with Cubist imitations. Some of these new Cubists, such as Piet Mondrian and Diego Rivera (who both then lived in Paris) were proceeding on their own paths, but others were merely imitators. "Neither Picasso nor I had anything to do with [Albert] Gleizes and [Jean] Metzinger and the others," Braque later said of those later known as the Salon Cubists. "Their idea was to systematize Cubism. . . . It was all intellectualism. They merely cubified what they painted."[45]

Increasingly, Picasso was gravitating to Montparnasse, joining friends at a favorite old haunt, the Closerie des Lilas, or at either of the two cafés at the intersection of Boulevard du Montparnasse and Boulevard Raspail (then called Carrefour Vavin, now Place Pablo-Picasso). These were the Café du Dôme and the Café de la Rotonde. All three were located within minutes of each other on Boulevard du Montparnasse, but the Closerie had been there the longest, having benefited from its location at the intersection of Boulevard du Montparnasse and Boulevard Saint-Michel, connecting Montparnasse with the Latin Quarter and the Right Bank. A longtime favorite with artists and students, it became a focus of weekly poetry readings that by 1905 attracted Picasso and his crowd, including André Salmon and Apollinaire. Fernande Olivier recalled walking with Picasso and Salmon clear across Paris from Montmartre to join in these drunken evenings at the Closerie, which ended only when the owner closed up and threw them out.

It was the completion of the Nord-Sud line of the Métro (finished by 1910 for most of the distance from Gare Montparnasse to Montmartre), together with the long-awaited cut-through of Boulevard Raspail to Boulevard du Montparnasse, that suddenly made the Carrefour Vavin a hot spot. Different nationalities congregated at one or another of the favored cafés, the Dôme or the newly expanded and refurbished Rotonde. Germans, Scandinavians, and Americans favored the Dôme, while everyone else gravitated to the Rotonde, "where painters, poets, and writers mixed with no regard for nationality, styles of painting, or schools of poetry."[46] In general, impoverished artists and writers could enjoy warmth and good company for hours at any of the three cafés, while nursing a mere *café crème*. "Innocent beverage!" rhapsodized André Salmon of the *café crème*, in his memoirs of Montparnasse, "ordered as a way of paying for the right to remain, for permission to reside a certain time, the most time possible, seated in front of a small table of this Bourse of the new artistic values, this temple of living Art!"[47]

Yet while Picasso was spending more time in Montparnasse, he kept a firm footing in Montmartre: in addition to his apartment, he rented another studio back at the Bateau-Lavoir, where he was free to paint and to conduct affairs as he pleased. When Gertrude Stein and Alice B. Toklas visited his Bateau-Lavoir studio in early 1912, they left their card for the absent painter and discovered upon their return that he had painted it into a recent still life, *The Architect's Table*, as well as adding the words *Ma Jolie* (the refrain from a then-popular song) to the painting. As Alice and Gertrude departed, Gertrude commented, "Fernande is certainly not ma jolie, I wonder who it is."[48] Soon they would find out.

The previous autumn, Fernande—always the flirt—had begun an affair with a handsome Italian painter, Ubaldo Oppi. For her go-between, Fernande chose her close friend, Eve Gouel, the mistress of Picasso's friend Louis Marcoussis. As it turned out, Fernande trusted where she should not have, and Eve made use of the opportunity to insinuate herself into Picasso's good graces, as well as his bed. Before long, Picasso had left Fernande for Eve (whom he called Eva) and began to include the words *Ma Jolie* in his paintings in tribute to her. Now that Fernande had compromised herself with Ubaldo Oppi, it was easy for Picasso to dump her, which he did, moving with Eva first to French Catalonia, then to Avignon, before settling back in Paris—this time in Montparnasse, on the other side of Paris from Montmartre.[49]

When Fernande tried to follow, Picasso left the terse message that "she can expect nothing from me, and I should be quite happy never to see her again."[50] By year's end, Picasso had proposed to Eva and been accepted. They would have married in Barcelona, had it not been for the death of Picasso's father, followed by signs of Eva's own impending illness. In the meantime, Fernande was left without any means of support (Picasso had left her with nothing, and she soon broke with Oppi, who had no money).

Eventually Fernande found a job as a salesperson with Paul Poiret. When Poiret retrenched during the war, she found work in an antiques shop, then as a nanny, a cashier in a butcher shop, and as manager of a cabaret. She found walk-on parts in plays and films, and even read horoscopes (thanks to Max Jacob's instruction). But she would always fall back on her ability to teach drawing and French, and although in her later years she often was penniless, she continued to find lovers to help finance her lifestyle.[51]

Unlike Montmartre, Montparnasse was not a distinctly defined quarter, with its own picturesque charm. Instead, when Picasso moved there it was a hodge-podge of shacks housing down-at-the-heels artists and poets interspersed with new buildings of more comfort but no distinct character for those who—like Picasso—could afford something better. Students from the Latin Quarter had long before named the area Mont-Parnasse, or Mount Parnassus, after the hilly slag-heap left by the quarries below. They and others came to drink and to dance there, at *guinguettes* and cafés such as the Grande Chaumière and the Closerie des Lilas. Yet one did not find painters painting street scenes in Montparnasse, such as Utrillo in Montmartre. Even by 1912, the quarter had not yet become fashionable, as it would between the wars, and by itself it did not offer inspiration—even if the people who inhabited it did.

During Chagall's early years in Paris—years at La Ruche, in the farthest corner of Montparnasse—his closest friend and unfailing supporter was the Swiss poet Blaise Cendrars (originally Frédéric Sauser). Cendrars "didn't just look at my paintings," Chagall recalled. "He used to swallow them."[52] Cendrars convinced Chagall that he need not be intimidated by the "proud cubists." Bolstered by Cendrars, Chagall was able to look at the Cubists and think: "Let them eat their fill of their square pears on their triangular tables!" Somewhat later, he declared that his art "is perhaps a wild art, a blazing quicksilver, a blue soul flashing on my canvases."[53]

Chagall's art vibrated with poetry, color, and musicality. Picasso, despite his sculptures and *papiers collés* of guitars, was not musically inclined. John Richardson writes that people who urged Picasso "to look more favorably on abstract art because it was the pictorial equivalent of music would be told, 'That's why I don't like music.'" Why then did "the unmusical Picasso paint so many musical instruments and instrumentalists?" Richardson speculates that Picasso may have "wanted his amazing eye to compensate for his insensitive ear."[54]

Picasso knew Chagall but was not impressed with his work, possibly because Chagall at this period had allied himself with some of those whom Picasso dismissively viewed as mere copyists of what he had already done, such as Robert Delaunay and Jean Metzinger. Delaunay, though, was in turn dismissive of Picasso's and Braque's monochrome paintings, remarking that "they paint with cobwebs, these fellows."[55] By 1912 Delaunay was breaking out of these cobwebs into the sort of vibrant color to which Chagall could relate. Apollinaire named Delaunay's movement into pure color and abstraction "orphism"—the incarnation of the mythical bard Orpheus.[56]

Late in his life and his career, Picasso told Françoise Gilot: "When Matisse dies, Chagall will be the only painter left who understands what color really is." Picasso was "not crazy about [Chagall's] roosters and asses and flying violinists and all the folklore, but his canvases are really painted, not just thrown together." Some of Chagall's latest works, in fact, had convinced Picasso "that there's never been anybody since Renoir who has the feeling for light that Chagall has."[57]

⌒

That autumn, Bernhardt returned to America for yet another "farewell tour," bringing her now twenty-nine-year-old lover, Lou Tellegen, with her. It was a sad tour, marked by old age and pain. Bernhardt could not bear to stand on her damaged knee, and she reduced the length of her performances accordingly, avoiding standing unaided. Some newspapers lauded her eternal genius, but others commented on her sad decline: "Time has taken its toll," the *New York World* wrote.[58]

That same autumn, Paris Singer began to lay plans for the theater he had promised Isadora. Curiously, he decided that the man to do the kind of job he wanted was Gordon Craig, who by this time was beginning to make his mark in the theater world as a man of vision, a man of the future. Singer offered Craig a princely sum to work on stage construction and lighting, and Craig at first accepted before suddenly withdrawing, ostensibly because of press reports that the theater was being built for Isadora Duncan—which of course he had known from the outset. "I have made it one of my rules lately to work for no performer however highly gifted or eminent," he informed Singer. Craig's prima donnish stance may have been prompted by the unresponsiveness of his and Isadora's daughter (who quite reasonably treated him as a stranger), as well as by the irritating presence of "Isadora and her millionaire."[59]

Still, Craig's departure left Isadora sad and dejected, and things soon became worse. During an opulent party at her Neuilly studio, Isadora and an admirer retreated to her apartment, where Singer found them "on the golden divan reflected in the endless mirrors." Singer stormed out and began to harangue the guests about her, saying "that he was going away, never to return."[60]

After all the flirtations and all the betrayals, Isadora had at last gone too far. She pleaded, but Singer's "curses fell upon my ears with the empty clanging of demon bells."[61] He finally agreed to meet with Isadora only in an automobile, and after berating her, he abruptly opened the door and pushed her out into the night.

This time, Singer meant what he said, and he reinforced his position by immediately leaving for Egypt. Isadora tried to make the best of it, but she was haunted by premonitions of disaster. Soon after, on a tour of Russia, she suddenly saw along the road "two rows of coffins, . . . the coffins of children." She clutched her companion's arm. "Look," she said, "all the children—all the children are dead!"[62] Her companion assured her that there was nothing but snow heaped up alongside the road, but Isadora could not shake the vision.

At the end of that night's performance, she unexpectedly told her accompanist to play Chopin's Funeral March. He protested that she had never danced it. Why now? But she insisted, and after she finished dancing, there was complete silence. Her accompanist took her hands in his, which were icy.

"Never ask me to play that again," he pleaded. "I experienced death itself."[63]

The Théâtre des Champs-Elysées. © J. McAuliffe

CHAPTER FIFTEEN

~

Fireworks

(1913)

On May 29, 1913, Igor Stravinsky's *The Rite of Spring* (*Le Sacre du printemps*) opened to an uproar at the Théâtre des Champs-Elysées, Gabriel Astruc's new theater on fashionable Avenue Montaigne. This new venue itself represented a breakthrough; it was a startlingly clean-lined structure made of reinforced concrete that provided plenty of controversy among the traditionalists. Still, Astruc's provocative new theater offered comfortable seating, clear acoustics, and generally excellent sightlines for the incendiary events to come.

The sculptor Antoine Bourdelle created the decorative friezes for the theater's exterior, including one celebrating a dance between Isadora Duncan and Nijinsky that had occurred only in the sculptor's imagination. Bourdelle had seen Duncan dance at the Théâtre du Châtelet in 1909 and never forgot the experience: "Each movement, each pose of this great artiste remained like flashes of lightning in my memory," he wrote. In his frieze, she leans her head and closes her eyes, to dance "in her pure emotion." As for Nijinsky, whom Bourdelle pictured as the faun, he "wrenches himself free of the marble with a savage movement, . . . but the marble block restrains this man who carries within himself the winged genius of birds!"[1]

Debussy also figured prominently at the new theater, which opened its Ballets Russes season with his ballet *Jeux* (*Games*), exactly a fortnight before Stravinsky's *Rite of Spring*. Unfortunately, *Jeux* was not a success. Stravinsky had been impressed with the music, which he called "Debussy's freshest, most youthful work of recent years,"[2] but audience response was tepid, possibly because of the modernist tilt of the production. The dancers appeared in re-alistic tennis togs rather than exotic costumes, and Debussy's score contained little in the way of traditional tunes and orchestral development (it did not do well even in concert version the following year). Yet to Debussy's way of thinking, it was Nijinsky's choreography that caused the trouble, and there were many who agreed.

Since the beginning of his association with Diaghilev, Debussy—much like Stravinsky—feared that Nijinsky's virtuosity as well as his primacy in Diaghilev's affections would lead to ballets in which the choreography would take a clear precedence over the music. On opening night of *Jeux*, Debussy was so repelled by Nijinsky's choreography that he left his box during the performance to smoke a cigarette at the night porter's lodge. Afterward, Debussy wrote a friend that, in his estimation, the production had been a meaningless event, "in which Nijinsky's perverse genius applied itself to a special branch of mathematics! The man adds up demisemiquavers with his feet, checks the result with his arms and then, suddenly struck with paralysis all down one side, glares at the music as it goes past. . . . It's awful!"[3]

Not surprisingly, *Jeux* marked the end of Debussy's association with Di-aghilev.

⌒

Diaghilev may have been worried about the rest of his season, but he need not have feared. Two weeks after *Jeux*, a seismic event ripped through the Théâtre des Champs-Elysées, creating a *succès de scandale* for Diaghilev and simultaneously making its mark on history.

The Rite of Spring had its origins in a dream Stravinsky had while compos-ing *The Firebird*. He later recalled that he had visualized "a scene of pagan ritual in which a chosen sacrificial virgin danced herself to death."[4] In 1911, after the first performances of *Petrushka*, he planned the scenario for this new ballet with Nicolay Roerich, who also designed the sets. They worked at the country estate of Princess Tenisheva near Smolensk, and then Stravinsky returned to Clarens, Switzerland, where he wrote almost the entire score in a closet-sized room barely big enough to hold a table, two chairs, and a small upright piano. He pushed himself to complete the score, hoping that Diaghi-lev would produce *The Rite of Spring* during the 1912 season; but, much to his disappointment, Diaghilev moved production off to 1913.

Oddly, Stravinsky recalled that he had not anticipated a riot at the first performance, even though Count Kessler recorded in his journal that follow-ing the dress rehearsal the common opinion at a dinner attended by Stravin-sky, Diaghilev, Nijinsky, Ravel, Misia Edwards, André Gide, Léon Bakst, and others was that "tomorrow evening the premiere would be a scandal."[5] In any case, there were rumblings of protest from the evening's outset. Stravinsky claimed he did not notice, having instead been keeping an eye on Debussy and Ravel, "who were not then on speaking terms, and who sat on opposite sides of the house," making it essential for Stravinsky (who wanted to remain on good terms with both) to sit directly behind the conductor to avoid showing partiality. Then, when the curtain rose on "the group of knock-kneed and long-braided Lolitas jumping up and down, the storm broke."[6]

The music, of course, was difficult, with complicated and rapidly changing rhythms and edgy dissonances that easily set unwary musicians adrift. "Everybody was confused,"[7] one of the double-bass players later recalled, and it had taken the conductor, Pierre Monteux, an extraordinary seventeen orchestral rehearsals as well as five stage rehearsals with the dancers to pull it together. Nijinsky's choreography was no less daunting. Advance publicity prepared the audience for a scandal, with Paris newspapers picking up on a press release that promised new thrills and a thoroughly savage evening to come. Yet it was the combination of music, choreography, and the strange appearance as well as movements of the dancers that sent shock waves through an audience well-prepared to be shocked.

The storm began almost immediately, with the opening bars of the prelude, which prompted derisive laughter. Boos and whistles quickly followed, along with raucous animal yelps. Cries of *"Ta gueule!"* ("Shut up!") broke out amid other yells, including one gentleman who erupted with, *"Taisez-vous grues* [whores] *du seizième!"*—a most unlikely slur on the society matrons of the sixteenth arrondissement, some of whom, including the elderly Comtesse de Pourtalès, took such affronts personally. Throughout the hall actual skirmishes broke out, while one gentleman suddenly realized that the man behind him had been pounding steadily on his head in response to the driving beat. Stravinsky was so angry at the outburst that he stalked out, slamming the door behind him. "I have never again been that angry," he recalled. "I loved [the music], and I could not understand why people who had not yet heard it wanted to protest in advance."[8]

Heading backstage, Stravinsky saw Diaghilev flicking the house lights in a vain effort to quiet the hall, and for the rest of the performance the composer stood in the wings, watching the spectacle. He could see Pierre Monteux, "apparently impervious and as nerveless as a crocodile," who somehow managed to bring the orchestra through to the end, while Nijinsky "stood on a chair shouting numbers to the dancers, like a coxswain,"[9] since the dancers could hear virtually nothing above the uproar. Stravinsky, who was holding the tails of Nijinsky's tailcoat, had all he could do to keep the furious choreographer from dashing onto the stage and creating an even bigger mess.

Afterward, according to Jean Cocteau, he and Stravinsky, Nijinsky, and Diaghilev piled into a cab and headed for the Bois de Boulogne. There, by the water, Diaghilev began to mutter Pushkin in Russian amid his tears. Although according to Cocteau, Stravinsky explained the Pushkin quote to him, the composer later said Cocteau's entire account was fictitious. Indeed, according to Stravinsky, Cocteau was not even present, and his story was only meant to make himself look important. What really happened, according to Stravinsky, was that he accompanied Diaghilev and Nijinsky (without Cocteau) to a restaurant, and Diaghilev—far from being in tears—was supremely contented. "Exactly what I wanted," is what he said, fully aware of the publicity value of what had taken place.[10]

Still, one cannot count Cocteau out of any nocturnal gathering of the Diaghilev clan. Count Kessler, who had attended the performance ("A thoroughly new vision," he wrote afterward, "something never before seen, enthralling, persuasive"), wrote that he had taken a late supper at Larue's with the "usual crowd," and then at 3 a.m. he and Diaghilev, Nijinsky, Bakst, and Cocteau "took a taxi and did a wild tour through the city at night, . . . Bakst waving his handkerchief on a walking stick like a flag, Cocteau and I high up on the roof of the automobile, Nijinsky in tails and a top hat, silently and happily smiling to himself."[11]

～

Gertrude Stein and Alice attended *The Rite of Spring* as guests of a friend. It was the second performance rather than the opening night, but—much to Gertrude's pleasure—the audience was almost as raucous as the opening night, hissing or applauding, depending on individual preference. She and Alice heard little or nothing of the music, because "one literally could not, throughout the whole performance, hear the sound of music." As for the dancing, it was "very fine," although their attention was distracted by an altercation between a disgruntled man in the box next to them and an enthusiast in the box beyond that. The first man brandished his cane throughout the performance and finally, enraged beyond endurance, smashed it down on the opera hat the other man had defiantly put on. "It was," Gertrude Stein reported with satisfaction, "all incredibly fierce."[12]

By this time, she was a veteran of explosive events, even if in absentia. That February and March, a mammoth art exhibition in New York's 69th Regiment Armory ignited a major cultural explosion in the art world and, in a curious chain of events, put Gertrude Stein's name in lights. The exhibition, soon simply known as the Armory Show, was sponsored by the Association of American Painters and Sculptors—a loose coalition of people "of varying tastes and predilections," as its explanatory statement put it. Many, including the group's director, Arthur B. Davies, were emphatically traditional in taste, but the group as a whole had decided "that the time has arrived for giving the public here an opportunity to see for themselves the results of new influences at work in other countries in the art way."[13]

The man who ended up having the most say in the show's selection was its secretary, Walt Kuhn, who borrowed unstintingly during a lengthy tour of Europe the year before. In making his choices, he leaned heavily in favor of Paris artists, thanks to the influence of Walter Pach, an American artist and art historian who had lived in Paris and was friend to a bevy of artists there. In the end, Kuhn selected more than thirteen hundred paintings, sculptures, and decorative works by more than three hundred European and American artists, with far more Europeans represented than American. It was a bonanza, and only a huge space could accommodate it. The cavernous Armory at Lexington Avenue and Twenty-fifth Street turned out to be just what the Association needed.

The exhibition's motto was "The New Spirit," and it certainly summed up the show's shattering impact. Public taste could tolerate some of the earlier artists represented (including Ingres, Goya, Delacroix, Corot, Courbet, and Puvis de Chavannes). Even works by Manet, Monet, Renoir, Degas, Mary Cassatt, Rodin, and Whistler no longer shocked. As for the rest, words could not describe the public's disbelief and horror. Cézanne, van Gogh, and Gauguin were bad enough, but what could one say about Kandinsky, Archipenko, and Picabia? Matisse's *Blue Nude* and other works (there were thirteen Matisses in the show) became special targets for wrath and derision, but it was Brancusi's goggle-eyed sculpture *Mademoiselle Pogany* and Marcel Duchamp's Cubist *Nude Descending a Staircase* (famously caricatured as *Explosion in a Shingle Factory*) that became vivid illustrations for what many believed was a major affront to civilization.

By the time the show moved on to the Chicago Art Institute, thousands had visited the New York Armory Show, and the waves of shock kept rippling outward. Thousands more Chicagoans flocked to see this latest example of European degeneracy, and they were just as outraged as New Yorkers by what they saw. Chicago school authorities declared the art "lewd," and the Illinois Senate's vice commission took it upon itself to investigate. Some offended students from the Chicago Art Institute even burned copies of Matisse's *Le Luxe* and *Blue Nude*. By this time, the show had moved on to Boston, and an alarmed Matisse (deemed a major instigator of all this immorality) had begged an American journalist to "please tell the American people that I am a devoted husband and father, with a comfortable home and a fine garden, just like any man."[14]

The Armory Show helped emancipate American artists and prepare the American public, especially collectors, for the future.[15] It also played a major role in launching Gertrude Stein's writing career. Stein's word portrait of Mabel Dodge (which displeased Leo) had overwhelmingly pleased Dodge, who jumped at an opportunity to write an article about Gertrude's work for the *New York Sun* just prior to the show's opening. The editor provided a preface to the article noting that "this article is about the only woman in the world who has put the spirit of post-impressionism into prose, and written by the only woman in America who fully understands it."[16] As a result, Gertrude Stein became known at the same time, and as part of the same tidal wave, that brought Europe's avant-garde artists to the fore of American consciousness. "Everybody wherever I go," Mabel wrote Gertrude excitedly, "is talking of Gertrude Stein!"[17] Gertrude was thrilled by the *gloire*, as she told Mabel, adding that she was "as proud as punch."[18]

Yet if Gertrude was pleased with the publicity, she was less than pleased with Mabel Dodge's love of the limelight ("if Gertrude Stein was born at the Armory Show," Dodge later wrote, "so was 'Mabel Dodge'").[19] Gertrude did not willingly take second place to anyone, and it would not be long before she would shed Mabel Dodge.

⌒

As with any major event, there were winners and losers at the Armory Show. Neither Picasso nor Braque had been well represented there, but at this point neither artist, especially Picasso, needed the Armory Show to further his career. Others, however, did. One of these was Modigliani, who had not even been invited to participate.

By this time Modigliani had labored for several years as a sculptor, but he still had no dealer or collectors. Rodin, as always, took the laurels, but even youngsters like Alexander Archipenko managed to have at least one entry in the Armory Show, while Modigliani's friend Brancusi had five—raising a furor with one sculpture in particular, his marble bust of *Mademoiselle Pogany*, which detractors likened to a hard-boiled egg balanced on a sugar cube.

Soon Modigliani would leave off stonecutting and return to painting, possibly because the dust damaged his lungs but also because of discouragement. Although his surviving sculptures have all skyrocketed in value, they had no buyers at the time. Modigliani, unlike Picasso, was broke.

Fortunately, he was about to find an art dealer, Guillaume Chéron, who would pay him a small but essential regular stipend. Soon after—with the assistance of Max Jacob—Modigliani would find a far more astute art dealer, Paul Guillaume. Guillaume was young and just starting on what would turn out to be a remarkable career (his collection now anchors Paris's Musée de l'Orangerie). He had vision, and he appreciated Modigliani.

With Guillaume's help, Modigliani would at last begin to clamber out of dire poverty.

⁓

Ravel and Stravinsky got to know one other during those heady years of *Firebird* (1910), *Petrushka* (1911), and *Daphnis et Chloé* (1912). They attended each other's openings, listened with interest to rehearsals of each other's music, and became friends. Their relationship became even closer when they jointly accepted Diaghilev's commission to adapt and re-orchestrate portions of Mussorgsky's incomplete opera *Khovantchina* (which was performed at the Théâtre des Champs-Elysées in June 1913, following Stravinsky's *Rite of Spring*).

The two worked together on the project during March and April 1913 at Stravinsky's home in Clarens, Switzerland. It was then that Stravinsky showed Ravel the manuscript of *Rite of Spring*, which prompted an impressed Ravel to write a friend: "I do hope that you will be there [in Paris] for the Russian season. You must hear Stravinsky's *Rite of Spring*. I believe it will be as important an event as the première of *Pelléas*."[20]

While Ravel's relationship with Stravinsky was increasingly warm and cordial, his relationship with Debussy continued to deteriorate. This unhappy state of affairs was aggravated that year when both (without prior knowledge of the other's activities) composed settings for three of Mallarmé's poems, and by coincidence chose two of the same poems (a "phenomenon of autosuggestion worthy of communication to the Academy of Medicine," Debussy remarked). Ravel completed his settings first and received exclusive permission from Mallarmé's son-in-law and executor, Dr. Edmond Bonniot, to use the poems' texts. Soon after, Dr. Bonniot refused permission for Debussy to use the same poems, on the grounds that he had just given the rights to Ravel. "Perhaps the Mallarmé family is afraid Nijinsky will invent some new choreography for these three songs?" Debussy commented acidly.[21]

Ravel and Debussy both had the same publisher, Jacques Durand, who now sent Ravel a "desperate letter." Not long before, Ravel had dived in to defend Debussy from critical attacks on *Images* by retorting in print that the critics had unsuccessfully attempted to turn younger composers "against their revered master [Debussy], and he against them."[22] Ravel immediately intervened in the Mallarmé affair as well, and asked Dr. Bonniot to reconsider, which Dr. Bonniot did. "I have settled everything," Ravel wrote Roland-Manuel in satisfaction.[23]

If Ravel anticipated that the two composers would create entirely different music for these texts, he was right. Ravel's delicate and effervescent settings (which were not performed until early 1914) showed the influence of Stravinsky and, through Stravinsky, Schoenberg's *Pierrot lunaire*. Debussy, who continued to be disturbed by the latest musical developments, nevertheless flirted with atonality in this magical song set, which would turn out to be his last.

⁓

That summer, Marie Curie—her health much improved—went hiking in the Swiss Engadine with Albert Einstein and their respective families. Madame Curie seems to have enjoyed herself, although Einstein found her overly serious.

That same summer, following the death of Picasso's father, Picasso himself became gravely ill with a fever that the doctor was unable to diagnose. It was then that Henri Matisse made the first overture to mend their friendship, frequently coming into town to visit the sick man and to bring him flowers and oranges.

Picasso recovered, and the rivals now were reconciled, with Picasso actually joining Matisse on his daily horseback rides through the woods near Matisse's home in Issy. Picasso was no horseman, and as one Matisse biographer has put it, "this was the equivalent of a public gesture of reconciliation between leaders of two warring countries."[24] The two continued to differ, but in a friendly manner, and now were in a position to compare notes and exchange ideas, much as leaders at an ongoing summit meeting. It was an amazing development, and their friends did not know what to make of it. Yet since Picasso and Matisse had obviously decided to forget the past, their colleagues could no longer regard them as deadly rivals. Instead, they soon would come to view Picasso and Matisse as joint leaders of modern art.

It was around this time that one or the other—no one remembers which—remarked: "We are both searching for the same thing by opposite means."[25]

⁓

In the autumn of 1913, Céleste Albaret—Proust's "dear Céleste"—went to work for Marcel Proust, "the monster of tyranny and goodness" whom she would love, enjoy, and put up with for the rest of his life. How could she have stood it, she was later asked, living only at night and with an invalid? "It was his charm," she replied, "his smile, the way he spoke, holding his delicate hand against his cheek."[26]

Céleste, who would eventually become Proust's housekeeper, first went to work for him as a last-minute replacement to distribute copies of *Swann's Way*, which was published on November 14, 1913. Her husband was Proust's chauffeur, and she was then a very young bride, new to Paris and homesick. Soon Proust (who seemed to understand exactly how she felt) suggested that she come during the late afternoon to cover for his manservant, Nicolas, while Nicolas went to visit his wife in the hospital. By then, Proust would already have had his *café au lait* and croissant that he sent for when he awakened, but a second croissant was always kept ready for his second cup.

Nicolas's instructions to Céleste were precise: If the bell rang twice and the disc for the bedroom turned white (there was a black disc for each room on a wall panel), then she should deliver the second croissant "on a special saucer that matched the coffee cup that would be left ready." In delivering the second croissant, she would see "a big silver tray on the table by the bed, with a little silver coffeepot, the cup, the sugar bowl, and the milk pitcher. Put the saucer with the croissant down on the tray," Nicolas instructed her, "and go." The most important instruction of all, though, was "whatever you do, don't say anything unless he asks you a question."[27]

Céleste waited for several successive afternoons without the bell ringing. Then one afternoon, there suddenly were two rings. She placed the second croissant on the appropriate saucer and headed across the hall and through the big drawing room. At the fourth door, she opened without knocking and pushed aside a heavy curtain on the other side. There, the smoke was so thick that she could scarcely see. "M. Proust, who suffered terribly from asthma, burned fumigation powder—but I wasn't prepared for this dense cloud." She could make out a little light from a bedside lamp, and a brass bedstead with a bit of white sheet. "All I could see of M. Proust was a white shirt under a thick sweater, and the upper part of his body propped against two pillows. His face was hidden in the shadows and the smoke from the fumigation, completely invisible except for the eyes looking at me." Intimidated, she made for the silver tray by the bed, placed the saucer with the croissant on the tray, and bowed toward the invisible face. He "gave a wave of the hand, presumably to thank me, but didn't say a word."[28]

It was only later, when she returned to the kitchen, that Céleste remembered the most striking thing about the room: "It was as if I'd been inside an enormous cork; there were panels of cork nailed everywhere to keep out the noise."[29]

And thus began Céleste's service at 102 Boulevard Haussmann.

⌁

Much to the surprise of Proust's publisher, *Swann's Way* was widely reviewed, for the most part favorably, and the publisher now contemplated a second printing—albeit with trepidation. It had taken five sets of proofs, in addition to galleys and mountains of complicated revisions, to bring *Swann's Way* to press—an editor's nightmare. Once in print, there still were a large number of errors and misprints that, in an odd turn of events, the impresario Gabriel Astruc helped correct for the second printing. Reverting to his early career as a proofreader, Astruc began to make corrections in his personal printed copy. Proust soon learned of Astruc's notated copy and asked to borrow it for the second printing. Astruc somewhat sheepishly agreed.

Yet despite such cheering developments on the literary front, Proust was in a morose mood. He spent December pining for his secretary and former chauffeur, Alfred Agostinelli, who had willingly accepted Proust's many favors but now fled from him, refusing to return. And so, feeling bereaved and misused, Proust sadly occupied himself in typing the second volume of his tome,[30] naming the girl who would become the unattainable object of the Narrator's desire Albertine.

Early on, Proust had decided on the name "Guermantes," and was relieved to discover that the last Comte de Guermantes had died in 1800, making the name available for fictional use. As for Proust's Duchesse de Guermantes, his primary model appears to have been the Countess Greffulhe, who stood at the pinnacle of Belle Epoque Parisian society, where she dispensed favor and largesse as a leading patron of the arts.[31] Proust had first glimpsed Elisabeth, Countess Greffulhe, during the early 1890s, when he led an active social life and ardently aspired to associate with members of the highest Parisian society ("his 'camellia button-hole' period," he later called it, adding that even his own mother "couldn't have introduced me into that sort of society").[32] The Countess Greffulhe was still in her young thirties and of impeccable social lineage. She also was rich—married to the Belgian banking tycoon Henri Greffulhe. More than this, she was beautiful, believed by many to be the most beautiful woman in Paris. After finally catching a glimpse of her at a ball, Proust wrote the Countess's cousin, the extravagantly refined Count Robert de Montesquiou: "The whole mystery of her beauty lies in the brilliance and especially the enigma of her eyes. I have never seen a woman so beautiful."[33]

Countess Greffulhe, 1907 (oil on canvas), by Philip Alexius de Laszlo. Private Collection / The Bridgeman Art Library. © The Bridgeman Art Library.

Proust was dazzled by the Countess Greffulhe in much the same way that Proust's Narrator idolizes the duchesse de Guermantes, following her on walks in the hope of encountering her. Yet in both the story and in real life, Proust and his Narrator learn that the woman they worship is far from a goddess. Apart from her great wealth, cultivation, and social position, she turns out to be unexpectedly ordinary and even vulnerable.

Paul Poiret, whose ego was second to none, saw only the arrogance that he in turn may well have provoked. "I did not know that you were capable of making a dress for a great lady," the Countess Greffulhe disdainfully told him after he dressed her to her satisfaction (in gold and ermine) for her daughter's wedding. "I thought that you only knew how to dress midinettes [seamstresses] and hussies."[34]

Yet Count Kessler saw something else. After witnessing a strained encounter between the countess and her husband, he asked why Rodin had never done a portrait bust of her. "Because my husband has never had the notion of having anything done of me," she replied. "I am the wife of a very rich man," she added, "but I have never considered his fortune as mine. I have a house and as long I will be there, I will be there. If ever I would lose it, I would have nothing." When Kessler asked if there were no paintings or pictures of her, she replied that there was "a pretty good photograph, taken last year in Brussels," but added, "No, nothing will remain of me." Kessler noted that "her voice was quite cold, but you sensed the fate beneath the words."[35]

It was a year of physical and financial challenge for a number of Paris's most prominent citizens. Sarah Bernhardt returned early in the year from her sad American tour and subsequently appeared on her own stage in a suitably moving role as the suffering mother in *Jeanne Doré*. It was a success, but a bittersweet one; the aging star was in pain, and it would be her last appearance in a full-length play.

Gabriel Astruc did not have much time to enjoy the successes of his Théâtre des Champs-Elysées: financial problems forced him to vacate in November the theater he had opened with such high expectations that spring. Filmmaker Georges Méliès also was broke and deeply in debt to Pathé. As if life had not dealt him enough blows, his wife now died, leaving him with a young son to raise. And Debussy, desperate for funds to pay for his sick mother's care as well as to maintain the lifestyle to which he and his family had become accustomed, wrote his publisher that he was "paralysed with worry. You can't possibly envisage the hours of torment I'm going through at present! I promise you, if my little Chouchou weren't here I'd blow my brain out, as stupid and ridiculous as that might be."[36]

On a happier note, late in the year the *Mona Lisa* unexpectedly came to light, in Italy. The thief, an Italian house painter who had been living and working in Paris, contacted a leading Florentine art dealer to request a substantial sum of money for living expenses, although he claimed that his real motive had been to return the painting to Italy. (The fellow was confused about the painting's provenance, having mistakenly thought that Napoleon had plundered it, when in actuality, France's King François I had acquired it legitimately some three centuries earlier.)

And how had the thief done the impossible? It had been easy, he told the judge. Having worked for the company that had the job of placing the *Mona Lisa* under glass, he had ample opportunity to see how the painting was hung and to become known to staff members. These recognized him when he appeared several months later in his work smock, even though he was not in fact employed at the Louvre at the time.

Slipping into the Salon Carré early one Monday morning, when the Louvre was closed to the public, the fellow waited until the guard disappeared, unhooked the *Mona Lisa* from the wall, and took off down an interior staircase. There he removed the lady from her frame, stowed her beneath his smock, and left. Despite all the theories that the French police had entertained for more than two years, the *Mona Lisa* had spent almost her entire absence in the thief's humble Paris apartment in the tenth arrondissement, wrapped in red silk and carefully stowed in the false bottom of a battered trunk.

All of France celebrated, especially when Italy agreed to return the lady to the Louvre. As for the thief, he went to jail, but only briefly. After serving in the Italian army during the war, he unaccountably returned to Paris. There, he opened a paint store.

～

In addition to battling a lingering illness early in the year, Rodin faced the challenge of mending some badly broken relationships with friends and family once Claire de Choiseul finally disappeared from his life. In particular, he returned to Rose, "the poor little flower of the field," as he called her, "which I almost crushed."[37] He also took it upon himself to improve relations with his son, Auguste Beuret, whom he had supported financially but always kept at a distance, never agreeing to recognize him—a situation that was deeply painful to Auguste, who worshiped his father. Auguste's financial need and illnesses had become pressing, and Rodin finally invited him and Auguste's longtime mistress to live at Meudon. There, the two lived under an assumed name in a house that Rodin provided, while Auguste (who showed significant skill as an artist in his own right) was classified and paid as an engraver, in addition to working as a guard.

Yet other shadows from the past continued to haunt Rodin. In March, following the death of Camille Claudel's father, who had provided her with financial and emotional support, Claudel's brother had her committed to an insane asylum. There (despite her doctors' reluctance, but in accord with her mother and brother's insistence), she would remain for the rest of her long life. Rodin tried to visit this former student and lover—a significant artist in her own right who had played such a vital part in his life—but Claudel's mother and brother managed to sequester her from receiving visits or mail from any but themselves. (For the record, her brother rarely visited, and her mother never came.) Eventually, Rodin would find a way to send her money (to provide "some comfort until she gets out of this hell"),[38] but in a more meaningful gesture, he promised to try to set aside a room for her work in the future Musée Rodin. Claudel's mother and brother were adamantly opposed to having her work shown, and so she never learned of this tribute. It was not until long after her death, when Paul Claudel donated four major works by his sister to the Musée Rodin, that Rodin's request could be honored.

～

While Rodin was working to mend the broken or frayed relationships in his life, Diaghilev's relationship with Nijinsky was rapidly deteriorating. After their final split, Nijinsky wrote that he had "begun to hate [Diaghilev] quite openly," and that Diaghilev had even hit him with his cane "because I wanted to leave him."[39] Diaghilev's appearance and age now repelled the much younger man, and Nijinsky claimed that he even took to locking the door of his hotel room to keep Diaghilev out. By summer, despite Diaghilev's attempts to hide the fact, his affair with Nijinsky had ended.

What came next, though, was a complete shock. The company departed on a scheduled tour of Latin America without Diaghilev, as planned (he was terrified of sea voyages, having once been told by a fortune-teller that he would die on the water; as it happened, he died in Venice). On shipboard, Nijinsky attracted the attention of Romola de Pulszky, a fledgling ballerina from Hungary who had taken classes with the Ballets Russes dancers and joined the company on its Latin American tour. They soon were seen everywhere together, but no one thought anything of it; despite some bumpy times, everyone assumed that Nijinsky still was Diaghilev's lover. But Nijinsky—or at least Romola—had other ideas, and a few days after landing in Buenos Aires, the two were married.

Nijinsky's mother was furious that her son had not sought her permission nor even informed her of his impending marriage. Diaghilev was almost hysterical with grief and rage. According to Misia (who was with him at the time he learned the news), he was "overcome with a sort of hysteria, ready to go to any extreme, sobbing and shouting."[40] And then he did what he could to avenge himself: he fired Nijinsky.

Nijinsky seems to have been floored by this response. He wrote Stravinsky, begging him to intercede with the irate impresario. Diaghilev "owes me a lot of money," Nijinsky pleaded. "For two years I wasn't paid anything at all for my dancing or for the new productions of *Faune* and *Jeux* and *Sacre*. I was working without a contract." Of course, as Diaghilev's lover, he had wanted for nothing. Yet now he had "lost everything."[41] It never had occurred to him that Diaghilev could do without him, whether as dancer, choreographer, or lover.

Change was everywhere. The last of the horse-drawn omnibuses now disappeared from the Grands Boulevards, taking an era with them. The skirts of women's day dresses, unlike the ballooning skirts of the recent past, had become so tight that they revealed the outlines of the thighs. And the automobile, only recently a new-fangled invention, had become a necessity—as was that intruder on private life, the telephone. Abbé Mugnier, who had managed to recover the social life he feared he had lost, marveled at the usefulness of automobiles and other inventions in connecting him with his many friends and acquaintances. "Ah, what a life is mine!" he exclaimed. "A life of automobiles and of pneumatics. A life of luncheons and of dinners."[42]

By early 1913, Lili Boulanger—dressed as fashionably as ever—once again was hard at work in preparing compositions for her end-of-semester exams at the Conservatoire, as well as preparing two works for performance. In March, she took time out to rest, but by April she was once again at work, preparing for the Prix de Rome competition. Her teacher, Paul Vidal, again reported on her extraordinary talent, but noted that most unfortunately she still suffered from poor health.

That May, Lili left Paris to go into seclusion in the Château de Compiègne for the first, or elimination, round of the Prix de Rome competition. Each of the thirteen contestants was required to compose an orchestrated chorus and fugue within strict constraints. The judges dictated the fugue's subject and the chorus's words, which were kept secret until announced to the contestants. Once given their musical challenge, the contestants were kept under strict surveillance, to ensure that they did not communicate with each other or with anyone outside, even their families.

Six days later, Lili submitted her composition, which won her entrance (with four others) to the next and final round, which required the composition of a cantata in the space of one month. As Lili and her fellow competitors once again went into seclusion, the press took due note of the fact that a woman (and the sister of a previous prize-winner) had made the cut. She was six years younger than the next-youngest contestant, and the only one who had never before competed in the final round. On June 5, she learned the results. She had done it. She was the overwhelming winner of the Prix de Rome for music, having received thirty-one out of thirty-six votes. It took the judges only forty-five minutes to reach their decision.

It was a stunning victory. At the age of nineteen, Lili Boulanger had become the first woman to win the Prix de Rome. And she had demolished the competition.

～

Back in Paris following her latest tour of Russia, Isadora Duncan continued to have premonitions of tragedy. She felt as if she was living "under a strange oppression," and one night, awakening with a start, she saw "a moving figure, draped in black, which approached the foot of the bed and gazed at me with pitiful eyes."[43] The figure vanished when Isadora turned on the light but reappeared at intervals.

On the doctor's recommendation, Isadora temporarily moved with the children and their governess to Versailles. It was while she was staying there that Singer unexpectedly returned and asked that she lunch with him and bring the children. She was delighted, and the four had a festive lunch at an Italian restaurant. After that they returned to her studio in Neuilly, where she planned to rehearse while the children and their governess went back to Versailles, so the children could rest.

Isadora's studio was located only a few hundred yards from an intersection with the boulevard that ran beside the Seine. By this time it was raining, and the chauffeur who was driving the children to Versailles had to brake hard to avoid a collision at the river's edge. At this, the car stalled, and the chauffeur got out to crank the engine. Afterward he insisted that he had left the car with the parking brake on and the gear in neutral, but when the engine started, the car shot forward across the boulevard, over the embankment, and into the river.

Several workmen at a nearby café responded to the cries for help, notifying the nearby fire brigades and diving into the water, but it was of no use. It took an hour and a half to locate the submerged automobile and haul it to shore. By that time Isadora's two children and their governess were long dead.

It was a tragedy beyond belief, and Isadora's life would never again be the same. For the moment, she was in complete shock. "Our little girl Deirdre was taken from us today without suffering," she telegrammed Craig in Florence. "My boy Patrick is taken with her," she added. "This sorrow is beyond any words."[44] She later wrote that "ever since then I have had only one desire—to fly—to fly—to fly from the horror of it, and my life has been but a series of weird flights from it all, . . . and all life has been to me but as a phantom ship upon a phantom ocean."[45]

Rebelling against what she called "the mummery of what one calls Christian burial," she had but one wish, "that this horrible accident should be transformed into beauty. The unhappiness was too great for tears."[46] In response to her ardent request, her brothers and sister surrounded the children with mountains of flowers, and students from the Ecole des Beaux-Arts brought armfuls of white blossoms. Refusing to put the children into the ground "to be devoured by worms," Isadora insisted on cremation—a controversial decision at the time, but the closest she could come to Byron's act of "burning Shelley's body on the pyre by the sea."[47]

Count Kessler represented Gordon Craig at the funeral service, which took place in Isadora's Neuilly studio. He brought, at Craig's request, two tiny bunches of flowers—two sprays of white lilacs to place on the white coffins. Afterward he wrote that he had "never seen a more moving ceremony. The absolute absence of words, of all the dreary, hypocritical jabbering of ordinary funeral services, did a great deal, and then the exquisite taste in the choice of music."[48] He added, "Everyone in Paris is moved to the depths of their hearts."[49]

Everyone, that is, except for a distasteful group who viewed the tragic events with a certain satisfaction, having construed the children's deaths as retribution for the regrettably immoral life of their mother.

⌒

That June, Bulgaria launched an attack on Greece and Serbia, in an attempt to even the territorial grab that its former allies had made in Macedonia. Soon Turkey and Rumania joined the fray, and—suddenly and unexpectedly surrounded—Bulgaria agreed to peace negotiations. The new treaty ending this second Balkan War rearranged the map of the Balkans, but managed to dissatisfy just about all the participants as well as some noncombatants, chiefly Italy. It did not bode well for the future.

It did, however, leave a wretched group of refugees, especially in Greece and Albania, and soon after the deaths of Isadora's children, she left Paris for Corfu, where her brother Raymond had established relief efforts during the first Balkan War. "It is terrible to see the results of war," she wrote Craig in late May. "If we can save some hundreds of little children I will say Deirdre & Patrick are doing it for me."[50] She later wrote, "We returned to our camp weary, yet a strange happiness crept into my spirit. My children were gone, but there were others—hungry and suffering. Might I not live for those others?"[51]

Yet by late July, she could not bear to "look at all this misery" any longer and returned to the empty house in Paris, where she fell into fits of weeping.[52] Distraught, she left Paris and drove alone across the Alps to Italy, where she joined Eleonora Duse, who helped her through her grief. "For the first time since [the children's] death," Isadora later wrote, "I felt I was not alone."[53]

With Duse's encouragement, Isadora found the courage to return to dancing. She also encountered a handsome young Italian sculptor with whom she had an affair. When she returned to Paris, it was to the promise of a new school: Singer had bought a large and beautiful mansion for her in Bellevue, on the outskirts of Paris, which she began to transform into a Temple of the Dance of the Future. She also returned to the promise of another child: thanks to her Italian lover, she was pregnant.

∽

Early the previous year, after two and a half years of virtual silence, Georges Clemenceau once again became politically active, helping to overthrow yet another government and bring in that of Rodin's friend, Raymond Poincaré.

Poincaré's election in early 1913 as president of the Republic put in place a man of firm convictions and wide experience—a man of center-right and increasingly conservative politics who was a lawyer, an economist, a former finance minister, prime minister, and foreign minister. He also was a man who was determined to make the office of the president as powerful as it once had been under Marshal MacMahon during the Third Republic's early days. In particular, Poincaré intended to dominate foreign policy, which meant a policy guided by suspicion of and antagonism toward Germany—a position he shared with Clemenceau, who otherwise intensely disliked him.

Under Poincaré's stewardship, French nationalism continued its rise, with public opinion siding decisively with the new Three-Year Law that extended the period of obligatory military service (aimed at raising an army comparable in size to Germany's). Patriotism had by now replaced pacifism, and increasingly bellicose nationalist demonstrations formed in Paris around the black-swathed statue of Strasbourg (the city lost to Germany in 1871) in the Place de la Concorde.

It was against this background that the French army engaged in its annual military maneuvers, which seemed to serve little purpose except to keep its soldiers occupied. Certainly these maneuvers (like their German counterparts, in which Count Kessler took part in late July) were no secret, especially as those that autumn involved the deployment of virtually the entire French army in an area near Toulouse. It was all very dignified and disciplined, with umpires declaring entire platoons eradicated and gun batteries wiped out. The German emperor even wrote the president of France that he was pleased the exercise had gone so well.

Yet in the background, the threat of real rather than mock warfare was growing, and to those who were watching carefully, it was clear that this would be a different kind of war from any that had gone before. Germany's General Staff still viewed aircraft as useful only for reconnaissance, but by 1913, the German War Ministry began to increase its contracts for aircraft, narrowing France's lead. The French army, too, was at first reluctant to consider using aircraft either for pursuit or bombardment. Nonetheless, Gabriel Voisin's factory already was shifting its manufacturing and sales toward supplying France's military, and the 1912 Voisin airplane, which its maker praised as "unequalled for observation," was about to become "the first of all the fighting aircraft."[54]

Crowd acclaiming the departure of the troops, Paris, 1914. Jacques Moreau / Archives Larousse, Paris, France / Giraudon / The Bridgeman Art Library. © The Bridgeman Art Library.

CHAPTER SIXTEEN

~

"Dear France, dear country"
(1914)

"It is pure delight for a soldier to see the national idea come into being, grow and increase on the field of battle," extolled a certain Captain H. de Malleray in 1905, on pilgrimage to the great medieval battle-site of Bouvines. "Dear France, dear country," he added, "you will doubtless live through some grave times."[1]

Grave times indeed were coming, but few Parisians in early 1914 seemed to sense this. In late spring, Georges Clemenceau told an American journalist that despite his drumbeat of editorials warning of the German threat, the readers of his newest newspaper, *L'Homme Libre*, "scoff at talk of war." He added, "Paris is gay, elegant, luxurious. . . . Paris is now the important place for unimportant things."[2]

As always, scandal ranked high in interest, and Henriette Caillaux's March assassination of Gaston Calmette, editor of *Le Figaro*, created a tidal wave of compelling reading. Calmette, during the course of his stormy career, had taken on Sergei Diaghilev and avant-garde morality, as well as the current minister of finance and former prime minister Joseph Caillaux, a powerful politician whom Calmette had accused of financial as well as marital irregularities. As leader of the Radicals (leftist republicans), Joseph Caillaux had long favored a policy of conciliation with Germany and, correspondingly, opposed the Three-Year Law, the highly popular extension of military conscription. He also staunchly advocated the conservatives' nightmare, an income tax, which now loomed (essentially in exchange for the Three-Year Law). For all these reasons, the conservative press, led by *Le Figaro*, heatedly and even libelously attacked him from 1913 through early 1914 as France's willing betrayer to socialism and to Germany. Yet it was the publication of letters from Henriette to Caillaux, while both still were married to their previous spouses, that tipped the balance. Rather than allow her second husband to challenge Calmette to a duel, Henriette took it upon herself to deal with the editor. Entering Calmette's *Le Figaro* office swathed in a fur coat and a muff, she pulled out a pistol and shot him.

The scandal was delicious, especially when Madame Caillaux was brought to trial for murder. Powerful members of the French political elite headlined the proceedings, which resulted in Madame Caillaux's acquittal—on the grounds that, as a woman, she had been unable to control her emotions in a crime of passion. It was not an outcome that feminists could cheer about, but Henriette Caillaux seems to have made no complaints.

As it happened, on June 28, the day that she was acquitted, a Serbian nationalist assassinated the Austrian archduke Franz Ferdinand and his wife in Sarajevo. The archduke was heir apparent to the Austro-Hungarian throne, but he was not especially well known in France—thus allowing news of Madame Caillaux's acquittal to eclipse this particular item, at least in Paris. There had been Balkan crises galore in recent years, all of them resolved or at least papered over. What could one more amount to?

⁓

Proust, who had dedicated *Swann's Way* to Calmette, was devastated by the news of his death—and equally devastated by the news of Madame Caillaux's acquittal.[3] For years Proust had assiduously courted Calmette, who was ready enough to socialize with the aspiring writer but (presumably engaged in more important matters) never bothered to acknowledge the dedication.

On the other hand, André Gide had experienced a dramatic change of heart about *Swann's Way*, writing apologetically to Proust: "For several days I have not put down your book; I am supersaturating myself in it, rapturously, wallowing in it." He even confessed that "the rejection of this book will remain the gravest mistake ever made by the NRF—and (for I bear the shame of being largely responsible for it) one of the most bitterly remorseful regrets of my life."[4] Gide proceeded to offer publication in the *Nouvelle Revue Française* for the next two volumes of what Proust then envisioned as a trilogy.[5] By this time, Proust's publisher, Grasset, had realized his client's worth and made a calculated bid to keep him, even while telling him that he was "free to choose." Morally as well as contractually bound to Grasset, Proust opted to stay with him, but on somewhat more favorable terms than originally.

Proust now was dealing with extremes in happiness and grief, for the object of his desire, Agostinelli, had recently crashed and died while taking flight lessons. By early June the *Nouvelle Revue Française* was publishing excerpts from Proust's upcoming volume, but Proust was too devastated by Agostinelli's death to care. As he told Gide, "I don't know how I can endure such grief."[6]

～

While Henriette Caillaux was capturing headlines, Isadora was hard at work starting up her new school at Bellevue, where by late spring she had admitted about twenty students. She also permanently moved her six best dancers (the so-called Isadorables, now in their teens) to the new location, where they served as dance instructors. There, her students' Friday afternoon performances attracted, among others, her near-neighbor Rodin as well as Jean Cocteau and Gordon Craig's famed mother, the actress Ellen Terry. On June 26, her students performed at the Trocadéro, while Isadora—now eight months pregnant—remained hidden from view. "I believed," Isadora later wrote, "that this school at Bellevue would be permanent and that I should spend there all the years of my life, and leave there all the results of my work."[7]

In late spring, Gertrude Stein also was making satisfying progress with her career, having published *Tender Buttons* with a small New York press that, most fortunately, had little interest in profits and, in its own words, specialized in "New Books for Exotic Tastes." The publisher's enthusiastic promotion touted Gertrude Stein as "a ship that flies no flag and . . . is outside the law of art, but she descends on every port and leaves a memory of her visits."[8] Reviewers split between those who regarded *Tender Buttons* as a revolutionary breath of fresh air and those who regarded it as nonsense (one reviewer said "he felt as if an eggbeater had been applied to his brain").[9] A slim book of prose poems divided into three sections (Objects, Food, Rooms), *Tender Buttons* has been described as the literary version of Cubism, especially in Cubism's later stage of synthesis or, more familiarly, collages. "I was very much struck at this period," Gertrude Stein later wrote, "with the way Picasso could put objects together and make a photograph of them. . . . To have brought the objects together already changed them to other things, not to another picture but to something else, to things as Picasso saw them."[10]

By this time, Leo and Gertrude Stein had definitively parted company, with Gertrude feeling spurned and badly used and Leo feeling morose but immeasurably superior in all ways, especially in intellect. Both claimed a need for independence. Yet although there was no explosion accompanying Leo's departure, they would not speak to one another again.

Leo left for Florence, and the two divided their paintings between them. Gertrude took the Picassos (except for the drawings, which went to Leo), while Leo claimed the Renoirs. They divided the Cézannes—although Leo expressed a particular wish for the Cézanne apples ("I'm afraid you'll have to look upon the loss of the apples as an act of God," he told her). Leo kept Matisse's *Joy of Life*, while Gertrude got Matisse's *Woman in a Hat*. Leo concluded his proposal with the patronizing comment, "I hope that we will all live happily ever after and maintain our respective and due proportions while sucking gleefully our respective oranges."[11]

Shortly before his own death, Leo took pains to refute the story that there had been a feud or quarrel between them. "We never quarreled except for a momentary spat," he wrote. "We simply differed and went our own ways."[12]

⁓

Amid his journal entries for numerous luncheons and dinners, Abbé Mugnier, back in the social whirl, noted on June 29, "Yesterday, the Archduke of Austria and his wife were assassinated."[13] The American writer Edith Wharton, who now was living in Paris, observed that "a momentary shiver" ran through the members of a garden party she was attending when the news broke. "But to most of us," she added, "the Archduke Ferdinand was no more than a name." Although one or two elderly diplomats shook their heads solemnly, "the talk wandered away to the interests of the hour, . . . the last play, the newest exhibition, the Louvre's most recent acquisitions."[14]

During the month that followed, the enormity of the crisis that this assassination unleashed was not yet clear, especially to the average Frenchman. Helen Pearl Adam, a British journalist then working in Paris, wrote in her diary for July, "In 1914, the people of France had decided that it could not be bothered with politics."[15] Still, by late July, Edith Wharton noted, "Everything seemed strange, ominous and unreal, like the yellow glare which precedes a storm,"[16] and Abbé Mugnier was writing of "grave rumors of war unleashed by the rupture between Austria and Serbia. If Russia defends its Slavic brothers against Austria, will not France be pulled in?"[17]

Austria had decided that the assassination of its heir apparent provided sufficient provocation and opportunity to swallow Serbia, much as it had swallowed Bosnia and Herzegovina only a few years before. Earlier that month, Germany had assured Austria of its support, if indeed Russia decided to defend its Slavic brothers. On July 28, Austria declared war against Serbia, and it began its attack on the following day. Russia immediately mobilized along its Austrian frontier, eliciting a German ultimatum. The French had already promised Russia to fulfill its treaty obligations by intervening militarily if Germany supported Austria-Hungary. Suddenly, all hell was about to break loose.

Jean Jaurès, the great socialist leader who had long worked for peace, had warned that in case of war, Germany was prepared to use its demographic advantage to the utmost, overwhelming France with sheer manpower. He was due to attend a conference of the International in early August, where he dearly hoped to persuade the belligerents to back down. But on July 31, as he sat in a café on Rue Montmartre, a twenty-nine-year-old French nationalist, Raoul Villain, shot and killed him.[18] Jaurès's assassination did not trigger a revolt by the workers, as France's leaders initially feared, but it did remove a powerful voice on behalf of peace—which was what his assassin intended.

At noon on Saturday, August 1, Germany's ultimatum to Russia expired in the face of Russian silence. At five o'clock, the Kaiser decreed general mobilization. Would France stay neutral in a Russo-German war? France had treaty obligations as well as self-interest to consider. That afternoon, France also declared mobilization, to begin at midnight. Bands played the Marseillaise, and a crowd tore the black mourning off the statue of Strasbourg in the Place de la Concorde. "Vive la France!" reverberated throughout the land, along with "Vive l'Alsace!"—in memory of the bitter defeat of 1871.

Misia Edwards rejoiced with other Parisians at the news. Caught up in the frenzy of excitement, "everybody kissed, sang, cried, laughed, trampled each other, hugged each other," she later recalled. "We were filled with compassion, generosity, noble feelings, ready for any sacrifice, and as a result of it all, wonderfully, unbelievably happy."[19] Yet Helen Pearl Adam reported that an hour after the first notice of mobilization was posted, "there were already groups of men with bundles on their shoulders marching to the railway stations," and "groups of weeping women everywhere."[20] Jules Bertaut, who lived through it, recalled that "as the evening drew on, Paris became calmer and graver. Shops put up the shutters which in many cases were not to be taken down for four years; uniforms that had not seen light for years appeared on the street; men linked arms and embraced each other, while others marched in slow file side by side. Passing by doors in quiet streets you could hear the sound of sobbing inside."[21]

In Brittany, at Sarah Bernhardt's vacation home of Belle-Isle-en-Mer, Sarah's granddaughter, Lysiane, made the rounds (in Sarah's car) to post the mobilization orders at nearby villages. "At each hamlet our appearance spread consternation," she later wrote. "The men shook their heads solemnly. The women crossed themselves and wept." Sarah herself, when she heard the news, could only exclaim, "Two wars in one lifetime! And to be able to do nothing: to be old and ill!"[22] Paul Poiret recalled that the taciturn men in the Brittany village where he was holidaying resolutely called to one another, as they returned from their fields: "Very well, then, we shall go and see him, [Kaiser] Wilhelm."[23]

"I still hope, non-believer though I am," Proust told a friend, "that some last-minute miracle will prevent the launching of the omni-death-dealing machine."[24] But as Count Kessler noted in his journal, "The storm is coming."[25]

⌒

While Europe was poised on the brink of war, Isadora Duncan was holed up in the elegant Hôtel de Crillon on the Place de la Concorde, where she awaited the birth of her child. It was hot, and she had her windows open. "Beneath my windows," she later wrote, "they were calling the news of the mobilization. . . . My cries, my sufferings, my agony were accompanied by the rolling of the drums and voice of the crier."[26]

She went into labor on August 3, as Germany declared war on France. Her doctor had been called up, and she spent the day in increasing agony, going from clinic to clinic in search of a responsible medic who could attend her childbirth. Finally, in despair, she headed back to Bellevue (passing through a military blockade en route). At the last minute a satisfactory doctor was found, who arrived in time to deliver the child—a boy, who did not live long enough to be named. As Isadora lay in her room she could hear "hammer-taps closing the little box which was my poor baby's only cradle." These sounds "seemed to strike on my heart the last notes of utter despair."[27]

Had she any sense, she later wrote, she would have remained at Bellevue and dedicated herself to Art. Yet, swept along with the fervor of those around her, she gave Bellevue to the Dames de France to use as a military hospital. "My Temple of Art was turned into a Calvary of Martyrdom and, in the end, into a charnel-house of bloody wounds and death."[28]

Then, like many other well-to-do Parisians, she escaped beyond the war zone to Deauville and the sea. Soon after, she left for safety in New York.

⌒

Anticipating war, in late July Count Kessler sent his mother and sister to safety in England. He, though, promptly returned to Berlin, where he took up his commission, ordered and purchased field equipment—boots, coat, and a revolver—and went to requisition horses.[29] Huge crowds of boys and girls were forming in the city, he noted, singing patriotic songs.

On the morning of August 1, Kessler wrote that "the uncertainty weighs, heavy and sultry, on the mood." Yet late that afternoon, when the German mobilization was announced, "the sultry pressure gave way, and a cool determination took its place." That night, the square in front of the palace was filled "by a mighty crowd of people" singing "Deutschland, Deutschland über Alles" and "The Watch on the Rhine," waving their hats.[30] He was well aware that the coming war "will be frightful, that we will suffer perhaps occasional setbacks," but he trusted that "the qualities of the German character—dutifulness, seriousness, and stubbornness—will in the end bring us victory." Everyone, he added, understood "that this war must result in Germany's world domination or its ruin. Since Napoleon there has been no gamble its like."[31]

⁓

Abbé Mugnier was not sleeping well, remembering the horrors of the Franco-Prussian War. Were times like that returning? And what, if anything, had the Church done to prevent them? "Nothing," he concluded morosely, noting the zeal expended on rites rather than on Christian charity. "Thou shalt not kill," he wrote in his journal, adding sadly that it becomes natural to kill thousands of people for a just cause. Yet was there a cause sufficiently just to be worth so much bloodshed?[32]

By the time he wrote, the blood had already begun to spill. On August 4, Germany crossed the frontier of neutral Belgium in the first stage of its Schlieffen Plan. This called for brazenly wheeling five German armies on a northern arc through Belgium, with the goal of quickly outflanking and destroying France's armies, grouped (as was expected) on France's eastern and northeastern frontiers, and laying siege to Paris. The Belgians unexpectedly put up a fight, but the French refused to come to their aid. Instead, the French followed their plan (initiated by General Ferdinand Foch and approved by France's commander-in-chief, General Joseph Joffre) to free Alsace and continue eastward across the Rhine to Berlin—a plan that led it directly into the German trap.

The French assumed that their offensive would be supported by a huge Russian advance from the east, as well as by aid from Great Britain, which had entered the war following Germany's violation of Belgian neutrality. Defense did not figure in France's plan; taking the offensive (the more spirited the better) was everything. As for defending the exposed portion of the Belgian frontier, it did not appear in French military options, even though an officer in the German General Staff had, years before, slipped an early version of the Schlieffen Plan to the French. As late as August 18, the French General Staff still firmly believed that "if the Germans commit the imprudence of an enveloping maneuver through northern Belgium, so much the better! The more men they have on their right wing, the easier it will be for us to break through their center."[33]

∼

Picasso and Juan Gris were Spanish nationals and noncombatants, but they were among the few of their age group to continue their lives as artists during the war. Picasso, who remained neutral during the conflict, saw Braque and Derain off at the station, but their eagerness to join the fight repelled him. Afterward, he said that he never saw either of them again—factually inaccurate, but metaphorically sound. Afterward, their relationship never was the same.[34]

Georges Braque became a sergeant in the infantry and was commissioned a lieutenant that December. André Derain, Maurice de Vlaminck, and Fernand Léger all were mobilized, while Apollinaire, although still a Polish subject, volunteered to join the French army. Swiss-born Blaise Cendrars and Polish-born Moïse Kisling joined the French Foreign Legion, while Russian-born Ossip Zadkine became a stretcher-bearer. The Norwegian artist Per Krohg joined a volunteer ambulance corps of Norwegian skiers for mountain fighting in the Vosges.

Cubism itself joined the military, in the form of camouflage. The French soon established a Section de Camouflage, headed by the painter Lucien-Victor Guirand de Scévola, who later commented that "in order to deform totally the aspect of an object, I had to employ the means that Cubists used to represent it."[35] One of this section's members was the Cubist painter Jacques Villon, who along with his brother, Marcel Duchamp, had exhibited at the famed New York Armory Show.

All the participants in the war quickly learned the importance of camouflaging airplanes, trucks, and gun positions (the latter, by using painted canvas tarpaulins), which became necessary to protect against the new threat of aerial reconnaissance. The British painted their ships in the disruptive Dazzle pattern, while the Germans were inspired by a range of modern artists (one German noted that the tarpaulins he painted to hide artillery emplacements "chart a development 'from Manet to Kandinsky.'")[36] In addition to the growing sophistication of French camouflage efforts, the French also reluctantly replaced their beloved but easily targeted army uniforms of baggy red trousers, red caps, and blue jackets with somber gray-blue uniforms.[37]

Matisse, despite his age (forty-four), was eligible to be called up, like other Frenchmen between the ages of eighteen and forty-eight. Prepared to leave for the front, he even bought himself a pair of army boots. But age and a weak heart put an end to this determined expression of patriotism. A second attempt to enlist brought the same results.

Among composers, Satie, at the age of forty-eight, served as a corporal in the local militia of Arcueil, while Debussy (fifty-two and ill) expressed his envy. "I'm nothing more than a wretched atom hurled around by this terrible cataclysm," he wrote Jacques Durand, "and what I'm doing seems to me so miserably petty! It makes me envious of Satie and his real job of defending Paris as a corporal." Still, despite his age and complete lack of military aptitude, if one more body was needed to ensure victory, "I'll offer mine without hesitation."[38]

Meanwhile, Maurice Ravel (thirty-nine) was going through agonies over his determination to serve his country. As a young man he had been exempted from military service due to frail health; but now that his brother Edouard and "virtually all of his friends" had enlisted, Maurice wanted to serve. Still, he was torn, largely because he felt responsible for his aged and ill mother. To one friend, he wrote: "If I leave my poor old mama, it would surely kill her. Moreover, France isn't waiting for me in order to be saved. . . . But that's all rationalization, and I feel it falling apart from hour to hour . . . and to hear no more of it, I'm working."[39] Finally, he wrote his brother, "As I felt I was going to go crazy, I took the wisest course: I'm going to enlist."[40] In the meantime, he frantically tried to finish his Trio before signing up, and managed to do so by August 7—completing in five weeks "the work of five months."[41]

Ravel was a small man and, much to his disappointment, the army medics found him underweight by about four pounds. Nevertheless he planned to apply again, this time among those previously rejected. If he didn't succeed at that, he planned to "try to finagle something when I return to Paris."[42] Yes, he told a friend, he was well aware that he was "working for the fatherland by writing music! At least, I've been told that enough times in the past two months to convince me of it; first to stop me from signing up, then, to console me for being rejected." This had little effect: "They didn't stop anything, and I'm not consoled." In the meantime, he served as best he could by caring for wounded soldiers where he then was located, in Saint-Jean-de-Luz. "The number, if not the variety of needs which forty gentlemen can have in the course of one night is incredible!"[43]

Dr. Robert Proust, Marcel Proust's brother, was among the first to be called up. To his family's dismay, Dr. Proust—who had become a distinguished surgeon—requested that he be sent to the front. When Marcel accompanied

Robert to the Gare de l'Est at midnight on August 2, he realized that he was sending his brother into the gravest of danger, even though the destination itself had not yet entered public consciousness. Dr. Robert Proust had been assigned to a place named Verdun.

Proust, by now a chronic invalid and exempted from military service, watched his friends disappear into the army or into a variety of service efforts and organizations. His dear friend Lucien Daudet, who had been declared unfit for army duty, was assigned to the Red Cross. Jean Cocteau, also classified as unfit for duty, decided to become a male nurse at the front—snappily dressed in a uniform designed by Paul Poiret. Poiret, in turn, left his fashion house for the war's duration, sent his family to Normandy for safety, and went to help streamline the army's uniform production.

Virtually everyone except for Rodin initially thought that the war would be over before Christmas. Yet by late August, the French army had been sufficiently pounded that, despite heavy censorship, the public's initial euphoria was shaken. Hundreds of Belgian refugees began to arrive in Paris, and soon the first German plane flew over the city, dropping bombs and killing or wounding several civilians. More bombers followed, prompting an enforced nighttime blackout.

Restaurants and theaters closed, and the Grand Palais (along with numerous schools and hotels) was turned into a hospital. The government moved to Bordeaux, and the streets of Paris acquired a sad and empty look, especially at night, when "the hush became acute."[44] Helen Pearl Adam, who stayed in Paris with her husband (a correspondent for *The Times*), wrote that the city had become strangely quiet, especially at night, when "almost the only sound heard was the curious note of the claxons of the Red Cross cars bearing wounded from the distributing stations in the suburbs." By the third week in August, she wrote that Paris was sweltering, "the streets were empty, and half the shops were shut. . . . One could have dined in the middle of the Place de l'Opéra. Every theatre and cinema was shut."[45] "Things aren't going very well," Marie Curie wrote her daughter Irène from Paris in late August.[46] Already, there was talk of a siege of Paris.

With the closing of so many hotels, restaurants, shops, and workrooms following the massive exodus of men into the army, equally vast numbers of women and children were left without means of support. In response, the government took the important step of paying a separation allowance to every needy family throughout France whose head had been mobilized. The amount was not large, but it was meaningful, and it may well have made the difference in bolstering the will of the French in holding out for what turned out to be more than four harrowing years.[47]

Private charities also played a large role in bolstering the home front. Edith Wharton immediately opened a workroom for unemployed Parisian seamstresses, and then she began the enormous job of helping to care for the French and Belgian refugees that were pouring into the city. Soon her workroom had about sixty women, and her American Hostels for Refugees would become even more extensive, including numerous houses and apartments throughout Paris, a lunchroom, a place for grocery and clothing distribution, a free clinic, coal delivery, day care for small children, classrooms, and even an employment agency. Within its first year, the American Hostels for Refugees provided lodging for thousands of refugees—supported by donations solicited by committees in America and Paris. In addition, Wharton's Children of Flanders Rescue Committee would soon be caring for more than seven hundred children, plus many elderly, in empty houses in Normandy and on the outskirts of Paris. Wharton also launched appeals for the victims of tuberculosis, which was on the rise, and opened fresh-air TB sanatoriums for refugees and soldiers. "I have plunged into work," she wrote her good friend, the art historian Bernard Berenson, on August 22.[48] On September 2, she wrote another friend that the stories of German atrocities were all true, and that "it is to America's interest to help stem this hideous flood of savagery. . . . No civilized race can remain neutral in feeling now."[49]

Soon Misia Edwards—who thrived on being at the center of things—took charge of one particularly useful effort, that of bringing first aid to the wounded at the front. Knowing that most of the fashion *couturiers* had virtually shut up shop for the war's duration, she persuaded them to donate their delivery vans, which she turned into ambulances. She then obtained authorization from the military governor of Paris to form a convoy of these ambulances to bring aid as close to the front as possible. Her tour of duty began in a burned-out railway station, where she attended to men so horribly burned that there was virtually nothing left of their faces. Her second outing, to Reims, brought her along a road "littered with the bodies of dead horses, fragments of men and animals thrown into the air by the explosions and remaining hanging on the branches of trees."[50]

Appalled by what she had seen, Misia was relieved to bow out gracefully after a short spell, gifting her fourteen vehicles to the Empress of Russia. In the meantime, the Red Cross amply filled the breach, and Marie Curie had begun to apply the results of her work on radium to treating the wounded at the front.

∼

From the outset, Marie Curie had no illusions: "What a massacre we are going to see," she wrote Irène, who remained (unwillingly) with her sister in their holiday cottage in Brittany. "What folly to have allowed it to be unchained!"[51] Yet despite her dread of what was coming, Marie Curie was committed to contributing to her adopted country.

She wanted to keep her children in relative safety in Brittany, but as for herself, she opted to remain in Paris—in large part to keep watch over her new research laboratory, jointly established by the Pasteur Institute and the University of Paris. In particular, she wanted to watch over the laboratory's valuable supply of radium, which Marie soon transported (in heavy lead casing) to safer quarters in Bordeaux.

Irène (who turned seventeen in September) was especially determined to return to Paris, since she felt useless and deprived of news in Brittany. "I understand now the difficulty that historians must have in establishing the facts," she wrote her mother, "when one can't even know what is happening at this very moment."[52] She was not alone in this complaint; wartime censorship in France was severe, not only for military information of possible value to the enemy, but for any information that might weaken morale at home. As a result, Swiss newspapers enjoyed a loyal readership among French cognoscenti, including Marcel Proust, who asked Céleste to take Le Journal de Genève regularly. Because of the censorship, he told her, it was the "only . . . paper now that is well informed."[53]

Still, only a small proportion of Parisians had access to this source of information, and according to French historian Jean-Jacques Becker, "there is no doubt that by leaving it in ignorance of the gravity of certain military defeats, of diplomatic failures and of the horrors of the war, censorship went a long way towards helping the French civilian front to stand firm."[54]

The Curies certainly were standing firm. By early autumn Irène and her sister, Eve, joined their mother in Paris, and Irène now took a nursing course so she could help her mother in her daring new venture of bringing X-rays to wounded soldiers at the front. It was a brilliant idea: equip regular automobiles with everything necessary to produce X-rays (the automobile engine, hooked to a generator, provided the power), thus creating highly mobile units. Soon, funded by generous individuals as well as by organizations such as the Patronage des Blessés [wounded] and the Union des Femmes de France, Marie Curie eventually had twenty such "little Curies." In addition, she would soon establish about two hundred permanent radiology posts as well as set up a school to train nurses as technicians.

The Battle of the Marne, in early September, became a turning point for her: as she saw the casualties inundating Paris hospitals, she became acutely aware of the necessity of bringing X-rays to the wounded at the front. The Battle of the Marne would in fact constitute a turning point in the entire course of the war—but not in the way that people first expected.

~

When war broke out, Monet made it clear that he intended to remain at Giverny. "I'm staying here," he wrote Gustave Geffroy, "and if those savages insist on killing me, they'll have to do it in the midst of my paintings."[55]

Unlike Monet, few who had a choice opted to stay in or even near Paris: during the war's early days, the city was almost emptied of those who could afford to leave and had a safe place to go. Helena Rubinstein sailed for New York, leaving her husband and two sons to pack up the valuables and follow. Gertrude Stein and Alice B. Toklas continued on in the English countryside, where they had been since July. Rodin and Rose left for England, where they stayed until November, when the prospect of an English winter drove them south to Italy (which had side-stepped its treaty obligations with Germany and Austria and, much to France's relief, declared itself a neutral). There, Rodin wanted to do a bust of the pope, although mainly he wanted to avoid the war. Finally, Rose's deteriorating health brought them back to Paris—although Rodin would make another Italian visit in the disappointing attempt to create a portrait bust of the Holy Father.

Anna de Noailles and her family (along with the French government) headed to Bordeaux, while Proust, along with Countess Greffulhe and her aesthetic cousin, Count Robert de Montesquiou, withdrew to Cabourg, on the Norman coast. There, surrounded by much of the same society they had frequented in Paris, they prepared to sit out the war. Proust (now largely recovered from his grief over Agostinelli) remained closeted in his hotel room, catered to by Céleste, while the great society ladies amused themselves with the latest in fashions. This meant Coco Chanel, who seemed to float with the tide, opening shops in Deauville[56] and Biarritz even while Paul Poiret and other leading designers were having to reduce or close their businesses in Paris. All the fashionable women who had retreated to these resort towns found Chanel fashions chic but sufficiently informal and adaptable to just about any circumstance, from fleeing the enemy to driving a car.

Anna de Noailles, Proust, and others would return to Paris once the imminent danger of enemy occupation subsided, but still others, such as Marc Chagall, could not. A great event in his life, his first solo exhibition, had drawn him to Berlin; from there he traveled to Vitebsk, where he married his beloved Bella—over the strenuous objections of her parents ("You'll starve with him, my daughter; you'll starve for nothing"). He was madly in love

("She seemed to float over my canvases for a long time, guiding my art"),[57] but once war broke out, he found himself stuck in Russia. Called up for military duty, he managed to serve in a military office in St. Petersburg rather than going to the front. It was a safe existence, at least for the moment, but soon life would become infinitely more precarious for him and countless other Russians.

While Gertrude Stein and Alice roamed the English countryside, Michael and Sarah Stein were enduring a major loss, albeit not in human life. They had loaned nineteen of their finest Matisses for a Berlin exhibition, which were promptly confiscated when Germany declared war on France.[58] Also in Berlin (for an air show) when war broke out, the renowned French pilot Roland Garros made a daring escape in his monoplane. He promptly flew to France, where he immediately enlisted.

⁓

On August 5, Lieutenant Charles de Gaulle wrote in his private journal: "Goodbye, my rooms, my books, my familiar objects. How much more intense life does seem, and how the smallest trifles stand out in relief when perhaps everything may be coming to an end."[59]

General Charles Lanrezac, commander of France's Fifth Army—of which Lieutenant de Gaulle's 33rd Infantry Regiment (RI) was a part—had little respect for France's military plan of action, including its underlying premise that a bold offense, fired by will and confidence, would inevitably lead to victory. "Are we to attack?" he commented contemptuously. "Then let us attack the moon!"[60] Soon after the outbreak of war, in response to his own reconnaissance reports of massive German forces coming through Belgium, he tried in vain to alert headquarters to the danger. Headquarters, still persuaded that the principal German attack would not come from the north, finally tried to fob him off by allowing him to shift his left corps (the Fifth Army's First Corps) to Dinant, a strategic river crossing in Belgium, on the River Meuse. When Lanrezac protested that his entire army should be shifted to the northwest, to prevent being encircled by the Germans, he was promptly denied.

So it was that Lieutenant Charles de Gaulle, now responsible for the 1st Platoon in the 11th Company of the 33rd Infantry Regiment's 1st Battalion (in turn part of the Fifth Army's First Corps), marched eastward from Arras toward the mountainous and heavily forested Ardennes. Lanrezac's army, most especially its First Corps, was on a collision course with hefty German forces intent on using the River Meuse as an entry into France. On August 13, with a German spotter plane watching overhead, de Gaulle and his fellow soldiers entered Belgium. On August 14 and 15 (as he later wrote from his hospital bed), "everyone feels we are going into battle, but everyone is determined and in high spirits." After a fifty-mile night march they entered Dinant, where the exhausted men fell asleep in the streets. And then, at six in the morning, "boom! boom! the music begins."[61]

The enemy soon seized the citadel that commanded the town and opened heavy rifle fire. Soon after, the first French wounded began to come in—at first a trickle, then a flood. The French artillery were not answering (indeed, had not yet arrived), and now the 11th Company, including de Gaulle's platoon, was ordered to go in with bayonet (and without artillery cover) to prevent the Germans from taking the bridge. "I shouted 'First platoon, advance with me!'" de Gaulle recalled, "and I raced forward, knowing that our only chance of success was acting very fast." But he had only advanced about twenty yards "when something struck my knee like a whip-lash," and he fell, with his sergeant on top of him, killed outright. He heard "an appalling hail of bullets all round me," and managed to extricate himself from his neighbors, "corpses or little better," and crawled along under a hail of bullets. Somehow, limping "and in a bad way," he dragged himself to the bridge, where he gathered together "what was left of the regiment in Dinant."[62] By night, some of the residents of Dinant removed the wounded in carts, and de Gaulle got into one of them. His entire company had been decimated. He would not see the ghastly German execution of more than six hundred men, women, and children of Dinant that followed.

De Gaulle was evacuated to Arras and then to Paris, where he was operated on. There, while recuperating, he wrote his account of the battle, including this dramatic conclusion, which represented a complete turnaround for him: "It is clear," he wrote, "that all the courage and valour in the world cannot prevail against gunfire."[63]

⁓

Everything continued to go badly for the French throughout the month of August. France's high command could no longer ignore the Germans' rapid advance through Belgium and into France, and after a series of disastrous encounters, the French, now joined by their British allies, were unable to prevent the Germans from pushing as far as Senlis, less than thirty miles from Paris. By August 29, gunfire "was audible in Paris."[64] It was a terrifying development, whose import the Germans had underscored by burning, massacring, and pillaging all along the way.[65] Paris, and all of France, awaited their arrival with terror and despair. The Germans had already spread the word that entire quarters of Paris might well be destroyed in the course of their invasion. The streets of Paris emptied, shops shuttered, and any remaining tourists vanished, leaving even the Ritz deserted.

The Allies had failed to stop the German onslaught—their efforts to shift the entire battle map westward to halt the Germans were too late, and now all that was left was the supreme effort to fight in retreat, hold off pursuit, and, ultimately, protect their armies from destruction.

Gathering its armies in retreat, France's high command prepared to make its last defense at the Seine. On September 3, the newly appointed military governor of Paris, Joseph-Simon Gallieni, issued a notice to the citizens of Paris that the Government of the Republic (ingloriously decamped to Bordeaux) had given him the mandate "to defend Paris against the invader," a mandate that he intended "to carry out to the end."[66] This included, as last resort, dynamiting the many bridges and other strategic structures at the city's periphery and center, including even the beloved Pont Neuf and the beautiful new Pont Alexandre III.

In addition, citizens previously not eligible for military duty were set to work erecting barricades across all entries to the city, including the sewers. Ammunition was stockpiled; bakers, butchers, and market gardeners were organized; cattle were brought to graze in the Bois de Boulogne. Among those senior citizens who did their part was Squadron Chief Alfred Dreyfus, now almost fifty-five and only partially recovered from his horrendous (and horrendously unjust) imprisonment on Devil's Island. Despite his remaining infirmities, Dreyfus returned to active service on behalf of his city and country. Although he requested assignment to the combat zone, he was at first assigned to the entrenched city's Artillery Staff.

According to the Schlieffen Plan, the Germans could count on victory over France between the thirty-sixth and the fortieth days following mobilization. It was on the thirty-fourth day, September 3, that a French reconnaissance plane definitely confirmed scattered reports of a gap that had opened in the German line as German General von Kluck, previously on a southward course toward Paris, swung southeast toward the River Marne in pursuit of the retreating French, exposing his flank. Soon a second French airplane confirmed the first report, followed by a third from British aviators. Suddenly, there was hope.

Without hesitation, Gallieni decided that now was the moment to launch an attack on the flank of the German right wing, and he successfully pressured the French high command to seize the opportunity. The Germans—whose troops were hungry and exhausted—were convinced that the French did not have it in them to mount a counteroffensive. French troops, who had been fighting and retreating for days, were as exhausted as the Germans.

Nevertheless, as Commander-in-Chief Joffre put it, the "supreme moment" had arrived. "Gentlemen," he told his assembled officers, "we will fight on the Marne."[67]

The French poured everything into this battle, including the six thousand reinforcing troops that six hundred Paris taxis rushed to the front—each taxi proudly carrying five soldiers and making the sixty-kilometer trip twice. The bloody battle that followed turned the tide and put an abrupt halt to German assumptions of a quick victory.

Yet as it soon became clear, the Battle of the Marne stopped short of achieving victory for France and its British ally. This and subsequent battles held the German line, but they did not extricate the Germans from Belgium or from the industrial heart of northern France. By year's end, the rival armies had dug in, confronting one another from opposing trenches along a front that stretched from Switzerland to the Channel.

Still, without anticipating the horrors that lay ahead, the Battle of the Marne figured as a miracle for the French. Like a bolt from heaven, the German juggernaut had been halted, and Paris was saved.

Gertrude Stein was not the only one who, on hearing news of the battle's outcome, wept with relief and joy.

Artists in the camouflage section painting a cannon (on the left, the painter Jean-Louis Forain) at Sailly-au-Bois (Pas-de-Calais), 1914–1915. Photo: Pascal Segrette. Musée de l'Armée, Paris, France. © Musée de l'Armée / Dist. RMN–Grand Palais / Art Resource, NY.

~

CHAPTER SEVENTEEN

"This war which never ends"

(1914–1915)

French casualties in the month of August 1914 alone (including those killed, wounded, and missing) reached more than two hundred thousand, and probably came closer to three hundred thousand. One French eighteen-year-old who was not mobilized due to illness found that by Christmas he was the only one of his class of twenty-seven boys who was still alive.[1]

By autumn, there was enough grief to touch virtually every household in France, and Paris's notables suffered with the rest. Clemenceau's son was wounded in August, while Renoir's two oldest sons, Jean and Pierre, were wounded in October. Jean Renoir was wounded again the following spring, this time more severely, and then became a reconnaissance pilot.

Monet, who had recently lost his wife and eldest son (who died early in the year after a long illness), now faced the uncertain fate of his younger son, Michel. Despite being declared physically unfit for military service, Michel nonetheless volunteered and soon would serve in active combat at Verdun.

Escoffier's younger son, Daniel, was killed in action on November 1, leaving four children whom his parents took in and raised. André Citroën's beloved brother, Bernard, died that October while trying to rescue a wounded comrade under fire, receiving a posthumous Croix de Guerre for his bravery. The poet Charles Péguy died in action, shot in the forehead the day before the Battle of the Marne. The painter Moïse Kisling was shot in the chest, and his fellow artist Georges Braque received a severe wound to the head and was left for dead after leading his platoon over the top. Found the next day by stretcher-bearers, Braque was trepanned in a field hospital and sent to Paris, where he remained blinded and was given little chance of surviving.

French and Belgian casualties included whole towns destroyed in the path of the German advance. The burning and sack of the medieval Belgian town of Louvain, including its irreplaceable library, aroused global disbelief and anger, as did the destruction of the treasured cathedral of Reims, which the Germans shelled in September, following the Battle of the Marne. "Oh, God!" wrote Ravel to Maurice Delage upon learning the news. "When I think that they just destroyed Rheims cathedral!"[2] Rodin was similarly despairing, and Debussy angrily wrote a former pupil, "I won't get on to the subject of German barbarity. It's exceeded all expectations."[3]

For the moment, Debussy found it impossible to compose, even though he and his wife had evacuated Paris for Angers. "Anyway," he added to Jacques Durand, he didn't "want this music played until the destiny of France is decided: she can't laugh or cry while so many of our men are dying heroes' deaths!"[4] It would be many months before Debussy would be able to compose again.

∿

By year's end, Paris had become a much sadder and quieter place, and the entire city appeared to be in mourning. Everyone wore black or the darkest blue, even those who had lost no one—yet.

Living in the apartment beneath Helen Pearl Adam were two elderly women from Normandy who, between their two families, had already lost fourteen dead plus twenty-six wounded and missing. And yet, Adam noted, "a lame sort of life goes on, with an air of wishing to be taken for normal."[5] Some department stores and a few luxury shops remained open, and the cinemas had recently reopened; but most theaters remained closed, except for special matinees to benefit war charities. All public buildings, including the museums, were closed, with the exception of the newly opened war museum at the Invalides, where crowds gathered to see trophies such as an airplane propeller or a collection of German helmets. Omnibuses were nonexistent (they would not run again until 1918), and although the Métro and the commuter boats still ran, it was on an erratic schedule. Food remained plentiful, but the prices for food and fuel had soared, causing considerable anxiety.

Stricter orders about lighting came in January 1915, and with the resulting complete blackout, streets at night were dark. "The physical beauty of the town is quite startling," wrote Adam, noting the more visible night sky. "The sky seems to have more colours, the night more stars than ever before." The Etoile district was "almost empty," she continued, except for hospitals and a few workshops. Without its "maddening glitter of lamps," the Place de la Concorde seemed "absolutely vast," capturing the imagination like never before.[6]

Entertaining simply was not done, "and if any one played the piano, protests were certain to be made by passersby against such frivolity."[7] Still, there were an abundance of canteens, where good, cheap meals were served and where, once a week, a musical and dramatic program might be given, usually by some of those very musicians and performers benefiting from the inexpensive meals.

Probably the most famous of these canteens was the one run by a former student of Matisse's, Marie Vassilieff. Aware that those artists who remained in Montparnasse were suffering as the art market dwindled and stipends dried up or failed to arrive, Vassilieff in early 1915 opened a canteen in her studio in the impasse at 21 Avenue du Maine. Vassilieff furnished her canteen with flea market finds and decorated it with paintings and drawings by Chagall, Modigliani, Picasso, and Léger, as well as sculptures by Zadkine. Somehow, with only a couple of burners, Vassilieff's cook made hearty meals for as many as forty-five hungry artists, who paid a pittance for soup, meat, vegetable, and salad or dessert. Saturdays featured planned concerts, but impromptu concerts frequently broke out throughout the week as the artists entertained one another.

Some of the larger restaurants remained open, but they were restricted to serving meals of only two courses. They struggled on, with greatly reduced staff and clientele, and were required to close by 10:30 p.m.—startlingly early by Paris standards. When Edith Wharton joined friends for a dismal dinner at the Ritz, they all had to sit on the same sofa to keep warm, while "a ghost of a waiter in a long apron shuffled up and down the endless empty vista of the hall."[8]

Absinthe was banned (by an overwhelming vote in the Chamber), leaving cafés as well as their clientele in the lurch. Women stopped buying clothes—many would wear the same clothing throughout the war—and an aura of dedication to troops and country pervaded the entire city. Most women and girls knitted or had some kind of work always at hand, and almost every street had a hospital, a workroom, and a storehouse of necessities for the combatants or their families.[9]

Parisians subscribed readily to that year's National Defense Loan and became accustomed to following the weather closely for the front, learning that too much rain prevented fighting, and too much wind hindered aerial observation. Wounded soldiers walked the streets, creating murmurs of sympathy as they passed. Jules Bertaut noted that "in the poorer parts of the town, the people would hang around all night, women with children in their arms, sitting on the ground, waiting for news, leaning against the walls, passing round rumours and airing their grievances." Yet there were "no general agitations, no outbursts, hardly a voice raised." Amazingly, for a city with as volatile a history as Paris, "the most catastrophic disasters were received silently and without public demonstration." Paris, and the nation, had realized that "the war had come to stay for a very long time."[10]

⁓

With the outbreak of war, François Coty—who had been placed in the active army reserves following his youthful years of obligatory military service—now rejoined his 19th Infantry Regiment of Ajaccio (Corsica). Like the rest of the French army, he soon found himself in the trenches. Yet by year's end he managed to extricate himself from this hellhole, on grounds of a worsening eye condition. He promptly returned to his headquarters in Suresnes, just outside of Paris, where he had left affairs in the capable hands of his mother-in-law, Virginie.

Since the war's outbreak, France's economy had quickly focused on wartime production, resulting in a scarcity of supplies for nonessentials such as perfume. Still, the prospects for purveyors of luxury goods remained relatively bright—at least for someone like Coty, who even in the midst of war saw opportunities for a "merchant of dreams."

Despite the dearth of supplies, Coty managed to double his wartime business, largely by packaging high-quality cosmetics, especially his "air-spun" face powder. By late 1914, Coty was selling thirty thousand compacts of this face powder daily to Americans alone—a huge market, and an especially important one now that European markets were suffering. His magnificent Coty Building on Fifth Avenue, with its Lalique-embossed windows, became the anchor for an international empire—one that shrewdly evaded heavy American duties for imported luxury goods by shipping its products in "detached pieces." This meant that from 1915 on, all Coty boxes, empty bottles, stoppers, and raw materials were shipped separately. A Coty specialist then manufactured Coty perfumes under license. The outcome was an enviable 60 percent profit margin for Coty, even during the height of war.

Coty was not the only Parisian-based businessman who profited during—and from—the war. André Citroën (newly married to the daughter of an Italian banker) entered the war as captain of the 2nd Heavy Artillery Regiment, stationed in the Argonne area on France's eastern border. There, as both sides dug in along the western front, he witnessed the French army's severe shortage of artillery and, even more critically, artillery shells. Not only were the French heavily outgunned, but (according to Citroën's estimates) they were within a few weeks of exhausting their stocks of shells.

The French government had hastily converted factories such as Renault's automobile firm and Citroën's gear company to produce munitions, but with the huge mobilization and consequent shortage of workers, these small factories could not produce nearly enough. Early in 1915, Citroën proposed that, given government backing, in four months he would build and equip a new kind of munitions factory, one that would dramatically increase the number of shells produced for the French army.

The government was interested, and—having been granted a leave of absence from the army—Citroën got to work. Funded by a large government contract, he designed and rapidly constructed a massive factory complex on thirty acres of land along the Quai de Javel (now the Quai André-Citroën), at Paris's southwest extremity. There he applied the scientific methods of production he had so admired at Henry Ford's plant in Michigan. Using the latest American machines and methods, Citroën followed the path of Ford and Frederick Winslow Taylor in organizing a self-sufficient factory with assembly-line production methods. Within two months the plant was sufficiently finished to begin production, and the entire complex was completed by June. By August, production was soaring, and soon the plant would be producing fifteen thousand shells a day (a total of almost twenty-three million shells by the war's end).

Although by now many men had been brought back from the front to work in munitions factories, there still was a shortage of manpower. Citroën consequently turned increasingly to women for his labor force, and by 1918, women constituted almost half of his twelve thousand workers. Unlike many of his peers, Citroën also provided significant worker benefits—a major factor in stabilizing production. He particularly grasped the importance of providing a support system for his women workers, covering pregnancy, birth, and paid leave while nursing, as well as providing an on-site nursery and kindergarten.

This, in addition to providing subsidized shops (a butcher, a baker, and a dairy), subsidized canteens, a medical and dental clinic, plus good ventilation and clean restrooms throughout, made Citroën's factory complex a reasonably attractive place to work, despite the stress of wartime production demands. Factories such as Citroën's typically went full tilt around the clock, with eleven-hour workdays (including one hour for a meal break) and no rest days or holidays except for Christmas. This was war, and although Citroën was unquestionably progressive and the wages he paid were attractively high, the work was demanding and relentless. It also was tedious. Each worker carried out her task again and again, for as many as five thousand times a day. Their individual tasks may not have been arduous, but the monotony of assembly-line production could quickly become mind-numbing.

⟵⟶

Louis Renault had little in common with André Citroën. Renault was fundamentally a mechanic who had become a businessman, while Citroën—although a product of the Ecole Polytechnique—was a businessman with an understanding of mechanics. He also was an attractive man who knew how to use his charm and who thoroughly enjoyed the social whirl. Renault, who was intensely private, abhorred socializing and detested publicity stunts, at which Citroën would prove increasingly adept. Renault also took pride in refusing to borrow even a sou. Citroën, however, borrowed without qualms for his escalating projects, both private and commercial.

Most critically, though, Renault differed from Citroën in his relation to his workers: whereas Citroën had readily introduced widespread social services for his workforce and encouraged group discussions between workers and their employer, Renault staunchly resisted such an approach. "The management of a firm," he commented, "should have nothing to do with social organizations."[11] Not surprisingly, by this time Renault was finding it difficult to maintain the convivial relations he had enjoyed with his workers during his enterprise's early days. Regarded as strict, albeit fair, he balked at discussing workers' grievances and maintained a stern and completely arbitrary order. As one man noted, after leaving Renault's firm for Citroën's: "I found I had left an Empire for a Republic."[12]

Both men had made their fortunes before the war even began: after all, the six hundred taxis that had raced reinforcement troops to the front during the Battle of the Marne had been Renaults, and Citroën had become wealthy with his management of the Mors auto company as well as with his original gear factory. At the war's outset, Renault had been supplying the French army with airplane engines for several years. He continued to do this, but by the early weeks of the war, the war ministry asked him to dedicate part of his automobile factory to the production of artillery shells. Other automobile makers were told to follow suit, and soon they formed a syndicate. It was now that Renault found himself working with André Citroën.

Renault later claimed that he paid little attention to Citroën at the time, except to note that Citroën had obtained a substantial government contract and that he produced his shells in large numbers using the Taylor method. Whether or not this was all he noted at the time, Renault certainly would have the opportunity to observe Citroën with considerably more care by the war's end.

⌒

Early in the year, the French Red Cross asked Edith Wharton to report on the needs of military hospitals near the front, and for several months she visited the front lines, her car "laden to the roof with bundles of hospital supplies." Given permission to visit "the rear of the whole fighting line, all the way from Dunkerque to Belfort," and even visiting some frontline trenches, she observed conditions, delivered medical supplies, and made it her business to find out what the troops needed.[13] At Châlons, where there were nine hundred cases of typhoid, she reported that "*everything* was lacking," and after emptying her car of supplies, she promised to return the next week with more. From there, she headed for Verdun, where "they said it was impossible—but the Captain had read one of my books, so he told the Colonel it was all right." The colonel replied, "Very well, but make it fast, for there is big fighting going on nearby." After several close encounters, she concluded that she intended to return in several days "with lots of things, now that I know what is needed." On subsequent journeys, which took her even closer to the fighting, she reported feeling "in the very gates of Hell."[14]

While trench warfare continued to chew up lives at an appalling rate, significantly worsened by the Germans' introduction of poison gas in April 1915, the fledgling battle in the air was beginning to open up a new dimension in warfare. At first limited to reconnaissance duties, airplanes soon took on a fighting mission with the discovery of a way to fire a machine gun through an airplane propeller—without, of course, shattering the wooden propeller.

During the war's early days, pilots and observers had armed themselves with rifles and pistols, and they had additionally made use of whatever was at hand, including bricks, darts, grenades, and even grappling hooks. Yet given the odds of hitting a moving target with any of these objects, or even with a rifle or pistol, the most practical approach remained the machine gun. By the end of 1914, machine guns were installed on the noses of French pusher aircraft, such as the Voisin III, where the propeller was safely in the rear. One daring pilot even mounted a machine gun on the top wing of his aircraft (this cool-headed fellow managed to clamber back into the cockpit and right his plane after the gun's weight flipped his airplane upside down).

In March 1915, Roland Garros, who had made a name for himself by flying across the Mediterranean and subsequently escaping from Berlin, got to work on the problem with Raymond Saulnier, and ended by attaching wedge-shaped metal deflectors on the propeller blades. Although this did not entirely eradicate the problem (deflected bullets could damage the plane or the pilot), Garros returned to the front in late March 1915 with a machine gun attached to his monoplane. During the next three weeks he proved a terror in the skies to opposing Germans, downing three German planes and achieving legendary status.

Then on April 18, German ground fire forced Garros down behind enemy lines. The Germans rushed his propeller to Anthony Fokker's factory, where the Dutch aircraft designer looked it over and improved on it, adding synchronization to the machine gun to prevent bullets from hitting the propeller blades.[15] The introduction of Fokker's Eindecker monoplane in July 1915 changed air combat, as German pilots began to shoot down Allied planes in what quickly became known as the "Fokker Scourge." By late in the year, the Germans had achieved air superiority, and the first German ace pilots, most notably the "Red Baron" (Manfred von Richthofen), now took to the skies.

⌒

Maurice Ravel wanted to fly. The romance of flight had captured his imagination, and although he harbored no hopes of becoming a pilot, it had become his dearest wish to serve his country by becoming a bombardier. In the spring of 1915, he managed to enlist in the 13th Artillery Regiment, and he promptly requested a bombardier appointment. Much to his disappointment, it was not granted. When, many months later, he received his assignment, it was as a truck driver—a far cry from what he had dreamed of. Still, Ravel was extremely proud of his new duties, signing his correspondence to friends, "Conducteur [Driver] Ravel," and naming his truck Adélaïde.[16]

In the meantime, a surreal calm had fallen over Paris. The French government returned from Bordeaux late in 1914, and a small portion of the city's social and artistic life correspondingly revived, but with marked restraint. The city was under blackout by night, as a precaution against air raids, and everyone kept one eye on the war—or at least on what they could learn of it from rumors, gossip, and heavily censured news reports.

Gertrude Stein and Alice returned from England in October 1914, where they tried to pick up where they had left off. Gertrude later claimed that she enjoyed wandering around the half-empty city, mostly because it was "wonderfully nice" simply to be in Paris.[17] And then one night in March 1915, Gertrude awakened Alice and whispered for her to come downstairs. Alarmed, Alice wanted to know what was happening, but all Gertrude could tell her was that she had been working in her studio (she usually wrote at night) and had heard an alarm. When Alice started to turn on a light, Gertrude stopped her. After all, Paris's military governor had issued strict orders requiring blackouts at night. "Give me your hand," she told Alice, "and I will get you down and you can go to sleep down stairs on the couch." Petrified, Alice followed, and just as she was settling down, they heard "a loud boom, then several more." After a bit, horns sounded, "and then we knew it was all over" and went to bed.[18]

Not long afterward, Gertrude and Alice experienced another bombing alarm, this time while Picasso and Eva were dining with them. By now the two women had learned that their small atelier offered no more protection than the little building where their bedroom was located, and so they all joined the concierge in her room, where they had six stout stories above them. It seemed a reasonable precaution, but soon they all got bored and went back to the atelier, where they lit a candle under the table so that it would not make much light. Eva and Alice tried to sleep, while Gertrude and Picasso talked until two in the morning, when the all clear sounded and the guests went home.

"It was not a very cheerful winter," Gertrude Stein concluded, and by spring she and Alice were ready to go away and "forget the war a little."[19] They left for Majorca, which pleased them so much that they remained there through the following winter. To raise funds for the journey, Gertrude sold her only remaining Matisse—the glorious *Woman in a Hat*—to her brother Michael for four thousand dollars.

⁓

Along with Gertrude Stein and Alice B. Toklas, Matisse returned that October to Paris, where he found his house occupied by French soldiers, along with signs of German shelling all around his Left Bank studio on the Quai St-Michel. He had left his family in the south of France, along with Juan Gris, who as a Spanish national had not been mobilized but whose income had vanished with the war. Gris's art dealer, the German Daniel-Henry Kahnweiler, had departed for Switzerland, and without the small monthly income that Kahnweiler provided, Gris was destitute. Matisse offered to find sponsors in Paris and persuaded Gertrude Stein (who in the past had bought several Gris paintings) to make a small monthly allowance to Gris. Matisse later learned that she went back on her agreement—a possible misunderstanding on his part, but a disappointment that added one more ice cube to the already-chilling relations between Matisse and Gertrude Stein.

October also brought Marcel Proust back to Paris, where he received news of his brother's heroism: Robert had managed to keep his field hospital in full operation while under enemy fire. He "goes out of his way to seek danger," Proust wrote a friend, and "is now in the Argonne, and gives me great concern."[20]

Proust returned to his writing, but now without a publisher; his publisher, along with many others, had ceased publication for the war's duration. It would be several more years before the second volume of Proust's novel (titled *A l'ombre des jeunes filles en fleurs*, or *In the Shadow of Young Girls in Bloom*) would appear,[21] and by then Proust had taken the opportunity to move to a more prestigious publisher.

He also had taken the opportunity to rethink his great work and greatly enlarge its central part, adding yet a fourth volume (*Sodom and Gomorrah*). There, he expanded his characters of Albertine and the Baron de Charlus (the former based in part on his maddening affair with Agostinelli, and the latter modeled largely on Count Robert de Montesquiou), and directly addressed the themes of male and female homosexuality. Virtually placing his vast cast of characters under a microscope, Proust carefully observed the social milieu into which he had so ardently worked to gain admission. "Listen, Céleste," he told his housekeeper on one occasion, as he read aloud a letter he had received from Montesquiou: "Listen for the hatred he breathes out between each word. He is terrific!" And then he laughed "as hard as he could."[22] Sweetly relentless in his own manipulation of friends and family, Proust's charm and invalidism now proved a convincing cover for his even more relentless—and lengthy—analysis of the connection between sex, status, and power among those he knew best.

Among Proust's acquaintances was young Jean Cocteau, whom he incorporated into *Search* as Octave, a young dandy holidaying at the seaside resort of Balbec (Cabourg, by another name). Proust's Narrator later discovers—much to his surprise—that this young idler is in fact a playwright of some significance and renown; indeed, Octave eventually becomes a star of Madame Verdurin's salon.

Of course, by the time Proust worked Octave's character development into the later volumes of *Search* (in *The Fugitive* and *Time Regained*), Cocteau's talents had become more evident, and his role in the avant-garde ballet *Parade* may well have provided impetus for Octave's fictional development. In addition, Cocteau's association with two of Proust's close friends, Lucien Daudet and Reynaldo Hahn, made friendship inevitable, at least on a certain level.[23] Yet Proust continued to be put off by Cocteau's theatrics and "showing off,"[24] and perhaps the fictional Octave's rise in esteem was tied, in Proustian fashion, to a joke: after all, Madame Verdurin's salon, in which Octave shone, was embarrassingly shallow.

Nonetheless, the war had a sobering influence on Cocteau, who at the fighting's outset embarked on a series of volunteer stints with ambulance units, from the Red Cross to Misia Edwards's private endeavor. These trips to the front brought the young man into direct contact with the horrors of war. The shelled cathedral of Reims, he wrote, "was a mountain of old lace," and the city around it a virtual desert of ruins, occupied primarily by the wounded. There was little food to be had in wartime Reims, and even less in the way of medical aid. He witnessed the deaths (by shelling) of two medical assistants just as they were about to amputate—without chloroform—the gangrenous leg of a wounded artilleryman. He saw 150 wounded men being cared for by nuns who had only "a cup of rancid milk apiece and a half a salami for all." He observed a priest going from pallet to pallet to administer the sacraments, sometimes having to "pry mouths open with a knife blade in order to insert the host."[25]

Despite his notorious Poiret-designed uniform and continued attention-getting adventures, including a series of noncombat flights with the dashing Roland Garros, Cocteau had earned the right to be taken seriously, at least as a witness to war. Yet he still was regarded as a flashy lightweight by much of the Paris he sought to impress. His *Le Dieu bleu* had been a failure, and his 1915 attempt at a circus-inspired production of *A Midsummer Night's Dream* never made it to opening night. What he needed was a major figure in his corner, such as Picasso, and so Cocteau set off on a complicated pursuit of the Cubist star, involving any number of friends and friends-of-friends, including the composer Edgard Varèse and Varèse's current mistress, the artist Valentine Gross (or Valentine Hugo, as she would be known after marrying the artist Jean Hugo, Victor Hugo's great-grandson).

With the help of these prominent members of Parisian bohemia, Cocteau finally pulled off his much-desired meeting with Picasso, which probably occurred in mid-1915 (although it may have taken place closer to the year's end). Picasso rebuffed him, but Cocteau persisted, applying flattery and charm. During that year, Picasso was ill (possibly with an ulcer), and he unquestionably was depressed over Eva's steady decline. Eva died in December, but Picasso had by this time taken another mistress, creating a plethora of complexities in his life. Although Cocteau was undeniably diverting, Picasso—for the moment—remained preoccupied and unattainable.

With the outbreak of war, Stravinsky had no need to return to Russia (having been exempted from military service), and so he holed up with his wife and children in Switzerland, eventually settling in Morges. There he composed, kept up his professional contacts (including meetings in London, Paris, and Italy), and corresponded with Paris friends, including Debussy, who at one point told him: "You are, I know, one of those who can fight and win against this kind of 'gas' [the destruction of our art], just as deadly as the other and against which we've had no 'masks' to protect us."[26]

As for Diaghilev, the impresario headed for Italy along with his new protégé, Léonide Massine, who served as an all-around replacement for Nijinsky. There, Diaghilev continued to plan for a 1915 season, with another Stravinsky ballet as the focal point. Yet by autumn 1914, with Stravinsky behind schedule and the company characteristically in need of money, Diaghilev signed on another young Russian composer, Sergei Prokofiev, for a ballet. When this did not progress as well as expected, Diaghilev (despite his famed aversion to water crossings) agreed to a 1916 U.S. tour, anchored (with an attractive advance) by a stint at the Metropolitan Opera. As it turned out, the Americans were not interested in seeing Léonide Massine dance; they wanted Nijinsky—an awkward situation that at length forced Diaghilev to try to bring back the prodigal.

It had been a difficult time for the young dancer. Upon breaking with Diaghilev, he formed his own troop and arranged for a spring 1914 booking in London. Unfortunately, his dancers' lack of preparation as well as Nijinsky's own shortcomings as a manager led to a dismal showing (quite possibly exacerbated by well-placed sabotage from Diaghilev). Nijinsky and his wife promptly retreated to Austria, where in June 1914, his wife gave birth to a daughter. Unfortunately, once war broke out, the authorities promptly placed him under house arrest, as a Russian in enemy territory. It would take months of intervention from the American ambassador in Vienna and U.S. Secretary of State Robert Lansing before Nijinsky was free to travel to America. Yet once there, he was not about to cooperate; before agreeing to dance for Diaghilev, he wanted his back wages—a considerable sum.

For that reason, as well as others, the tour was not the financial success that Diaghilev had hoped for. Still, Americans all along the lengthy tour route loved the Ballets Russes—especially after Nijinsky appeared on stage. It was a promising beginning.

∿

Isadora Duncan returned to dancing early in 1915, in New York. There her indignation at Americans' apparent indifference to the war found few sympathizers, except for left-wing artists and intellectuals. Adding to her woes, younger competitors had by now entered the modern dance scene (among them, Martha Graham and Doris Humphrey, who trained with Ruth St.

Denis and Ted Shawn). The emergence of these young and vibrant competitors, plus a new craze for jazz dancing (fox trot, turkey trot, and more), made Isadora's evocations of classical Greece look tired and dated. Perhaps most devastating of all, Isadora had aged and put on weight; neither she nor her dancing was as attractive as they once had been.

Increasingly arbitrary and erratic, Isadora alternately wooed and insulted her would-be supporters. At length, out of money and out of patience with America, she decided to leave. Two days before she sailed, a German submarine torpedoed the British liner *Lusitania*, killing nearly twelve hundred passengers and crew, but Isadora was not deterred. Relying on a last-minute donation to pay her way, she had virtually no money when she left for Naples on May 9, 1915. At the dock, her dear friend Mary Desti Sturges impulsively joined her on board, dashing up the gangplank (with no baggage, passport, or money) after hastily telling her by now teenage son, Preston: "Do the best you can darling. Keep things going. I'll send you some money as soon as I can!"[27]

By the time Isadora arrived in Naples, Italy had entered the war on the side of the Allies. By December 1915, after many adventures, she returned to Paris, where she partied continuously and gave a sold-out performance to cheering Parisians, capped by dancing to the Marseillaise. She had not danced in Paris since the death of her children, and it was a triumph.

⌇

Old age, the enemy of actors and dancers, is especially harsh on women, as Sarah Bernhardt could readily testify. She had managed to maintain the fiction of youth long past anyone's expectations, but now, at the age of seventy, her bad knee threatened to do her in. When war broke out, she refused to leave Paris—in part because she feared to leave the surgeon she trusted. Finally, in response to the pleas of her old friend Georges Clemenceau, she at last capitulated and left in early 1915 for a tiny fishing village near Bordeaux. There, with her leg in a cast, she impatiently waited for the painful knee to heal.

When it did not, she wrote her Paris doctor in February, begging him to amputate her leg a little above the knee. "Do not protest," she told him. "I have perhaps ten or fifteen years left. Why condemn me to constant suffering?" She added, "I cannot bear to be useless, confined to a chair as I have been for six months." With her typical spirit, she concluded, "If you refuse me I'll shoot a bullet into my knee and then it will have to be cut off."[28]

Bernhardt got her way, although the surgeon who agreed to perform the operation was not her beloved doctor, but one of his former students. All went well, except that she had no patience with the wooden legs sent her, and instead ordered a sedan chair (decorated in sumptuous Louis XV style) in which she could be carried about. It was now, with the city apparently out of immediate danger, that she agreed to return to Paris. Immersing herself in war work, she appeared that October in a patriotic scenario during which she somehow managed to raise herself to her full height to deliver her final, ringing, lines: "Weep, weep Germany! The German Eagle has fallen into the Rhine."[29] And then, undaunted by her recent amputation, she set out to entertain the troops.

A group of young actors from the Comédie-Française accompanied her, skeptical that she would last more than a day. Soon they were left gasping in admiration at her stamina and pluck. At their first performance, Bernhardt's dressing room was a small lean-to with an earthen floor. She was delighted with it. Their stage was a platform reached by a ten-rung ladder; Bernhardt made little fuss and simply directed her associates to hoist her up, depositing her in an old armchair. She faced an audience of three thousand young men who, for the most part, had never heard of her and were completely unimpressed by her presence. She proceeded to do what she had always done, win them over. "With a rhythm that surged like the sounding of the charge," she evoked the glories of those throughout history who had died for France. And then, maintaining that same driving cadence, she culminated in a final cry, "Aux Armes!," which brought them, cheering, to their feet.[30]

Her courage, "which laughed at adversity," and her triumph of the spirit over frail flesh "changed our pity into admiration," one of her fellow actors later recalled. Of all Bernhardt's many triumphs throughout a lifetime of achievements, it was this last act that stood out above all: this "old woman of genius, who clumped along on her poor leg and in her little sedan chair, to give her blazing heart and valiant smile to the men who were suffering for us."[31]

⌒

Like Sarah Bernhardt, Marie Curie was ready to give her utmost for the soldiers of France. In addition to reading anatomical treatises and perfecting her ability to use the X-ray machinery, she learned to drive a car, received her driver's license, and became adept at auto repairs—essential when driving over bad roads to remote destinations. She could change a tire, clean a dirty carburetor, or carry heavy apparatus, all without fuss. She could eat or sleep anywhere, and did. Only when a kidney attack laid her low did she allow herself to stay in bed. Otherwise, she was out and about, on the front or in one of the three or four hundred French and Belgian hospitals that she visited during the course of the war.

While Marie lived a nomad's life, her daughters continued their studies—Irène receiving her degrees from the Sorbonne in math (1915), physics (1916), and chemistry (1917), all with distinction. While excelling at school, Irène managed to help her mother at the front and taught technicians-in-training to use the X-ray machinery. It was a schedule that rivaled that of her indefatigable mother.

While the Curies, mother and daughter, were serving their country by bringing X-rays to the wounded, the Boulanger sisters, Nadia and Lili, worked to help musicians and actors on active duty, whether by sending them letters, food, clothing, and news about one another, or by sending assistance to their families. Lili initiated the idea. Following her Prix de Rome victory (and after yet another bout of illness), she went to study and compose at the Villa Médicis in Rome, where she was living when war broke out. It was there that she began an extensive correspondence with fellow musicians that rapidly burgeoned into a support network for musicians serving in the war.

Nadia soon joined the effort, and after obtaining the backing of several American artists and diplomats, the two sisters formed a French-American support group (the Comité Franco-Américain du Conservatoire National de Musique et de Déclamation), enlisting a member of the Académie des Beaux-Arts to raise funds in the United States. It was thanks to these American contacts made during the course of this war work that American students would play such a prominent role in Nadia Boulanger's remarkable postwar teaching career.

⁓

Quite suddenly, after a long dry period following the outbreak of war, Debussy began to compose again—in what would prove to be one of the most productive periods of his career. As he told his friend, the composer and conductor D. E. Inghelbrecht: "The emotional satisfaction one gets from putting the right chord in the right place can't be equaled in any of the other arts. Forgive me. I sound as if I've just discovered music. But, in all humility, that's rather what I feel like."[32]

Earlier in the year, Debussy had agreed to revise Chopin's complete works, given the unavailability of the German editions after the war's outbreak. Initially, he found this work "terrifying,"[33] but eventually it would help him alleviate his war-inspired panic. By summer, Chopin's work would inspire him to write his own *Etudes*, which in turn he dedicated to Chopin.

From July to October 1915, in a cozy vacation house by the sea, Debussy wrote a series of sonatas for different combinations of instruments. In addition, he composed those twelve astonishing piano *Etudes*, five of which are so difficult that, for years, even the most acclaimed pianists refused to record them (Debussy conceded that he, too, had difficulty playing passages of some). And yet Debussy viewed these studies with humor as well as with "passion and faith": "There's no need to make technical exercises over-sombre just to appear more serious," he wrote his publisher; "a little charm never spoilt anything." He supported this viewpoint with his description of the daunting Etude, *For Sixths*: "For a long time," he told Durand, "the continuous use of sixths reminded me of pretentious young ladies sitting in a salon, sulkily doing their tapestry work and envying the scandalous laughter of the naughty ninths." And so he wrote this study, "in which my concern for sixths goes to the lengths of using no other intervals to build up the harmonies." "Not bad," he added cheerfully.[34]

He had not forgotten the war, he told his friends. Yet he had come to believe in the necessity for recreating a little of the beauty that the Germans were destroying. He kept working "at full tilt," but by December his illness became dramatically worse, requiring an operation. "As one never knows the outcome of even the simplest event," he wrote his wife, "I want to tell you one last time how much I love you."[35]

He survived the operation, but from then on, his creativity would ebb, along with his health and strength.

~

In mid-October 1914, Charles de Gaulle returned to the 33rd Infantry Regiment in Champagne, near Reims, where the opposing armies had been entrenched for several weeks. There, as commander of the regiment's 7th Company, he had little patience with the prevailing attitude of "leave the enemy alone, and he will not bother us." Instead, de Gaulle pressed his company to take aggressive action—an approach that seems to have dismayed his men but impressed his commanding officer, who offered him the post of adjutant. Ironically, this position offered de Gaulle substantially more safety, putting him well behind the trenches in regimental staff quarters.

Still, as de Gaulle wrote his mother, it was "something of a wrench to leave my 7th Company. I had only commanded it in the trenches but it had satisfied me entirely." During the two months the company was under his command, it had lost twenty-seven killed or wounded—a number which, de Gaulle told his mother, "is in no way excessive."[36]

By early 1915, however, Marie Curie's nephew, Maurice Curie, was coming to a different conclusion. At the war's outset he had been enthusiastically patriotic, eager to serve. After the Battle of the Marne, he walked north to join the front near Reims—"one hundred and thirty kilometers on foot, sack on back, rain and mud, hardly any food, across the mass graves of Epernay, Montmirail, etc. It is unbearable." Yet at that point he still wanted to join the infantry, to "take a more active part." He would spend a full year on the front lines, much of it near Verdun, but he soon became distressed by the mind-numbing destruction he saw everywhere around him. He witnessed the bombed remains of Reims cathedral, and wrote with despairing cynicism of a small village caught in the conflagration, a village that before the war was remarkable only for its insignificance. "I am going back down now into the trenches," he wrote later, "in keeping with my custom of serving breakfast [mortar fire] daily to these Messieurs Boches [the Germans]; they are used to it and this morning they didn't respond, which makes the job much easier—because it has become a job, this war which never ends."[37]

Memorial to
the Lafayette
Escadrille, Paris. ©
J. McAuliffe

CHAPTER EIGHTEEN

~

"Ils ne passeront pas"
(1916)

The Battle of Verdun began in February 1916. By the time it ended in December, the French had held the Germans, but more than seven hundred thousand troops had been killed or wounded, and three-quarters of the entire French army on the western front had fought there.[1] It became as close to hell as anything any of the troops had ever seen, and they referred to it as a furnace, or inferno. "As soon as I saw the battlefield," one infantryman recalled, "even though I had already spent fourteen months at the front, I thought: 'If you haven't seen Verdun, you haven't seen anything of war.'"[2]

Although the town of Verdun occupied a wedge that projected across the German front, it was a strongly fortified place that seemed impervious to attack—so much so that, by early February, the French high command had compounded its earlier neglect by actually reducing its defenses. Still, the very fact that Verdun jutted into German territory made it vulnerable on three sides, and the Germans took due note. France's high command, preparing for a huge offensive on the Somme and ignoring warnings from intelligence, was oblivious to the danger. When the ferocious German attack began, the relatively small number of defenders at Verdun managed to hold on until help arrived, in the form of Philippe Pétain (who by now was General Pétain). General Joffre may have loathed Pétain, but desperate times called for desperate measures, and Joffre now summoned Pétain to defend Verdun.

Pétain demanded—and received—reinforcement troops and munitions, and he immediately put into practice his firm belief in artillery barrages. Rather than leave his infantrymen (the famed *poilu*) in the trenches for months on end, he rotated troops in and out of action. Key to Pétain's demands for a continuous supply of fresh troops and materiel was a narrow road, dubbed the *Voie sacrée*, which was the only surviving access into Verdun. Soon an endless line of trucks barreled round-the-clock over this shell-pocked Sacred Way, which immediately became an essential lifeline in France's desperate effort to hold the Germans at bay. At its peak, when twelve thousand vehicles were employed there, one passed every fourteen seconds, day and night. This meant shifts of up to seventy-five hours at the wheel for these drivers, who were judged either too old or insufficiently hardy to fight.

Because of wartime censorship, it is difficult to know exactly where Maurice Ravel was driving at this time, but it is clear that by the spring of 1916 he was in the Verdun vicinity at the front. He wrote his mother that everything reminded one of this fact: "The airplanes going there, the convoys filled with soldiers, and at every turn in the road, you see the same sign: V . . . . . and an arrow"[3] (the "V" that he could not name in full, for security reasons, being "Verdun").

It is also clear that he was exposed to considerable danger. In writing the transcriber and arranger Lucien Garban, Ravel spoke of the risks and of his exhaustion: "I went through 5 days—and almost as many nights—of exhausting, insane, and perilous service, which consisted of going to look for damaged trucks over muddy or rough roads."[4] In another letter, this time to Major A. Blondel, Ravel elaborated: "For a week, I was driving day and night—without lights—on unbelievable roads, often with a load twice too heavy for my truck. And yet you couldn't drag along [slow down], because shells were falling all around. . . . One of them, an Austrian 130, sent the residue of its powder right into my face."[5]

He and his truck, Adélaïde, "escaped with only some shrapnel," but at length the worn-out truck refused to go any further. Fortunately, at this point Ravel was within range of a truck encampment. During the days he waited to be evacuated, he slept in his truck, washed in a nearby spring, and coaxed food from the encampment cooks. Unfortunately, the weather turned cold and nasty, leaving him to "play . . . Robinson Crusoe for 10 days" until he could be rescued.[6]

It all was unquestionably challenging. Yet it was a very different sort of encounter, with "a nightmarish city, horribly deserted and mute," that provided an even more disturbing experience. "Undoubtedly, I will see things which will be more frightful and repugnant," Ravel wrote Jean Marnold. "[Yet] I don't believe I will ever experience a more profound and stranger emotion than this sort of mute terror."[7]

～

By February 25, Charles de Gaulle's 33rd Infantry Regiment had moved to the outskirts of Verdun, where it was assigned a particularly dangerous sector, north of Douaumont. On March 1, de Gaulle (who had been injured a second time the previous year, awarded a Croix de Guerre, and promoted to captain) was told that the German offensive was over, and received orders to reconnoiter the regiment's position. Yet in conducting his reconnaissance, de Gaulle concluded that the German threat was far from over and that, indeed, a second attack was imminent.

He was right. Starting at daybreak on March 2, the Germans' heavy artillery began to roar across the entire sector, lobbing shells for as far as two miles. The noise was so deafening that communications became impossible—"an absolute hell, a never-ending thunder," as one of de Gaulle's men later recalled.[8] It was in the thick of this assault that (according to his commanding officer) Captain de Gaulle's 10th Company charged straight into the enemy, where he and his men engaged the Germans in hand-to-hand combat. De Gaulle's commanding officer later wrote that Captain de Gaulle and his men continued the fight, even after they were completely surrounded. The young captain was presumed dead—"an incomparable officer," as General Pétain noted in his dispatches.[9]

However, de Gaulle survived. He had been brave, but the accounts by his commanding officers, including that of General Pétain, were overblown. According to de Gaulle's own account (as told to his son), the German attackers had isolated and surrounded the surviving defenders of his 10th Company, heading off his attempts to establish contact with the nearest French unit. It was as he dived for cover in a shell-hole that a German gave him a bayonet thrust in his thigh, causing him to pass out from the pain. When de Gaulle regained consciousness, he was a German prisoner.

∼

On March 16, at four o'clock in the afternoon, Guillaume Apollinaire was sitting in a trench on the war front near Berry-au-Bac, in northern France. A shell came close, and he ducked before going back to reading the latest *Mercure de France*. Suddenly blood started to drip onto the page; shrapnel had pierced his helmet, wounding his head.

He wrote his fiancée, Madeleine (an attractive young teacher), that there was no cause for alarm, it was not serious. But it was serious. Paralysis set in, and soon he was moved to Paris, where he was trepanned. After the operation, he appeared to recover, but his friends noticed that he had changed. Not only did he abruptly end his engagement to Madeleine, but his personality seemed altered. In fact, his abrupt mood swings made his friends wonder whether his brain had been damaged, either by the wound or by the operation.

Meanwhile Georges Braque, who had also undergone trepanning, was sufficiently recovered that, in 1916, he went back to the army (this time, behind the lines). Soon he was invalided out and lived through the rest of the war quietly, with the exception of the riotous banquet given in his honor at Marie Vassilieff's studio-canteen, where he was lauded by dozens of friends, including Apollinaire, Picasso, Matisse, Max Jacob, and Juan Gris. In a more decorous fashion, he also received the Croix de Guerre and was made a Chevalier of the Legion of Honor.

While French artists, musicians, and writers were doing their utmost for their country, their German counterparts were doing the same for their own, including the aristocrat, Count Harry Kessler, whose keen interest in French culture did not prevent him from wholeheartedly embracing the German cause. This in turn did not blind him to a certain type of German careerist, "smug to the point of madness," with "competent, but puffed-up, empty, subaltern minds." Noting the prevalence of this type among the military and political leadership, he implored, "God save us from being ruled by such people after the war."[10]

In the spring of 1916, Kessler's regiment was transferred back from the eastern front to Verdun. After a stopover in Berlin, where he noted the lack of food as well as the growing discouragement about the war, he reached Verdun in May, where he witnessed the slaughter during the assault on Mort Homme (Dead Man) and Hill 304. Called back to Berlin, he spent the summer there before going to a posting in Bern, Switzerland, as cultural attaché to the German embassy—a sufficiently cushy position that it served to substantiate a long-circulating rumor that he was the illegitimate son of none other than the old Kaiser himself. After all, Kessler's mother, a striking beauty, had noticeably attracted the attention of Kaiser Wilhelm I, who became godfather to Kessler's little sister. Tongues wagged, but a more likely explanation for Kessler's Swiss posting is that, after two years of fighting, Count Harry Kessler was suffering severe fatigue or possibly even a nervous breakdown, requiring time to mend.

Another notable among France's enemies was the Austrian concert pianist Paul Wittgenstein, who was wounded early in the war, leading to the amputation of his right arm. It was a ghastly fate for a pianist, but after capture by the Russians, Wittgenstein was exchanged and returned to Vienna. There, in the autumn of 1916, he astounded audiences by resuming his concert career. In the years to come, he would commission works for the left hand, including Maurice Ravel's ravishing Piano Concerto for the Left Hand.

⁓

It was while Ravel was at the front that he first learned of the efforts of an organization called the National League for the Defense of French Music, which proposed to ban all public performance of music by German and Austrian composers not yet in the public domain. In other words, the ban would apply to works of contemporary or recently born composers, such as Schoenberg, and exclude works of composers such as Mozart and Beethoven. About eighty French musicians had already become members, including d'Indy and Saint-Saëns, but Ravel politely refused to join them. Although he wholeheartedly endorsed their commitment to French victory—after all, he pointed out, he had joined the war effort despite an easy excuse not to do so—he did not believe that such a regulation of music would safeguard France's artistic heritage. Even the proposed exception for "classical master-works" did not mollify him. It would be dangerous, he stated, "for French composers to ignore systematically the productions of their foreign colleagues, and thus form themselves into a sort of national coterie."[11]

It was a courageous position for Ravel to take, but one that he took without hesitation. After all, as he wrote Jean Marnold in June, "after having fought the militarist element of modern Germany, it would be intolerable to return home and have admiration or aversion imposed by decree."[12]

Debussy was of similar mind. Despite his use of the descriptive title, "Debussy, *musician français*," he did not hold with the chauvinism of d'Indy and Saint-Saëns. In late 1916, in a preface for a series of essays, *Pour la musique française*, he wrote that "Strange statements are to be heard about Beethoven who—Flemish or German—was a great musician, and about Wagner, who was a greater artist than a musician." His point was that "not everyone is able to write 'la grande musique,' but everyone attempts to do so."[13] He was not persuaded that anyone should be prevented from so doing.

Debussy had declared his musical independence from German hegemony since the 1890s, when Erik Satie bluntly told him that Frenchmen ought to free themselves "from the Wagnerian adventure," and that "we ought to have our own music—if possible without *choucroute* [sauerkraut]."[14] By 1916, Satie still was living in Arcueil, south of Paris, and walked home every night across the city, a bowler hat always on his head and an umbrella in his hand. As Jean Cocteau later put it: "Another poet whom the angels guide, cherish and torment is Erik Satie, who walks every night from Montmartre or Montparnasse to his home at Arcueil-Cachan—a miracle which cannot be explained unless the angels carry him."[15]

Cocteau first encountered Satie in 1915. A year later, prompted by a performance of Satie's *Three Pieces in the Shape of a Pear* (despite the title, the work actually contains seven pieces), Cocteau invited the "hermit of Arcueil" to collaborate with him in a ballet. By this time, Satie had become something of a celebrity in Parisian musical circles, notwithstanding his strange behavior and the odd titles of his compositions. His work was published and performed, and critics wrote favorable reviews. Debussy and especially Ravel expressed their admiration. Cocteau, who had been frantically trying to catch Diaghilev's attention with a sufficiently daring production, had until now encountered nothing but reversals on all fronts, including rejection by Stravinsky, Cocteau's composer of choice (Diaghilev, always proprietorial, may have encouraged Stravinsky to keep his distance). It was after hearing Satie play his *Three Pieces in the Shape of a Pear* with Ricardo Viñes (four-hand version) that Cocteau's idea for *Parade* began to take shape—as "a burlesque scene played outside a sideshow booth to entice spectators inside."[16]

With the help of Satie's and Cocteau's mutual friend Valentine Gross, Cocteau made his pitch to the composer, who was somewhat mystified but intrigued. "You are the *idea* man. Bravo!" he wrote Cocteau,[17] adding (in a note to Gross) that he did not understand what Cocteau had in mind, but hoped that Cocteau did not intend to rely only on Satie's previous works. "Let's do something new, no?" he proposed.[18]

While Cocteau was on leave from the front, where he was working with yet another private ambulance unit, he assiduously paid court to Picasso—who took him to the popular Montparnasse café, the Rotonde, located near Picasso's Rue Schoelcher studio. Cocteau later wrote that "our promenade took us to the Café de la Rotonde. The Rotonde, the Dôme, and a restaurant at the corner of boulevards Raspail and Montparnasse formed a town square, where the vegetable sellers stopped their small carts and grass grew between the paving stones."[19]

Cocteau was amused by the reception he received from the Rotonde's regulars: "Gloves, cane and collar astonish these artists in shirtsleeves—they have always regarded them as the emblems of feeble-mindedness."[20] Yet Cocteau was already envisioning a role for himself as a bridge between the Beau Monde (situated in Paris's most fashionable districts) and Bohemia, now located in Montparnasse. "I was on the way to what seemed to me the intense life," he later wrote, "toward Picasso, toward Modigliani, toward Satie, a little later toward the young men who were to become 'Les Six.'" He endured suspicion from Picasso's friends because Picasso himself took him around to meet everyone. "His authority was such," Cocteau added, "that I could quickly make contact with people who might have been slow to accept me if it had not been for him."[21]

Still, Picasso had made no commitment to Cocteau's latest project, and by May, Cocteau had returned to the front, where he eventually was posted to the second great battle of that year, the Battle of the Somme. Suddenly his blithe insouciance disappeared, replaced by the horror and depression that marked his earlier descriptions of the wounded in Reims. "Too dispirited to write," he told Valentine Gross. He and his colleagues were "hunting for the dead—horrible deliveries of wretches battered to pulp—blood flows—the very sheds are groaning."[22]

It seems to have shaken his health, perhaps even caused a breakdown. "I'm paying for the war trauma," he wrote Valentine Gross, "ridding myself of immense fatigue and disgust. Tics, dizziness, toxic smells that cling to my hands."[23] It may have been a breakdown, or it may simply have been a ruse to get him back to Paris, where Picasso still was playing hard-to-get. Misia Edwards had gotten wind of the project—a dangerous situation, since her usual mode of operation was to undermine any artistic endeavor involving *her* artists (she counted Satie as one) that dared to function outside her control. She and Diaghilev were going to take *Parade* away from Cocteau, Misia told him, and "begin all over again with Satie," whom she claimed as her own personal discovery.[24] She even enlisted Stravinsky in the fight.

Cocteau and Satie immediately got to work in pacifying Misia ("Tante Brutus," as Cocteau privately called her) by considerable stroking, including the fiction that *Parade* was entirely her idea—a story that only temporarily put her off. Yet by late August they had persuaded Picasso to join them, as designer of sets and costumes. In early autumn, they persuaded Diaghilev to back them, and contracts to that effect were signed early in 1917. Diaghilev in turn decided that Léonide Massine would dance the role of the Chinese magician and would also serve as the ballet's choreographer.

Somewhere along the way, Misia appears to have been mollified—perhaps because Satie refused to knuckle under, and possibly because Diaghilev (who was much impressed with Picasso) overrode her objections. In the meantime, danger appeared on another front: Picasso and Satie threatened to pair off and exclude Cocteau from the planning. Still, despite these hazards, the project continued to move briskly ahead. As for Cocteau, he managed to pull enough strings that he now held down a desk job in army staff headquarters in Paris. It was not a permanent solution—the job bored him. But for the moment, it would do.

∼

"The war continues—as you know," Debussy wearily wrote a friend in February, "but it's impossible to see why. . . . When will hate be exhausted?"[25]

So many of Paris's artists, musicians, and writers had departed for the front. Foreign dealers and collectors had also left, publishers shut down, and galleries closed. Concerts had virtually disappeared, and even the Salon d'Automne and the Salon des Indépendants had canceled. There were too few people to perform or to attend, and besides, it seemed frivolous.

Of course, there always were those who simply sought distraction and escape in the face of war. Helen Pearl Adam noted that "while Paris prided herself on having suppressed all unseemly gaiety during war-time, a small section of her population . . . took measures to secure its own amusement." There were places where, if you knew the password, one could dance the latest dances from America until the wee hours—private clubs not being subject to the curfew.[26] French and Allied servicemen on leave, airmen passing through, and war profiteers of all sorts, came to taste the proverbial delights of Paris. By 1916, "the town had become the capital of pleasure, to the great scandal of those who were suffering from the war."[27]

It was in the midst of the war's endless slaughter, and the raw Parisian nightlife that accompanied it, that culture began to take a stand. This was not a backward-looking movement, draped in the gentle aura of turn-of-the-century salons, but a harbinger of the future, anticipating the postwar years. Not long after Satie's 1916 performance of *Three Pieces in the Shape of a Pear* prompted the beginnings of the ballet *Parade*, the writer and critic André Salmon enlisted the *couturier* Paul Poiret—an avid art collector—in presenting what Salmon named the Salon d'Antin. This ambitious cultural event (held in July in Poiret 's extensive couture salon at 26 Avenue d'Antin) included literary and musical matinees, timed to avoid the evening blackout. Apollinaire and Blaise Cendrars read their poetry; Beatrice Hastings read an excerpt from her unfinished semi-autobiographical novel *Minnie Pinnikin*, based on her affair with Modigliani; and several young musicians (including Darius Milhaud, Georges Auric, and Arthur Honegger) performed works by Debussy, Satie, and Stravinsky. Yet from the outset it was the art exhibition that drew the most attention. "Would you ever have believed that we would be coming to an opening in wartime?" one attendee was said to have remarked, while another responded, "Artists have to live, like other people, and France, more than any other nation, needs art."[28]

Poiret's sister, Germaine Bongard, had led the way a few months earlier by opening part of her own dress shop to a group exhibition. Normally Picasso did not exhibit anywhere but at his art dealer's gallery, but Kahnweiler's departure for Switzerland made alternatives seem more attractive. Picasso, along with Matisse, Modigliani, André Derain, and Fernand Léger, participated in Germaine Bongard's small group exhibition in December 1915. Now, in July 1916, he presented—for the first time in public—his seismic *Les Demoiselles d'Avignon* at the Salon d'Antin.

Naturally, *Demoiselles* scandalized the Salon's visitors and became the star of the show.[29] Coming at the height of war, the Salon d'Antin's exhibition of modern art was already preparing the way for the postwar world.

～

During the months while so many of their friends had been serving their country, Gertrude Stein and Alice B. Toklas were enjoying themselves in Majorca. It was pleasant, yet the news of Verdun made it impossible to stay on holiday any longer. Feeling miserable, they decided to return to Paris. There they signed on with the American Fund for French Wounded, which required them to travel about from hospital to hospital, delivering supplies in their own automobile.

Gertrude did not have enough money to purchase the required auto, and so she wired relatives in New York, who raised the funds and had a Ford shipped over. She promptly christened it "Auntie," in honor of her Aunt Pauline, who "always behaved admirably in emergencies and behaved fairly well most times if she was properly flattered."[30] A friend had taught Gertrude how to drive his Paris taxi, and she now took on the driving duties with enthusiasm (except for driving in reverse, which she never mastered). Auntie repeatedly broke down, but Gertrude Stein (unlike Marie Curie) did not take pride in her self-reliance; she always managed to wangle help, sometimes from the unlikeliest sources.

Much like Gertrude Stein and Alice B. Toklas, the Princesse Edmond de Polignac (née Winnaretta Singer) had been staying with friends in England when war broke out in 1914. It was an agreeable place to be and, having completely underestimated the gravity of the situation, she remained there until she realized that the advancing German armies might well block her route home. She made it, but upon arriving in Paris she was shocked to see the flood of Parisians fleeing town. Unshaken by the German threat, she lent her car to Anna de Noailles and Anna's mother, who were leaving for the south; for her part, she decided to stay.

The princess promptly threw herself into war relief efforts, helping to finance Marie Curie's X-ray units and organizing major fund-raising efforts on behalf of soldiers on the front. She soon realized that many composers and musicians were now in great financial distress and needed help. Stravinsky, in particular, seemed in trouble, having lost his Russian lands (and the income from them) to Austro-German armies; in addition, he was having a difficult time collecting fees and royalties, especially from Diaghilev, who typically was hard up.

Early in 1916, the princess met with Stravinsky and offered him a substantial fee to write something for her. Her only specification was that the work be orchestral and for a chamber-sized group. Stravinsky's chamber opera-ballet, *Renard*, was the result. That spring, the princess also commissioned Erik Satie to write a work on a subject and with a form and size of his own choice. The mezzo-soprano Jane Bathori, who was responsible for introducing Satie to the princess, later recalled that Satie "was particularly fond of the dialogues of Plato and he chose three passages . . . making up a portrait of Socrates."[31] The Princesse de Polignac, who had read Plato's *Dialogues* in the original Greek, may have been the one to suggest the subject, but in any case, patron and composer were of one mind. This commission, in addition to encouraging Satie to write a work that would prove of major significance, would also prove a financial lifesaver for him.

⌢

Isadora Duncan's return to Paris consisted of one long party, during which she entertained the usual A-list as well as hundreds of soldiers. Soon her coffers were running dry, making it necessary to dance again just to pay the bills. She performed in Paris to wild acclaim, and then in May she left on tour of Latin America, where she continued her nonstop love affairs and champagne binges. She also played the diva, throwing tantrums in Buenos Aires and responding to newspaper insults about her weight by in turn insulting her audience, stopping the program to tell them that they were "primitive and uneducated," and capping her harangue with painfully racist epithets.[32] Angered, the management canceled the rest of her engagement.

Although her personal life remained out of control, Isadora's subsequent performances in Rio and Montevideo went well, leaving her audiences cheering. Unfortunately her school, temporarily located in Switzerland, now ran out of money. To pay their debts, Isadora's young dancers, the Isadorables, gave a dance performance—a daring action, since they took it without her permission. Given the success of this venture, they then organized a tour through Switzerland, under the management of Isadora's brother Augustin. It was their first break for freedom. "Much as we loved Isadora and venerated her as an artist and teacher," one of her students later wrote, "we nevertheless ardently wished to be independent."[33]

By year's end, Isadora once again was in New York, where she gave a benefit performance at the Metropolitan Opera for the families of needy French artists. Paris Singer once again came to her rescue, booking the Met for her, but once again Isadora baited him mercilessly, dancing an astonishing tango with an unidentified stranger during the after-performance party. Singer, who was furious, seized the considerably smaller man and carried him out the door. Equally furious, Isadora ripped off the fabulous diamond necklace that Singer had given her, scattering diamonds across the floor.

The lovers made up, much as in the past, and Singer agreed to bring the Isadorables from Switzerland to New York. He also took an option on Madison Square Garden, which he offered to Isadora for her school. Earlier, she had expressed interest in the venue, but now she was sarcastic and insulting. Singer said nothing, but abruptly left the room. "He'll come back," Isadora said complacently to the party of family and friends around her. "He always does."[34]

Yet this time, he did not. It was the end of the long and troubled relationship between Isadora Duncan and Paris Singer. And with it, all funding from Singer finally ended.

⁓

As Charles de Gaulle wrote his mother from prison camp: "For a French officer, the state of being a prisoner is the worst of all."[35] In this spirit, after recovery from his wound, de Gaulle made his first attempt at escape, in a boat on the Danube. His captors quickly caught up with him, and he promptly was sent to a punishment camp in Lithuania. There he made friends with a former engineer in the French Department of Mines—a tunnel specialist who, in an additional stroke of luck, spoke Russian.

Unfortunately, prison guards soon detected the hole that de Gaulle and his colleague were digging, leading to punishments for all their fellow prisoners as well as a transfer for de Gaulle and his friend to Fort IX, a high-security camp in Bavaria. Here, the Germans had gathered together one hundred or so of their most difficult prisoners (including the famed pilot, Roland Garros). So far as the camp's commander was concerned, they all were criminals and were treated accordingly. The prisoners responded by doing their best to disrupt the place: setting fire to straw mattresses, throwing water bombs, and performing "concerts" on food tins at all hours of the night.

De Gaulle soon decided that, given the fort's layout and surveillance, the best way to escape was by getting himself sent to the garrison's hospital. Deliberately swallowing the entire bottle of picric acid that his mother had sent him for his chilblains, he became sufficiently ill that he was sent to the hospital, where he discovered that the prisoner's wing was almost as well guarded as the fortress. Still, the adjoining hospital for German casualties was not guarded, and after he and a colleague with similar intent managed to pile up food and civilian clothes (thanks to well-placed bribery of a German guard and effective pleas to a French electrician), they managed to escape, with de Gaulle escorted out by his colleague, who was disguised in a male nurse's coat. Their goal was Switzerland, two hundred miles away.

The two escapees traveled by night, through a steady downpour of rain. Unfortunately, by the eighth day their rag-bag appearance gave them away, and they were arrested—having traveled almost two-thirds of their long journey. Brought back to Fort IX, de Gaulle now decided on a course of good behavior, in the hope that this would get him transferred to a place where it would be easier to break out.

For the rest of the year, he became a model prisoner, reading, writing, and giving lectures. In what would become characteristic de Gaulle fashion, these analyzed and leveled serious criticism of France's leadership of the war. All the while, he carefully watched for further opportunities to escape.

⌣

Throughout the year, Monet worked on huge canvases (three feet high and between nine and fifteen feet wide) of his garden's water lilies. He now was working in a new studio large enough to accommodate them and enable him to work indoors throughout the winter. He called these canvases his *Grandes Décorations*, and from now on he would be almost totally preoccupied with what he referred to as "The Work."

Monet swung back and forth between hope and despair as he painted his *Grandes Décorations*, aware that his age and declining eyesight were operating against him. Still, he remained hopeful that he would somehow be able to complete this enormous project, which obsessed him. Perhaps what he was attempting was "sheer madness," he wrote Gustave Geffroy in November, but it served to distract him from the war's constant anxieties. "I was extremely worried about my son Michel," he told Geffroy in September, adding that Michel "had three terrible weeks at Verdun." Presently Michel was on leave at Giverny, Monet added, but only for six days. "How long-drawn-out and painful it all is!" he exclaimed.[36]

The pain was not lessening. The Battle of Verdun dragged on, while the equally devastating Battle of the Somme ground through hundreds of thousands of British as well as French troops during the second half of the year. In response to the steady barrage of bad news and the sound of distant guns, Parisians pulled together, in an attempt to console one another and help each other through the anguish. Edith Wharton found that many of the women with whom she was in contact "found their vocation in nursing the wounded, or in other philanthropic activities."[37] For his part, the poet Blaise Cendrars met Erik Satie regularly at the home of the widow of a mutual friend who had recently been killed at Verdun. Cendrars, who had lost an arm the previous year at the front, later recalled that the widow was from Marseilles, and on Friday mornings she often received a basket of fish from her hometown. On those evenings, she ate bouillabaisse with Satie, Cendrars, and Georges Auric, a young musician who would soon become part of the Group des Six. They talked "of this and that," Cendrars later recalled, but the main thing was the companionship, a small effort to relieve the gloom.[38]

By now the high seas were becoming almost as dangerous as the field of battle, thanks to Germany's strategy of unrestricted submarine warfare. In March, a German sub torpedoed the passenger ferry *Sussex* in the English Channel, with the loss of many lives, including the Spanish pianist and composer Enrique Granados. Although no American citizens were among those lost, President Wilson warned that if Germany continued this practice, the United States would break off relations. Fearing U.S. entry into the war, Germany agreed that henceforth it would not target passenger ships. It was against the backdrop of this precarious agreement that, in October, Sarah Bernhardt dared once again to cross the Atlantic.

Rapturously welcomed by Americans, Bernhardt toured indefatigably, playing ninety-nine cities in fourteen months. Accommodating her disability, she performed short scenes designed to win sympathy for her beleaguered nation, and she spoke at Red Cross rallies, benefits, and just about any other public venue where she could urge America to join the Allies in the fight. "How many cities there are," she wrote her son, Maurice, well into the tour. "Some fine, some ghastly."[39] She also showed a spirited sensitivity for human rights, praising a suffragette convention for its support of a black woman who wished to attend, and stating flatly, "I think that the ostracism in which blacks are held by the whites is odious."[40]

After months of touring, Bernhardt became seriously ill and had to undergo a kidney operation. Yet even after this setback, she soon was up and touring again. "Never stop," was her motto; "never stop; otherwise you die."[41] Colette, the writer and erstwhile music hall entertainer who had fought her way out of crushing difficulties of her own, would put it another way: what she later noticed, even as Bernhardt approached her eightieth year, was Bernhardt's "indomitable, endless desire to please, to please again, to please even unto the gates of death."[42] In other words, Bernhardt was a performer, and she would perform to the end.

〜

The war was taking its toll among Paris's artists, musicians, and writers. Not only had Apollinaire and Braque received serious head wounds, and Blaise Cendrars lost an arm, but the artist Fernand Léger suffered a near-fatal exposure to mustard gas during the autumn of 1916. That year, the sculptor Raymond Duchamp-Villon, one of the famous Duchamp brothers, contracted typhoid on the front and died. The sculptor Ossip Zadkine, who served as a stretcher-bearer from 1916 through 1917, was gassed while transferring the wounded. After a lengthy hospitalization, he was invalided out.

Maurice Ravel did not escape harm, even though he was not injured; by early autumn he had become seriously ill with dysentery, leading to an operation. He was apprehensive about the surgery, telling Madame Dreyfus, the mother of his friend Roland-Manuel, that he knew "from the example of many comrades here—that I will suffer horribly for some time, but I prefer that to discomfort and pain for the rest of my life."[43] The operation went well, and afterward, a more characteristically upbeat Ravel told Jean Marnold that he experienced no aftereffects from the chloroform, but "on the contrary, as soon as I woke up, I needed a cigarette, because I was dying of hunger."[44]

Madame Dreyfus had been serving as Ravel's *marraine de guerre*, or wartime godmother—a correspondent who "adopted" a soldier and sent packages and letters. It was a fortunate development for Ravel, because his own mother had become too ill and weak to write either of her sons. In late July, when Ravel was still at or near the front, he received a letter from her that was so "frail, . . . incoherent, almost illegible," that it caused him great sadness.[45] Although he still hoped for improvement, it was becoming increasingly unlikely.

Some, like Debussy's friend, the composer and conductor André Caplet, managed to keep up their spirits, even in the trenches. Caplet, who had survived an alarmingly tempestuous seduction by Isadora Duncan (on the floor, beneath the piano, within Paris Singer's hearing),[46] now faced far graver dangers. As Debussy described it, Caplet was a liaison officer in Verdun who "toys with death from morning till night and manages to keep in high spirits." Much to Debussy's delight, Caplet had "a collapsible piano in the trenches with him!"[47] Unfortunately, life in the trenches was not so jolly as Caplet made it sound; not long after, he was severely gassed and later died from the effects.

Debussy himself was not doing well, and he became ever more exasperated with his illness as the months wore on. In February, he wrote Robert Godet, "I've just started a new treatment. . . . I'm asked to be patient. . . . Good God! Where am I to find patience?"[48] In June, he wondered, "Will I ever again know what it is to be well?"[49] In September, he told Godet, "I watch the days go past, minute by minute, as cows watch trains go past." In December, he wrote, "Naturally, I don't take this poor tattered body for walks any more, in case I frighten little children and tram conductors."[50]

Auguste Rodin was not doing well, either, having suffered a series of strokes during the year. Once again, he was the target of manipulative females, this time Jeanne Bardey and her daughter, Henriette, Frenchwomen from Lyon. Bardey, who was a talented painter and sculptor, had encountered Rodin several years earlier but had made little progress in the face of firm opposition from Claire de Choiseul. Now Bardey's husband was dead, and Choiseul was safely out of the picture. "I want to be your slave," Jeanne Bardey assured Rodin. "My dear little papa Rodin," twenty-one-year-old Henriette addressed him.[51] Rodin, by now an ailing old man with a weakness for pretty women, was "easy prey."[52] Although he planned to give his entire oeuvre to France, there still were plenty of other goodies to be nabbed, such as reproduction rights to those works.

With Rodin so clearly in his dotage, the state now found the time amid the chaos of war to ensure the transfer of his massive donation to France, including the provision that the Hôtel Biron would henceforth be called the Musée Rodin. By autumn, the bequest was formally executed, although Parliament reserved its right to debate acceptance of the gift. Unfortunately there were some right-wing extremists who opposed the idea, on grounds that France had no need for yet another museum, and certainly not one that desecrated the memory of the Convent of the Sacré-Coeur, which had occupied the Hôtel Biron prior to the Convent's expulsion. Most opposition, though, focused on the nature of Rodin's art, which his critics described as decadent, vulgar, and "tending toward the pornographic."[53] Fortunately, when the final vote was taken, the bequest was overwhelmingly approved.

In the meantime, other interested parties ensured the departure of Madame Bardey and her daughter, and guards were posted around the Hôtel Biron to prevent her entry and the disappearance of any works of art. As with the Duchesse de Choiseul, drawings and small bronzes were rumored to have disappeared.

⌒

Gustave Eiffel had abruptly retired in the 1890s, following his humiliating involvement in the Panama Canal scandal, but he did not put his feet up during the remaining three decades of his life. During these years, some of his many projects may have come to nothing (such as constructing an astronomical observatory on Mont Blanc, or a tunnel beneath the English Channel), but others, especially those involving his iconic tower, had remarkable results.

Eiffel had always believed that his tower offered great possibilities for scientific research, and by the early years of the century, the Eiffel Tower had become the center for military experiments in communications. By 1908, the French army was able to use it to establish contact with its bases throughout France, as well as with foreign destinations of interest—notably Berlin. One of the Eiffel Tower's most famous exploits was the early 1917 interception of a message between Berlin and Spain that led to the identification and conviction of Mata Hari as a spy. (She was executed by firing squad later in the year.)

Eiffel also was intrigued by the effects of wind—a study that had large payoffs in the new field of aviation, especially when he extended his research by building a wind tunnel. He demonstrated that aircraft lift came about largely by airflow over rather than under the wing surface, and he also made a major discovery in propeller design. After the neighbors along the Champ de Mars complained about the noise, Eiffel moved his wind tunnel west, to Auteuil. There, he built a laboratory that contributed significantly to the effectiveness of French military aircraft during the war.

Despite their fragility, these early planes had to undergo rough conditions. As Gabriel Voisin later wrote, it was "necessary to land and to take off heavily loaded on broken ground, and our landing gear was the only one able to undertake easily this sort of intensive duty."[54] The Voisin III pusher plane became the fighter and reconnaissance plane of choice for the French during the war's early years, and its steel frame construction gave it the strength to serve as a light bomber—at least until more powerful engines were added in 1916.

Critically, the Germans had held air superiority at the outset of the Battle of Verdun, but the Allies quickly learned to change tactics to meet the so-called Fokker Scourge by providing escort for reconnaissance aircraft and by forming fighter squadrons. Prior to Verdun, the Germans had used their air superiority to conduct highly detailed photographic reconnaissance of French positions and to deny the French the opportunity to do the same over German lines. Initially, this policy served the Germans well, but the Germans then made the mistake of continuing their aerial blockade—wasting resources that could have been used to break up the French supply line along the all-important and vulnerable Voie Sacrée. The French, for their part, ramped up their fighter and reconnaissance units in Verdun (including the Lafayette Escadrille, largely made up of American volunteer fighter pilots), and by late summer had regained control of the skies above Verdun.

～

The Battle of Verdun ended in victory for the French, who had prevented the Germans from capturing the city and who had inflicted enormous losses on the enemy. "Ils ne passeront pas" ("They shall not pass") had proved a stirring inspiration for French defenses throughout the terrible ordeal.[55] Yet French casualties over the course of the year-long battle had also been enormous, and there still was no sign of an end to this murderous war.

At the year's close, Paris remained a city essentially under siege, occasionally bombarded by German Zeppelins and suffering increasing deprivation. Food shortages were common, food prices were rising dramatically, and rationing (beginning with sugar) was about to begin. Temperatures fell close to zero degrees Fahrenheit that winter, and coal was at a premium. Late in the year, Jean Cocteau would write Stravinsky, "Here we are freezing for lack of coal."[56]

On Christmas Eve, Debussy wrote a note to his wife, telling her, "Never has your love been more precious or more necessary to me." And then he despairingly concluded: "Noël! Noël! The bells are cracked. Noël! Noël! They have wept too long."[57]

Woman worker on machinery in the French Métro, Paris, France, March 28, 1917. Photo Credit: The Art Archive at Art Resource, NY. © Art Resource, NY.

~

CHAPTER NINETEEN

Dark Days

(1917)

"This life in which you have to fight for a lump of sugar or for manuscript paper, not to mention your daily bread, needs stronger nerves than mine," Debussy wrote despairingly in the spring of 1917.[1]

Paris was dark and cold in the winter and early spring of 1917, and Parisians took it quietly when news came that the Germans had begun to evacuate their positions on the Somme. "We knew by then," wrote Helen Pearl Adam, "that more than such a retirement was necessary to bring victory into sight." In addition, "what attention we had to spare for ourselves was entirely devoted to keeping warm."[2] Fuel was scarce, and the unremitting cold had frozen water pipes throughout the city, adding water to the list of scarcities. "I've adopted as my motto a variant of Wilson's 'Too proud to fight' which runs 'Too cold to sleep,'" Edith Wharton wrote Bernard Berenson, adding that her warm feelings for him were "the only thing left of me that's not below zero, after so many days of this inexorable cold."[3]

In the midst of the cold and gloom, life went on, sometimes with an undertone of grim mockery. On January 29, after more than fifty years of cohabitation, Auguste Rodin finally married Rose Beuret—apparently at the instigation of those among his closest friends and supporters who wished to quiet any remaining disgruntlement over the unsanctified relationship. One does not know what Rodin made of this event; he was too old by this time to register much, or at least to put up much of a protest. As for Rose, she too was well past her mental prime. It had always been difficult to know exactly what Rose thought, and in any case, the marriage that she may have longed for did not last long. Soon after the hasty wedding at their stark and unheated home in Meudon, Rose became ill and died.

Early that same January, Maurice Ravel's beloved mother passed away. Although she had been ill for some time, her death devastated him. "My captain keeps telling me that 'I've got to snap out of it,'" Ravel wrote his wartime godmother, Madame Dreyfus. Yet despite efforts to get over his grief, Ravel remained severely depressed. His mother's death, added to all that he had seen and experienced during the war, deeply affected him. "Physically, I'm still all right," he assured Madame Dreyfus. But "spiritually, it's dreadful."[4] In fact, Ravel was not in good health either physically or emotionally, leading to a temporary discharge from military service that became permanent. In June, while recuperating at the home of Madame Dreyfus, he completed his lovely *Le Tombeau de Couperin*, each of whose six movements is dedicated to a fallen friend or friends.[5] He would compose nothing new for three years, and comparatively little after that for the remainder of his life.

∾

By the spring of 1917, France had succeeded in staggering through almost three years of devastating warfare, in alliance with Great Britain, Russia, and, more recently, Italy (Italy declared war against the Austro-Hungarian Empire in 1915 and against Germany in 1916). It was Russia in the east and the United States in the west that now provided equal measures of hope and despair in this war without end.

Strikes and armed clashes broke out in war-torn and demoralized St. Petersburg in February, followed by a mutiny of the troops and the abdication of the czar. In New York, Isadora Duncan draped herself on stage in the French flag as she played to packed houses, rejoicing in Russia's emergence from autocracy and urging the United States to join the Allies in stopping the German tide. "At that time," she later wrote, "I believed . . . that the whole world's hope of liberty, regeneration, and civilization depended on the Allies winning the war."[6]

Although Russia's new provisional government pledged to continue the fight, the Bolsheviks demanded an end to participation in the war, and anarchy rapidly spread throughout Russia's badly demoralized troops. Lenin's arrival in Russia, followed by rapidly escalating upheaval and the Bolshevik Revolution, would by March 1918 result in a peace treaty with the Central Powers—("The very Russia that dragged us into this war!" an outraged Abbé Mugnier exclaimed at the news.)[7] This removed Russia's already-disintegrating opposition on Germany's eastern front, making American entry into the war even more imperative. German resumption of unrestricted submarine warfare, and British interception of German plans to ally with Mexico and Japan against the United States (the famous Zimmermann note), prompted the United States to sever relations with Germany and then, in early April 1917, to declare war.

The French were relieved and grateful, even though America was not yet on a war footing—Wilson had sought to signal his nation's neutrality by abstaining from war preparations. Still, according to Adam, "France went quite mad about Americans," and Paris was at the center of this national feeling.[8] The Stars and Stripes joined the Tricolor at the top of the Eiffel Tower, accompanied by a 101-gun salute. General Pershing soon arrived in Paris, where at Lafayette's tomb, he (or possibly his aide) uttered the moving words, "Lafayette, we are here." That July 4, Parisians enjoyed a good look at an infantry regiment of American soldiers marching through their streets, prompting enthusiastic comments about the Americans' "magnificent appearance." The "tall, square" American soldier "became an immediate success in France," Adam wrote. "He had come at a moment of stress, and we were grateful to him."[9]

The stress she spoke of was an understatement. France's badly demoralized soldiers had been going to the slaughter for too long, with only heavy losses and defeat to show for the bloodbath. France's government was perceptibly floundering, and in May 1917, French troops along the front began to mutiny.

Late the previous year, the French government had finally managed to remove General Joffre as commander-in-chief, where he had taken almost total control over the conduct of the war—to the dismay of an increasing number of critics, who were appalled by his blind certainty of imminent victory and his willingness to sacrifice ever larger numbers of soldiers to achieve it. To appease him, Joffre was elevated to Marshal of France, where he occupied a largely ceremonial position and became a technical adviser to the government, while General Nivelle took his place.

Unfortunately Nivelle, who had an ambitious offensive plan of his own, was not much of an improvement. His plan relied on coordinated attacks by the Allies, but the prolonged cold and that year's first Russian revolution, of February and March, set these back. The Italians' decision to wait it out for a more propitious moment left the French and British very much on their own to face the Germans' surprise unfurling of the Siegfried (or Hindenburg) Line—a falling-back, it was true, but to a ferociously defended line between Cambrai and the Chemin des Dames, the latter being a long and narrow ridge between two river valleys to the north of Paris. Deciding that this made little difference to the success of his plan, General Nivelle went ahead—despite grave doubts from the minister of war and from General Pétain, the only military commander to question the advisability of Nivelle's offensive.

Squadron Chief Alfred Dreyfus was one of the hundreds of thousands of men who took part in this doomed offensive. That February, after repeated requests, fifty-seven-year-old Dreyfus received a transfer from essentially home-guard duty in the Paris area to the front, where he took command of an artillery group on the Chemin des Dames sector. The war had eaten through enough young lives that the older soldiers now were being called into frontline action.

The weather was "glacial," Dreyfus recorded in his notebook, with driving rain and wind, and he found himself serving under Colonel Georges Larpent, a royalist, anti-Semite, and nationalist of the Ligue d'Action Française, who had published vociferously and extensively (under a pseudonym), including a *Précis de l'Affaire Dreyfus* that had become a major reference source for the anti-Dreyfusards. In spite of these difficulties, Dreyfus made no complaints and, for the most part, kept his spirits up. "Here, despite the mud, the rain, the snow, the absolute lack of comfort, I carry on wonderfully, and the morale of my men is good," he wrote a friend, adding that his letters were necessarily banal because of censorship.[10]

Amid continued icy rains and biting wind, Dreyfus and his men underwent increasing cannon bombardment as the battle approached. "All night," he wrote briefly in his notebook for April 15, "the formidable rumbling of cannons of all caliber." During that night, he received orders for the offensive that was about to begin. He and his men were to cross the River Aisne at the Pont de Bourg-et-Comin and take part in the assault of the crest of the Chemin des Dames. His division, part of the 20th Corps of the Sixth Army, left promptly at six in the morning, but was caught in an immense crowd of other infantry divisions on the banks of the Aisne. Fortunately, Dreyfus noted, the Germans on the heights were sufficiently preoccupied with the French attack that they did not take aim at them, "otherwise it would have been a disaster for the munitions sections." Two days later, caught in driving rain, he and his men still had not crossed the Aisne. "We're in the mud up to our necks," Dreyfus scribbled in his notebook.[11]

Nivelle was so sure of success that he had invited a group of legislators to watch this battle. It quickly turned into a disaster for the French, with enormous casualties. Still, Nivelle persisted in believing that the Germans had suffered disproportionately, and he continued to launch other attacks along the Siegfried Line, with similar results. Early on, Dreyfus was reporting heavy losses to the 20th Corps, and by May 12 they were pulling back, under heavy cannon and airplane bombardment. Nivelle's offensives had failed.

With that, Parliament abruptly replaced Nivelle with General Pétain. Yet by this time, mutiny had broken out in the French army, starting at the killing fields where these most recent offensives had taken place. The mutinies began in early May, as troops refused to go into battle, and the movement quickly spread. Before it was over, some thirty or forty thousand soldiers had participated, including two regiments that decided to march on Paris to force Parliament to end the war. The generals blamed this outbreak on revolutionaries, pointing to incidents where red flags were waved and the Internationale was sung. What the generals failed to see was that these uprisings were simply a vast protest movement against their own incompetence and the ruinous way the war was being waged. Since Pétain was in fundamental agreement with his troops, it was relatively easy for him to bring the mutinies to a close by ending Nivelle's disastrous offensive. He punished the most flagrant of the offenders (forty-nine of the mutineers were executed), but he took care to show his interest in his troops' welfare, including restoring their leave (which had been suspended). By mid-June, the mutinies were over.

～

That July, Charles de Gaulle and three of his comrades from Fort IX were transferred to a prison fortress at Rosenberg, built at the edge of a sheer wall of rock. By way of reinforcement, the prisoners' quarters were surrounded by two walls and two moats. The walls did not look like much of a problem to de Gaulle and his cohorts, but the perpendicular descent down the rock face gave them pause, especially since they had no idea of how high up they were or how long their rope would have to be. Taking the average calculated by those they talked with about it, they made their rope ninety feet long, using strips of sheets. They also constructed an eighteen-foot ladder that could be dismantled.

One rainy night in October, when the sentries were sitting cozily in their boxes and unlikely to venture out, the men decided to make their break. By ten o'clock they had reached the top of the cliff and lowered one of the team over the edge, where they discovered that the rope was not long enough. Hauling him up, they began again, finding another spot where they could do the deed in two stages. By midnight, they were on their way for the Swiss border—this time, nearly three hundred miles away.

After ten days of marching, they were worn out and decided to find shelter in a dovecote. Unfortunately, peasants working in the fields heard them and warned a soldier, who called for aid and hauled them in. Knowing that this latest escapade would send them promptly back to Fort IX, de Gaulle and one colleague decided to move quickly. Sawing through a bar in their window, they climbed out while a friend replaced the bar and retrieved their rope. Dressed in civilian clothes they had somehow wangled, they walked off, this time aiming for the Dutch border via the train. Again, they were spotted and were arrested in the station. Promptly sent back to Fort IX, de Gaulle was punished by "shuttered windows, no light, special diet, nothing to read, no writing materials, half an hour's exercise a day in a court measuring a hundred square yards." He was bitterly depressed. "When one is formed for action," he wrote his parents that December, "being so totally and irremediably useless . . . is the cruelest [position] for a man and a soldier that can be imagined!"[12]

∿

Stravinsky, who was trying to make ends meet in Switzerland, and Diaghilev, who was trying to keep his Ballets Russes afloat while his star, Nijinsky, was sinking into psychosis, did not yet realize that the Russia they had always known was rapidly vanishing. Stravinsky's first impulse, upon hearing of the February revolution, was to go home—to "our dear, liberated Russia."[13] Diaghilev was similarly sympathetic to the new Kerensky regime, but he turned down an opportunity to become its minister of culture. By the year's end, the Bolshevik Revolution had changed his Russia forever, while it deprived Stravinsky of "the last resources which had still from time to time been reaching me from my country, and I found myself . . . face to face with nothing, in a foreign land and right in the middle of the war."[14]

Chagall, on the other hand, was caught inside Russia during that year of upheaval. "On Znamensky Square in front of the great monument of Alexander III," he wrote, "people began to whisper: 'Lenin has arrived.' . . . 'Lenin from Geneva?' 'The very same.'" And in Vitebsk, a group of actors and painters gathered to found a ministry of arts. Chagall's wife wept when she heard that he had been selected as its head. "She warned me it would all end badly," Chagall later wrote. Instead of "peacefully painting" his pictures, he founded a school of fine arts and became "its director, its president and everything else."[15] At first he thought it a lucky break, but from the outset, his wife thought otherwise.

In time he came to realize that "Lenin turned [Russia] upside down the way I turn my pictures."[16]

∿

Meanwhile, Matisse was desperate for news of his mother and other family members, who were stuck behind German lines in northeastern France. He had learned that they were subjected to prisoner rations while the Germans stripped their homes and lands of everything edible or otherwise usable in the war. His brother, first deported to a German prison camp, had been sent home with other deportees to do forced labor. Matisse responded to intermittent word from his brother by canvassing actively in the United States as well as Paris to raise funds from a series of his etchings for the relief of French prisoners. Matisse's wife, Amélie, became a whirlwind of activity for relief distribution, especially food and knitted socks.

In addition to these family anxieties, Matisse's oldest son, Jean, who had disappointed him by wanting to work as an airplane mechanic, turned eighteen and received his mobilization orders—as an airplane mechanic. When Matisse visited Jean in his training camp a few months later, he was shocked to find the young man and his fellow conscripts hungry, cold, dirty, and "living like pigs." Somehow they managed to survive in ankle-deep mud, without access to latrines or showers.[17]

Late in 1917, after Jean was posted to an airfield near Marseilles, Matisse immediately caught the overnight train to Marseilles, where—despite his precautions of having gotten an introduction to the camp commandant—it took four days for permission to see Jean. When Matisse finally got through, he discovered that, much as he had feared, it was "a prison camp." He finagled a twenty-four-hour pass for Jean, fed him well, and sent him back wearing clean, dry clothes. It was all he could do for the moment, although he would continue to send food parcels and try to pull all possible connections to arrange for a transfer.

By 1917, Helen Pearl Adam noticed more and more women in the workplace, something that was "very remarkable" in France. France had never had the women's auxiliaries of the armed services during World War I as in Britain, and Adam noted that at one time there even was a groundswell to withdraw young women from service in French hospital wards, "on the grounds that the sights they saw there were not fit for 'well-brought-up young girls.'"[18] It remained permissible for older women to serve in the various branches of the Red Cross. Yet women in any sort of uniform drew curious eyes in Paris, even toward the end of the war.

Still, by 1917 Adam noted that women were delivering the mail in Paris—conservatively dressed in black overalls and black straw hats, and carrying little square boxes. She also noted a growing trend of tram conductresses, women ticket collectors, and women watering the public gardens—the latter dressed in black overalls, big hats, and sabots.

Women—as well as older male workers—had by now filled the ranks in a variety of occupations. When strikes broke out in a number of wartime factories in 1917, around the same time as mutinies broke out on the front, women played a prominent role. These strikers were largely motivated by rising prices rather than antiwar sentiment, although grim news from the front had by now filtered back to Paris, dashing hopes that the war's end was near. In André Citroën's munitions factory, it was the women who went on strike, demanding higher pay and shorter working hours. Citroën managed to defuse the situation by listening to his workers' grievances and referring the dispute to arbitration by a council presided over by the socialist minister of armaments. This council soon negotiated a settlement and return to work.

Meanwhile, women's fashion had followed women into the workplace. Skirts went up, hair went back into neat buns or even (daringly) was cropped, and styles featured increasingly easy and comfortable movement. At the forefront of this formidable fashion trend was Coco Chanel, whose first shirtwaist dress made as much news as her jersey jackets, straight skirts, and sailor blouses, drawing the raves of *Harper's Bazaar* for her emphasis on stylish simplicity. Chanel later commented that "fashion should express the place, the moment." For her, this particular place and moment in fashion encompassed far more than an accommodation to wartime stringencies. Instead, she was "witnessing the death of luxury, the passing of the nineteenth century, the end of an era."[19]

While Chanel was revolutionizing fashion, François Coty continued to revolutionize his perfume as well as his perfume business. Despite the horrors of war, this was the year he presented his famous Chypre perfume, one that aficionados consider his masterpiece. Coty was betting that, in the face of constant death and destruction, women needed something to remind them of art, beauty, and seduction. He also was busy propping up and expanding his perfume and cosmetics empire, which that year suffered the huge loss of its Moscow branch, destroyed by the Bolsheviks—for whom he would retain an abiding hatred. To mollify critics of his burgeoning wealth and easy escape from military duty, Coty helped found an association to aid the war wounded and installed a military hospital in his château at Montbazon.

Like Citroën rather than Coty or Chanel, Gabriel Voisin and Louis Renault were profiting directly from rather than despite the war—Voisin from the manufacture of airplanes, and Renault from the production of trucks and a wide range of war materiel. By 1917, Renault's contribution to the war effort starred his invention and production of the first functional lightweight armored tank.

Others had envisioned and developed tanks, and the British had launched a cumbersome thirty-ton monster the year before, at the Somme. Yet unlike its rivals, Renault's six-ton version was sufficiently lightweight to climb slopes, crush barbed wire and trench revetments, and maneuver well, all the while its gunner (preferably less than five feet eight inches in height) fired the gun. The army first ordered one thousand, then increased the order to thirty-five hundred. The premature use of the British tanks had alerted the Germans, who used the intervening months to develop armor-piercing bullets and other devices. Still, the Germans did not anticipate anything quite so mobile or fast, and the arrival of these lightweight tanks on the front in 1918 would be a much-needed response to the final German offensive of the war.

Another much-needed response was the development of sonar for submarine detection—although it came a little late for use in this particular war. One of the key figures here was Paul Langevin, who pursued his scientific career with much the same dedication as Marie Curie pursued hers after their disastrous affair ended in 1911. He and Constantin Chilowski filed for U.S. patents for ultrasonic submarine detection in 1916 and 1917.

Langevin and Marie Curie never resumed their love affair, but in one of those coincidences that may not be a coincidence at all, given the closeness of the scientific community, Langevin's grandson, Michel Langevin (a nuclear physicist), married Marie Curie's granddaughter, the nuclear physicist Hélène Langevin-Joliot. Their son, Yves, is an astrophysicist. Langevin's remains, as well as those of Pierre and Marie Curie, are enshrined in the Panthéon.[20]

On the afternoon of May 18, 1917, Diaghilev and the Ballets Russes presented the premiere of *Parade*—the joint production of Cocteau, Satie, Picasso, and Massine—at a gala benefit for several war charities at the Théâtre du Châtelet. It was the first Paris season for the Ballets Russes since 1914, and Misia Edwards (looking like the mother of the bride, as Cocteau waspishly observed)[21] had come around sufficiently to agree to subsidize the production. The young Swiss conductor Ernest Ansermet presided, while Apollinaire contributed a program note in which he described the ballet as "*surréaliste*," thus giving a name to the surrealist movement soon to come.[22]

In a short article appearing that day, Cocteau wrote that "laughter is natural to Frenchmen: it is important to keep this in mind and not to be afraid to laugh even at this most difficult time."[23] It was indeed a most difficult time, for *Parade* was premiering during the height of the slaughter on the western front, which at that very moment was creating widespread mutiny among the troops. Yet beyond *Parade's* dalliance with the volatile moods of wartime Paris, it was the audience's incomprehension of what was happening on stage as well as in the orchestra that caused the trouble.

A mad mix of the circus and the streets, Satie's music combined the sounds of the music hall and ragtime with the noise of typewriters, sirens, and airplane propellers. This, along with Picasso's Cubist set and costumes (described as "ambulant chunks of Cubist scenery") and Massine's bizarre dance steps, created bedlam in the theater. Montparnasse and Montmartre artists bellowed their approval of Picasso, and young musicians such as Francis Poulenc and Georges Auric shouted "*Vive Satie!*," but less enlightened members of the audience were simply bewildered and appalled. Still, Diaghilev's challenge to Cocteau, to astound him, had at last found an answer. "Finally, in 1917," Cocteau wrote, "the opening night of *Parade*, I did astound him."[24]

Parade may have inspired the degree of scandal that Cocteau longed for, but it certainly bombed with the critics, especially Jean Poueigh, who lambasted Satie so thoroughly that Satie sent him a series of postcards in which he vulgarly told Poueigh what he thought of him. Poueigh immediately sued Satie for libel, on the grounds that Satie's postcards had publicly humiliated him, having been open to the eyes of Poueigh's concierge and, thereby, having exposed Poueigh to the ridicule of his entire neighborhood. The young Swiss composer Arthur Honegger, who was present at the trial, wrote home to his parents that "it was hilarious listening to the cards being read out indignantly by Poueigh's lawyer and repeated in judgment by the president, who looked distinctly cross at being obliged to read out such epithets."[25] Of course the last word resided with the court, which by this time seemed entirely out of sorts with the defendant and his noisy supporters. Satie lost the case and was sentenced to a week in prison plus a stiff one-hundred-franc fine and one thousand francs in damages. In the aftermath, Cocteau slugged Poueigh's lawyer and in turn was roughed up by the police.

Fortunately, Satie's prison sentence was suspended and the Princesse de Polignac paid the fine and damages, but the entire episode deeply depressed him. He had enjoyed being at the center of an artistic scandal, especially in league with such renowned collaborators, but the threat of bankruptcy and a police record alarmed him. Although he eventually won his appeal, this did not come until late November, leaving him under a cloud for many months. Fortunately the appeal judge also waived the damages, leaving the perpetually broke Satie with an unexpected windfall at year's end, which the Princesse de Polignac graciously allowed him to keep as an advance on *Socrate*.

Still, Satie was as notoriously thin-skinned as he was poverty-stricken, and Debussy's reaction to *Parade* stung him. They had been friends—often at a distance, but still friends—for many years. Satie had even served as a witness at Debussy's first marriage, in 1899. Louis Laloy later noted that their friendship was "turbulent but indissoluble," a "brotherhood" and yet a "rivalry"—one exacerbated by Debussy's success.[26] Debussy's opinion clearly mattered to Satie, and Debussy—who attended *Parade*—did not like it or what it portended for music's future. He never reviewed *Parade*, but word of his disenchantment reached Satie, who was infuriated. Opinions differ on whether they made up before Debussy's death.[27]

Despite opposition and opprobrium, *Parade*'s enthusiasts continued their support, organizing an homage to Satie in June in Montparnasse's tiny Salle Huyghens, an artist's studio that had become the venue for the newest in new music as well as in poetry and art. As Cocteau later wrote, "We listened to music and poetry standing—not as a matter of respect, but owing to a lack of chairs."[28]

Cocteau had successfully linked the world of fashionable society to Bohemia, with Misia and José Sert and all the others crowding together, much to the amazement of the elegant and wealthy young writer Paul Morand, who noted that Cocteau "is completely at ease in this milieu that is quite new to me."[29] It was from this energized gathering that there emerged a loose affiliation of young avant-garde composers led by Satie, who named them the Nouveaux Jeunes. Starting with Georges Auric, Louis Durey, and Arthur Honegger, they would soon include Germaine Tailleferre, Francis Poulenc, and Darius Milhaud—the future Groupe des Six. As Georges Auric pointed out: "Art continues to go forward and no one can prevent her."[30]

⌐⌐

It was not until the last week in April that the cold finally disappeared, only to be replaced by sweltering summer heat. By that time, Debussy's health was rapidly deteriorating. He had already declined a request from Fauré to perform, "due to the simple reason that I can no longer play the piano well enough to risk a performance of the *Etudes*. . . . I haven't enough fingers any more."[31] Although he would play the first performance of his sonata for violin and piano on May 5 (for the benefit for blind soldiers), it would be his last concert in Paris.

Sleep did not come easily, and he wryly noted that he had taken to reading the Civil Code in hope of nodding off—a remedy that did little good, as he found the Code sufficiently disturbing to keep him awake. More relaxing was G. K. Chesterton, especially *The Napoleon of Notting Hill*, which Debussy recommended for its "delightful imaginative touches."[32]

Another who notoriously found sleep difficult was Marcel Proust, who was known to awaken sleeping friends with a midnight visit ("to verify some fact or idea or to see again one of the models for one of his characters," as Céleste Albaret recalled).[33] Or he occasionally roused a particular quartet of musicians from their beds to come and play soothingly for him. Yet sometime during 1916 or 1917, friends noticed a change in him. Proust now began to socialize more, astonishing those who had not seen him in years. Some attributed this turnaround to the increasing danger from German attacks on Paris, which they concluded had flushed Proust out of his reclusive ways. But a more likely cause was that it was about this time that Proust completed *In Search of Lost Time.*

His housekeeper and confidante, Céleste Albaret, recalled that the momentous date when Proust finally wrote the words "The End" to his huge novel was in the early spring of 1922, but she may have been mistaken—she had not kept a diary or other exact record of these years.[34] Proust biographer William Carter argues for an earlier date, falling somewhere between 1916 and 1919—with the addendum that Proust (as always) made changes, additions, and corrections right up until the last minute.[35] Certainly by early 1918, Proust was anticipating a six-volume work.[36] If he had indeed given his masterwork its ultimate, if not final, shape by 1916 or 1917, that would explain the remarkable change in his routine starting around this time. Once again he could be seen several times a week at his own or others' much-diminished dinner parties at the Ritz or the Hôtel de Crillon, or at private soirées around town.

It was at one of these dinner parties at the Ritz that Proust first encountered Abbé Mugnier, who was as delightfully witty, engagingly literate, and shabbily dressed as ever. Jean Cocteau had earlier praised *Swann's Way* at a dinner that Mugnier attended,[37] and Mugnier was eager to make Proust's acquaintance. They talked of cathedrals, especially those of Chartres and Reims (whose angel statues "have da Vinci smiles"),[38] and discovered common interests in Chateaubriand, George Sand, and flowers—in particular Proust's beloved hawthorns. It was the start of a friendship that would continue to bloom throughout the remaining years of Proust's life.

⁓

Art struggled to survive during these difficult months. Monet continued hard at work on his grand paintings of water lilies (in his studio during the winter, in his garden during the summer), and Modigliani had his first one-man show in the tiny gallery of Berthe Weill, who had long ago discovered and championed Picasso and Matisse. Yet Georges Méliès's reverses grew increasingly heartbreaking. During 1917, the French army turned his main studio into a hospital and confiscated many of the original prints of his films, melting them down for their silver and celluloid content and using the reduction to make heels for army boots. Pathé took over his business, and in despair, Méliès burned most of his archive of film negatives as well as his extraordinary sets and costumes. Driven out of business, he would at length resort to running a small candy and toy shop in the Gare Montparnasse.[39]

There were too many funerals this year—not only of the fallen in battle, but also of giants from days gone by: Mirbeau in February and Degas in September, followed by Rodin on November 17. An age was passing.

In the south of France, an unlikely friendship took hold late in the year when Henri Matisse met and became firm friends with Pierre-Auguste Renoir, one of the titans among Matisse's predecessors—and one of the few who still was alive. Renoir had retired to the south of France several years earlier, for his health—although he never had enjoyed northern winters ("Even if you can stand the cold, why paint snow? It is a blight on the face of Nature").[40] Over the course of Renoir's remaining months of life, the two would chat endlessly about their work, analyze each other's paintings, and probe their differences in a spirit of ever-growing friendship and respect. It was a golden gift in the twilight of Renoir's life, and a blessing for Matisse.[41]

Meanwhile, the spotlight had turned on yet another major figure from the past: the famed Tiger, Georges Clemenceau, who in November 1917, at the age of seventy-six, became prime minister of France for the second time in his long career. It was without question the most difficult challenge of his entire life, and he was ready for it. As everyone knew, he was a feared fighter, with no tolerance for defeat—in war or in anything else. He had contemptuously refused to join previous wartime coalitions, which he lambasted for wishy-washiness, and flatly rejected any talk of a compromise peace. Now it was his turn, and he took to the leadership of wartime France with gusto. American support had not yet arrived, Italy was doing badly, and Russian participation had virtually ended, with every indication that Russia was preparing to make a separate peace with Germany. Yet upon presenting his governmental team to the Chamber, Clemenceau unhesitatingly declared: "We present ourselves to you with one thought—total war. . . . Just war, war, and nothing but war."[42]

He kept the all-important post of minister of war for himself, and indeed kept all important decisions in his own hands. Devoting himself to the prosecution of the war, Clemenceau now would firmly lead his country through the difficult months to come.

French Prime Minister Georges Clemenceau and British Field Marshal Sir Douglas Haig review an honor guard in Paris after the Second Battle of Cambrai, from "L'Illustration," 1918. French photographer Private Collection / Ken Welsh / The Bridgeman Art Library. © The Bridgeman Art Library.

CHAPTER TWENTY

~

Finale

(1918)

"Misfortune dogged us during the winter," wrote Helen Pearl Adam of that terrible winter of 1917–1918. Italian resistance was crumbling against the Austro-German offensive, all help from Russia had disappeared, and Germany now was prepared to throw its entire military strength onto its western front. "They meant to attack as soon as they were ready, and with the utmost possible force," Adam recorded in her diary.[1]

After a hiatus of almost two years, German bombs began to fall once more on Paris. On the night of January 30–31, thirty planes dropped 144 bombs containing 7,400 pounds of high explosives—the largest raid so far of the entire war. Subsequent nights were almost as bad. The idea was to soften up and demoralize the city prior to and during Germany's great offensive on the Arras–Saint-Quentin front in March, where the Germans expected to break through, opening their way to Paris.

In March, in coordination with its attack on the British army in the Saint-Quentin sector, Germany stepped up its aerial assault, bombarding the city by day with a frightening new weapon, its so-called Paris Gun. Little for certain is known about the construction of this siege gun, which the Germans destroyed before it could fall into Allied hands. What is known is that it was capable of hurling two-hundred-pound shells great distances, arcing in a trajectory that reached an altitude of twenty-five miles above the earth before descending into Paris, seventy-five miles away. When the first of these shells hit, early on the morning of March 21, 1918, the explosion rocked a large portion of the city. It landed on the Quai de la Seine, in northeastern

Paris, followed by others at close intervals (twenty-one on that first day, and about twenty per day for many days thereafter). Distraught Parisians at first assumed that these were bombs dropped from airplanes flying too high to be heard or seen, but soon sufficient evidence showed that this new assault was from shells, not bombs.

But how? And from where? Parisians were familiar with Big Bertha, the monster that chewed through fortresses along the Germans' relentless advance through Belgium into France, and quickly decided that this was the culprit. Yet given Big Bertha's size and limited range, this meant that German agents were firing it from just outside the city, or even within the city itself. When French air reconnaissance finally pinpointed the source, the truth turned out to be far more devastating. The Germans had constructed a weapon so powerful that it launched its shells into the stratosphere (the first man-made objects to do so prior to V-2 flights). No wonder that Parisians had little or no warning before these missiles streaked downward, wreaking havoc.

On March 29, one of these shells hit the Right Bank church of Saint-Gervais-Saint-Protais during its Good Friday service, collapsing the roof, crumpling a stone vault and support pillar, and sending tons of stone down on the hundreds of kneeling worshippers. Eighty-eight people died, and sixty-eight more were wounded in this disaster.[2] Many more would die and even more would be wounded before the Germans withdrew the gun in August, just ahead of Allied advances.

Despite fears that the Germans might at any moment decimate treasures such as Notre-Dame and the Eiffel Tower, the Paris Gun never was sufficiently accurate to aim so precisely. Given the extent of its range, its gunners were hard-pressed to target with any more precision than the city itself.

Yet accuracy mattered little; what the Germans sought was the destruction of morale. A great number of Parisians now left the city, but as for the rest, Germany was largely unsuccessful. After "two days of stupor," reported Adam, the rest of the population "settled to 'sticking it.'"[3] For his part, Clemenceau, surrounded by his anxious deputies, announced: "I am going to tell you a secret. Last night I slept, I slept well."[4]

⌒

"Perhaps the most startling thing about Clemenceau's present position," wrote Adam in 1918, "is the fact that he might have been a pillar of the French Government all his days. . . . We seem to have been looking to him for guidance and reassurance for many years."[5]

Yet throughout the length of Clemenceau's long career in politics and journalism, his reputation had been an edgy one. He had begun his career as a fire-eater, as a left-wing republican loosely grouped with other left-wingers under the rubric of "radical." He had earned a reputation for bringing down governments, not for leading them, and in more recent years he had turned against his labor constituency with a memorable sweep of strong-armed strike-breaking. A champion duelist with both words and weapons, he had not been nicknamed "the Tiger" for nothing.

All this seemed forgotten throughout the terrible first seven months of 1918, when Clemenceau not only remained in power but buoyed the entire nation, visiting the *poilus*, or infantrymen, in the trenches, and fairly prickling with determination to resist—and win. *Le Père la Victoire* (Father Victory), they called him, an affectionate appellation that conveyed both respect and trust. Steadfastly rallying the French, he never showed the smallest measure of doubt during Germany's final effort to break through the four-year-long stalemate and achieve victory before American troops and materiel arrived in meaningful numbers on the western front.

France faced multiple crises during these months, but never more severe than those of March and early June, when the German armies under General Erich Ludendorff pushed closer to Paris—and to victory—than at any time since the opening of the war. Germany no longer was fighting on two major fronts and could afford to throw its entire weight into the war in the west. Its assault on the Somme sector (Battle of Saint-Quentin) on March 21, timed to coincide with the first pummeling of Paris with the long-range Paris Gun, routed the British and allowed the Germans to advance almost forty miles—a devastating development for the Allies. The Allies (who now, at long last, agreed to a joint command, with General Foch as commander-in-chief) were able to regroup and hold the German forces until May 27. Then the Germans broke through at Chemin des Dames, and by May 30—in a repeat of the terrors of 1914—they reached the River Marne, less than forty miles from Paris.

"The worst days of 1914 seemed come again," wrote Helen Pearl Adam. "After four years of heroism and endurance, after four years of civilian patience, after four years of tested faith in victory, the solid ground beneath our feet threatened to fail." No one spoke of it, she added. "The people who remained in Paris kept their flag flying." But Paris banks sent their securities and their safe deposit boxes southward, as did various ministries and embassies, while Parisians "held furtive consultations as to what arrangements we could make if we had to walk out of Paris at one gate while the Germans walked in at another."[6]

∼

Claude Debussy was too weak to be carried to the cellar during the Germans' bombardment of Paris. "During his last days he listened to the dismal sound of explosions," his good friend Louis Laloy later recalled.[7] Debussy's suffering at last ended on March 25, when he died quietly in his bed.

The most touching account of Debussy's last moments came from his twelve-year-old daughter, Chouchou, in a letter she wrote to her half-brother, Raoul Bardac. "Papa was asleep," she recounted, "breathing regularly but very shallowly. He went on sleeping like that until 10 o'clock in the evening and then, gently, like an angel, he went to sleep forever." She wanted to burst into tears, "but I forced them back because of Mama."[8]

The funeral took place on March 28, the day before Good Friday, and included only a few of Debussy's oldest friends. Many had left Paris or were at the front; others, like Pierre Louÿs, Erik Satie, and René Peter, had become estranged. Debussy's brother Alfred had gotten leave from the trenches, and Louis Laloy was also present in his soldier's uniform. Laloy later wrote: "The Minister of Education took his place at the head of the procession. Side by side, . . . the two conductors of our great philharmonic societies, Camille Chevillard [Orchestre Lamoureux] and Gabriel Pierné [Concerts Colonne], walked in silence. . . . The sky was overcast. There was a rumbling in the distance. Was it a storm, the explosion of a shell or the guns at the front?"[9]

At the cemetery, the war's dismal presence precluded orations. All that Chouchou could think of was, "'I mustn't cry because of Mama.' I summoned up all my courage. . . . Tears restrained are worth as much as tears shed, and now it is night for ever. Papa is dead."[10]

They buried him at Père-Lachaise, but the following year he was reinterred at Passy cemetery. There, Chouchou would soon join him.[11]

⌒

The bombings of Paris devastated Lili Boulanger, who had collapsed following her success in the Prix de Rome. Ever the extrovert, Lili thoroughly enjoyed her new celebrity, accepting public performances and social engagements even while she continued to compose prolifically. Yet her health and strength were not up to this kind of activity, and by mid-1917, she once again became severely ill. An operation did not help, and by late 1917 she was rapidly declining.

Returning to Paris, she suffered so intensely from the bombings that her mother took her to the countryside to escape. Nadia and their friends braved the bombardments to travel to and from to see her, bringing ice to relieve her pain and delivering medical assistance.

Yet they could do little to help. On March 15, 1918, Lili Boulanger died, at the age of twenty-four. Her friends and family were devastated, but it was Lili's sister, Nadia, who would promote Lili's works throughout the course of her own long and remarkable career as a teacher, lecturer, conductor, and soloist (of both piano and organ). In this capacity, the older of the two pioneering Boulanger sisters would continue to help the younger, working to secure at least a small space for the musical legacy of a talented woman who died much too young.

～

One night in the midst of the German bombardments, Proust decided to pay a visit to the poet Francis Jammes, who lived on the other side of the Seine, near the Invalides. Proust was successful in finding a taxi to take him (not an easy undertaking in wartime Paris), but he walked all the way home, his way lit by "the searchlights and the shellbursts in the sky and the reflections in the river." When he reached the Place de la Concorde, he encountered a man who quickly fell into step beside him. They walked along like that, chatting, until they reached the Place de la Madeleine, where Proust was within a short distance of his residence and thanked the man for seeing him home. "He was a bad lot," Proust later told Céleste. "I guessed it right away, but I didn't show it until we parted." After thanking him, Proust asked the fellow why he hadn't attacked him. The answer? "Oh, not someone like you, monsieur"—which pleased Proust enormously.[12]

Céleste was taken aback by this encounter, especially after she began to put away Proust's coat and hat. "When I got to the hat," she recalled, "I couldn't help exclaiming. The brim was full of bits of shrapnel. 'Monsieur, look at all this metal!'. . . 'Weren't you afraid?'"

"No, Céleste," he replied. "Why should I be? It was such a beautiful sight."[13]

At about this time, Proust wrote a friend, "As for guns and Gothas, I assure you that I never give them a thought; I'm afraid of far less dangerous things—mice, for instance—and, not being frightened by air-raids . . . it would be an affectation on my part to pretend to a fear of them."[14]

～

It was during one of the last and worst of the bombardments that Blaise Cendrars encountered Erik Satie lying at the foot of the obelisk in the Place de la Concorde. Alarmed, Cendrars leaned over what he thought was a dead body and discovered that it was Satie, very much alive. What was he doing there? asked Cendrars. Satie replied that he realized that he was not under shelter, "but you know, that thing goes up into the sky and I have the feeling of being under shelter." In any case, he added, "I'm composing a piece of music for the obelisk. A good idea, don't you think?"

Cendrars replied that he thought it was quite a good idea, so long as it wasn't a military march. No danger of that, Satie told him; he was composing a piece for the pharaoh's wife who was buried there. "No one ever gives her a thought."

Actually, Cendrars told him, it was Cleopatra's mummy that was down there. "Impossible," Satie retorted, and then hummed the tune he had composed. He added, "It's only because of those damned guns that I'm here now—for the first time."[15]

⌢

That spring, Jean Cocteau published Le Coq et l'Arlequin (The Cock and the Harlequin), a pamphlet of witty aphorisms that made Cocteau into the spokesman for the musicians Satie had dubbed Les Nouveaux Jeunes, soon to become known as Les Six. In it, Cocteau pleaded for a purely French music, much as Satie had done all those years before. This new music, declared Cocteau, "shuns the colossal. That is what I call 'escaping from Germany.'"[16] Cocteau proclaimed Satie the leader of this musical breakthrough and, perhaps surprisingly, attacked Debussy and Stravinsky as well as Wagner and Germany—Debussy, for his "impressionist polyphonies" and preoccupation with the sublime; Stravinsky, for his corruption by the theater. "I consider the 'Sacre du Printemps' a masterpiece," Cocteau conceded, "but I discern in the atmosphere created by its execution a religious complicity existing among the initiated, like the hypnotism of Bayreuth."[17]

Cocteau and his musical compatriots were quite willing, of course, to allow the infiltration of American jazz into their purely French music. The whole point of their aesthetic was freshness and originality, and the breezes that were blowing from across the Atlantic brought exactly what Cocteau longed for. He enthused over Mitchell's Jazz Kings, whom he heard in a cabaret in the Casino de Paris, leading a critic to write that Cocteau's artistic sensibility "fluctuated between Cubism and vaudeville."[18]

Misia Edwards Sert once famously remarked that Cocteau "needs to make himself liked by everybody at the same time."[19] Yet despite Cocteau's maddening contradictions, it was clear that with Le Coq's resounding rejection of the past, he had emerged as a leading figure of Paris's artistic future.

⌢

In May 1918, while Cocteau and his colleagues were debating the future of French music, Charles de Gaulle and his determined companions were transferred to the great fortress of Wülzburg. There he continued to hold what one fellow prisoner described as "an unquestionable ascendency over those around him." Although de Gaulle was unaffected, "he knew how to keep people at a distance." Everyone else addressed one another with the familiar *tu*. But "no one ever said *tu* to de Gaulle."[20]

De Gaulle now decided to re-attempt an escape operation that he had tried before—being escorted out by someone disguised in a German uniform. All that was necessary was to break into the tailor's shop that provided the guards' uniforms and pretend that de Gaulle was being transferred elsewhere. Successfully negotiating the break-in and departure, and changing afterward into civilian clothes, he and his ersatz escort walked for a day and night toward Nuremberg, where they planned to take a train to Frankfurt. All went well until they were stopped by a patrol asking to see their papers. Back they went to Wülzburg.

So now, de Gaulle decided on another approach. Unable to climb the ramparts, he decided to hide in the huge basket of dirty laundry, slipping inside during those few moments between when the quartermaster checked the basket's contents and when it was sent off, padlocked, to the nearby town. Having comrades who by this time were accomplished at picking locks, de Gaulle chose his moment after the quartermaster went off to search for the sentries to accompany the padlocked basket. The clever accomplices even supplied de Gaulle with a cable that allowed him to hold on firmly when the basket was lifted.

De Gaulle managed the escape perfectly, and after emerging from the basket (in civilian clothes), he mingled with the crowds, hid in the forest outside town, and then walked toward Nuremberg, which he reached in three days. Unfortunately a bad stomach flu now hit him. Instead of waiting for a less-watched night train, he had to take the first train out, where he encountered military police. Once again, he failed.

⁓

In July, General Ludendorff threw his troops into yet another massive attack, in what became known as the Second Battle of the Marne, and now the Americans massively entered the fray.

American soldiers had begun to arrive in France the previous year; some of them took part in that year's July 4 celebration in Paris. After training in that summer's rain and mud, they were first deployed with French and British troops in relatively quiet sectors to break them in to the rigors of combat.[21]

By late May and early June 1918, American soldiers (by now flooding into France at the astounding rate of almost ten thousand a day) were beginning to make their presence felt on the battlefield, although they still were fighting within the French and British armies.

"On the fourth of July," recounted Helen Pearl Adam, "Paris went mad," with stars and stripes everywhere. Adam noted that her cook "says wisely that if America wins the war for us, what remains for us to say?" But her housemaid, "almost in tears, cries: 'But we've fought for four years!'" Americans, a bit embarrassed by the accolades, "say that they wish they had already earned it, as they mean to do."[22]

That fourteenth of July, Bastille Day—France's own Fête Nationale— "echoed with the tread of marching squadrons, . . . the crash of military music, the voices of children chanting so high that it seemed . . . that 'le jour de gloire est arrivé.'"[23] Then at midnight, "a deep, baying clamour broke the darkness." Parisians, wakened, waited for the sirens, but there were none. Adam suddenly understood that this was no air raid. "The immense symphony of drums that sounded . . . was no barrage," nor were the lights from Paris's anti-aircraft defense.[24] Edith Wharton realized that she had heard this "level throb of distant artillery"[25] during her expeditions to the front, but never before in Paris. It was the sound of the long-awaited German offensive, just a few short miles away.

⁓

On July 12, just before this dreaded offensive began, Pablo Picasso got married. His bride was the lovely Ballets Russes dancer Olga Khokhlova, with whom he fell in love the previous year in Rome, while working on the sets and costumes for *Parade*. "Russians marry," Diaghilev had warned him,[26] but Picasso did not shy from the prospect. He was thirty-seven years old and thought himself quite ready to become a husband and father.

He wed his bride in Paris's Russian Orthodox Church (later, Cathedral) of Saint-Alexandre-Nevski, a traditional onion-domed edifice that had been the social as well as religious center for homesick Russians in Paris ever since the mid-nineteenth century—a function that it would embrace with special fervor during the years of the great exodus of Russians to Paris following the Bolshevik Revolution. Stravinsky, for whom the church would play an important role during the 1930s, thought of it as "an island of Russian colour in its drab Parisian neighbourhood."[27]

Jean Cocteau, Max Jacob, and Apollinaire served as witnesses for the marriage, and the newlyweds honeymooned glamorously in Biarritz, in the villa of Picasso's new patron, the Chilean heiress Eugenia Errázuriz (who by this time was supplying him with a thousand francs a month). When Picasso and Olga returned, they moved from Montparnasse to a large Right Bank apartment on Rue La Boétie, between Boulevard Haussmann and the Champs-Elysées. Just as Picasso had permanently left Montmartre for Montparnasse, he now left Montparnasse forever.

Only two months earlier, Picasso and Ambroise Vollard had served as witnesses at Apollinaire's marriage to Jacqueline Kolb at the Church of Saint-Thomas-d'Aquin, near Apollinaire's quarters on the Boulevard Saint-Germain. Ostensibly it was a joyous occasion, but the war was at its peak, and Apollinaire himself was suffering more and more from headaches, depression, and vertigo. Something was wrong, but no one quite knew what. He certainly wasn't his old self. Perhaps his head wound had not properly healed? Or had his brain been permanently damaged?

Modigliani, too, was ill—although his illness was a recurrence of the tuberculosis that had plagued him since childhood. A year or so before, Beatrice Hastings had exited his life and another woman, Jeanne Hébuterne, had quietly entered. Jeanne was a gifted artist almost sixteen years Modigliani's junior, from a proper, if artistically inclined, bourgeois home. By May 1917, they had become lovers, and by the spring of 1918, she was pregnant. Soon after, they left Paris for Nice, where Jeanne's mother joined them—presumably to care for her daughter and imminent grandchild, but prompting Modigliani to move into his own space.

Modigliani had never taken much concern for the welfare of his lovers, or of the children they bore (at least one of which clearly was his). Years before, he had argued that "people like us [artists] . . . have different rights, different values than do normal, ordinary people because we have different needs which put us . . . above their moral standards." According to his view of things, everything—including Jeanne and the child—was secondary to his art. According to a close friend, "he had no other attachment."[28]

Several years earlier, in contemplating the shambles of his second marriage, Debussy had argued that "an artist is by definition a man accustomed to dreams and living among apparitions. . . . It's pointless expecting this same man to follow strictly all the observances of daily life, the laws and all the other barriers erected by a cowardly, hypocritical world."[29] Yet Ravel, who never married or—to anyone's knowledge—had an intimate relationship with anyone, had long before reached a different conclusion. Soon after the war's end, he responded to the news of friends' marital troubles by observing: "Artists are not made for marriage. We are rarely normal, and our lives are even less so." Given that, he chose to hold himself aloof from intimate relationships. "Morality," he noted, "this is what I practice, and what I am determined to continue." He added, "Life does hurt us, doesn't it?"[30]

⁓

As the war ground on, Stravinsky remained in Switzerland, where he was supporting an ever-growing horde of destitute Russian in-laws on his much-diminished income.[31] "You had to see him at the piano," recalled one of the soloists in The Soldier's Tale, which occupied Stravinsky during the first part of the year. There he was, "hammering the keys with nervous hands and sustaining his dynamism with an improbable number of kirsches, gulping them down one after the other, then correcting their sometimes too drastic effects with a no less enormous intake of aspirin."[32]

Matisse, too, found the stress of the war almost unbearable, especially with one son, Jean, soon to be posted to the front and his youngest, Pierre, about to be mobilized. Matisse was still in Nice when the long-range March shelling began on Paris, and he wrote a friend that "there's a wave of panic in Nice just now," with everyone assuming—and hoping—that there was a mistake in the radio transmission about the new weapon's astonishing range. Communications were disrupted, and he had little word from Amélie (who had returned to Paris for Marguerite's regular medical treatment), except to tell him to stay where he was. Rising early each morning to read the latest dispatches in the newspapers, Matisse wrote in late March that "the atmosphere isn't at all reassuring here—and as I haven't worked today, I've lost my usual ballast."[33]

The panic diminished during April and May but surged once more during the crisis of late May and early June, as the Germans pushed to the Marne. Even painting did not calm Matisse now, and he daily took the tram downtown to wait for the communiqué posted every afternoon—drinking coffee and, to calm his nerves, beer while he waited. While Matisse remained anxiously on the sidelines, Amélie prepared their Paris home for evacuation, burying sculpture in the garden and rolling up batches of paintings to travel south. In the meantime, Paris hospitals had been evacuated, surgeons throughout France had been drafted for duty on the front, and facilities nearer Nice were inadequate for Marguerite's medical care.

It was in the midst of this furor that Pierre Matisse celebrated his eighteenth birthday and, jubilant about being saved from endless hours of violin practice (upon which his father insisted), raced to enlist. Unfortunately he soon took ill in a cholera outbreak that killed a number of his colleagues. Matisse, who had already managed to return to Paris to move Marguerite closer to her surgeons (and consequently spent several nights with his family in their cellar during a resumption of the shelling), now raced to Pierre in Cherbourg. Pierre, as it turned out, only suffered from the flu, but taking no chances, Matisse managed to win leave for him and take him home.

That April, Manfred von Richthofen—the "Red Baron"—who was credited with an awe-inspiring eighty air victories or kills, was in turn killed in action. France's René Fonck then became the man of the moment, earning the title "Ace of Aces" for his seventy-five confirmed air victories.

In the meantime, the daring pilot Roland Garros at last escaped his prisoner-of-war camp and now encountered Isadora Duncan, who in April returned to Paris after a lengthy stint abroad (including a homecoming in San Francisco, an acrimonious and expensive stay in New York, and an unsuccessful attempt to seduce George Bernard Shaw in London). She and Garros watched a night-time burst of shells in the Place de la Concorde, where Isadora danced to the sound of the shells and Garros applauded, "his melancholy dark eyes lit up by the fire of the rockets that fell and exploded quite near us." That night, he told Isadora that he "only saw and wished for death"—a death wish that Isadora said she identified with, calling it "Incurable Sorrow & Heartbreak. I rush about the world trying to find a remedy—There is none."[34]

Garros returned to the front,[35] and Isadora consoled herself with a new lover, the famed concert pianist Walter Rummel, who shared her American roots (being a grandson of Samuel Morse). For the next three years Rummel would become Isadora's accompanist and musical adviser, receiving equal billing in what were described as joint recitals. Her association with Rummel would bring Isadora a period of unaccustomed calm, as well as a surge of fine reviews.

And then, in the midst of despair, good news at long last came. On July 18, Helen Pearl Adam reported that all news of the relentless German offensive seemed to have disappeared, replaced, amazingly enough, by news of an Allied offensive. Strong French and American resistance had held the Germans at the Marne, and on July 18, Foch ordered a counterattack. Suddenly the Allies were pushing the Germans back, and back farther yet, until by the end of August, they had withdrawn to the Hindenburg Line. In September, American forces, attacking on both sides of the Saint-Mihiel salient, captured some fifteen thousand of the enemy, and the news kept getting better as the counterattack spread. At last, at long last, the initiative had passed to the Allies.

Ludendorff's nerve now cracked, and he began to probe possibilities for an armistice. Clemenceau's nerve, though, never cracked. He had maintained the morale of France's troops and of the entire nation during the long difficult months when victory seemed beyond reach. Following Germany's devastating victory over the Allies on March 21, Clemenceau had remarked that after news like that, "you need an iron-bound spirit to retain your confidence."[36]

Pétain's pessimism had swung Clemenceau in favor of Foch for the command of Allied armies, and Foch, too, inspired as well as coordinated. Yet it was Clemenceau's own confidence as well as his presence, as near to the front lines as he could get, that bolstered sagging morale when it was most needed. Not only his mental but his physical endurance was remarkable for a man of his age. But it was his disregard for danger that brought him into instant rapport with the fighting men in the trenches.

One encounter in particular stood out in Clemenceau's mind: "They came to meet [me]," he later recalled, "vague shapes all white with the dust, who made the gesture of lining up to give the military salute while their leader stepped forward and in staccato tones shouted out, '1st Company, 2nd battalion, 3rd regiment, present'!" And then, touchingly, the soldier offered Clemenceau a little bouquet of dusty flowers. "Ah, those frail dried-up stalks," Clemenceau recollected. "The Vendée will see them; for I have promised that they will go to the grave with me."[37]

And they did. For these dry and dusty flowers remained in Clemenceau's study until his death, when they were placed in his coffin.

Another touching ceremony took place in early autumn, when Squadron Chief Alfred Dreyfus, after having served fourteen months on the front, was posted to duty behind the lines, having reached the age of fifty-nine. In his new post, he received an excellent report from his commanding general, leading to his promotion, at long last, to the rank of lieutenant-colonel. Marking the occasion, Dreyfus found on his desk a "superb bouquet of flowers," accompanied by a touching note of congratulations from the women he employed in the work of destroying grenades. Two days later, a delegation of civil workers from the armaments workshops under his command presented him with a "ravishing bronze" of a Gallic cock crushing a Prussian helmet under its feet. The oldest member of the delegation then read Dreyfus a "heartfelt speech." This demonstration of respect and even affection was perhaps not surprising, given the encouragement that Dreyfus showed his subordinates (on at least one occasion noting that his men at the front were "admirable" and "'exceptional,' not a complaint, not a murmur").[38] Yet Dreyfus was deeply moved and wrote his son, Pierre, of these developments, including the text of his promotion.[39]

～

By September, the news from the front continued to be good, but Paris took the change quietly. "It is like a city created in a dream between sleeping and waking," Helen Pearl Adam wrote. "Like lovers united after many years of unhappiness, France and Victory talk together in low tones." In October, she wrote, "We are half afraid to be as happy as we are!"[40]

As soon as the Germans departed, Matisse rushed north to his hometown of Bohain, to rescue his mother and brother and his brother's family, who had suffered terribly during their years under the German army's yoke. In contrast, Charles de Gaulle anticipated his own release with despair. "If I cannot get into the fighting again between now and the end of the war," he wrote his mother on September 1, "shall I stay in the army? And what commonplace kind of a future would I have there?"[41] Having missed so much of the fighting, his future career as an army officer looked bleak.

The global flu pandemic, which first surfaced at the beginning of the year, now reappeared in a far deadlier form, sweeping through Paris that autumn. One of its first victims was Apollinaire, who, weakened as he was by his war wound, died on November 9 at the age of thirty-eight. Among the many other deaths in Paris, Sarah Bernhardt's beloved playwright, Edmond Rostand, the author of Cyrano de Bergerac and L'Aiglon, succumbed to the flu in December. And there were many, many more.

Yet despite the pandemic's dismal impact, the end of the war was drawing near. Germany was pressing for an armistice, and at this, Clemenceau "nearly went mad, mad with joy. . . . I had seen too much of the front, too many of those water-filled holes where men had lived for four years."[42] In early November, when victory was sure, he recalled that he was the last survivor of those in the National Assembly who had signed the protest against the treaty of 1871 that relinquished Alsace-Lorraine to Germany. It had taken almost fifty years and a war of unimaginable proportions, but France had emerged victorious. She had repelled Germany's invasion, and in the end, Alsace-Lorraine once again was hers.

On the morning of November 11, Edith Wharton was startled to hear the sound of church bells at an unusual hour. "Through the deep expectant hush," she later wrote, "we heard, one after another, the bells of Paris calling to each other." For a moment, "our hearts wavered and doubted. Then, like the bells, they swelled to bursting, and we knew the war was over."[43]

Celebration in Paris, France, for the signing of the armistice, November 11, 1918. © Excelsior–L'Equipe / Roger-Viollet / The Image Works.

That same morning, Sarah Bernhardt and her granddaughter, Lysiane, sailed into port in Bordeaux, returning from their long tour in America. A large crowd on the wharf was shouting and gesturing, and it was a while before anyone on board could make out what they were saying. "It's the armistice!" Sarah's doctor finally cried. "They're shouting 'Armistice!' Can't you hear them?"

Lysiane ran to tell her grandmother, but she was jostled and held up by the other passengers, "who were mad with excitement." Her father, racing on board from shore, beat her to it, and when Lysiane reached their cabin, he was holding Sarah in his arms. "Mama! It's the armistice!" he exclaimed. "The war is over!"[44]

At that, Sarah Bernhardt and her family wept.

On November 11, at 11 a.m. (the eleventh hour of the eleventh day of the eleventh month), guns sounded the Armistice, and Parisians celebrated for three days. "No one who saw the boulevards on the Sunday when we were waiting for the news, the Monday when the Armistice was signed, or the Tuesday when we heard its terms, and the lights went up at dusk along the splendid thoroughfare for the first time in four years, will ever forget the sight," wrote Adam.[45] People poured into the Place de la Concorde, where they climbed on the enemy cannons and gathered around the Strasbourg memorial—"an immense, unorganized, intoxicated crowd, driven by a desire to shout, to cry aloud, to run or to climb up something."[46] This jubilant throng downed champagne and anything else that was bottled, but they remained in good order. About the worst crime committed by the Paris populace in those three days was the theft of Allied flags, once the shops sold out.

Isadora Duncan and Walter Rummel watched the victory march through the Arc de Triomphe and shouted, "The world is saved."[47] Paul Poiret gave an enormous victory party, while Claude Monet wrote to his good friend Georges Clemenceau to tell him that he was on the verge of finishing two water lilies panels, which he wanted to sign on Victory Day. Could they, he wanted to know, be offered to the state? "It's little enough," he added, "but it's the only way I have of taking part in the victory."[48]

Despite the relief and the euphoria that came with victory, Clemenceau clearly recognized the problems that lay ahead. That evening, after reading the text of the armistice in both the Chamber and the Senate, he remarked quietly to a friend, "We have won the war: now we have to win the peace, and it may be more difficult."[49]

~

Some months later, when a young American soldier visited Gertrude Stein and Alice B. Toklas in Paris, they took him to see the sights. Afterward, he told them solemnly, "I think all that was worth fighting for."[50]

Virtually every Parisian would have fervently agreed. And yet the cost had been horrendous. To achieve victory, France had lost almost one and a half million men, with at least another three million wounded—many so severely that they would be unable to work or function normally again. The loss of property—homes, fields, shops, and factories—was incalculable. Moreover, the trauma of more than four years of warfare would affect the nation for years to come.

It was as France began to realize the depth of its war-inflicted wounds that its prewar world increasingly acquired the aura of a golden age. This was of course an illusion, as Proust so clearly realized while depicting and dissecting a society and a way of life that (in Céleste Albaret's words) "was disappearing then and is now gone forever."[51]

The Belle Epoque had never been a golden age, especially for those who did not share the wealth and privilege of society's upper echelons. Yet even for those who belonged to these rarified strata, the Belle Epoque had never been as radiantly perfect as enshrined in memory. Tensions and fault lines had shadowed the era's extraordinary achievements, and dramatic break-throughs had inevitably heralded change. Those who enjoyed the comforts and pleasures that their rank and wealth commanded saw their world rapidly disappearing, in the kind of last throes that Ravel's La Valse would evoke. This world was dying, and it would at last be swept away by war.

"Ah, Céleste," Proust told his sympathetic housekeeper, as he pondered the pre-war world he had known so well and portrayed so uncompromisingly. "All that is crumbling to dust. It is like a collection of beautiful antique fans on a wall. You admire them, but there is no hand now to bring them alive. The very fact that they are under glass proves that the ball is over."[52]

~

Notes

1 Enter the King (1900)

Selected sources for this and subsequent chapters are listed, by chapter, in the approximate order in which they informed the text: Josep Palau i Fabre, *Picasso: The Early Years, 1881–1907*, trans. Kenneth Lyons (New York: Rizzoli, 1981); John Richardson, *A Life of Picasso: The Prodigy, 1881–1906* (New York: Knopf, 2012); Janet Flanner, *Men and Monuments* (New York: Harper, 1957); Robert Boardingham, *The Young Picasso* (New York: Universe, 1997); Jiri Mucha, *Alphonse Mucha: His Life and Work* (New York: St. Martin's, 1974); Jiri Mucha, *Alphonse Mucha: His Life and Art* (London: Academy Editions, 1989); Claude Berton and Alexandre Ossadzow, *Fulgence Bienvenüe et la construction du métropolitain de Paris* (Paris: Presses de l'Ecole nationale des ponts et chausses, 1998); Frédéric Descouturelle, André Mignard, and Michel Rodriguez, *Le Métropolitain d'Hector Guimard* (Paris: Somogy editions d'art, 2004); Maurice Rheims, *Hector Guimard*, trans. Robert Erich Wolf, phot. Felipe Ferré (New York: Abrams, 1988); Alain Clément and Gilles Thomas, *Atlas du Paris souterrain: La doublure sombre de la ville lumière* (Paris: Editions Parigramme, 2001); Clive Lamming, *Métro insolite: Promenades curieuses, lignes oubliées, stations fantômes, metros imaginaires, rames* (Paris: Parigramme, 2001); Ghislaine Sicard-Picchiottino, *François Coty: Un industriel corse sous la IIIe République* (Ajaccio, France: Albiana, 2006); Elisabeth Barillé, *Coty: Parfumeur and Visionary*, trans. Mark Howarth (Paris: Editions Assouline, 1996); Bill Mallon, *The 1900 Olympic Games: Results for All Competitors in All Events, with Commentary* (Jefferson, N.C.: McFarland, 1998); Mike O'Mahony, *Olympic Visions: Images of the Games through History* (London: Reaktion Books, 2012); Stephanie Daniels and Anita Tedder, *"A Proper Spectacle": Women Olympians, 1900–1936* (Houghton Conquest, UK: ZeNaNA Press, 2000); Mike Dyreson, *Making the American Team: Sport, Culture, and the Olympic Experience* (Urbana: University of Illinois Press, 1998); Anthony Rhodes, *Louis Renault: A Biography* (New York: Harcourt, Brace & World, 1970); Jean-Noël Mouret, *Louis Renault* (Paris: Gallimard, 2009); Arbie Orenstein, *Ravel: Man and Musician* (New York: Columbia University Press, 1975); Maurice Ravel, *A Ravel Reader: Correspondence, Articles, Interviews*, comp. and ed. Arbie Orenstein (Mineola, N.Y.: Dover, 2003);

Mary McAuliffe, *Dawn of the Belle Epoque: The Paris of Monet, Zola, Bernhardt, Eiffel, Debussy, Clemenceau, and Their Friends* (Lanham, Md.: Rowman & Littlefield, 2011); Paul Poiret, *King of Fashion: The Autobiography of Paul Poiret*, trans. Stephen Haden Guest (Philadelphia: J. B. Lippincott, 1931); Cornelia Otis Skinner, *Elegant Wits and Grand Horizontals: Paris—La Belle Epoque* (London: Michael Joseph, 1962); Valerie Steele, *Paris Fashion: A Cultural History*, 2nd rev. ed. (New York: Oxford University Press, 1998).

1. The Gare d'Orsay, now transformed into the Musée d'Orsay, was built especially to accommodate the crowds attending the Paris exposition.

2. It is now preserved in the Musée Carnavalet, the museum of the history of Paris (23 Rue de Sévigné, Paris).

3. This is now Métro Line 1, which then extended from Porte de Vincennes in the east to Porte Maillot in the west, minus several stations that would be built later. It took approximately thirty minutes for a passenger to travel its 10.6 kilometers.

4. The majority of these establishments were quite small, employing fewer than ten people. Among the largest, Guerlain was the most prestigious, with Houbigant and Lubin close behind.

5. Rhodes, *Louis Renault*, 26.

6. Ravel quoted from a 1933 article in *Ravel Reader*, 399. Here he would add that his own *Bolero* (written in 1928) "owed its inception to a factory," and he mused that someday he would "like to play it with a vast industrial works in the background."

7. Debussy won the Prix de Rome in 1884 and hated every minute of his Rome years (see McAuliffe, *Dawn of the Belle Epoque*).

8. Ravel to Dumitru Kiriac, 21 March 1900, in *Ravel Reader*, 57. The Institut de France, which included the Académie des Beaux-Arts, was the official body overseeing the Prix de Rome competition.

9. Ravel to Dumitru Kiriac, 21 March 1900, in *Ravel Reader*, 57. See also *Ravel Reader*, 35n15 and 57n2.

10. Saint-Saëns praised Ravel's 1901 Prix de Rome cantata, which presented Ravel in his most traditional mode (Ravel, *Ravel Reader*, 107n2).

11. Madame de Saint-Marceaux's comment from her diary, in Orenstein, *Ravel*, 21.

12. Poiret, *King of Fashion*, 19.

13. Poiret, *King of Fashion*, 23.

14. Poiret, *King of Fashion*, 40.

15. Poiret, *King of Fashion*, 24.

16. Poiret, *King of Fashion*, 65.

17. Poiret, *King of Fashion*, 67.

2 Bohemia on the Seine (1900)

Selected sources for this chapter: Palau i Fabre, *Picasso: The Early Years*; Richardson, *Life of Picasso: The Prodigy*; Boardingham, *Young Picasso*; Jaime Sabartès, *Picasso: An Intimate Portrait*, trans. Angel Flores (New York: Prentice Hall, 1948); Flanner, *Men and Monuments*; McAuliffe, *Dawn of the Belle Epoque*; Robert Orledge, ed., *Satie Remembered*, trans. Roger Nichols (Portland, Ore.: Amadeus Press, 1995); Jean Renoir, *Renoir, My Father*, trans. Randolph Weaver and Dorothy Weaver (Boston: Little, Brown, 1962); Charles Rearick, *Paris Dreams, Paris Memories: The City and Its Mystique* (Stanford, Calif.: Stanford University Press, 2011); Hilary Spurling, *The Unknown Matisse, A Life of Henri Matisse: The Early Years, 1869–1908*

(New York: Knopf, 2005); Alfred H. Barr Jr., *Matisse: His Art and His Public* (New York: Museum of Modern Art, 1951); Henri Matisse, *Matisse on Art*, rev. ed., ed. Jack Flam (Berkeley: University of California Press, 1995); Ruth Butler, *Rodin: The Shape of Genius* (New Haven, Conn.: Yale University Press, 1993); Poiret, *King of Fashion*; Claude Monet, *Monet by Himself: Paintings, Drawings, Pastels, Letters*, ed. Richard R. Kendall, trans. Bridget Strevens Romer (London: Macdonald, 1989); Daniel Wildenstein, *Monet, or the Triumph of Impressionism*, vol. 1, trans. Chris Miller and Peter Snowdon (Cologne, Germany: Taschen/Wildenstein Institute, 1999); Robert Gottlieb, *Sarah: The Life of Sarah Bernhardt* (New Haven, Conn.: Yale University Press, 2010); Jean Lacouture, *De Gaulle: The Rebel, 1890–1944*, trans. Patrick O'Brian (New York: Norton, 1993); Charles Williams, *The Last Great Frenchman: A Life of General de Gaulle* (New York: Wiley, 1993); Jean-Marie Mayeur and Madeleine Rebérioux, *The Third Republic from Its Origins to the Great War, 1871–1914*, trans. J. R. Foster (Cambridge, UK: Cambridge University Press, 1989); Frederick Brown, *Zola: A Life* (New York: Farrar, Straus & Giroux, 1995); William C. Carter, *Marcel Proust: A Life* (New Haven, Conn.: Yale University Press, 2000); Marcel Proust, *Selected Letters*, vol. 1 (1880–1903), ed. Philip Kolb, trans. Ralph Manheim (Garden City, N.Y.: Doubleday, 1983); Marcel Proust, *Selected Letters*, vol. 3 (1910–1917), ed. Philip Kolb, trans. Terence Kilmartin (London: HarperCollins, 1992); Marcel Proust, *The Guermantes Way* (Vol. 3, *In Search of Lost Time*), trans. C. K. Scott Moncrieff and Terence Kilmartin, rev., D. J. Enright (New York: Modern Library, 1993); Céleste Albaret, *Monsieur Proust: A Memoir*, rec. Georges Belmont, trans. Barbara Bray (New York: McGraw-Hill, 1976); Arthur Gold and Robert Fizdale, *Misia: The Life of Misia Sert* (New York: Morrow, 1981); Misia Sert, *Misia and the Muses: The Memoirs of Misia Sert*, trans. Moura Budberg (New York: John Day, 1953); Peter Kurth, *Isadora: A Sensational Life* (Boston: Little, Brown, 2001); Isadora Duncan, *My Life* (New York: Liveright, 2013); Gale Murray, ed., *Toulouse-Lautrec: A Retrospective* (New York: Hugh Lauter Levin, 1992); Henry Adams, *The Education of Henry Adams* (New York: Random House, 1931); Gabriel Voisin, *Men, Women, and 10,000 Kites*, trans. Oliver Stewart (London: Putnam, 1963); Harry Kessler, *Journey to the Abyss: The Diaries of Count Harry Kessler, 1880–1918*, ed. and trans. Laird M. Easton (New York: Knopf, 2011).

1. The father's family name was Ruiz and the mother's was Picasso (her family originally came from Genoa). It was usual in Spain for the child's legal name to combine both parents' names, but with the child called by the father's family name. Until about the age of seventeen Picasso signed his pictures "P. Ruiz Picasso." After that, he opted to be known as Picasso.

2. Richardson, *Life of Picasso: The Prodigy*, 160–61.

3. Richardson, *Life of Picasso: The Prodigy*, 161.

4. The exposition's enormous fine arts display, housed in the newly built Grand Palais and Petit Palais, was divided into three sections: an exhibition of French art to 1800; an exhibition of French art from 1800 to 1889 (the year of the previous Paris exposition); and a contemporary exhibition, where works by artists from the exclusive and tradition-minded Salon (the official exhibition of the Académie des Beaux-Arts) for the first time mingled with artists from the Société Nationale des Beaux-Arts, which had been formed several years earlier as an alternative to the Salon.

5. Contamine de Latour's reminiscences appeared in the August 3, 5, and 6, 1925, issues of the French journal *Comoedia*. From Orledge, *Satie Remembered*, 26.

6. At this time Paris's original twelve arrondissements, or administrative units, expanded to the twenty that exist today. Note that the Bois de Boulogne and the Bois de Vincennes,

at the eastern and western edges of Paris, lie outside these arrondissements, even though they belong to the city.

7. Orledge, *Satie Remembered*, 26.

8. As told to his son, Jean Renoir (*Renoir, My Father*, 197).

9. Swags of similar gilded leaves can still be seen in the courtyard of the Petit Palais.

10. Spurling, *Unknown Matisse*, 46.

11. Matisse to the Museum of the City of Paris at the Petit Palais, 10 November 1936, in *Matisse on Art*, 124. This painting still hangs in the Museum of Beaux-Arts of the City of Paris, in the Petit Palais.

12. Butler, *Rodin*, 439.

13. Poiret, *King of Fashion*, 27.

14. Falguière received the nod from the Société des Gens de Lettres for a Balzac sculpture when the society famously rejected Rodin's monument of Honoré de Balzac.

15. See note 4.

16. Monet to his gardener, [February 1900?], in *Monet by Himself*, 187.

17. Monet to Alice Monet, 28 March 1900, in *Monet by Himself*, 190.

18. Gottlieb, *Sarah*, 179–80.

19. King Louis Philippe I was forced to abdicate in 1848, and Emperor Napoleon III, nephew of Napoleon Bonaparte, was deposed in 1870.

20. The amnesty did not go into effect until 1901. For background on the Dreyfus Affair, see McAuliffe, *Dawn of the Belle Epoque*.

21. Brown, *Zola*, 778. *L'Aurore* was the newspaper in which Zola published his famous defense of Dreyfus, "J'accuse."

22. Carter, *Marcel Proust*, 294.

23. Proust never seems to have been a practicing Catholic, and he referred to himself as a nonbeliever. But at the end of his life he expressed the wish that Abbé Mugnier pray at his deathbed and that Proust's housekeeper, Céleste Albaret, place in his hands a rosary brought by a friend from Jerusalem (Albaret, *Monsieur Proust*, 207).

24. As when the Duchesse de Guermantes complains: "I went to see Marie-Aynard a couple of days ago. It used to be so nice there. Nowadays one finds all the people one has spent one's life trying to avoid, on the pretext that they're against Dreyfus, and others of whom you have no idea who they can be" (Proust, *Guermantes Way*, 321).

25. Proust to Madame de Noailles, 1? May 1901, in Proust, *Selected Letters*, 1:219. Proust recommended flattering Anna de Noailles, as "she is at once divinely simple and sublimely proud" (Proust to Jean Cocteau, 30 or 31 January 1911, in Proust, *Selected Letters*, 3:28).

26. Kurth, *Isadora*, 70.

27. Kurth, *Isadora*, 72.

28. Brown, *Zola*, 786.

29. Adams, *Education of Henry Adams*, 380, 388.

30. Voisin later insisted that Ader, in his first aircraft, the *Eole*, had in 1890 been the first to leave the ground "under his aircraft's own power, from a level surface, without the aid of up-currents" and had flown "about 260 feet (80 meters) in a straight line at a height of from three to six feet" (Voisin, *Men, Women and 10,000 Kites*, 104–5).

31. Voisin, *Men, Women and 10,000 Kites*, 100.

32. Kessler, 8 July 1900, in *Journey to the Abyss*, 230.

33. Kessler, 22 July 1900, in *Journey to the Abyss*, 231.

3 Death of a Queen (1901)

Selected sources for this chapter: Monet, *Monet by Himself*; Wildenstein, *Monet, or the Triumph of Impressionism*, vol. 1; Palau i Fabre, *Picasso*; Richardson, *Life of Picasso: The Prodigy*; Boardingham, *Young Picasso*; Murray, *Toulouse-Lautrec*; Julia Frey, *Toulouse-Lautrec: A Life* (London: Weidenfeld and Nicolson, 1994); Orenstein, *Ravel*; Ravel, *Ravel Reader*; Claude Debussy, *Debussy Letters*, ed. François Lesure and Roger Nichols, trans. Roger Nichols (Cambridge, Mass.: Harvard University Press, 1987); Edward Lockspeiser, *Debussy: His Life and Mind*, vol. 2, *1902–1918* (New York: Macmillan, 1965); Roger Nichols and Richard Langham Smith, *Claude Debussy: Pelléas et Mélisande* (Cambridge, UK: Cambridge University Press, 1989); Roger Nichols, *The Life of Debussy* (Cambridge, UK: Cambridge University Press, 1998); Rhodes, *Louis Renault*; Mouret, *Louis Renault*; John Reynolds, *André Citroën: The Man and the Motor Cars* (Thrupp, Stroud, UK: Sutton, 1996); Jacques Wolgensinger, *André Citroën* (Paris: Flammarion, 1991); Alex Danchev, *Georges Braque: A Life* (New York: Hamish Hamilton, 2005); Flanner, *Men and Monuments*; Brown, *Zola*; Matthew Josephson, *Zola and His Time* (Garden City, N.Y.: Garden City Publishing, 1928); Jean-Denis Bredin, *The Affair: The Case of Alfred Dreyfus*, trans. Jeffrey Mehlman (New York: George Braziller, 1986); Mayeur and Rebérioux, *The Third Republic from Its Origins to the Great War*; Abbé (Arthur) Mugnier, *Journal de l'Abbé Mugnier: 1879–1939* (Paris: Mercure de France, 1985); David Robin Watson, *Georges Clemenceau: A Political Biography* (New York: David McKay, 1974); Carter, *Marcel Proust*; Proust, *Selected Letters*, vol. 3 (1910–1917); Léon Daudet, *Memoirs of Léon Daudet*, ed. and trans. Arthur Kingsland Griggs (New York: L. MacVeagh, Dial Press, 1925); Kurth, *Isadora*; Isadora Duncan, *My Life*; Michael de Cossart, *The Food of Love: Princesse Edmond de Polignac (1865–1943) and Her Salon* (London: Hamish Hamilton, 1978); Butler, *Rodin*; André Tuilier, *Histoire de l'Université de Paris et de la Sorbonne*, 2 vols. (Paris: Nouvelle Librairie de France, 1994).

1. Monet to Alice Monet, 2 February 1901, in *Monet by Himself*, 190.
2. Monet, 2 February 1901, in *Monet by Himself*, 190.
3. Natanson in Murray, *Toulouse-Lautrec*, 179.
4. Natanson in Murray, *Toulouse-Lautrec*, 316.
5. Despite the collaboration, this two-piano score indicates that Ravel alone did these transcriptions (Ravel, *Ravel Reader*, 59n1). Debussy's complete *Nocturnes*, including *Sirènes*, would first be performed on October 27, 1901. Reception was mixed, especially for *Sirènes*, whose female chorus unfortunately was a bit out of tune.
6. Ravel to Lucien Garban, 26 July 1901, in *Ravel Reader*, 60. Jules Massenet was a prominent French composer.
7. Saint-Saëns to Charles Lecocq, 4 July 1901, in Ravel, *Ravel Reader*, 61n3.
8. By the turn of the century the Opéra-Comique was a substantial rival to the Paris Opera and offered a similar repertoire, although the Opéra-Comique found a competitive niche by offering contemporary works such as Debussy's *Pelléas et Mélisande*.
9. Debussy to Georges Hartmann, 23 July 1898, in *Debussy Letters*, 98. Adding to Debussy's woes, Gabriel Fauré wrote incidental music for an 1898 performance of the Maurice Maeterlinck play on which Debussy's opera was based. By that time Debussy had been at work on his opera for several years and had also turned down the commission that Fauré accepted.
10. Debussy to Pierre Louÿs, 5 May 1901, in *Debussy Letters*, 120.
11. Arthur Symons, *Annotations by the Way*, quoted in Nichols and Smith, *Claude Debussy: Pelléas and Mélisande*, 1.

12. Debussy quoted in Nichols and Smith, *Claude Debussy: Pelléas and Mélisande*, 28–29.

13. Rhodes, *Louis Renault*, 29.

14. Rhodes, *Louis Renault*, 29.

15. Josephson, *Zola and His Time*, 491.

16. Abbé Mugnier, 30 August 1901, in *Journal*, 128.

17. Abbé Mugnier, 28 August 1901, in *Journal*, 128.

18. Abbé Mugnier, 30 August 1901, in *Journal*, 128–29.

19. Technically Clemenceau was mayor of the eighteenth arrondissement, which comprised Montmartre.

20. In 1899, Waldeck-Rousseau granted Dreyfus a pardon but not an acquittal (see McAuliffe, *Dawn of the Belle Epoque*, 323). In 1900, the Senate granted amnesty to all the Affair's participants, which went into effect in 1901 (see chapter 2 of this book).

21. This was Alexandre Millerand, as minister of commerce.

22. Daudet, *Memoirs of Léon Daudet*, 267.

23. Carter, *Marcel Proust*, 302.

24. Kurth, *Isadora*, 79.

25. Isadora Duncan, *My Life*, 74.

26. Richardson, *Life of Picasso: The Prodigy*, 200.

27. By that autumn Germaine had taken up with Ramon Pichot, whom she would eventually marry. Picasso now lived briefly with a young woman only known to history as Blanche.

28. Richardson notes that "Vollard, to name only one potential buyer, disdained the Blue period until it found favour with the Steins" (*Life of Picasso: The Prodigy*, 226).

4 Dreams and Reality (1902)

Selected sources for this chapter: Debussy, *Debussy Letters*; Nichols and Smith, *Claude Debussy: Pelléas et Mélisande*; Nichols, *Life of Debussy*; Lockspeiser, *Debussy*, vol. 2; Orenstein, *Ravel*; Ravel, *Ravel Reader*; Orledge, *Satie Remembered*; Spurling, *Unknown Matisse*; Barr, *Matisse*; Danchev, *Georges Braque*; Flanner, *Men and Monuments*; Eve Curie, *Madame Curie: A Biography*, trans. Vincent Sheean (Garden City, N.Y.: Garden City Publishing, 1940); Susan Quinn, *Marie Curie: A Life* (New York: Simon & Schuster, 1995); Alan E. Walter, *Radiation and Modern Life: Fulfilling Marie Curie's Dream* (Amherst, N.Y.: Prometheus Books, 2004); Josephson, *Zola and His Time*; Brown, *Zola*; Mayeur and Rebérioux, *The Third Republic from Its Origins to the Great War*; Jack D. Ellis, *The Early Life of Georges Clemenceau, 1841–1893* (Lawrence: Regents Press of Kansas, 1980); Watson, *Georges Clemenceau*; Williams, *The Last Great Frenchman*; John McManners, *Church and State in France, 1870–1914* (London: SPCK, 1972); Reynolds, *André Citroën*; Rhodes, *Louis Renault*; Mouret, *Louis Renault*; Descouturelle, Mignard, and Rodriguez, *Le Métropolitain d'Hector Guimard*; Berton and Ossadzow, *Fulgence Bienvenüe et la construction du métropolitain de Paris*; Maurice Bessy and Lo Duca, *Georges Méliès, mage* (Paris: Jean-Jacques Pauvert, 1961); Butler, *Rodin*; Bernard Champigneulle, *Rodin*, trans. J. Maxwell Brownjohn (London: Thames and Hudson, 1967); Isadora Duncan, *My Life*; Kurth, *Isadora*; Mary Desti, *The Untold Story: The Life of Isadora Duncan, 1921–1927* (New York: Da Capo, 1981); Preston Sturges, *Preston Sturges*, ed. Sandy Sturges (New York: Simon & Schuster, 1990); Richard Nelson Current and Marcia Ewing Current, *Loie Fuller: Goddess of Light* (Boston: Northeastern University Press, 1997); Richardson, *Life of Picasso: The Prodigy*.

1. Maeterlinck's diatribe, published on 14 April 1902 in a letter to *Le Figaro*, is quoted in Nichols and Smith, *Claude Debussy: Pelléas et Mélisande*, 143.

2. Debussy to Robert Godet, 13 June 1902, in *Debussy Letters*, 128.

3. Satie (according to Jean Cocteau) quoted in Orledge, *Satie Remembered*, 46. Orledge notes that "although Cocteau did not meet Satie until 1915, his retrospective account of Satie's career was undoubtedly prepared with the composer's assistance" (Orledge, *Satie Remembered*, 45).

4. Saint-Saëns quoted in Nichols and Smith, *Claude Debussy: Pelléas et Mélisande*, 148.

5. Georges Sagnac to Pierre Curie, in Eve Curie, *Madame Curie*, 186–87.

6. Marie Curie quoted in Eve Curie, *Madame Curie*, 204–5.

7. Josephson, *Zola and His Time*, 489.

8. Brown, *Zola*, 786.

9. Josephson, *Zola and His Time*, 510.

10. The left-wing bloc had a clear parliamentary majority but a relatively small popular majority (see Mayeur and Rebérioux, *The Third Republic from Its Origins to the Great War*, 221).

11. Nichols, *Life of Debussy*, 107.

12. Butler, *Rodin*, 375.

13. Butler, *Rodin*, 402.

14. Butler, *Rodin*, 403.

15. This Beaux-Arts sculpture, by Louis-Ernest Barrias, was destroyed in 1942 during the German Occupation.

16. Desti, *The Untold Story*, 25.

17. Isadora Duncan, *My Life*, 75.

5 Arrivals and Departures (1903)

Selected sources for this chapter: Spurling, *Unknown Matisse*; Matisse, *Matisse on Art*; Barr, *Matisse*; Camille Pissarro, *Letters to His Son Lucien*, ed. John Rewald, with assistance of Lucien Pissarro, trans. Lionel Abel (Santa Barbara, Calif.: Peregrine Smith, 1981); John Rewald, *Camille Pissarro* (New York: Abrams, 1963); Richard R. Brettell and Joachim Pissarro, *The Impressionist and the City: Pissarro's Series Paintings*, ed. Mary Anne Stevens (New Haven, Conn.: Yale University Press, 1992); David Sweetman, *Paul Gauguin: A Life* (New York: Simon & Schuster, 1995); Butler, *Rodin*; Kurth, *Isadora*; Isadora Duncan, *My Life*; John Malcolm Brinnin, *The Third Rose: Gertrude Stein and Her World* (Reading, Mass.: Addison-Wesley, 1987); Brenda Wineapple, *Sister Brother: Gertrude and Leo Stein* (New York: Putnam, 1996); Gertrude Stein, *The Autobiography of Alice B. Toklas* (New York: Vintage, 1990); Leo Stein, *Appreciation: Painting, Poetry, and Prose*, ed. Brenda Wineapple (Lincoln: University of Nebraska Press, 1996); Rhodes, *Louis Renault*; Mouret, *Louis Renault*; Berton, *Fulgence Bienvenüe et la construction du métropolitain de Paris*; Descouturelle, Mignard, and Rodriguez, *Le Métropolitain d'Hector Guimard*; Brown, *Zola*; Debussy, *Debussy Letters*; Orenstein, *Ravel*; Ravel, *Ravel Reader*; Nichols, *Life of Debussy*; Eve Curie, *Madame Curie*; Quinn, *Marie Curie*.

1. The older son, Jean, had stayed with his paternal grandparents in Bohain, while Pierre had gone to his mother's relations in Rouen.

2. Pissarro to Lucien, 8 and 22 September 1903, in *Letters to His Son Lucien*, 475.

3. Spurling, *Unknown Matisse*, 134.

4. Pissarro to Lucien, 22 September 1903, in *Letters to His Son Lucien*, 475.

5. Pissarro to Lucien, 30 March 1903; Pissarro to Esther [Lucien's wife], 30 June 1903, in *Letters to His Son Lucien*, both on 470.

6. Rewald, *Camille Pissarro*, 45.

7. Butler, *Rodin*, 384.

8. Kurth, *Isadora*, 108.

9. Kurth, *Isadora*, 105.

10. They would meet for the first time in Paris.

11. Gertrude Stein tells this story in *Autobiography of Alice B. Toklas*, 79, but Wineapple finds little evidence to corroborate it; James gave Stein an A for her laboratory work, but in his seminar, he gave her an A at midyear and a C at the end (including that final exam), averaging the two into a B overall (Wineapple, *Sister Brother*, 82).

12. Brinnin, *Third Rose*, 22.

13. Gertrude Stein, *Autobiography of Alice B. Toklas*, 81.

14. Her devil-may-care version of the experience thirty years later (*Autobiography of Alice B. Toklas*, 82–83) may have distorted the facts: Wineapple, in *Sister Brother*, 142–43, finds evidence of Stein's fear of failure and her disappointment at not receiving her degree. Yet even at the time, Stein's friends certainly felt that she "did not seem to care a rap" (Wineapple, *Sister Brother*, 149).

15. Debussy to Messager, 29 June 1903, in *Debussy Letters*, 135.

16. Ravel quoted in Orenstein, *Ravel*, 39.

17. Ravel to Jane Courteault, 11 September 1903, in *Ravel Reader*, 65.

18. Orenstein, *Ravel*, 40.

19. Ravel to Jane Courteault, 11 September 1903, in *Ravel Reader*, 65. Fauré's exclusion would not in fact be permanent, but it would take several years and a lot of persuasion on the part of his supporters before he became a member.

20. Nichols, *Life of Debussy*, 109. It is perhaps curious that Claude Debussy would feel this way, given his father's failure at just about everything *he* undertook. Still, the father once had dreams of Claude becoming a concert pianist, which Claude had not managed to achieve. This seemed to make up for everything.

21. Eve Curie, *Madame Curie*, 202.

22. Marie Curie to Joseph Sklodovski, 11 December 1903, in Eve Curie, *Madame Curie*, 211.

23. Until her daughter Irène won the prize in 1935, Marie Curie would be the only female Nobel Prize winner in the sciences.

24. Marie to Bronya, 25 August 1903, in Eve Curie, *Madame Curie*, 190–91. Bronya was a medical doctor.

25. According to a biographer, Susan Quinn, Marie Curie was five months pregnant at the time (*Marie Curie*, 183–84).

26. Marie to Bronya, 25 August 1903, in Eve Curie, *Madame Curie*, 190–91.

6 Alliances and Misalliances (1904)

Selected sources for this chapter: Debussy, *Debussy Letters*; Nichols, *Life of Debussy*; Gold and Fizdale, *Misia*; Butler, *Rodin*; Helene von Nostitz, *Dialogues with Rodin*, trans. H. L. Ripperger (New York: Duffield & Green, 1931); Richardson, *Life of Picasso: The Prodigy*; Pierre Villoteau, *La vie Parisienne à la Belle Epoque* ([Genève, Switzerland]: Cercle du bibliophile, 1968); Spurling, *Unknown Matisse*; Flanner, *Men and Monuments*; Barr, *Matisse*; Brinnin, *Third Rose*; Wineapple, *Sister Brother*; Gertrude Stein, *Autobiography of Alice B. Toklas*; Leo Stein, *Appreciation*; Isadora Duncan, *My Life*; Kurth, *Isadora*; Francis Steegmuller, ed., *"Your Isadora": The Love Story of Isadora Duncan and Gordon Craig* (New York: Random House and New York Public Library,

1974); Francis Steegmuller, *Cocteau: A Biography* (Boston: Little, Brown, 1970); Jean Cocteau, *Souvenir Portraits: Paris in the Belle Epoque*, trans. Jesse Browner (New York: Paragon House, 1990); Sicard-Picchiottino, *François Coty*; Barillé, *Coty*; Diana Holmes and Carrie Tarr, eds., *A "Belle Epoque"? Women in French Society and Culture, 1890–1914* (New York: Berghahn Books, 2006); Skinner, *Elegant Wits and Grand Horizontals*; Reynolds, *André Citroën*; Wildenstein, *Monet, or the Triumph of Impressionism*, vol. 1; Pierre-Antoine Donnet, *La saga Michelin* (Paris: Seuil, 2008); Stephen L. Harp, *Marketing Michelin: Advertising and Cultural Identity in Twentieth-Century France* (Baltimore: Johns Hopkins University Press, 2001); Auguste Escoffier, *Memories of My Life*, trans. Laurence Escoffier (New York: Van Nostrand Reinhold, 1997); Timothy Shaw, *The World of Escoffier* (New York: Vendome Press, 1995); Eve Curie, *Madame Curie*; Quinn, *Marie Curie*; Current and Current, *Loie Fuller*; Butler, *Rodin*; Kessler, *Journey to the Abyss*; Monet, *Monet by Himself*; Sabartès, *Picasso*; McManners, *Church and State in France*; Mugnier, *Journal*; Mayeur and Rebérioux, *Third Republic from Its Origins to the Great War*.

1. Debussy to Lilly, 16 July 1904, in *Debussy Letters*, 147–48.
2. Debussy to Jacques Durand, [July 1904], in *Debussy Letters*, 148–49.
3. Debussy to André Messager, 19 September 1904, in *Debussy Letters*, 149.
4. Spurling, *Unknown Matisse*, 273. Level would buy another Matisse, two Picassos, and a Gauguin for the Peau de l'Ours that year. In March 1914, when the syndicate auctioned off its holdings, its investors quadrupled their investment.
5. Flanner, *Men and Monuments*, 80.
6. Gertrude Stein, *Autobiography of Alice B. Toklas*, 31–32.
7. Leo Stein, *Appreciation*, 157.
8. Gertrude Stein, *Autobiography of Alice B. Toklas*, 21. The spelling and punctuation are her own.
9. Picasso sold *La Vie* to a Parisian collector, Jean Saint-Gaudens, soon after completing it, but little further is known about the collector or the transaction. *La Vie* is now in the Cleveland Museum of Art.
10. Kurth, *Isadora*, 117.
11. Isadora Duncan, *My Life*, 159.
12. Kurth, *Isadora*, 130.
13. Steegmuller, *Cocteau*, 8.
14. Steegmuller, *Cocteau*, 9. There have been persistent rumors that Cocteau *père* was secretly homosexual, leading to doubts about Jean's paternity. See Steegmuller, *Cocteau*, 10 (note).
15. Madame Singer quoted in Steegmuller, *Cocteau*, 9.
16. Barillé, *Coty*, 112. Coty named his perfume after Docteur Jacqueminot, the owner of the pharmacie Jacqueminot where Coty first discovered his perfume-making abilities.
17. There would be no fine dining stars until 1926.
18. Escoffier, *Memories of My Life*, 9.
19. Escoffier, *Memories of My Life*, 84.
20. Escoffier, *Memories of My Life*, 113.
21. Contrary to legend, the Curies do not appear to have visited the Folies Bergère to see their friend perform. Instead, she brought her act to them, at their Boulevard Kellermann home, including the lighting essential to her act. According to what Marie later told Eve, it took hours to set up, during which she and Pierre escaped to their laboratory (Eve Curie, *Madame Curie*, 232).

22. Kessler, 11 May 1902, in *Journey to the Abyss*, 279–80.

23. Vernon is the nearest train station to Giverny, which is located a short distance across the Seine from Vernon.

24. Kessler, 20 November 1903, in *Journey to the Abyss*, 309.

25. Bazille, one of the early Impressionist painters, was killed during the Franco-Prussian War.

26. Monet quoted in Kessler, 20 November 1903, in *Journey to the Abyss*, 311, 312.

27. Monet to Georges Durand-Ruel, 3 [July] 1905, in *Monet by Himself*, 196.

28. Sabartès, *Picasso*, 78.

29. Sabartès recalled that Place Ravignan, now Place Emile-Goudeau, was at that time "a veritable desert," with "no lights, no sidewalks, no cobblestones" (*Picasso*, 72).

30. Mugnier, 17 July 1904, in *Journal*, 148.

7 Wild Beasts (1905)

Selected sources for this chapter: Flanner, *Men and Monuments*; Spurling, *Unknown Matisse*; Barr, *Matisse*; Gertrude Stein, *Autobiography of Alice B. Toklas*; Leo Stein, *Appreciation*; Wineapple, *Sister Brother*; Brinnin, *Third Rose*; Richardson, *Life of Picasso: The Prodigy*; Palau i Fabre, *Picasso: The Early Years*; Fernande Olivier, *Picasso and His Friends*, trans. Jane Miller (London: Heinemann, 1964); Fernande Olivier, *Loving Picasso: The Private Journal of Fernande Olivier*, trans. Christine Baker and Michael Raeburn (New York: Abrams, 2001); Jean-Paul Crespelle, *La vie quotidienne à Montmartre au temps de Picasso, 1900–1910* (Paris: Hachette, 1978); Villoteau, *La vie Parisienne à la Belle Epoque*; Carter, *Marcel Proust*; Marcel Proust, *Selected Letters*, vol. 2 (1904–1909), ed. Philip Kolb, trans. Terence Kilmartin (New York: Oxford University Press, 1989); Edith Thomas, *Louise Michel*, trans. Penelope Williams (Montréal: Black Rose Books, 1980); Mayeur and Rebérioux, *Third Republic from Its Origins to the Great War*; Jean Lacouture, *De Gaulle: The Rebel*; Lysiane Sarah Bernhardt and Marion Dix, *Sarah Bernhardt, My Grandmother* (London: Hurst & Blackett, 1949); Arthur Gold and Robert Fizdale, *The Divine Sarah: A Life of Sarah Bernhardt* (New York: Vintage Books, 1992); Gottlieb, *Sarah*; Steegmuller, *Cocteau*; Cocteau, *Souvenir Portraits*; Nichols, *Life of Debussy*; Debussy, *Debussy Letters*; Orledge, *Satie Remembered*; Rollo H. Myers, *Erik Satie*, rev. ed. (New York: Dover, 1968); Alan M. Gillmor, *Erik Satie* (Boston: Twayne, 1988); Orenstein, *Ravel*; Ravel, *Ravel Reader*; Gold and Fizdale, *Misia*; Butler, *Rodin*; Champigneulle, *Rodin*; Steegmuller, *"Your Isadora"*; Kurth, *Isadora*; Sjeng Scheijen, *Diaghilev: A Life*, trans. Jane Jedley-Prôle and S. J. Leinbach (New York: Oxford University Press, 2010); Isadora Duncan, *My Life*; Poiret, *King of Fashion*; Reynolds, *André Citroën*; Barillé, *Coty*; Sicard-Picchiottino, *François Coty*; Ruth Brandon, *Ugly Beauty: Helena Rubinstein, L'Oréal, and the Blemished History of Looking Good* (New York: HarperCollins, 2011); McManners, *Church and State in France*; Mugnier, *Journal*.

1. The Cone sisters' collection ultimately went to the Baltimore Museum of Art.

2. Leo Stein, *Appreciation*, 158.

3. Leo Stein, *Appreciation*, 170.

4. Gertrude Stein, *Autobiography of Alice B. Toklas*, 46.

5. Leo Stein, *Appreciation*, 170.

6. Gertrude Stein, *Autobiography of Alice B. Toklas*, 47.

7. Gertrude Stein, *Autobiography of Alice B. Toklas*, 47.

8. Richardson, *Life of Picasso: The Prodigy*, 362.

9. Proust to Anna de Noailles, 27 September 1905, in Proust, *Selected Letters*, 2:207.

10. Proust to Montesquiou, soon after 28 September 1905, in Proust, *Selected Letters*, 2:208.

11. Lacouture, *De Gaulle: The Rebel*, 3. Péguy was about to become an ardent nationalist as well as a devout Catholic.

12. As told by Sarah Bernhardt's granddaughter, Lysiane, who as a nine-year-old witnessed the event (Lysiane Sarah Bernhardt and Marion Dix, *Sarah Bernhardt, My Grandmother*, 180–81).

13. Gold and Fizdale, *Divine Sarah*, 302.

14. Cocteau, *Souvenir Portraits*, 109. De Max "realized his blunder [and] took us away, removed our curls and our make-up, and dropped us at our respective homes" (109).

15. Lysiane Sarah Bernhardt and Marion Dix, *Sarah Bernhardt, My Grandmother*, 193.

16. Nichols, *Life of Debussy*, 115–16.

17. Debussy to Durand, [January 1905], in *Debussy Letters*, 150.

18. Debussy to Laloy, 14 April 1905, in *Debussy Letters*, 152.

19. Satie and Louÿs had been witnesses at Debussy and Lilly's wedding in 1899.

20. Debussy to Durand, 7 August 1905, in *Debussy Letters*, 154.

21. Nichols, *Life of Debussy*, 118.

22. According to Hélène Jourdan-Morhange, in Orledge, *Satie Remembered*, 97.

23. Myers, *Erik Satie*, 40.

24. Rolland to Paul Léon, 26 May 1905, in Ravel, *Ravel Reader*, 66–67. Rolland's letter was addressed to the art historian Paul Léon, who at the time was an undersecretary of the Académie des Beaux-Arts.

25. Orenstein, *Ravel*, 44n55.

26. Debussy to Fauré, 28 June 1905, in *Debussy Letters*, 153.

27. Ravel to Maurice Delage, 24 June 1905, in *Ravel Reader*, 70.

28. Ravel to Maurice Delage, 5 July 1905, in *Ravel Reader*, 70. According to Ravel, the foundry he visited, in Ahaus, Germany, employed twenty-four thousand men working round the clock.

29. Ravel to Madame René de Saint-Marceaux, 23 August 1905, in *Ravel Reader*, 75.

30. Champigneulle, *Rodin*, 239.

31. Butler, *Rodin*, 376.

32. Champigneulle, *Rodin*, 240.

33. Although how much of an impact Duncan made on Fokine's choreography is subject to debate (see Kurth, *Isadora*, 147–48, 154–55, and Scheijen, *Diaghilev*, 173).

34. Isadora Duncan, *My Life*, 140. She may well have invented this recollection. Joan Acocella writes, in the introduction to the 2013 edition of Duncan's *My Life*, that "her story of arriving in St. Petersburg in 1905 in time to see, out of her cab window, the funeral procession of the victims of the Bloody Sunday massacre . . . is demonstrably false." But "she needed such stories, to make sense of her life" (xviii).

35. Steegmuller, "*Your Isadora*," 69.

36. Duncan to Craig, [probably Berlin, 10–15 March 1905], in Steegmuller, "*Your Isadora*," 83.

37. "I wonder what this was?" Craig scrawled on the first of Isadora's two letters to him. "Jealousy?" (Steegmuller, "*Your Isadora*," 81). Eventually Craig's mother, Ellen Terry, would pay May Gibson's alimony after May's divorce from Craig.

38. Poiret, *King of Fashion*, 76.

39. Poiret, *King of Fashion*, 93.

40. Consecration of Sacré-Coeur, initially scheduled for October 1914 but delayed by the war, took place in October 1919.

41. McManners, *Church and State in France*, 141.

42. Mugnier, 6 September 1905, in *Journal*, 155.

8 *La Valse* (1906)

Selected sources for this chapter: Ravel, *Ravel Reader*; Orenstein, *Ravel*; Gold and Fizdale, *Misia*; Proust, *Selected Letters*, vol. 2; Kurth, *Isadora*; Isadora Duncan, *My Life*; Steegmuller, "*Your Isadora*"; Martin Shaw, *Up to Now* (London: Oxford University Press, 1929); Kathleen Scott, *Self-Portrait of an Artist: From the Diaries and Memoirs of Lady Kennet, Kathleen, Lady Scott* (London: Murray, 1949); Olivier, *Loving Picasso*; Olivier, *Picasso and His Friends*; Richardson, *Life of Picasso: The Prodigy*; Louis Laloy, *La musique retrouvée, 1902–1927* (Paris: Desclée de Brouwer, 1974); François Lesure, "'L'Affaire' Debussy-Ravel," in *Festschrift Friedrich Blume zum 70. Geburtstag*, ed. Anna Amalie Abert and Wilhelm Pfannkuch, 231–34 (Kassel, Germany: Bärenreiter, 1963); Nichols, *Life of Debussy*; Debussy, *Debussy Letters*; Brown, *Zola*; Josephson, *Zola and His Time*; Watson, *Georges Clemenceau*; Mayeur and Rebérioux, *Third Republic from Its Origins to the Great War*; Michel Winock, *La Belle Epoque: La France de 1900 à 1914* (Paris: Perrin, 2003); McManners, *Church and State in France*; McAuliffe, *Dawn of the Belle Epoque*; Mugnier, *Journal*; Michael Burns, *Dreyfus: A Family Affair, 1789–1945* (New York: HarperCollins, 1991); Bredin, *The Affair*; Georges Journas, *Alfred Dreyfus, officier en 14–18: Souvenirs, lettres, et carnet de guerre* (Orléans, France: Regain de lecture, 2011); Butler, *Rodin*; Champigneulle, *Rodin*; von Nostitz, *Dialogues with Rodin*; Gertrude Stein, *Autobiography of Alice B. Toklas*; Leo Stein, *Appreciation*; Brinnin, *Third Rose*; Wineapple, *Sister Brother*; Matisse, *Matisse on Art*; Spurling, *Unknown Matisse*; Flanner, *Men and Monuments*; Lacouture, *De Gaulle: The Rebel*; Williams, *Last Great Frenchman*; Justin D. Murphy, *Military Aircraft, Origins to 1918* (Santa Barbara, Calif.: ABC CLIO, 2005); Voisin, *Men, Women, and 10,000 Kites*; Guillermo de Osma, *Mariano Fortuny: His Life and Work* (New York: Rizzoli, 1980); Proust, *Selected Letters*, vol. 3; Quinn, *Marie Curie*; Eve Curie, *Madame Curie*.

1. Ravel to Jean Marnold, 7 February 1906, in *Ravel Reader*, 80.

2. Ravel to Misia Edwards, 19 July 1906, in *Ravel Reader*, 83.

3. Proust to Reynaldo Hahn, [second half of August 1907], in Proust, *Selected Letters*, 2:324.

4. Martin Shaw, *Up to Now*, 59–60.

5. Isadora Duncan, *My Life*, 170.

6. Duncan to Craig, in Steegmuller, "*Your Isadora*," 128–29.

7. See Isadora Duncan, *My Life*, for her unforgettable account of the birth. "I suppose that, perhaps with the exception of being pinned underneath a railway train," she wrote, "nothing could possibly resemble what I suffered" (*My Life*, 171). Her companion, Kathleen Bruce Scott, later wrote that "the cries and sights of a slaughter-house could not be more terrible" (*Self-Portrait of an Artist*, 64).

8. Scott, *Self-Portrait of an Artist*, 60–61. Kathleen Bruce later married the Antarctic explorer Captain Robert Scott, and upon his death was granted the rank of Lady Scott. When her second husband, Edward Hilton Young, was made Baron Kennet, she became Lady Kennet.

9. Duncan to Craig, in Steegmuller, "*Your Isadora*," 142.

10. Scott, *Self-Portrait of an Artist*, 63.

11. Kurth, *Isadora*, 198.

12. Olivier, *Loving Picasso*, 170.

13. Olivier, *Loving Picasso*, 137, 139.

14. Olivier, *Loving Picasso*, 141.

15. Olivier, *Loving Picasso*, 154.

16. Picasso appears to have smoked opium from around 1904 to mid-1908 (Richardson, *Picasso: The Prodigy*, 312, 324–25).

17. Olivier, *Loving Picasso*, 174.

18. Olivier, *Loving Picasso*, 178.

19. Lalo quoted in Ravel, *Ravel Reader*, 79n1.

20. Ravel to Pierre Lalo, 5 February 1906, in *Ravel Reader*, 79.

21. Marnold quoted in Ravel, *Ravel Reader*, 81n1.

22. Orenstein, *Ravel*, 51. See also 51n11.

23. Claude Debussy to Louis Laloy, 8 March 1907, in Ravel, *Ravel Reader*, 87.

24. Lalo quoted in Ravel, *Ravel Reader*, 89n2.

25. Ravel to the editor of *Le Temps*, late March [printed in *Le Temps* on 9 April 1907], in *Ravel Reader*, 88–89.

26. Lalo quoted in Ravel, *Ravel Reader*, 89n3. In this article Lalo quoted part of Ravel's 5 February 1906 letter to him (see above), in which Ravel had compared *Jeux d'eau* favorably with Debussy's early piano works.

27. Laloy, *La musique retrouvée*, 166–67.

28. Ravel, "Regarding Claude Debussy's *Images*," reprinted from *Les Cahiers d'aujourd'hui* (February 1913), in *Ravel Reader*, 367–68.

29. Debussy to Louis Laloy, 10 March 1906, in *Debussy Letters*, 167.

30. Debussy to Raoul Bardac, 24 and 25 February 1906, in *Debussy Letters*, 166.

31. See McAuliffe, *Dawn of the Belle Epoque*, 172–73.

32. Mugnier, 1 and 2 February 1906, in *Journal*, 157–58.

33. Burns, *Dreyfus*, 313–14.

34. Among these, Abbé Mugnier wrote: "It is the reparation of a huge judicial error" (14 July 1906, in *Journal*, 160), while Marcel Proust read the newspaper accounts of the ceremony with "tears in [his] eyes" (Proust to Madame Straus, 21 July 1906, in Proust, *Selected Letters*, 2:222).

35. Butler, *Rodin*, 390.

36. Butler, *Rodin*, 378.

37. It is now in the gardens of the Musée Rodin.

38. Helene von Nostitz, *Dialogues with Rodin*, 62. He also wrote her: "I am tired and yet I cannot withdraw from the burden which I carry" (72).

39. See Richardson, *Life of Picasso: The Prodigy*, 413.

40. Leo Stein, *Appreciation*, 171.

41. Gertrude Stein, *Autobiography of Alice B. Toklas*, 53.

42. Richardson, *Life of Picasso: The Prodigy*, 417.

43. Leo Stein, *Appreciation*, 174.

44. Gertrude Stein, *Autobiography of Alice B. Toklas*, 53, 57. Picasso made her a gift of the work, which now hangs in New York's Metropolitan Museum of Art.

45. Gertrude Stein, *Autobiography of Alice B. Toklas*, 63.

46. Gertrude Stein, *Autobiography of Alice B. Toklas*, 64.
47. Wineapple, *Sister Brother*, 234, 269.
48. Gertrude Stein, *Autobiography of Alice B. Toklas*, 50.
49. Lacouture, *De Gaulle: The Rebel*, 9.
50. See chapter 2, note 30, for Gabriel Voisin's argument on behalf of Clément Ader.
51. In early 1916 Proust asked a female friend, "Do you know . . . whether for his dressing-gowns Fortuny ever used as motifs those coupled birds . . . which are so recurrent on the Byzantine capitals in St. Mark's. And do you also know whether there are pictures in Venice . . . showing cloaks or dresses from which Fortuny drew (or might have drawn) inspiration" (Proust to Madame de Madrazo, 6 February 1916, in Proust, *Selected Letters*, 3:335).
52. Isadora Duncan, *My Life*, 181.
53. Duncan to Craig, 19 December [1906], in Steegmuller, *"Your Isadora,"* 168.
54. Isadora Duncan, *My Life*, 181.
55. Quinn, *Marie Curie*, 219.
56. Quinn, *Marie Curie*, 231.
57. Marie [Curie] to Bronya, 1899, in Eve Curie, *Madame Curie*, 172.
58. Quinn, *Marie Curie*, 231.

9 Winds of Change (1907)

Selected sources for this chapter: Scheijen, *Diaghilev*; Hilary Spurling, *Matisse the Master, A Life of Henri Matisse: The Conquest of Colour, 1909–1954* (New York: Knopf, 2007); Debussy, *Debussy Letters*; Lockspeiser, *Debussy*, vol. 2; Nichols, *Life of Debussy*; Carter, *Marcel Proust*; Proust, *Selected Letters*, vol. 2; Monet, *Monet by Himself*; Wildenstein, *Monet, or the Triumph of Impressionism*, vol. 1; Mayeur and Rebérioux, *Third Republic from Its Origins to the Great War*; Matisse, *Matisse on Art*; Barr, *Matisse*; Spurling, *Unknown Matisse*; Richardson, *Life of Picasso: The Prodigy*; John Richardson, *A Life of Picasso: The Cubist Rebel, 1907–1916* (New York: Knopf, 2012); Olivier, *Loving Picasso*; Olivier, *Picasso and His Friends*; Flanner, *Men and Monuments*; Danchev, *Georges Braque*; Pierre Assouline, *An Artful Life: A Biography of D. H. Kahnweiler, 1884–1979*, trans. Charles Ruas (New York: G. Weidenfeld, 1990); Gertrude Stein, *Autobiography of Alice B. Toklas*; Leo Stein, *Appreciation*; Wineapple, *Sister Brother*; Brinnin, *Third Rose*; Meryle Secrest, *Modigliani: A Life* (New York: Knopf, 2011); Orledge, *Satie Remembered*; Butler, *Rodin*; Kurth, *Isadora*; Isadora Duncan, *My Life*; Steegmuller, *"Your Isadora"*; Quinn, *Marie Curie*; Eve Curie, *Madame Curie*; Mugnier, *Journal*; Reynolds, *André Citroën*; Rhodes, *Louis Renault*; Jules Bertaut, *Paris, 1870–1935*, trans. R. Millar, ed. John Bell (London: Eyre and Spottiswoode, 1936); Brandon, *Ugly Beauty*; Cocteau, *Souvenir Portraits*; Steele, *Paris Fashion*; Osma, *Mariano Fortuny*; Poiret, *King of Fashion*; Barillé, *Coty*; Kessler, *Journey to the Abyss*; Murphy, *Military Aircraft*; Voisin, *Men, Women and 10,000 Kites*.

1. According to the London impresario Charles B. Cochran, quoted in Spurling, *Matisse the Master*, 229.
2. Scheijen, *Diaghilev*, 122.
3. Diaghilev to Benois, 1897, in Scheijen, *Diaghilev*, 80. Although Diaghilev also wrote: "If I should fail at all—O then the wounds will reopen and everything will be set down against me" (80).
4. Diaghilev to Benois, 16 October 1905, in Scheijen, *Diaghilev*, 137.

5. Scheijen, *Diaghilev*, 159.

6. Debussy to Sylvain Dupuis, 8 January 1907; Debussy to Jacques Durand, 7 January 1907; Debussy to Louis Laloy, 23 January 1907; all in *Debussy Letters*, 174–76.

7. See chapter 8.

8. Proust to Lucien Daudet, early February 1907, Proust, *Selected Letters*, 2:252.

9. Anna de Noailles to Proust, 18 June 1907, Proust, *Selected Letters*, 2:293n1. She had referred to a review by Proust that included this passage.

10. Monet to Gustav Geffroy, 8 February 1907, in Monet, *Monet by Himself*, 197. *Olympia* was transferred to the Louvre, where it hung in the Salle des Etats opposite Ingres' *Odalisque*. It now hangs, with other treasures of Impressionist art, in the Musée d'Orsay.

11. Wildenstein, *Monet, or the Triumph of Impressionism*, 1:353. During the 1890s, only three thousand people in France had incomes of more than a hundred thousand francs (Mayeur and Rebérioux, *Third Republic from Its Origins to the Great War*, 68).

12. From introduction to "Notes of a Painter," in *Matisse on Art*, ed. Flam, 32.

13. Barr, *Matisse*, 38.

14. The painting would not acquire the name *Les Demoiselles d'Avignon* until 1916, when Picasso finally allowed the painting to be shown in public. Much to Picasso's annoyance, André Salmon, who organized the 1916 show, substituted "demoiselles" ("damsels") as a euphemism for "bordel" or "brothel" (Richardson, *Life of Picasso: The Cubist Rebel*, 18–19).

15. Leo Stein, *Appreciation*, 175. See also Richardson, *Picasso: The Cubist Rebel*, 45.

16. Flanner, *Men and Monuments*, 134. Similar reports of Braque's response came from Fernande Olivier, André Salmon, and D. H. Kahnweiler (Danchev, *Georges Braque*, 52).

17. Assouline, *Artful Life*, 49.

18. John Richardson thinks this event, recalled by Fernande Olivier, was unlikely to have happened: "Apart from the unlikelihood of Matisse's promoting the sale of paintings he had condemned by a rival he resented to a patron he wanted to keep to himself, there is no evidence that Shchukin was in Paris at this time, or that he began buying Picassos until 1909." If it did happen, Richardson adds, it would have been at an earlier date, when "far from acquiring any Picassos, Shchukin was predictably horrified by what he saw, as Matisse doubtless hoped he would be" (*Life of Picasso: The Cubist Rebel*, 106).

19. Spurling, *Unknown Matisse*, 346.

20. Gertrude Stein, *Autobiography of Alice B. Toklas*, 68.

21. Gertrude Stein, *Autobiography of Alice B. Toklas*, 56.

22. Wineapple, *Sister Brother*, 212.

23. Matisse, *Matisse on Art*, 42.

24. Gertrude Stein, *Autobiography of Alice B. Toklas*, 58.

25. Rodin worked in clay, not directly in stone.

26. Secrest, *Modigliani*, 129.

27. Kurth, *Isadora*, 213.

28. Duncan to Craig, [January 1907], in Steegmuller, *"Your Isadora,"* 185.

29. Isadora Duncan, *My Life*, 183.

30. Duncan to Craig, [September 1907], in Steegmuller, *"Your Isadora,"* 261.

31. Duncan to Craig, [5 September 1907], in Steegmuller, *"Your Isadora,"* 259n1.

32. Duncan to Craig, [November 1907], in Steegmuller, *"Your Isadora,"* 272.

33. Quinn, *Marie Curie*, 240.

34. Quinn, *Marie Curie*, 235.

35. That year, Andrew Carnegie bestowed a series of annual scholarships that made it possible for her to bring some novice assistants to the laboratory. According to Eve Curie, "They joined the assistants paid by the university and some benevolent volunteer workers" (*Madame Curie*, 275).

36. Quinn, *Marie Curie*, 243. She would be promoted to the titular professorship in 1908 (Eve Curie, *Madame Curie*, 274–75).

37. Eve Curie, *Madame Curie*, 275.

38. Mugnier, 17 June 1907, in *Journal*, 167.

39. Rhodes, *Louis Renault*, 41, 42, 48.

40. According to Jules Bertaut, "The first autobus plied between the Bourse and the Cours de la Reine on December 8th 1905, and the first regular service, Montmartre–St. Germain-des-Prés, dates from June 1906" (Bertaut, *Paris, 1870–1935*, 210).

41. Rhodes, *Louis Renault*, 50.

42. Rhodes, *Louis Renault*, 55.

43. Cocteau, *Souvenir Portraits*, 65, 67.

44. Poiret, *King of Fashion*, 76.

45. Kessler, 26 November 1907, in *Journey to the Abyss*, 429.

46. Voisin, *Men, Women and 10,000 Kites*, 143.

47. Kessler, 8 July 1907, in *Journey to the Abyss*, 419.

10 Unfinished Business (1908)

Selected sources for this chapter: Brown, *Zola*; Josephson, *Zola and His Time*; Burns, *Dreyfus*; Debussy, *Debussy Letters*; Nichols, *Life of Debussy*; Ravel, *Ravel Reader*; Orenstein, *Ravel*; Scheijen, *Diaghilev*; Gold and Fizdale, *Misia*; Sert, *Misia and the Muses*; Spurling, *Unknown Matisse*; Barr, *Matisse*; Flanner, *Men and Monuments*; Butler, *Rodin*; Champigneulle, *Rodin*; Proust, *Selected Letters*, vols. 1 and 2; Carter, *Marcel Proust*; William C. Carter, *The Proustian Quest* (New York: New York University Press, 1992); Marcel Proust, *Swann's Way* (Vol. 1, *In Search of Lost Time*), trans. Lydia Davis (New York: Viking, 2003); Marcel Proust, *Sodom and Gomorrah* (Vol. 4, *In Search of Lost Time*), trans. John Sturrock (New York: Viking, 2002); P. F. Prestwich, *The Translation of Memories: Recollections of the Young Proust* (London: Peter Owen, 1999); Jane Bennett and William Connolly, "The Crumpled Handkerchief," in *Time and History in Deleuze and Serres*, ed. Bernd Herzogenrath (New York: Continuum, 2012); Frank Arntzenius, *Space, Time, and Stuff* (New York: Oxford University Press, 2012); Sara Danius, *The Senses of Modernism: Technology, Perception, and Aesthetics* (Ithaca, N.Y.: Cornell University Press, 2002); Kessler, *Journey to the Abyss*; Charles Harvard Gibbs-Smith, *The Rebirth of European Aviation, 1902–1908: A Study of the Wright Brothers' Influence* (London: Her Majesty's Stationery Office, 1974); Voisin, *Men, Women, and 10,000 Kites*; Murphy, *Military Aircraft*; Harp, *Marketing Michelin*; Donnet, *La saga Michelin*; Berton and Ossadzow, *Fulgence Bienveniie*; Gérard Roland, *Stations de metro, d'Abbesses à Wagram* (Clermont-Ferrand, France: Christine Bonneton, 2008); Descouturelle, Mignard, and Rodriguez, *Le Métropolitain d'Hector Guimard*; Brandon, *Ugly Beauty*; Barillé, *Coty*; Gertrude Stein, *Autobiography of Alice B. Toklas*; Wineapple, *Sister Brother*; Richardson, *Life of Picasso: The Cubist Rebel*; Roger Shattuck, *The Banquet Years: The Origins of the Avant Garde in France, 1885 to World War I*; Alfred Jarry, *Henri Rousseau, Erik Satie, Guillaume Apollinaire* (New York: Vintage, 1968); Olivier, *Picasso and His Friends*; Watson, *Georges Clemenceau*; Mayeur and Rebérioux, *Third Republic from Its Origins* to the Great War; Lenard R. Berlanstein, *The Working People of Paris, 1871–1914* (Baltimore: Johns Hopkins University Press, 1984); John M. Merriman, *The Dynamite Club: How a Bombing in Fin-de-Siècle Paris Ignited the Age of Modern Terror* (Boston: Houghton Mifflin Harcourt, 2009); Winock, *La Belle Epoque*; Timothy Shaw, *World of Escoffier*; Peter M. Wolf, *Eugène Hénard and the Beginning of Urbanism in Paris, 1900–1914* (The Hague: International Federation for Housing and Planning; Paris, Centre de recherche d'urbanisme, 1968); Mugnier, *Journal*; Lacouture, *De Gaulle: The Rebel*.

1. Josephson, *Zola and His Time*, 517.
2. This defense won him an acquittal, thanks to the jury's decision that it had been a crime of passion committed in devotion to France.
3. See Debussy to Louis Laloy, 10 September 1906, in *Debussy Letters*, 173.
4. Debussy to Victor Segalen, 15 January 1908, in *Debussy Letters*, 186.
5. Debussy to Paul-Jean Toulet, 22 January 1908, in *Debussy Letters*, 187.
6. Ravel to Ralph Vaughan Williams, 3 March 1908, in *Ravel Reader*, 93.
7. Ralph Vaughan Williams's recollections, in Ravel, *Ravel Reader*, 94n1.
8. Ravel to Ida Godebska, 9 March 1908, in *Ravel Reader*, 94.
9. Orenstein, *Ravel*, 58.
10. Ravel to Cipa Godebski, 26 March 1908, in *Ravel Reader*, 95.
11. Ravel to Ida Godebska, 22 May or 5 June 1908, in *Ravel Reader*, 96 and 97n5.
12. Barr, *Matisse*, 118.
13. Butler, *Rodin*, 457, 469.
14. Butler, *Rodin*, 458.
15. *A la recherche du temps perdu* was originally translated into English as *Remembrance of Things Past*, but recently has been more closely translated as *In Search of Lost Time*.
16. Proust to Antoine Bibesco, 20 December 1902, in Proust, *Selected Letters*, 1:284.
17. Carter, *Marcel Proust*, 358, 362.
18. Proust to Maurice Barrès, 13, 14, or 15 March 1904, in Proust, *Selected Letters*, 2:33–34.
19. Carter, *Marcel Proust*, 367.
20. Carter, *Marcel Proust*, 392.
21. Picasso's art dealer, Daniel-Henry Kahnweiler, later said that with Cubism, "the artist painted several aspects of the object simultaneously—the theory of the space-time continuum—according to several angles of vision, and even projected onto it his own personal vision" (Flanner, *Men and Monuments*, 147).
22. In 1884, the International Prime Meridian Conference standardized time worldwide, creating twenty-four time zones, with the longitude of Greenwich, England, as zero degrees longitude.
23. Carter, *Marcel Proust*, 789, 773–74.
24. Proust, *Sodom and Gomorrah* (Vol. 4, *In Search of Lost Time*), 416–17.
25. Proust was "fascinated by airplanes" as early as 1909 (Carter, *Proustian Quest*, 183).
26. In fairness to the unbelievers, it should be noted that the Wrights had been notoriously publicity-shy, afraid that others would steal their technology. Instead of public demonstrations and other corroborations, the Wrights had focused on getting patents and contracts.
27. Kessler, 24 October 1908, in *Journey to the Abyss*, 470.
28. Barillé, *Coty*, 112.
29. Barrilé, *Coty*, 119.

30. According to Berlanstein, the "value of inherited property [in Paris] in 1911 was six times that of 1847" (*Working People of Paris*, 35).

31. For more on Hénard, see Wolf, *Eugène Hénard and the Beginning of Urbanism in Paris, 1900–1914*.

32. See chapter 9.

33. Mugnier, 4 December 1908, in *Journal*, 174.

34. Lacouture, *De Gaulle: The Rebel*, 10.

11 Idyll (1909)

Selected sources for this chapter: Steegmuller, *Cocteau*; Cocteau, *Souvenir Portraits*; Butler, *Rodin*; Champigneulle, *Rodin*; Kessler, *Journey to the Abyss*; Spurling, *Unknown Matisse*; Spurling, *Matisse the Master*; Barr, *Matisse*; Matisse, *Mattisse on Art*; Flanner, *Men and Monuments*; Danchev, *Georges Braque*; Edward F. Fry, *Cubism* (New York: Oxford University Press, 1978); Richardson, *Life of Picasso: The Cubist Rebel*; Gertrude Stein, *Autobiography of Alice B. Toklas*; Isadora Duncan, *My Life*; Kurth, *Isadora*; Cossart, *Food of Love*; Scheijen, *Diaghilev*; Stephen Walsh, *Stravinsky: A Creative Spring; Russia and France, 1882–1934* (Berkeley: University of California Press, 2002); Gold and Fizdale, *Misia*; Carter, *Marcel Proust*; Caroline Potter, *Nadia and Lili Boulanger* (Burlington, Vt.: Ashgate, 2006); Debussy, *Debussy Letters*; Lockspeiser, *Debussy*, vol. 2; Nichols, *Life of Debussy*; Nichols and Smith, *Claude Debussy*; Ravel, *Ravel Reader*; Orenstein, *Ravel*; Murphy, *Military Aircraft*; Ferdinand Collin, *Parmi les précurseurs du ciel* (Paris: J. Peyronnet, 1948); Eileen F. Lebow, *Before Amelia: Women Pilots in the Early Days of Aviation* (Washington, D.C.: Brassey's, 2002); Williams, *Last Great Frenchman*; Watson, *Georges Clemenceau*; Mayeur and Rebérioux, *Third Republic from Its Origins to the Great War*; Winock, *Belle Epoque*; Ghislain de Diesbach, *L'Abbé Mugnier: Le confesseur du tout-Paris* (Paris: Perrin, 2003); Mugnier, *Journal*.

1. Probably 1909, although Cocteau is difficult to pin down on dates.

2. Many of these have since been repurchased or reconstructed.

3. Cocteau, *Souvenir Portraits*, 126–27.

4. See chapter 7.

5. Steegmuller, *Cocteau*, 36.

6. Butler, *Rodin*, 461.

7. Kessler, 9 October 1909, in *Journey to the Abyss*, 494–95.

8. Kessler, 12 October 1909, in *Journey to the Abyss*, 495–96.

9. Kessler, 21 August 1904, in *Journey to the Abyss*, 323.

10. Kessler, 25 August 1904, *Journey to the Abyss*, 325.

11. Matisse, *Matisse on Art*, 37–43.

12. Matisse, *Matisse on Art*, 42. In the same essay, Matisse also wrote: "Composition is the art of arranging in a decorative manner the diverse elements at the painter's command to express his feelings" (*Matisse on Art*, 38).

13. Picasso's art dealer Daniel-Henry Kahnweiler, quoted in Flanner, *Men and Monuments*, 138.

14. Edward F. Fry, *Cubism*, 13.

15. He also rejected the Impressionism that preceded them both: "It is not possible for me to copy nature in a servile way," he wrote, regarding Impressionism. "I am forced to interpret nature and submit it to the spirit of the picture" (*Matisse on Art*, 40).

16. Spurling, *Matisse the Master*, 36.

17. Richardson, *Life of Picasso: The Cubist Rebel*, 105.

18. Flanner, *Men and Monuments*, 134–35.

19. Flanner, *Men and Monuments*, 134–35, 74.

20. Richardson, *Life of Picasso: The Cubist Rebel*, 101. Kahnweiler promptly decided to give a one-man show of Braque's work, which thereby became the first Cubist exhibition, elevating Kahnweiler to the role of standard-bearer for the new movement.

21. Gertrude Stein, *Autobiography of Alice B. Toklas*, 58.

22. It now is located in the gardens of the Musée Rodin.

23. Butler, *Rodin*, 453.

24. Isadora Duncan, *My Life*, 202.

25. Isadora Duncan, *My Life*, 205, 209–10.

26. Isadora Duncan, *My Life*, 211, 212.

27. Scheijen, *Diaghilev*, 173. Although by 1912, Diaghilev already found Duncan old-fashioned. The Ballets Russes, he said, needed to "search for new trends in movement, but one that will circumvent Isadora Duncan, who doesn't appear to be old-fashioned simply because her talent is so forceful" (Kurth, *Isadora*, 248).

28. Walsh, *Stravinsky, A Creative Spring*, 132.

29. Anna de Noailles quoted in Scheijen, *Diaghilev*, 183.

30. Carter, *Marcel Proust*, 491.

31. She returned to the Ballets Russes after two weeks, at the end of her own tour.

32. Scheijen, *Diaghilev*, 187. This story has been repeated in endless variations. Isadora did not believe in marriage, and repeatedly refused Paris Singer's marriage proposals. Some stories simply have her proposing to bear Nijinsky's child.

33. Steegmuller, *Cocteau*, 71.

34. Steegmuller, *Cocteau*, 73.

35. Ernest Boulanger, an opera composer who spent much of his career as a singing teacher at the Paris Conservatoire, was more than forty years older than his wife and died in 1900 at the age of eighty-five.

36. Potter, *Nadia and Lili Boulanger*, 8.

37. Debussy to Durand, 18 July 1909; Debussy to Laloy, 30 July 1909, both in *Debussy Letters*, 206, 210.

38. Debussy quoted in Lockspeiser, *Debussy*, 2:170.

39. Ravel to Mme René de Saint-Marceaux, 27 June 1909, in *Ravel Reader*, 107.

40. Ravel to Charles Koechlin, 16 January 1909, in *Ravel Reader*, 102.

41. Nichols, *Life of Debussy*, 107; Nichols and Smith, *Claude Debussy*, 153.

42. Debussy to Jacques Durand, 18 May 1909; Debussy to his parents, 23 May 1909, both in *Debussy Letters*, 199, 200.

43. Debussy to André Caplet, 20 July 1909, in *Debussy Letters*, 208.

44. According to Debussy biographer Roger Nichols, "the evidence suggests" that this may have been the first sign of the cancer that would kill him nine years later (Nichols, *Life of Debussy*, 119).

45. Lebow, *Before Amelia*, 14.

46. Williams, *Last Great Frenchman*, 217.

47. Lockspeiser, *Debussy*, 2:110–11.
48. "From the beginning of 1907 to the autumn of 1908 there was hardly a socialist or anarchist group or trade union in which motions were not passed denigrating [Clemenceau] and
rejoicing in his imminent hanging" (Mayeur and Rebérioux, *Third Republic from Its Origins to
the Great War*, 264).
49. Diesbach, *L'Abbé Mugnier*, 166.
50. Diesbach, *L'Abbé Mugnier*, 168.
51. Mugnier, 25 August 1909, *Journal*, 184.
52. Mugnier, 23 October 1909, *Journal*, 186.
53. Mugnier, 1 November 1909, *Journal*, 187.

12 Deep Waters (1910)

Selected sources for this chapter: Jeffrey H. Jackson, *Paris under Water: How the City of Light
Survived the Great Flood of 1910* (New York: Palgrave Macmillan, 2010); Berton and Os-
sadzow, *Fulgence Bienvenüe*; Ravel, *Ravel Reader*; Carter, *Marcel Proust*; Wildenstein, *Monet*,
vol. 1; Orenstein, *Ravel*; Spurling, *Matisse the Master*; Rhodes, *Louis Renault*; Monet, *Monet by
Himself*; Diesbach, *L'Abbé Mugnier*; Mugnier, *Journal*; Quinn, *Marie Curie*; Eve Curie, *Madame
Curie*; André Langevin, *Paul Langevin, mon père: L'homme et l'oeuvre* (Paris: Les Editeurs Fran-
çais Réunis, 1971); Debussy, *Debussy Letters*; Nichols, *Life of Debussy*; Walsh, *Stravinsky: A
Creative Spring*; Igor Stravinsky, *An Autobiography* (New York: Norton, 1998); Igor Stravinsky
and Robert Craft, *Memories and Commentaries* (New York: Faber and Faber, 2002); Scheijen,
Diaghilev; Lysiane Sarah Bernhardt and Dix, *Sarah Bernhardt*; Steegmuller, *Cocteau*; Cossart,
Food of Love; Gold and Fizdale, *Misia*; Kessler, *Journey to the Abyss*; Lockspeiser, *Debussy*, vol.
2; Proust, *Selected Letters*, vol. 2; Proust, *Selected Letters*, vol. 3; Gold and Fizdale, *Divine Sarah*;
Bessy and Duca, *Georges Méliès*; Butler, *Rodin*; Wineapple, *Sister Brother*; Isadora Duncan, *My
Life*; Kurth, *Isadora*; Flanner, *Men and Monuments*; Olivier, *Picasso and His Friends*; Danchev,
Georges Braque; Barr, *Matisse*; Richardson, *Life of Picasso: The Cubist Rebel*; Mayeur and Rebéri-
oux, *Third Republic from Its Origins to the Great War*; Lacouture, *De Gaulle: The Rebel*; Williams,
Last Great Frenchman.

1. For more on the 1910 flood and its aftermath, see Jackson, *Paris under Water*.
2. He remains, even though the bridge has been rebuilt above him.
3. Marie Ravel to Maurice Ravel, 27 January 1910, in Ravel, *Ravel Reader*, 109.
4. Proust would later suffer from the methods used to dry out and disinfect his building,
which worsened his asthma attacks, as well as from the noise caused by the building repairs
(Carter, *Marcel Proust*, 489).
5. Mirbeau to Monet, in Wildenstein, *Monet*, 1:391–92.
6. Orenstein, *Ravel*, 60.
7. Monet to Paul Durand-Ruel, 10 February 1910, in *Monet by Himself*, 242–43.
8. Monet to Paul Durand-Ruel, 15 April 1910, in *Monet by Himself*, 243.
9. 13 August 1910, *Journal*, 190.
10. 19 August 1910, *Journal*, 191.
11. André Langevin, *Paul Langevin, mon père*, 63.
12. Quinn, *Marie Curie*, 262, 263.
13. Debussy to Jacques Durand, 8 July 1910, in *Debussy Letters*, 220.

14. Debussy to Jacques Durand, 8 July 1910, in *Debussy Letters*, 220. See also Debussy to Georges Hartmann, 14 July 1898 (*Debussy Letters*, 98), in which Debussy despaired of "the barriers erected by law to separate those who strive for their own kind of happiness"; and Debussy to Lilly Texier, 3 July 1899 (*Debussy Letters*, 105–6), in which Debussy told her that they should never demean their love "with those constricting little rules fit only for nonentities."

15. Debussy to Chouchou, 2 December 1910, in *Debussy Letters*, 229.

16. Debussy to Jacques Durand, 4 December 1910, in *Debussy Letters*, 231.

17. Stravinsky, *Autobiography*, 30.

18. Stravinsky, *Autobiography*, 30.

19. Stravinsky and Craft, *Memories and Commentaries*, 77.

20. Kessler, 9 June 1910, in *Journey to the Abyss*, 500.

21. Steegmuller, *Cocteau*, 83; also, in a somewhat different translation, in Scheijen, *Diaghilev*, 201.

22. Stravinsky and Craft, *Memories and Commentaries*, 77.

23. Stravinsky and Craft, *Memories and Commentaries*, 78.

24. Debussy to Jacques Durand, 8 July 1910; Debussy to Robert Godet, 18 December 1911, both in *Debussy Letters*, 221, 250.

25. Nichols, *Life of Debussy*, 134.

26. Stravinsky and Craft, *Memories and Commentaries*, 78.

27. Lysiane Bernhardt and Marion Dix, *Sarah Bernhardt*, 194–95.

28. Many of Méliès's films were two hundred and four hundred meters long rather than the more usual twenty to thirty meters. During this period Méliès even produced a so-called fantasy based on the Dreyfus Affair, in ten films of twenty meters each, including the "Suicide du Colonel Henry" (Bessy and Duca, *Georges Méliès*, 51, 52, 54).

29. Ravel to Michel D. Calvocoressi, 3 May 1910, in *Ravel Reader*, 116.

30. Proust went to Cabourg while his apartment "was echoing with the noise of hammer and saw" (Proust to Maurice Duplay, [shortly before 8 September 1910], in Proust, *Selected Letters*, 3:16–17).

31. Wineapple, *Sister Brother*, 299.

32. Isadora Duncan, *My Life*, 215. Duncan's *dahabeah*, or houseboat, included a Steinway piano and an English pianist who entertained her and Singer each evening with recitals of Bach and Beethoven.

33. Isadora Duncan, *My Life*, 216.

34. Isadora Duncan, *My Life*, 169.

35. Flanner, *Men and Monuments*, 140.

36. Braque later said that Matisse "had found his own truth for himself, and . . . altogether missed out on what we were doing" (Flanner, *Men and Monuments*, 143–44).

37. Olivier, *Picasso and His Friends*, 154.

38. Lacouture, *De Gaulle: The Rebel*, 16.

39. Lacouture, *De Gaulle: The Rebel*, 17. The Constable was the supreme commander of the French armies during the monarchy.

40. Lacouture, *De Gaulle: The Rebel*, 19.

41. Lacouture, *De Gaulle: The Rebel*, 13.

42. Lockspeiser, *Debussy*, 2:110.

43. Count Harry Kessler collaborated with the poet Hugo von Hofmannsthal on the libretto for *The Rosenkavalier*, although Hofmannsthal was initially reluctant to acknowledge Kessler's role (*Journey to the Abyss*, 376, 503).

44. Diesbach, *L'Abbé Mugnier*, 207. Given the diametrically different personalities and politics of Barrès and Anna de Noailles, it seemed an unlikely liaison from the start.

45. Mugnier, 1 December 1910, *Journal*, 197.

46. Mugnier, 22 November and 6 December 1910, *Journal*, 196, 200.

13 Between Heaven and Hell (1911)

Selected sources for this chapter: Carter, *Marcel Proust*; Proust, *Selected Letters*, vol. 3; Gold and Fizdale, *Misia*; Crespelle, *La vie quotidienne à Montmartre au temps de Picasso*; Nichols, *Life of Debussy*; Debussy, *Debussy Letters*; Quinn, *Marie Curie*; Eve Curie, *Madame Curie*; André Langevin, *Paul Langevin, mon père*; Mayeur and Rebérioux, *Third Republic from Its Origins to the Great War*; Murphy, *Military Aircraft*; Bertaut, *Paris, 1870–1935*; Kessler, *Journey to the Abyss*; Lacouture, *De Gaulle: The Rebel*; Williams, *Last Great Frenchman*; Shattuck, *Banquet Years*; Olivier, *Loving Picasso*; Richardson, *Life of Picasso: The Cubist Rebel*; Milton Esterow, *The Art Stealers* (New York: Macmillan, 1966); Marc Chagall, *My Life*, trans. Elizabeth Abbott (New York: Da Capo Press, 1994); Jackie Wullschläger, *Chagall: A Biography* (New York: Knopf, 2008); Voisin, *Men, Women and 10,000 Kites*; Valérie Bougault, *Paris, Montparnasse: The Heyday of Modern Art, 1910–1940* (Paris: Editions Pierre Terrail, 1997); Scheijen, *Diaghilev*; Walsh, *Stravinsky: A Creative Spring*; Stravinsky and Craft, *Memories and Commentaries*; Stravinsky, *Autobiography*; Sert, *Misia and the Muses*; Orledge, *Satie Remembered*; Myers, *Erik Satie*; Gillmor, *Erik Satie*; Ravel, *Ravel Reader*; Orenstein, *Ravel*; Isadora Duncan, *My Life*; Kurth, *Isadora*; Poiret, *King of Fashion*; André Salmon, *Souvenirs sans fin (1903–1940)* (Paris: Gallimard, 2004); Spurling, *Matisse the Master*; Barr, *Matisse*; Wineapple, *Sister Brother*; Brinnin, *Third Rose*; Gertrude Stein, *Autobiography of Alice B. Toklas*; Gertrude Stein, *The Making of Americans: Being a History of a Family's Progress* (Normal, Ill.: Dalkey Archive Press, 1995); Gertrude Stein, *Gertrude Stein on Picasso*, ed. Edward Burns (New York: Liveright, 1970); Butler, *Rodin*; Camille Saint-Saëns, *Camille Saint-Saëns on Music and Musicians*, ed. and trans. Roger Nichols (New York: Oxford University Press, 2008); Steegmuller, *Cocteau*; Monet, *Monet by Himself*; Wildenstein, *Monet*, vol. 1; Cocteau, *Souvenir Portraits*.

1. Proust to Lucien Daudet, 10 January 1911, in Proust, *Selected Letters*, 3:27.

2. Nichols, *Life of Debussy*, 137. See also Debussy, *Debussy Letters*, 240n3.

3. Quinn, *Marie Curie*, 277.

4. Quinn, *Marie Curie*, 278.

5. The Academy of Sciences is one of five academies in the Institut de France.

6. In Eve Curie, *Madame Curie*, 277.

7. Quinn, *Marie Curie*, 317. Langevin's son later wrote: "The xenophobes, the antifeminists, and the ultra-nationalists of the era organized a hateful campaign against Marie Curie and my father, whose baseness I insist on underlining" (André Langevin, *Paul Langevin, mon père*, 13).

8. Quinn, *Marie Curie*, 328, 329–30.

9. Paul Langevin was an attentive father, says his son André, taking them to museums, concerts, the theater, and on hikes around Paris—and eventually farther afield (*Paul Langevin, mon père*, 63).

10. Kessler, 28 November 1910, in *Journey to the Abyss*, 502.

11. Bertaut, *Paris, 1870–1935*, 230.

12. Kessler, 9 September 1911, *Journey to the Abyss*, 561.

13. Lacouture, *De Gaulle: The Rebel*, 19.

14. Olivier, *Loving Picasso*, 275. As foreigners, both Picasso and Apollinaire were justifiably afraid of being deported.

15. Voisin, *Men, Women, and 10,000 Kites*, 128.

16. Bougault, *Paris, Montparnasse*, 41.

17. In his memoirs, Chagall incorrectly dates his arrival as 1910. Private correspondence more accurately dates his departure from Russia and arrival in Paris (see Wullschläger, *Chagall*).

18. Chagall, *My Life*, 107.

19. Chagall, *My Life*, 103.

20. Chagall, *My Life*, 113.

21. Chagall, *My Life*, 104–5.

22. Chagall, *My Life*, 106.

23. Stravinsky, *Autobiography*, 31, 32.

24. Walsh, *Stravinsky: A Creative Spring*, 163.

25. Stravinsky and Craft, *Memories and Commentaries*, 83.

26. Stravinsky quoted in Orledge, *Satie Remembered*, 105.

27. Ravel, *Ravel Reader*, 122n3.

28. Myers, *Erik Satie*, 42.

29. "That [Debussy's upcoming concert] is something I owe to you. Thanks." (Erik Satie to Ravel, 4 March 1911, in Ravel, *Ravel Reader*, 121).

30. Gillmor, *Erik Satie*, 144, and Myers, *Erik Satie*, 43.

31. 16 March 1911, unsigned interview in *The Musical Leader*, in Ravel, *Ravel Reader*, 410.

32. 16 March 1911, unsigned interview in *The Musical Leader*, in Ravel, *Ravel Reader*, 410.

33. Debussy to Jacques Durand, 19 July 1911, in *Debussy Letters*, 244.

34. Debussy to Jacques Durand, 26 August 1911, in *Debussy Letters*, 246.

35. Debussy to André Caplet, [October 1911], in *Debussy Letters*, 247.

36. Debussy to André Caplet, 22 December 1911, in *Debussy Letters*, 252.

37. Debussy to Robert Godet, 18 December 1911, in *Debussy Letters*, 250.

38. Kurth, *Isadora*, 280.

39. Isadora Duncan, *My Life*, 231.

40. Poiret, *King of Fashion*, 193.

41. Poiret, *King of Fashion*, 194.

42. Salmon, *Souvenirs sans fin*, 629.

43. Spurling, *Matisse the Master*, 63.

44. Kessler, 26 May 1911, in *Journey to the Abyss*, 535.

45. Spurling, *Matisse the Master*, 91.

46. Five hundred copies were published in 1925; of these, one hundred were exported for an American edition published by Albert and Charles Boni in 1926 (Gertrude Stein, *The Making of Americans*, xxxvi).

47. Wineapple, *Sister Brother*, 328.

48. Gertrude Stein, *Gertrude Stein on Picasso*, 23.

49. Wineapple, *Sister Brother*, 332.

50. Monet to Paul Durand-Ruel, 18 May 1911, in *Monet by Himself*, 243.

51. It is now located in the Cité de la Musique in the Parc de la Villette (19th).

52. Saint-Saëns, *Camille Saint-Saëns on Music and Musicians*, 49.

53. Her books included *Le Coeur innombrable* (1901), *L'Ombre des jours* (1902), and *Les Eblouissements* (1907).

54. Steegmuller, *Cocteau*, 47.

55. Steegmuller, *Cocteau*, 57.

56. "The utmost intimacy . . . reigns between Lucien and Cocteau," Proust reported to Reynaldo Hahn in March (Proust to Hahn, 4 March 1911, in Proust, *Selected Letters*, 3:34).

57. Cocteau, *Souvenir Portraits*, 139.

14 Dancing on the Edge (1912)

Selected sources for this chapter: Poiret, *King of Fashion*; Scheijen, *Diaghilev*; Lockspeiser, *Debussy*, vol. 2; Nichols, *Life of Debussy*; Debussy, *Debussy Letters*; Kessler, *Journey to the Abyss*; Butler, *Rodin*; Champigneulle, *Rodin*; Laloy, *La musique retrouvée*; Stravinsky and Craft, *Memories and Commentaries*; Walsh, *Stravinsky*; Ravel, *Ravel Reader*; Orenstein, *Ravel*; Steegmuller, *Cocteau*; Arthur King Peters, *Jean Cocteau and André Gide: An Abrasive Friendship* (New Brunswick, N.J.: Rutgers University Press, 1973); Carter, *Marcel Proust*; Albaret, *Monsieur Proust*; Proust, *Selected Letters*, vol. 3; Brandon, *Ugly Beauty*; Justine Picardie, *Coco Chanel: The Legend and the Life* (New York: itbooks, 2010); Barillé, *Coty*; Reynolds, *André Citroën*; Rhodes, *Louis Renault*; Murphy, *Military Aircraft*; Harp, *Marketing Michelin*; Bertaut, *Paris, 1870–1935*; Lacouture, *De Gaulle: The Rebel*; Williams, *Last Great Frenchman*; Watson, *Georges Clemenceau*; Mayeur and Rebérioux, *Third Republic from Its Origins to the Great War*; Quinn, *Marie Curie*; Eve Curie, *Madame Curie*; Wildenstein, *Monet*, vol. 1; Monet, *Monet by Himself*; Potter, *Nadia and Lili Boulanger*; Léonie Rosenstiel, *The Life and Works of Lili Boulanger* (Cranbury, N.J.: Associated University Presses, 1978); Wineapple, *Sister Brother*; Brinnin, *Third Rose*; Gertrude Stein, *Autobiography of Alice B. Toklas*; Ernest Hemingway, *A Moveable Feast* (New York: Touchstone, 1996); Flanner, *Men and Monuments*; Richardson, *Life of Picasso: The Cubist Rebel*; William Rubin, *Picasso and Braque: Pioneering Cubism* (New York: Museum of Modern Art, 1989); Olivier, *Loving Picasso*; Olivier, *Picasso and His Friends*; André Salmon, *Montparnasse: Mémoires* (Paris: Arcadia, 2003); Billy Klüver and Julie Martin, *Kiki's Paris: Artists and Lovers, 1900–1930* (New York: Abrams, 1989); Crespelle, *La vie quotidienne à Montmartre au temps de Picasso*; Bougault, *Paris, Montparnasse*; Dan Franck, *The Bohemians: The Birth of Modern Art: Paris, 1900–1930*, trans. Cynthia Hope Liebow (London: Weidenfeld & Nicolson, 2001); Chagall, *My Life*; Wullschläger, *Chagall*; Françoise Gilot and Carlton Lake, *Life with Picasso* (New York: McGraw-Hill, 1964); Gold and Fizdale, *Divine Sarah*; Kurth, *Isadora*; Isadora Duncan, *My Life*.

1. Poiret, *King of Fashion*, 204, 205.

2. Nichols, *Life of Debussy*, 141.

3. Calmette quoted in Kessler, *Journey to the Abyss*, 600n.

4. Lockspeiser, *Debussy*, 2:265. By the second performance, Nijinsky had changed the gesture, and instead of lying on the veil, he now knelt (Kessler, 31 May 1912, *Journey to the Abyss*, 601).

5. In fact, Marx forged Rodin's signature, although Rodin stood by the article, which he said reflected his views (Scheijen, *Diaghilev*, 249).

6. This indeed happened. The current Musée Rodin is located in the former Hôtel Biron.

7. Butler, *Rodin*, 475. Another of Rodin's biographers quotes him as saying: "That woman was my evil genius. . . . She took me for a fool and people believed her" (Champigneulle, *Rodin*, 244).

8. Laloy, *La musique retrouvée*, 213.

9. Debussy to Stravinsky, [5 November 1912], in *Debussy Letters*, 265.

10. Nichols, *Life of Debussy*, 141.

11. Stravinsky and Craft, *Memories and Commentaries*, 148.

12. Ravel to Ralph Vaughan Williams, 7 June 1914, in *Ravel Reader*, 146.

13. Shortly after the two performances of *Daphnis et Chloé*, Fokine permanently broke with Diaghilev and the Ballets Russes.

14. Ravel to Rouché, 7 October 1912, in *Ravel Reader*, 132. According to Ravel, that spring's season, especially *Daphnis et Chloé*, "left me in a pitiful condition," and he had to repair to the country for a rest cure (Ravel to Ralph Vaughan Williams, 5 August 1912, in *Ravel Reader*, 132). Ravel would experience more problems with Diaghilev in 1914, when Diaghilev cut the choral sections in a London production of *Daphnis et Chloé*, over Ravel's strenuous objections. Ravel finally published these objections in the London press (Ravel to Ralph Vaughan Williams, 7 June 1914, in *Ravel Reader*, 146–47).

15. Lockspeiser, *Debussy*, 2:267.

16. Debussy to Igor Stravinsky, [5 November 1912], in *Debussy Letters*, 265.

17. Debussy to Jacques Durand, 9 August 1912, in *Debussy Letters*, 260–61.

18. Debussy to André Caplet, 25 August 1912, in *Debussy Letters*, 261–62.

19. Ravel, "Les 'Tableaux symphoniques' de M. Fanelli," in *Ravel Reader*, 350.

20. Steegmuller, *Cocteau*, 82.

21. Steegmuller, *Cocteau*, 82.

22. Gide won the Nobel Prize in Literature in 1947.

23. Steegmuller, *Cocteau*, 81–82.

24. Later, a contrite Gide confessed to Proust as having "thought of you . . . [as] a dilettante socialite" (Gide to Proust, [10 or 11 January 1914], in Proust, *Selected Letters*, 3:225).

25. Proust to René Blum, [5, 6, or 7 November 1913], in Proust, *Selected Letters*, 3:207.

26. Early in 1913, he wrote Madame Straus that he had been trying to arise sufficiently early to be able to "stop in front of the St Anne portal [the right-hand portal] of Notre Dame," but had been unable to do so. He needed a model for the church porch at Balbec, and according to the editor's note, several days after writing Madame Straus he "stood for two hours, his fur-lined coat over his nightshirt, in front of the St Anne portal" (Proust to Madame Straus, 14 January 1913, in Proust, *Selected Letters*, 3:143 and 145n4).

27. Brandon, *Ugly Beauty*, 25.

28. Picardie, *Coco Chanel*, 70.

29. The building, at 714 Fifth Avenue, is now occupied by Henri Bendel, which has carefully restored the windows.

30. By 1914, France was second only to the United States in automobile production (Mayeur and Rebérioux, *Third Republic from Its Origins to the Great War*, 327).

31. From *Crowds: A Study of the Popular Mind*, by Gustave le Bon, quoted in Rhodes, *Louis Renault*, 73.

32. Bertaut, *Paris, 1870–1935*, 237.

33. Bertaut, *Paris, 1870–1935*, 236.

34. Lacouture, *De Gaulle: The Rebel*, 20.

35. Quinn, *Marie Curie*, 337.

36. Wildenstein, *Monet*, 1:396.

37. Wildenstein, *Monet*, 1:396.

38. Monet to G. and J. Bernheim-Jeune, 16 April 1912; Monet to Paul Durand-Ruel, 10 May 1912; Monet to Gustave Geffroy, 7 June 1912, all in *Monet by Himself*, 245.

39. The American violinist Albert Spalding quoted in Rosenstiel, *Life and Works of Lili Boulanger*, 62.

40. Hemingway, *Moveable Feast*, 14.

41. *Two: Gertrude Stein and Her Brother* was completed by mid-1912 but not published until after her death.

42. Wineapple, *Sister Brother*, 350, 354, 355, 358.

43. Wineapple, *Sister Brother*, 363.

44. Gertrude Stein, *Autobiography of Alice B. Toklas*, 96.

45. Flanner, *Men and Monuments*, 145. Interestingly, it was around this time, following the affair of the African statuettes and his imprisonment, that Apollinaire changed his allegiance and began wholeheartedly to extoll the Salon Cubists, whom he had previously reviled (Richardson, *Life of Picasso: The Cubist Rebel*, 207).

46. Klüver and Martin, *Kiki's Paris*, 63.

47. Salmon, *Montparnasse*, 127.

48. Gertrude Stein, *Autobiography of Alice B. Toklas*, 111.

49. They moved to 242 Boulevard Raspail, in a ground-floor apartment adjoining the Montparnasse Cemetery. They remained there for only a year and then moved to a larger apartment at 5 bis Rue Schoelcher, which also overlooked the cemetery.

50. Quoted in John Richardson, "Epilogue," in Olivier, *Loving Picasso*, 279.

51. In 1957, when she was in her mid-seventies and broke, Fernande Olivier was able to coerce Picasso into giving her a sizable amount of money to prevent her from publishing during his lifetime yet another memoir of their years together. *Souvenirs intimes* (published in English as *Loving Picasso*) was first published in French in 1988, after both of their deaths (Richardson, *Life of Picasso: The Cubist Rebel*, 232).

52. Bougault, *Paris, Montparnasse*, 52.

53. Chagall, *My Life*, 110.

54. Richardson, *Life of Picasso: The Cubist Rebel*, 165, 189.

55. Richardson, *Life of Picasso: The Cubist Rebel*, 217.

56. This was perhaps a marketing ploy on the part of Apollinaire, who had just published *Bestiaire*, subtitled *Cortège d'Orphée*.

57. Gilot and Lake, *Life with Picasso*, 282. "Long after that," Gilot wrote, "Chagall gave me his opinion of Pablo. 'What a genius, that Picasso,' he said. 'It's a pity he doesn't paint.'" (Françoise Gilot was the mother of Picasso's two youngest children, Claude and Paloma.)

58. Gold and Fizdale, *Divine Sarah*, 311.

59. Kurth, *Isadora*, 287.

60. Isadora Duncan, *My Life*, 231.

61. Isadora Duncan, *My Life*, 232.

62. Isadora Duncan, *My Life*, 233.

63. Isadora Duncan, *My Life*, 234.

15 Fireworks (1913)

Selected sources for this chapter: Lockspeiser, *Debussy*, vol. 2; Gaston Varenne, *Bourdelle par lui-même: Sa pensée et son art* (Paris: Fasquelle, 1937); Nichols, *Life of Debussy*; Debussy, *Debussy Letters*; Steegmuller, *Cocteau*; Stravinsky and Craft, *Memories and Commentaries*; Stravinsky, *Autobiography*; Walsh, *Stravinsky: A Creative Spring*; Scheijen, *Diaghilev*; Kessler, *Journey to the Abyss*; Modris Eksteins, *Rites of Spring: The Great War and the Birth of the Modern Age* (Boston: Houghton Mifflin, 1989); Alex Ross, *The Rest Is Noise: Listening to the Twentieth Century* (New York: Farrar, Straus & Giroux, 2007); Gertrude Stein, *Autobiography of Alice B. Toklas*; Wineapple, *Sister Brother*; Brinnin, *Third Rose*; Quinn, *Marie Curie*; Eve Curie, *Madame Curie*; Flanner, *Men and Monuments*; Barr, *Matisse*; Spurling, *Matisse the Master*; Richardson, *Life of Picasso: The Cubist Rebel*; Butler, *Rodin*; Secrest, *Modigliani*; Ravel, *Ravel Reader*; Orenstein, *Ravel*; Albaret, *Monsieur Proust*; Proust, *Selected Letters*, vol. 3; Carter, *Marcel Proust*; Proust, *The Guermantes Way*; Carter, *Proustian Quest*; Proust, *Selected Letters*, vol. 1; Poiret, *King of Fashion*; Gold and Fizdale, *Divine Sarah*; Esterow, *Art Stealers*; Butler, *Rodin*; Champigneulle, *Rodin*; Odile Ayral-Clause, *Camille Claudel: A Life* (New York: Abrams, 2002); Sert, *Misia and the Muses*; Gold and Fizdale, *Misia*; Mugnier, *Journal*; Rosenstiel, *Life and Works of Lili Boulanger*; Potter, *Nadia and Lili Boulanger*; Isadora Duncan, *My Life*; Steegmuller, *"Your Isadora"*; Kurth, *Isadora*; Irma Duncan, *Duncan Dancer* (New York: Books for Libraries, 1980); Watson, *Georges Clemenceau*; Mayeur and Rebérioux, *Third Republic from Its Origins to the Great War*; Philippe Bernard and Henri Dubief, *The Decline of the Third Republic, 1914–1938*, trans. Anthony Forster (New York: Cambridge University Press, 1988); Williams, *Last Great Frenchman*; Murphy, *Military Aircraft*; Voisin, *Men, Women, and 10,000 Kites*.

1. Varenne, *Bourdelle par lui-même*, 168, 169.
2. Walsh, *Stravinsky: A Creative Spring*, 188.
3. Debussy to Robert Godet, 9 June 1913, in *Debussy Letters*, 272.
4. Stravinsky and Craft, *Memories and Commentaries*, 87.
5. Kessler, 28 May 1913, *Journey to the Abyss*, 619.
6. Stravinsky and Craft, *Memories and Commentaries*, 90, 91.
7. Walsh, *Stravinsky: A Creative Spring*, 202.
8. Stravinsky and Craft, *Memories and Commentaries*, 91. The first concert performance of *The Rite of Spring*, conducted by Pierre Monteux at the Casino de Paris a year later (5 April 1914), was received much more favorably. Louis Laloy reported that the audience listened to the music "in the most respectful silence, and [it] was endlessly acclaimed" (Walsh, *Stravinsky: A Creative Spring*, 232). According to Ravel (who wasn't there): "Apparently it was a triumph. When I think of all those idiots who booed it less than a year ago!" (Ravel to Ida Godebska, 8 April 1914, in *Ravel Reader*, 146).
9. Stravinsky and Craft, *Memories and Commentaries*, 91. Like Debussy, Stravinsky had a low regard for Nijinsky's choreography. Stravinsky considered the choreography for *The Rite of Spring* "a very labored and barren effort rather than a plastic realization flowing simply and naturally from what the music demanded. How far it all was from what I had desired!" (Stravinsky, *Autobiography*, 48).
10. Stravinsky and Craft, *Memories and Commentaries*, 91.
11. Kessler, 29 May 1913, *Journey to the Abyss*, 619–20.
12. Gertrude Stein, *Autobiography of Alice B. Toklas*, 137.
13. Brinnin, *Third Rose*, 179.

14. Flanner, *Men and Monuments*, 92.

15. By purchasing Cézanne's 1887 *View of the Domaine Saint-Joseph* from the Armory Show, the Metropolitan Museum of Art in New York became the first American museum to acquire a Cézanne.

16. Brinnin, *Third Rose*, 185.

17. Wineapple, *Sister Brother*, 174.

18. Brinnin, *Third Rose*, 186.

19. Brinnin, *Third Rose*, 187.

20. Ravel to Lucien Garban, 28 March 1913, in *Ravel Reader*, 134.

21. Debussy to Jacques Durand, 8 August 1913, in *Debussy Letters*, 277.

22. Ravel, "Regarding Claude Debussy's *Images*," [originally published in *Les Cahiers d'aujourd'hui*, February 1913], in *Ravel Reader*, 367–68.

23. Ravel to Roland-Manuel, 27 August 1913, in *Ravel Reader*, 140.

24. Spurling, *Matisse the Master*, 138.

25. Spurling, *Matisse the Master*, 138.

26. Albaret, *Monsieur Proust*, 2.

27. Albaret, *Monsieur Proust*, 15.

28. Albaret, *Monsieur Proust*, 16.

29. Albaret, *Monsieur Proust*, 17.

30. As of November 1913, Proust envisioned *Swann's Way* as the first volume of a three-volume work under the general title of *A la recherche du temps perdu*, with the second and third volumes being *The Guermantes Way* and *Time Regained*, although he already was contemplating naming the second volume *In the Shadow of Young Girls in Bloom* [later translated as *Within a Budding Grove*] (Proust to René Blum, [5, 6, or 7 November 1913], in Proust, *Selected Letters*, 3:207).

31. Others whom Proust drew upon for this character were the Countess de Chevigné ("her bearing and her clothes," according to Céleste Albaret) and Proust's good friend Geneviève Straus, for her wit (Albaret, *Monsieur Proust*, 244–45). William Carter calls Madame Straus "the primary model for the duchesse de Guermantes" (Carter, *Proustian Quest*, 134).

32. Albaret, *Monsieur Proust*, 148, 149.

33. Proust to Robert de Montesquiou, [2? July 1893], in Proust, *Selected Letters*, 1:51.

34. Poiret, *King of Fashion*, 177–78.

35. Kessler, May 24, 1913, *Journey to the Abyss*, 618. Countess Greffulhe, a talented amateur artist, painted her own portrait as well as that of the Abbé Mugnier (both now in Paris's Musée Carnavalet).

36. Debussy to Jacques Durand, 30 August and 3 September 1913, in *Debussy Letters*, 277–78.

37. Champigneulle, *Rodin*, 244.

38. Ayral-Clause, *Camille Claudel*, 198.

39. Scheijen, *Diaghilev*, 277–78.

40. Sert, *Misia and the Muses*, 120.

41. Scheijen, *Diaghilev*, 283.

42. Mugnier, 23 May 1911, *Journal*, 215. "Pneumatics" were pneumatic tubes, powered by compressed air and used for quickly transporting messages, business accounts, and small packages over short distances (often within a single building).

43. Isadora Duncan, *My Life*, 237.

44. Isadora Duncan to Gordon Craig, 19 April 1913, in Steegmuller, *"Your Isadora,"* 317.

45. Isadora Duncan, *My Life*, 236.

46. Isadora Duncan, *My Life*, 245.

47. Isadora Duncan, *My Life*, 245, 246.

48. Kessler, 21 April 1913, *Journey to the Abyss*, 615–16n.

49. Kessler to Craig, quoted in a letter from Craig to his mother, Ellen Terry (28 April), in Steegmuller, *"Your Isadora,"* 321.

50. Isadora to Gordon Craig, 31 May 1913, in Steegmuller, *"Your Isadora,"* 323.

51. Isadora Duncan, *My Life*, 250.

52. Isadora Duncan, *My Life*, 251, 259.

53. Isadora Duncan, *My Life*, 260.

54. Voisin, Men, *Women and 10,000 Kites*, 183.

16 "Dear France, dear country" (1914)

Selected sources for this chapter: Mayeur and Rebérioux, *Third Republic from Its Origins to the Great War*; Bernard and Dubief, *Decline of the Third Republic*; Jean-Jacques Becker, *The Great War and the French People*, trans. Arnold Pomerans (Dover, N.H.: Berg, 1985); Butler, *Rodin*; Watson, *Georges Clemenceau*; Proust, *Selected Letters*, vol. 3; Carter, *Marcel Proust*; Kurth, *Isadora*; Isadora Duncan, *My Life*; Brinnin, *Third Rose*; Wineapple, *Sister Brother*; Gertrude Stein, *Autobiography of Alice B. Toklas*; Gertrude Stein, *Three Lives and Tender Buttons* (New York: Signet, 2003); Gertrude Stein, *Gertrude Stein on Picasso*; Mugnier, *Journal*; Edith Wharton, *A Backward Glance* (New York: Appleton, 1934); Edith Wharton, *Fighting France, from Dunkerque to Belfort* (New York: Charles Scribner's Sons, 1919); Helen Pearl Adam, *Paris Sees It Through: A Diary, 1914–1919* (New York: Hodder and Stoughton, 1919); Shari Benstock, *Women of the Left Bank: Paris, 1900–1940* (Austin: University of Texas Press, 1986); Barbara Tuchman, *The Guns of August* (New York: Ballantine Books, 1994); Alistair Horne, *The Price of Glory: Verdun, 1916* (New York: St. Martin's, 1962); Ian Ousby, *The Road to Verdun: France, Nationalism, and the First World War* (London: Jonathan Cape, 2002); Kessler, *Journey to the Abyss*; Flanner, *Men and Monuments*; Klüver and Martin, *Kiki's Paris*; Timothy Newark, *Camouflage* (New York: Thames and Hudson, 2007); Spurling, *Matisse the Master*; Richardson, *Life of Picasso: The Cubist Rebel*; Myers, *Erik Satie*; Debussy, *Debussy Letters*; Ravel, *Ravel Reader*; Orenstein, *Ravel*; Steegmuller, *Cocteau*; Sert, *Misia and the Muses*; Bertaut, *Paris, 1870–1935*; Lysiane Sarah Bernhardt and Marion Dix, *Sarah Bernhardt, My Grandmother*; Poiret, *King of Fashion*; Danchev, *Georges Braque*; Edith Wharton, *The Letters of Edith Wharton*, ed. R. W. B. Lewis and Nancy Lewis (New York: Scribner, 1988); Hermione Lee, *Edith Wharton* (London: Chatto & Windus, 2007); Gold and Fizdale, *Misia*; Quinn, *Marie Curie*; Eve Curie, *Madame Curie*; Albaret, *Monsieur Proust*; Cossart, *Food of Love*; Monet, *Monet by Himself*; Brandon, *Ugly Beauty*; Picardie, *Coco Chanel*; Chagall, *My Life*; Wullschläger, *Chagall*; Bougault, *Paris, Montparnasse*; Murphy, *Military Aircraft*; Lacouture, *De Gaulle: The Rebel*; Williams, *Last Great Frenchman*; Journas, *Alfred Dreyfus*; Burns, *Dreyfus*.

1. Mayeur and Rebérioux, *Third Republic from Its Origins to the Great War*, 290–91.

2. Butler, *Rodin*, 490–91. The first number of Clemenceau's daily, *L'Homme Libre*, appeared on May 5, 1913, and was influential despite its small circulation (Watson, *Georges Clemenceau*, 246).

3. Proust signed a petition protesting the verdict, published in *Le Figaro* on August 1. But by then, events had already overtaken this once-inflammatory case.

4. André Gide to Proust, 10 or 11 January 1914, in Proust, *Selected Letters*, 3:225.

5. Gide to Proust, 20 March 1914, in Proust, *Selected Letters*, 3:237. On the number of volumes Proust then envisioned, see chapter 15, note 30.

6. Proust to Gide, 10 or 11 June 1914, in Proust, *Selected Letters*, 3:268.

7. Isadora Duncan, *My Life*, 268.

8. Brinnin, *Third Rose*, 158.

9. Wineapple, *Sister Brother*, 384.

10. Gertrude Stein, *Gertrude Stein on Picasso*, 24, 27.

11. Brinnin, *Third Rose*, 197.

12. Brinnin, *Third Rose*, 207.

13. Mugnier, *Journal*, 29 June 1914, 265.

14. Wharton, *A Backward Glance*, 336–37.

15. Adam, *Paris Sees It Through*, 1. Adam was the daughter of C. E. Humphrey, one of the first women journalists in Britain, and was married to George Adam, a correspondent for *The Times*. Both she and her husband served as war correspondents in Paris and France throughout the war.

16. Wharton, *A Backward Glance*, 338.

17. Mugnier, *Journal*, 25 July 1914, 266.

18. Ten years after Jaurès's death, his remains were transferred to the Panthéon. Villain was later tried and acquitted but was killed in 1936 during the Spanish civil war.

19. Sert, *Misia and the Muses*, 136.

20. Adam, *Paris Sees It Through*, 19.

21. Bertaut, *Paris, 1870–1935*, 241.

22. Lysiane Sarah Bernhardt and Marion Dix, *Sarah Bernhardt, My Grandmother*, 208.

23. Poiret, *King of Fashion*, 215.

24. Proust to Lionel Hauser, Sunday evening, 2 August 1914, in Proust, *Selected Letters*, 3:275. Proust added, "I wonder how a believer, a practicing Catholic like the Emperor Francis-Joseph, convinced that after his impending death he will appear before his God, can face having to account to him for the millions of human lives whose sacrifice it was in his power to prevent" (275). The emperor died on November 21.

25. Kessler, 27 July 1914, in *Journey to the Abyss*, 640.

26. Isadora Duncan, *My Life*, 273.

27. Isadora Duncan, *My Life*, 274.

28. Isadora Duncan, *My Life*, 276.

29. Kessler, 31 July and 4 August 1914, in *Journey to the Abyss*, 641, 642. At the war's outset, Kessler served as commander of an artillery munitions column (three officers, 179 junior officers and men, 186 horses, and a number of supply wagons) (643n).

30. Kessler, 1 August 1914, in *Journey to the Abyss*, 641.

31. Kessler, 3 August 1914, in *Journey to the Abyss*, 642.

32. Mugnier, 29 July and 11 August 1914, in *Journal*, 266–67, 268–69.

33. General Henri-Mathias Berthelot, Joffre's assistant chief of staff, quoted in Tuchman, *Guns of August*, 223–24.

34. Although Alex Danchev points out that Picasso arrived at Braque's bedside after Braque's almost-deadly battlefield injury in 1915, and argues that "the differences between them were not easily reducible to the ancient schisms of combatant and non-combatant" (*Georges Braque*, 127).

35. Newark, *Camouflage*, 72. Gertrude Stein recalled that, upon first seeing a camouflaged army truck on Boulevard Raspail, Picasso cried out, "Yes, it is we who made it, this is cubism" (Gertrude Stein, *Gertrude Stein on Picasso*, 18).

36. Newark, *Camouflage*, 68.

37. Helen Pearl Adam noted that by April 1915, the soldiers seen in Paris "wore at least a dozen shades of blue, for experiments were being made as to the most invisible tint. . . . For a while, the official choice fell upon 'Joffre' blue, a curious colour formed by interwoven threats of red, white, and blue. Finally, 'horizon' blue came to stay" (Adam, *Paris Sees It Through*, 55).

38. Debussy to Durand, 8 and 18 August 1914, in *Debussy Letters*, 291, 292.

39. Ravel to Maurice Delage, 4 August 1914, in *Ravel Reader*, 150.

40. Ravel to Edouard Ravel, 8 August 1914, in *Ravel Reader*, 151.

41. Ravel to Roland-Manuel, 26 September 1914, in *Ravel Reader*, 154. Ravel would later dedicate the "Menuet" from *Le Tombeau de Couperin* to Roland-Manuel's stepbrother, Jean Dreyfus, who was killed in the war (*Ravel Reader*, 155n5).

42. Ravel to Roland-Manuel, 26 September 1914, in *Ravel Reader*, 154.

43. Ravel to Roland-Manuel, 1 October 1914, in *Ravel Reader*, 155.

44. Wharton, *Fighting France*, 23.

45. Adam, *Paris Sees It Through*, 21, 31.

46. Marie to Irène, 28 and 31 August 1914, in Eve Curie, *Madame Curie*, 292.

47. Becker notes that the allowance "was not enough to make up the wages lost by a skilled worker, . . . but it was a sizeable amount for day labourers and even more so for agricultural labourers" (*The Great War and the French People*, 17).

48. Wharton to Berenson, 22 August [1914], in *Letters of Edith Wharton*, 334. See also 330 and 393n1. By the war's end, Wharton wrote, "we had, in addition to five thousand refugees permanently cared for in Paris, and four big colonies for old people and children, four large and well-staffed sanatoria for tuberculosis women and children" (*Backward Glance*, 349). In recognition of her work for refugees, France in 1916 made Wharton a Chevalier of the Legion of Honor.

49. Wharton to Sara Norton, 2 September [1914], in *Letters of Edith Wharton*, 335.

50. Sert, *Misia and the Muses*, 137–38.

51. Quinn, *Marie Curie*, 355.

52. Quinn, *Marie Curie*, 356–57.

53. Albaret, *Monsieur Proust*, 203.

54. Becker, *The Great War and the French People*, 63.

55. Monet to Geffroy, 1 September 1914, in *Monet by Himself*, 248.

56. By 1916, Helen Pearl Adam reported that Deauville had become "a perfect orgy of wealth and amusement" (*Paris Sees It Through*, 86).

57. Chagall, *My Life*, 122, 123.

58. A German former student and friend of Matisse managed to retrieve these paintings after the war, but Sarah and Michael had already secretly sold them, at bargain prices, to a Danish collector—probably out of fear of never seeing them again (see Spurling, *Matisse the Master*, 222). Gertrude Stein later sold Matisse's *Femme au chapeau* to Michael. She had kept it when she and Leo split up (Richardson, *Life of Picasso: The Cubist Rebel*, 372).

59. Lacouture, *De Gaulle: The Rebel*, 29.

60. Lacouture, *De Gaulle: The Rebel*, 23.

61. De Gaulle quoted in Lacouture, *De Gaulle: The Rebel*, 29–30.

62. De Gaulle quoted in Lacouture, *De Gaulle: The Rebel*, 30.

63. De Gaulle quoted in Lacouture, *De Gaulle: The Rebel*, 31.

64. Adam, *Paris Sees It Through*, 33.

65. Count Kessler, while in Liège, described the savagery of German reprisals and the increased incidence of drunkenness among German soldiers. However, he blamed the brutality of German reprisals on the Belgians themselves—"return payment" for their alleged actions (22 August 1914, *Journey to the Abyss*, 647)—an echo of the official German position. Kessler would not remain in Belgium and France very long; in late August, his corps was transferred to East Prussia and the eastern front (26 August 1914, *Journey to the Abyss*, 649).

66. Tuchman, *Guns of August*, 409.

67. Tuchman, *Guns of August*, 433–34.

17 "This war which never ends" (1914–1915)

Selected sources for this chapter: Bernard and Dubief, *Decline of the Third Republic*; Tuchman, *Guns of August*; Becker, *The Great War and the French People*; Jean Renoir, *Renoir: My Father*; Wildenstein, *Monet*; Monet, *Monet by Himself*; Timothy Shaw, *World of Escoffier*; Flanner, *Men and Monuments*; Danchev, *Georges Braque*; Klüver and Martin, *Kiki's Paris*; Ravel, *Ravel Reader*; Butler, *Rodin*; Debussy, *Debussy Letters*; Adam, *Paris Sees It Through*; Wharton, *Letters of Edith Wharton*; Wharton, *Fighting France*; Lee, *Edith Wharton*; Bertaut, *Paris, 1870–1935*; Sicard-Picchiottino, *François Coty*; Barillé, *Coty*; Reynolds, *André Citroën*; Wolgensinger, *André Citroën*; Rhodes, *Louis Renault*; Wharton, *A Backward Glance*; Murphy, *Military Aircraft*; Voisin, *Men, Women, and 10,000 Kites*; Orenstein, *Ravel*; Ravel, *Ravel Reader*; Wineapple, *Sister Brother*; Brinnin, *Third Rose*; Gertrude Stein, *Autobiography of Alice B. Toklas*; Proust, *Selected Letters*, vol. 3; Spurling, *Matisse the Master*; Marcel Proust, *Within a Budding Grove* (Vol. 2, *In Search of Lost Time*), trans. C. K. Moncrieff and Terence Kilmartin, rev. D. J. Enright (New York: Modern Library, 1998); Proust, *Sodom and Gomorrah* (Vol. 4, *In Search of Lost Time*); Marcel Proust, *The Captive* and *The Fugitive* (Vols. 5 and 6, *In Search of Lost Time*), trans. C. K. Scott Moncrieff and Terence Kilmartin, rev. D. J. Enright (New York: Modern Library, 1999); Proust, *Time Regained* (Vol. 7, *In Search of Lost Time*), trans. Andreas Mayor and Terence Kilmartin, rev. D. J. Enright (New York: Modern Library, 1993); Albaret, *Monsieur Proust*; Carter, *Marcel Proust*; Steegmuller, *Cocteau*; Richardson, *Life of Picasso: The Cubist Rebel*; Walsh, *Stravinsky: A Creative Spring*; Stravinsky, *Autobiography*; Scheijen, *Diaghilev*; Isadora Duncan, *My Life*; Kurth, *Isadora*; Sturges, *Preston Sturges*; Gold and Fizdale, *Divine Sarah*; Lysiane Sarah Bernhardt and Marion Dix, *Sarah Bernhardt, My Grandmother*; Gottlieb, *Sarah*; Béatrix Dussane, *Reines de Théâtre, 1633–1941* (Lyon, France: H. Lardanchet, 1944); Quinn, *Marie Curie*; Eve Curie, *Madame Curie*; Potter, *Nadia and Lili Boulanger*; Rosenstiel, *Life and Works of Lili Boulanger*; Lockspeiser, *Debussy*, vol. 2; Nichols, *Life of Debussy*; Lacouture, *De Gaulle: The Rebel*; Williams, *Last Great Frenchman*.

1. This young man, André Varagnac, was a nephew of Marcel Sembat, the socialist minister of public works (Tuchman, *Guns of August*, 439n). Despite Varagnac's fragile health, he enlisted in 1915, and during the following year he was twice buried alive in the trenches—severely damaging his already poor health. Hospitalized in the summer of 1918, he was demobilized at the war's end.

2. Ravel to Maurice Delage, 21 September 1914, in *Ravel Reader*, 155n6.

3. Debussy to Nicolas Coronio, [September 1914], in *Debussy Letters*, 292–93. Stravinsky joined the many other composers and artists who protested the destruction of Louvain and the bombardment of Reims cathedral (Walsh, *Stravinsky: A Creative Spring*, 244).

4. Debussy to Jacques Durand, 9 October 1914, in *Debussy Letters*, 294.

5. Adam, *Paris Sees It Through*, 38.

6. Adam, *Paris Sees It Through*, 40.

7. Adam, *Paris Sees It Through*, 42–44. Edith Wharton got around this, in response to a plea by Vincent d'Indy, by giving a series of fund-raising chamber concerts in her apartment "for the poor musicians who are starving" (Wharton to Mary Berenson, 12 January [1915], in *Letters of Edith Wharton*, 346).

8. Wharton to Mary Berenson, 12 January [1915], in *Letters of Edith Wharton*, 347.

9. Adam, *Paris Sees It Through*, 57.

10. Bertaut, *Paris, 1870–1935*, 245, 246, 250.

11. Rhodes, *Louis Renault*, 114.

12. Rhodes, *Louis Renault*, 114.

13. Wharton, *A Backward Glance*, 352.

14. Wharton to Henry James, 28 February and 14 May 1915, in *Letters of Edith Wharton*, 348, 350, 356. A subsequent tour of war-ravaged Belgium led her to found the Children of Flanders Rescue Committee, and in early 1916 she helped start a program aimed at curing those soldiers who had contracted tuberculosis in the trenches (*Letters of Edith Wharton*, 330, 393n1).

15. Fokker had already been experimenting with synchronization designs when he was shown Garros's propeller.

16. The name of Ravel's orchestrated version of *Valses nobles et sentimentales* (*Adélaïde, ou le langage des fleurs*).

17. Gertrude Stein, *Autobiography of Alice B. Toklas*, 156.

18. Gertrude Stein, *Autobiography of Alice B. Toklas*, 157.

19. Gertrude Stein, *Autobiography of Alice B. Toklas*, 158, 161.

20. Proust to Georges de Lauris, 30 November 1914, in Proust, *Selected Letters*, 3:294. Dr. Proust had received a commendation and promotion due to his "courage and efficiency under fire" (Proust, *Selected Letters*, 3:280n9).

21. Later translated as *Within a Budding Grove*.

22. Albaret, *Monsieur Proust*, 201.

23. As evidenced by a warm and friendly letter from Proust to Jean Cocteau, 30 or 31 January 1911, in Proust, *Selected Letters*, 3:28. Proust had already written Cocteau that he regretted his superficiality—"the lack of appetite of someone who has been paying New Year visits all day long and eaten too many marrons glacés [candied chestnuts, a typical Parisian holiday treat]. This . . . is the stumbling-block to be feared for your marvelous but sterilized gifts." Nevertheless, Proust added, "your desires are at present capable of evolving" (Proust to Cocteau, 25 December 1910, in Proust, *Selected Letters*, 3:25–26).

24. Albaret, *Monsieur Proust*, 124.

25. Steegmuller, *Cocteau*, 125.

26. Debussy to Igor Stravinsky, 24 October 1915, in *Debussy Letters*, 308.

27. Sturges, *Preston Sturges*, 127.

28. Gold and Fizdale, *Divine Sarah*, 315–16.

29. Gold and Fizdale, *Divine Sarah*, 318.

30. Dussane, *Reines de Théâtre*, 199–200.
31. Dussane, *Reines de Théâtre*, 200, 201.
32. Debussy to D. E. Inghelbrecht, 30 September 1915, in *Debussy Letters*, 302.
33. Debussy to Jacques Durand, 24 February 1915, in *Debussy Letters*, 296.
34. Debussy to Jacques Durand, 28 August 1915, in *Debussy Letters*, 300.
35. Debussy to Emma, 6 December 1915, in *Debussy Letters*, 310.
36. Lacouture, *De Gaulle: The Rebel*, 33.
37. Maurice Curie quoted in Quinn, *Marie Curie*, 371, 372.

18 "Ils ne passeront pas" (1916)

Selected sources for this chapter: Horne, *Price of Glory*; Ousby, *Road to Verdun*; Bernard and Dubief, *Decline of the Third Republic*; Ravel, *Ravel Reader*; Orenstein, *Ravel*; Lacouture, *De Gaulle: The Rebel*; Williams, *Last Great Frenchman*; Shattuck, *Banquet Years*; Flanner, *Men and Monuments*; Danchev, *Georges Braque*; Kessler, *Journey to the Abyss*; Bertaut, *Paris, 1870–1935*; Lockspeiser, *Debussy*, vol. 2; Debussy, *Debussy Letters*; Myers, *Erik Satie*; Gillmor, *Erik Satie*; Orledge, *Satie Remembered*; Steegmuller, *Cocteau*; Richardson, *Life of Picasso: The Cubist Rebel*; Gold and Fizdale, *Misia*; Scheijen, *Diaghilev*; Adam, *Paris Sees It Through*; Billy Klüver, *A Day with Picasso: Twenty-four Photographs by Jean Cocteau* (Cambridge, Mass.: MIT Press, 1997); Secrest, *Modigliani*; Gertrude Stein, *Autobiography of Alice B. Toklas*; Cossart, *Food of Love*; Walsh, *Stravinsky: A Creative Spring*; Stravinsky and Craft, *Memories and Commentaries*; Mary E. Davis, *Classic Chic: Music, Fashion, and Modernism* (Berkeley: University of California Press, 2006); Poiret, *King of Fashion*; Mugnier, *Journal*; Isadora Duncan, *My Life*; Kurth, *Isadora*; Irma Duncan, *Duncan Dancer*; Monet, *Monet by Himself*; Wildenstein, *Monet*, vol. 1; Wharton, *A Backward Glance*; Gottlieb, *Sarah*; Gold and Fizdale, *Divine Sarah*; Lysiane Sarah Bernhardt and Marion Dix, *Sarah Bernhardt, My Grandmother*; Nichols, *Life of Debussy*; Gaston-Louis Marchal, *Ossip Zadkine: La sculpture—toute une vie* (Rodez, France: Editions du Rouergue, 1992); Benstock, *Women of the Left Bank*; Butler, *Rodin*; Champigneulle, *Rodin*; David I. Harvie, *Eiffel: The Genius Who Reinvented Himself* (Stroud, UK: Sutton, 2004); Murphy, *Military Aircraft*; Voisin, *Men, Women, and 10,000 Kites*.

1. According to Ousby (*Road to Verdun*, 5), there were 708,777 casualties (including both sides), with 162,440 French and 143,000 Germans killed.
2. Ousby, *Road to Verdun*, 9.
3. Ravel to Madame Joseph Ravel, 19 March 1916, in *Ravel Reader*, 161.
4. Ravel to Lucien Garban, 8 May 1916, in *Ravel Reader*, 165.
5. Ravel to Major A. Blondel, 27 May 1916, excerpted in *Ravel Reader*, 167–68n3.
6. Ravel to Major A. Blondel, 27 May 1916, excerpted in *Ravel Reader*, 168n3.
7. Ravel to Jean Marnold, 4 April 1916, in *Ravel Reader*, 162–63.
8. Samson Delpech quoted in Lacouture, *De Gaulle: The Rebel*, 39. Delpech added that, while crouching in his trench, he "had to make a little hole in the ground with the front of my helmet to protect my head from splinters of every kind; so did my comrades" (Lacouture, *De Gaulle: The Rebel*, 39–40.
9. Lacouture, *De Gaulle: The Rebel*, 38.
10. Kessler, 7 August 1915, in *Journey to the Abyss*, 692–93.

11. Ravel to the Committee of the National League for the Defense of French Music, 7 June 1916, in *Ravel Reader*, 169.

12. Ravel to Jean Marnold, 24 June 1916, in *Ravel Reader*, 173.

13. Lockspeiser, *Debussy*, 2:216.

14. Myers, *Erik Satie*, 32.

15. Cocteau in Myers, *Erik Satie*, 48.

16. Steegmuller, *Cocteau*, 146.

17. Gillmor, *Erik Satie*, 195.

18. Satie in Steegmuller, *Cocteau*, 147.

19. Cocteau in Klüver, *Day with Picasso*, 5.

20. Richardson, *Life of Picasso: The Cubist Rebel*, 388.

21. Steegmuller, *Cocteau*, 149.

22. Steegmuller, *Cocteau*, 157.

23. Steegmuller, *Cocteau*, 159.

24. Steegmuller, *Cocteau*, 162.

25. Debussy to Robert Godet, 4 February 1916, in *Debussy Letters*, 314.

26. Adam, *Paris Sees It Through*, 86–87.

27. Bernard and Dubief, *Decline of the Third Republic*, 44.

28. Klüver, *A Day with Picasso*, 65. From Salmon's column, "Nos Echos," in the 16 July 1916 *L'Intransigeant*.

29. Afterward, with the exception of Paul Guillaume's Picasso-Matisse exhibit in early 1918, where Abbé Mugnier would describe it as "undecipherable" (*Journal*, 7 February 1918, 329), *Demoiselles* disappeared from public view for many years. In 1924, Picasso sold it to the *couturier* Jacques Doucet, whose art collection (recently upended to focus on modern art) was far more impressive than Paul Poiret's. After Doucet's death, *Demoiselles* made its way to New York and to the Museum of Modern Art, where it has remained.

30. Gertrude Stein, *Autobiography of Alice B. Toklas*, 172.

31. Jane Bathori quoted in Orledge, *Satie Remembered*, 175. Barthori served as the wartime director of the Théâtre du Vieux-Coumbier, where she helped popularize the works of Satie and the Nouveaux Jeunes.

32. Kurth, *Isadora*, 352. Of this episode, Duncan simply says that "the audiences were cold, heavy, unappreciative" (*My Life*, 291).

33. Irma Duncan, *Duncan Dancer*, 163.

34. Kurth, *Isadora*, 359.

35. Lacouture, *De Gaulle: The Rebel*, 42.

36. Monet to Gustave Geffroy, 11 September 1916, in *Monet by Himself*, 250.

37. Wharton, *A Backward Glance*, 356.

38. Blaise Cendrars quoted in Orledge, *Satie Remembered*, 96.

39. Gold and Fizdale, *Divine Sarah*, 321.

40. Gottlieb, *Sarah*, 175.

41. Lysiane Sarah Bernhardt and Marion Dix, *Sarah Bernhardt, My Grandmother*, 222.

42. Gold and Fizdale, *Divine Sarah*, 325.

43. Ravel to Madame Fernand Dreyfus, 29 September 1916, in *Ravel Reader*, 176.

44. Ravel to Jean Marnold, 7 October 1916, in *Ravel Reader*, 177–78n7.

45. Ravel to Jean Marnold, 24 July 1916, in *Ravel Reader*, 174.

46. See chapter 13.

47. Debussy to Robert Godet, 4 September 1916, in *Debussy Letters*, 318.

48. Debussy to Robert Godet, 4 February 1916, in *Debussy Letters*, 314. According to Roger Nichols, "when the doctors operated on 7 December [1915], it was clear to them that the cancer they found had gone too far to be cured. For the remaining two and a quarter years of his life Debussy used a colostomy" (Nichols, *Life of Debussy*, 156).

49. Debussy to Victor Segalen, 5 June 1916, in *Debussy Letters*, 315.

50. Debussy to Robert Godet, 4 September and 11 December 1916, in *Debussy Letters*, 317 and 320.

51. Butler, *Rodin*, 504.

52. Champigneulle, *Rodin*, 268.

53. Butler, *Rodin*, 507.

54. Voisin, *Men, Women and 10,000 Kites*, 191.

55. Credited to General Robert Nivelle, who took General Pétain's place as commander of the French Second Army at Verdun when Pétain was promoted in May. Nivelle would later replace Joffre as commander-in-chief.

56. Steegmuller, *Cocteau*, 159.

57. Debussy to Emma, 24 December 1916, in *Debussy Letters*, 322.

19 Dark Days (1917)

Selected sources for this chapter: Debussy, *Debussy Letters*; Adam, *Paris Sees It Through*; Wharton, *Letters of Edith Wharton*; Butler, *Rodin*; Champigneulle, *Rodin*; Ravel, *Ravel Reader*; Orenstein, *Ravel*; Bernard and Dubief, *Decline of the Third Republic*; Isadora Duncan, *My Life*; Kurth, *Isadora*; Journas, *Alfred Dreyfus*; Burns, *Dreyfus*; Lacouture, *De Gaulle: The Rebel*; Williams, *Last Great Frenchman*; Walsh, *Stravinsky: A Creative Spring*; Stravinsky, *Autobiography*; Scheijen, *Diaghilev*; Chagall, *My Life*; Wullschläger, *Chagall*; Spurling, *Matisse the Master*; Reynolds, *André Citroën*; Picardie, *Coco Chanel*; Barillé, *Coty*; Sicard-Picchiottino, *François Coty*; Rhodes, *Louis Renault*; André Langevin, *Paul Langevin, mon père*; Walter, *Radiation and Modern Life*; Steegmuller, *Cocteau*; Myers, *Erik Satie*; Gillmor, *Erik Satie*; Orledge, *Satie Remembered*; Cossart, *Food of Love*; John Richardson, *A Life of Picasso: The Triumphant Years, 1917–1932* (New York: Knopf, 2007); Gold and Fizdale, *Misia*; Ross, *The Rest Is Noise*; Lockspeiser, *Debussy*, vol. 2; Nichols, *Life of Debussy*; Carl B. Schmidt, *Entrancing Muse: A Documented Biography of Francis Poulenc* (Hillsdale, N.Y.: Pendragon Press, 2001); Klüver, *A Day with Picasso*; Carter, *Marcel Proust*; Marcel Proust, *Selected Letters*, vol. 4, ed. Philip Kolb, trans. Joanna Kilmartin (London: HarperCollins, 2000); Albaret, *Monsieur Proust*; Mugnier, *Journal*; Jean Renoir, *Renoir, My Father*; Wildenstein, *Monet*, vol. 1; Bessy and Duca, *Georges Méliès*; Secrest, *Modigliani*; Flanner, *Men and Monuments*; Ambroise Vollard, *Renoir: An Intimate Record*, trans. Harold L. Van Doren and Randolf T. Weaver (New York: Knopf, 1925); Watson, *Georges Clemenceau*; Bernard and Dubief, *Decline of the Third Republic*.

1. Debussy to Robert Godet, 7 May 1917, in *Debussy Letters*, 325.

2. Adam, *Paris Sees It Through*, 89.

3. Wharton to Berenson, 4 February [1917], in Wharton, *Letters of Edith Wharton*, 389.

4. Ravel to Mme Dreyfus, 9 February 1917, in *Ravel Reader*, 180.

5. These included Jean Dreyfus, Madame Dreyfus's son, in addition to Pierre and Pascal Gaudin, two brothers killed by the same shell.

6. Isadora Duncan, *My Life*, 299.

7. Mugnier, 29 November 1917, in *Journal*, 321.

8. Adam, *Paris Sees It Through*, 94.

9. Adam, *Paris Sees It Through*, 93.

10. Dreyfus to the Marquise Arconati-Visconti, 27 February 1917, in Journas, *Alfred Dreyfus*, 69.

11. Dreyfus, 15, 16, 17, and 18 April [1917], in Journas, *Alfred Dreyfus*, 77, 79.

12. Lacouture, *De Gaulle: The Rebel*, 50. Despite the punishment's stipulation of "no writing materials," de Gaulle evidently had access to the pen and paper with which he wrote his parents.

13. Walsh, *Stravinsky: A Creative Spring*, 275.

14. Stravinsky, *Autobiography*, 70.

15. Chagall, *My Life*, 136, 137.

16. Chagall, *My Life*, 137.

17. Spurling, *Matisse the Master*, 202.

18. Adam, *Paris Sees It Through*, 99.

19. Chanel quoted in Picardie, *Coco Chanel*, 79.

20. Marie Curie's ashes entered the Panthéon in 1995. She was the first woman to be included among the Panthéon's luminaries on her own merits, although it took more than fifty years for this to happen (she died in 1934).

21. Gold and Fizdale, *Misia*, 195.

22. Amid his praise for Satie, Picasso, and Massine, Apollinaire failed to mention Cocteau's role as originator of *Parade*—an omission that seems to have been deliberate and was indicative of the lack of regard in which Cocteau still was widely held.

23. Steegmuller, *Cocteau*, 183.

24. Steegmuller, *Cocteau*, 83. The Abbé Mugnier slyly noted, though, that "Jean Cocteau is swollen with pride in imagining that [*Parade*] is the equivalent of the première of [Hugo's] *Hernani!*" (Mugnier, 5 June 1917, *Journal*, 312).

25. Honegger letter quoted in Orledge, *Satie Remembered*, 172.

26. Laloy quoted in Orledge, *Satie Remembered*, 98–99.

27. See Orledge, *Satie Remembered*, 99 and 99n.

28. Schmidt, *Entrancing Muse*, 55.

29. Klüver, *A Day with Picasso*, 80.

30. Myers, *Erik Satie*, 51.

31. Debussy to Gabriel Fauré, 29 April 1917, in *Debussy Letters*, 324.

32. Debussy to Robert Godet, 11 December 1916, in *Debussy Letters*, 321.

33. Albaret, *Monsieur Proust*, 67.

34. Albaret, *Monsieur Proust*, 335–37.

35. Carter, *Marcel Proust*, 629.

36. Proust to Abbé Mugnier, 14 February 1918, in Proust, *Selected Letters*, 4:22.

37. Mugnier, 12 January 1914, in *Journal*, 4:259.

38. Mugnier, 23 April 1917, in *Journal*, 309–10. See also 5 June 1917, 312–13.

39. Brian Selznick's *The Invention of Hugo Cabret* and the Martin Scorsese film *Hugo* are fictional stories based on Méliès's life.

40. Vollard, *Renoir*, 51–52.

41. Adding to their friendship, both men had sons named Jean and Pierre who were serving in, or about to join, the army. Jean Renoir had fought in the infantry until wounded and then served as a reconnaissance pilot. Jean's older brother, Pierre, "had his arm shattered by a bullet" and was invalided out of the army (Jean Renoir, *Renoir, My Father*, 4). Matisse's older

son, Jean, was still operating as a airplane mechanic, and his younger son, Pierre, was scheduled in the autumn of 1918 to be posted to the front as a driver in an artillery regiment (Spurling, *Matisse the Master*, 214).

42. Bernard and Dubief, *Decline of the Third Republic*, 59.

20 Finale (1918)

Selected sources for this chapter: Adam, *Paris Sees It Through*; Henry W. Miller, *The Paris Gun: The Bombardment of Paris by the German Long Range Guns and the Great German Offensives of 1918* (New York: Jonathan Cape & Harrison Smith, 1930); Bernard and Dubief, *Decline of the Third Republic*; Watson, *Georges Clemenceau*; Edward M. Coffman, *The War to End All Wars: The American Military Experience in World War I* (Lexington: University Press of Kentucky, 1998); Nichols, *Life of Debussy*; Lockspeiser, *Debussy*, vol. 2; Debussy, *Debussy Letters*; Potter, *Nadia and Lili Boulanger*; Rosenstiel, *Life and Works of Lili Boulanger*; Orledge, *Satie Remembered*; Gertrude Stein, *Autobiography of Alice B. Toklas*, Albaret, *Monsieur Proust*; Proust, *Selected Letters*, vol. 4; Steegmuller, *Cocteau*; Gillmor, *Erik Satie*; Myers, *Erik Satie*; Peters, *Jean Cocteau and André Gide*; Lacouture, *De Gaulle: The Rebel*; Williams, *Last Great Frenchman*; Richardson, *Life of Picasso: The Triumphant Years*; Wharton, *A Backward Glance*; Flanner, *Men and Monuments*; Klüver, *Day with Picasso*; Scheijen, *Diaghilev*; Roland Penrose, *Picasso: His Life and Work* (Berkeley: University of California Press, 1981); Stravinsky and Craft, *Memories and Commentaries*; Shattuck, *Banquet Years*; Secrest, *Modigliani*; Ravel, *Ravel Reader*; Walsh: *Stravinsky: A Creative Spring*; Spurling, *Matisse the Master*; Journas, *Alfred Dreyfus*; Burns, *Dreyfus*; Isadora Duncan, *My Life*; Kurth, *Isadora*; Lysiane Sarah Bernhardt and Marion Dix, *Sarah Bernhardt, My Grandmother*; Gold and Fizdale, *Misia*; Monet, *Monet by Himself*; Wildenstein, *Monet*, vol. 1; Georges Clemenceau, *Claude Monet: The Water Lilies*, trans. George Boas (Garden City, NY: Doubleday, Doran, 1930); Bertaut, *Paris, 1870–1935*.

1. Adam, *Paris Sees It Through*, 146.
2. A memorial chapel in the rebuilt church commemorates this catastrophe.
3. Adam, *Paris Sees It Through*, 222.
4. From the war diary of Romain Rolland, in Lockspeiser, *Debussy*, 2:222.
5. Adam, *Paris Sees It Through*, 198.
6. Adam, *Paris Sees It Through*, 226, 227, 229.
7. Laloy quoted in Nichols, *Life of Debussy*, 160.
8. Chouchou to Raoul Bardac, 8 April 1918, in Debussy, *Debussy Letters*, 335.
9. Laloy quoted in Lockspeiser, *Debussy*, 2:224–25.
10. Chouchou to Raoul Bardac, 8 April 1918, in Debussy, *Debussy Letters*, 335.
11. She died the following year, at the age of thirteen, after receiving the wrong treatment for diphtheria.
12. Albaret, *Monsieur Proust*, 93–94.
13. Albaret, *Monsieur Proust*, 93–94.
14. Proust to Madame Soutzo, 9 April 1918, in *Selected Letters*, 4:37.
15. Blaise Cendrars' memories of Satie, quoted in Orledge, *Satie Remembered*, 78.
16. Cocteau quoted in Myers, *Erik Satie*, 53.
17. Gillmor, *Erik Satie*, 210. Bayreuth was the home of Wagner, and continues to be the home of the Wagner Festival, known as the Bayreuth Festival.
18. Steegmuller, *Cocteau*, 207.

19. Steegmuller, *Cocteau*, 197.
20. Lacouture, *De Gaulle: The Rebel*, 50.
21. The 26th Infantry Division (nicknamed the Yankee Division) of National Guardsmen from New England was among the first to arrive in France. Early in 1918, it served at Chemin des Dames, which then was a quiet sector. In April, the 26th left Chemin des Dames, and in July it was sent into action at Château-Thierry. I was privileged to visit the underground quarters at Chemin des Dames (an extensive former quarry) where members of the 26th Division lived and rested when not in the trenches. Their wall carvings are extraordinary, ranging from humorous (an imaginary Red Sox–Yankees score, with the Red Sox clobbering the Yankees) to deeply moving tributes to loved ones back home.
22. Adam, *Paris Sees It Through*, 236, 238.
23. From France's national anthem, the Marseillaise (Adam, *Paris Sees It Through*, 240).
24. Adam, *Paris Sees It Through*, 240, 241.
25. Wharton, *A Backward Glance*, 358–59.
26. Flanner, *Men and Monuments*, 214. Khokhlova reportedly refused to sleep with Picasso before marriage (Scheijen, *Diaghilev*, 335; Richardson, *Life of Picasso: The Triumphant Years*, 5), although she appears to have capitulated by the time he brought her to Barcelona to introduce her to his mother (Richardson, *Life of Picasso: The Triumphant Years*, 60). Picasso had gone to Rome to join Diaghilev, Massine, and the Ballets Russes. Cocteau, and eventually Stravinsky, joined them. Satie did not come.
27. Stravinsky and Craft, *Memories and Commentaries*, 170.
28. Secrest, *Modiligiani*, 259–60, 276.
29. Debussy to Jacques Durand, 8 July 1910, in *Debussy Letters*, 220. See chapter 12.
30. Ravel to Madame Alfredo Casella, 19 January 1919, in *Ravel Reader*, 185.
31. Although by the war's end, Eugenia Errázuriz was supplying him, like Picasso, with a thousand francs a month.
32. Walsh, *Stravinsky*, 290.
33. Spurling, *Matisse the Master*, 208–9.
34. Isadora Duncan, *My Life*, 310; Kurth, *Isadora*, 379.
35. He died in October, killed in action.
36. Watson, *Georges Clemenceau*, 302.
37. Watson, *Georges Clemenceau*, 314.
38. Dreyfus to the Marquise Arconati-Viscoti, 20 July 1917, in Journas, *Alfred Dreyfus*, 88.
39. Journas, *Alfred Dreyfus*, 123. Alfred Dreyfus's son, Pierre, an engineer, had served at the front since the war's outset, first at Mulhouse, then at the Marne, at Verdun, and the Somme, for which he received citations and the Croix de Guerre.
40. Adam, *Paris Sees It Through*, 246, 250.
41. Lacouture, *De Gaulle: The Rebel*, 53.
42. Watson, *Georges Clemenceau*, 326.
43. Wharton, *A Backward Glance*, 359.
44. Lysiane Sarah Bernhardt and Marion Dix, *Sarah Bernhardt, My Grandmother*, 222.
45. Adam, *Paris Sees It Through*, 253. By "thoroughfare," Adam probably was referring to the Champs-Elysées, although she simply may have omitted an "s" from a more general reference to "thoroughfares."
46. Bertaut, *Paris, 1870–1935*, 270.
47. Isadora Duncan, *My Life*, 313.

48. Monet to Clemenceau, 12 November 1918, in *Monet by Himself*, 252. Monet originally proposed that these be placed in the Musée des Arts Décoratifs.

49. Watson, *Georges Clemenceau*, 327.

50. Gertrude Stein, *Autobiography of Alice B. Toklas*, 176.

51. Albaret, *Monsieur Proust*, 155.

52. Albaret, *Monsieur Proust*, 159.

Bibliography

Adam, Helen Pearl. *Paris Sees It Through: A Diary, 1914–1919*. New York: Hodder and Stoughton, 1919.

Adams, Henry. *The Education of Henry Adams*. New York: Random House, 1931. First published 1918.

Albaret, Céleste. *Monsieur Proust: A Memoir*. Recorded by Georges Belmont. Translated by Barbara Bray. New York: McGraw-Hill, 1976.

Arntzenius, Frank. *Space, Time, and Stuff*. New York: Oxford University Press, 2012.

Assouline, Pierre. *An Artful Life: A Biography of D. H. Kahnweiler, 1884–1979*. Translated by Charles Ruas. New York: G. Weidenfeld, 1990.

Ayral-Clause, Odile. *Camille Claudel: A Life*. New York: Abrams, 2002.

Barillé, Elisabeth. *Coty: Parfumeur and Visionary*. Translated by Mark Howarth. Paris: Editions Assouline, 1996.

Barr, Alfred H., Jr. *Matisse: His Art and His Public*. New York: Museum of Modern Art, 1951.

Becker, Jean-Jacques. *The Great War and the French People*. Translated by Arnold Pomerans. Dover, N.H.: Berg, 1985.

Bennett, Jane, and William Connolly. "The Crumpled Handkerchief." In *Time and History in Deleuze and Serres*. Edited by Bernd Herzogenrath. New York: Continuum, 2012.

Benstock, Shari. *No Gifts from Chance: A Biography of Edith Wharton*. New York: Scribner, 1994.

———. *Women of the Left Bank: Paris, 1900–1940*. Austin: University of Texas Press, 1986.

Berlanstein, Lenard R. *The Working People of Paris, 1871–1914*. Baltimore: Johns Hopkins University Press, 1984.

Bernard, Philippe, and Henri Dubief. *The Decline of the Third Republic, 1914–1938.* Translated by Anthony Forster. New York: Cambridge University Press, 1988. First published in English, 1985.

Bernhardt, Lysiane Sarah, and Marion Dix. *Sarah Bernhardt, My Grandmother.* London: Hurst & Blackett, 1949.

Bertaut, Jules. *Paris, 1870–1935.* Translated by R. Millar. Edited by John Bell. London: Eyre and Spottiswoode, 1936.

Berton, Claude, and Alexandre Ossadzow. *Fulgence Bienvenüe et la construction du métropolitain de Paris.* Paris: Presses de l'Ecole nationale des ponts et chausses, 1998.

Bessy, Maurice, and Lo Duca. *Georges Méliès, mage.* Paris: Jean-Jacques Pauvert, 1961.

Boardingham, Robert. *The Young Picasso.* New York: Universe, 1997.

Bonthoux, Daniel, and Berard Jégo. *Montmartre: Bals et Cabarets au temps de Bruant et Lautrec.* Paris: Musée de Montmartre, 2002.

Bougault, Valérie. *Paris, Montparnasse: The Heyday of Modern Art, 1910–1940.* Paris: Editions Pierre Terrail, 1997.

Bourdelle. Dossier de l'Art 10 (Janvier–Février 1993).

Brandon, Ruth. *Ugly Beauty: Helena Rubinstein, L'Oréal, and the Blemished History of Looking Good.* New York: HarperCollins, 2011.

Bredin, Jean-Denis. *The Affair: The Case of Alfred Dreyfus.* Translated by Jeffrey Mehlman. New York: George Braziller, 1986.

Brettell, Richard R., and Joachim Pissarro. *The Impressionist and the City: Pissarro's Series Paintings.* Edited by Mary Anne Stevens. New Haven, Conn.: Yale University Press, 1992.

Brinnin, John Malcolm. *The Third Rose: Gertrude Stein and Her World.* Reading, Mass.: Addison-Wesley, 1987.

Brown, Frederick. *Zola: A Life.* New York: Farrar, Straus & Giroux, 1995.

Burns, Michael. *Dreyfus: A Family Affair, 1789–1945.* New York: HarperCollins, 1991.

Butler, Ruth. *Rodin: The Shape of Genius.* New Haven, Conn.: Yale University Press, 1993.

Carter, William C. *Marcel Proust: A Life.* New Haven, Conn.: Yale University Press, 2000.

———. *The Proustian Quest.* New York: New York University Press, 1992.

Chagall, Marc. *My Life.* Translated by Elizabeth Abbott. New York: Da Capo Press, 1994. Republication of 1960 edition.

Champigneulle, Bernard. *Rodin.* Translated by J. Maxwell Brownjohn. London: Thames and Hudson, 1967.

Clemenceau, Georges. *Claude Monet: The Water Lilies.* Translated by George Boas. Garden City, N.Y.: Doubleday, Doran, 1930.

Clément, Alain, and Gilles Thomas. *Atlas du Paris souterrain: La doublure sombre de la ville lumière.* Paris: Editions Parigramme, 2001.

Cocteau, Jean. *Souvenir Portraits: Paris in the Belle Epoque.* Translated by Jesse Browner. New York: Paragon House, 1990. First published 1935.

Coffman, Edward M. *The War to End All Wars: The American Military Experience in World War I*. Lexington: University Press of Kentucky, 1998. First published 1968.

Collin, Ferdinand. *Parmi les précurseurs du ciel*. Paris: J. Peyronnet, 1948.

Cossart, Michael de. *The Food of Love: Princesse Edmond de Polignac (1865–1943) and Her Salon*. London: Hamish Hamilton, 1978.

Crespelle, Jean-Paul. *La vie quotidienne à Montmartre au temps de Picasso, 1900–1910*. Paris: Hachette, 1978.

Curie, Eve. *Madame Curie: A Biography*. Translated by Vincent Sheean. Garden City, N.Y.: Garden City Publishing, 1940. First published 1937.

Current, Richard Nelson, and Marcia Ewing Current. *Loie Fuller: Goddess of Light*. Boston: Northeastern University Press, 1997.

Danchev, Alex. *Georges Braque: A Life*. New York: Hamish Hamilton, 2005.

Daniels, Stephanie, and Anita Tedder. *"A Proper Spectacle": Women Olympians, 1900–1936*. Houghton Conquest, UK: ZeNaNA Press, 2000.

Danius, Sara. *The Senses of Modernism: Technology, Perception, and Aesthetics*. Ithaca, N.Y.: Cornell University Press, 2002.

Daudet, Léon. *Memoirs of Léon Daudet*. Edited and translated by Arthur Kingsland Griggs. New York: L. MacVeagh, Dial Press, 1925.

Davis, Mary E. *Classic Chic: Music, Fashion, and Modernism*. Berkeley: University of California Press, 2006.

Debussy, Claude. *Debussy Letters*. Edited by François Lesure and Roger Nichols. Translated by Roger Nichols. Cambridge, Mass.: Harvard University Press, 1987.

Descouturelle, Frédéric, André Mignard, and Michel Rodriguez. *Le Métropolitain d'Hector Guimard*. Paris: Somogy editions d'art, 2004.

Desti, Mary. *The Untold Story: The Life of Isadora Duncan, 1921–1927*. New York: Da Capo, 1981. First published 1929.

Diesbach, Ghislain de. *L'Abbé Mugnier: Le confesseur du tout-Paris*. Paris: Perrin, 2003.

Donnet, Pierre-Antoine. *La saga Michelin*. Paris: Seuil, 2008.

Duncan, Irma. *Duncan Dancer*. New York: Books for Libraries, 1980. First published 1965.

Duncan, Isadora. *My Life*. New York: Liveright, 2013. First published 1927.

Dussane, Béatrix. *Reines de Théâtre, 1633–1941*. Lyon, France: H. Lardanchet, 1944.

Dyreson, Mike. *Making the American Team: Sport, Culture, and the Olympic Experience*. Urbana: University of Illinois Press, 1998.

Easton, Laird M. *The Red Count: The Life and Times of Harry Kessler*. Berkeley: University of California Press, 2002.

Eksteins, Modris. *Rites of Spring: The Great War and the Birth of the Modern Age*. Boston: Houghton Mifflin, 1989.

Ellis, Jack D. *The Early Life of Georges Clemenceau, 1841–1893*. Lawrence: Regents Press of Kansas, 1980.

Escoffier, Auguste. *Memories of My Life*. Translated by Laurence Escoffier. New York: Van Nostrand Reinhold, 1997.

Esterow, Milton. *The Art Stealers*. New York: Macmillan, 1966.

Flanner, Janet. *Men and Monuments*. New York: Harper, 1957.

Franck, Dan. *The Bohemians: The Birth of Modern Art: Paris, 1900–1930*. Translated by Cynthia Hope Liebow. London: Weidenfeld & Nicolson, 2001.

Frèrejean, Alain. *André Citroën, Louis Renault: Un duel sans merci*. Paris: Albin Michel, 1998.

Frey, Julia. *Toulouse-Lautrec: A Life*. London: Weidenfeld and Nicolson, 1994.

Fry, Edward F. *Cubism*. New York: Oxford University Press, 1978.

Gibbs-Smith, Charles Harvard. *The Rebirth of European Aviation, 1902–1908: A Study of the Wright Brothers' Influence*. London: Her Majesty's Stationery Office, 1974.

Gibson, Ralph. *A Social History of French Catholicism, 1789–1914*. New York: Routledge, 1989.

Gillmor, Alan M. *Erik Satie*. Boston: Twayne, 1988.

Gilot, Françoise. *Matisse and Picasso: A Friendship in Art*. New York: Doubleday, 1990.

Gilot, Françoise, and Carlton Lake. *Life with Picasso*. New York: McGraw-Hill, 1964.

Gold, Arthur, and Robert Fizdale. *The Divine Sarah: A Life of Sarah Bernhardt*. New York: Vintage Books, 1992.

———. *Misia: The Life of Misia Sert*. New York: Morrow, 1981.

Gordon, Robert, and Andrew Forge. *Degas*. With translations by Richard Howard. New York: Abrams, 1988.

Gottlieb, Robert. *Sarah: The Life of Sarah Bernhardt*. New Haven, Conn.: Yale University Press, 2010.

Harp, Stephen L. *Marketing Michelin: Advertising and Cultural Identity in Twentieth-Century France*. Baltimore: Johns Hopkins University Press, 2001.

Harvie, David I. *Eiffel: The Genius Who Reinvented Himself*. Stroud, UK: Sutton, 2004.

Hemingway, Ernest. *A Moveable Feast*. New York: Touchstone, 1996. First published 1964.

Holmes, Diana, and Carrie Tarr, eds. *A "Belle Epoque"? Women in French Society and Culture, 1890–1914*. New York: Berghahn Books, 2006.

Horne, Alistair. *The Price of Glory: Verdun, 1916*. New York: St. Martin's, 1962.

Jackson, Jeffrey H. *Paris under Water: How the City of Light Survived the Great Flood of 1910*. New York: Palgrave Macmillan, 2010.

Jones, Colin. *Paris: Biography of a City*. New York: Viking, 2005.

Josephson, Matthew. *Zola and His Time*. Garden City, N.Y.: Garden City Publishing, 1928.

Journas, Georges. *Alfred Dreyfus, officier en 14–18: Souvenirs, lettres et carnet de guerre*. Orléans, France: Regain de lecture, 2011.

Jullian, Philippe. *Prince of Aesthetes: Count Robert de Montesquiou, 1855–1921*. Translated by John Haylock and Francis King. London: Secker & Warburg, 1967.

Kessler, Harry. *Journey to the Abyss: The Diaries of Count Harry Kessler, 1880–1918*. Edited and translated by Laird M. Easton. New York: Knopf, 2011.

Klüver, Billy. *A Day with Picasso: Twenty-four Photographs by Jean Cocteau.* Cambridge, Mass.: MIT Press, 1997.

Klüver, Billy, and Julie Martin. *Kiki's Paris: Artists and Lovers, 1900–1930.* New York: Abrams, 1989.

Kurth, Peter. *Isadora: A Sensational Life.* Boston: Little, Brown, 2001.

Lacouture, Jean. *De Gaulle: The Rebel, 1890–1944.* Translated by Patrick O'Brian. New York: Norton, 1993.

Laloy, Louis. *La musique retrouvée, 1902–1927.* Paris: Desclée de Brouwer, 1974.

Lamming, Clive. *Métro insolite: Promenades curieuses, lignes oubliées, stations fantômes, metros imaginaires, rames.* Paris: Parigramme, 2001.

Langevin, André. *Paul Langevin, mon père: L'homme et l'oeuvre.* Paris: Les Editeurs Français Réunis, 1971.

Lebow, Eileen F. *Before Amelia: Women Pilots in the Early Days of Aviation.* Washington, D.C.: Brassey's, 2002.

Lee, Hermione. *Edith Wharton.* London: Chatto & Windus, 2007.

Lesure, François. "'L'Affaire' Debussy-Ravel." In *Festschrift Friedrich Blume zum 70. Geburtstag.* Edited by Anna Amalie Abert and Wilhelm Pfannkuch, 231–34. Kassel, Germany: Bärenreiter, 1963.

Lockspeiser, Edward. *Debussy: His Life and Mind.* Vol. 2, *1902–1918.* New York: Macmillan, 1965.

Maclellan, Nic, ed. *Louise Michel.* Melbourne, N.Y.: Ocean Press, 2004.

Mallon, Bill. *The 1900 Olympic Games: Results for All Competitors in All Events, with Commentary.* Jefferson, N.C.: McFarland, 1998.

Marchal, Gaston-Louis. *Ossip Zadkine: La sculpture—toute une vie.* Rodez, France: Editions du Rouergue, 1992.

Matisse, Henri. *Matisse on Art.* Rev. ed. Edited by Jack Flam. Berkeley: University of California Press, 1995.

Mayeur, Jean-Marie, and Madeleine Rebérioux. *The Third Republic from Its Origins to the Great War, 1871–1914.* Translated by J. R. Foster. Cambridge, UK: Cambridge University Press, 1989.

McAuliffe, Mary. *Dawn of the Belle Epoque: The Paris of Monet, Zola, Bernhardt, Eiffel, Debussy, Clemenceau, and Their Friends.* Lanham, Md.: Rowman & Littlefield, 2011.

McManners, John. *Church and State in France, 1870–1914.* London: SPCK, 1972.

Merriman, John M. *The Dynamite Club: How a Bombing in Fin-de-Siècle Paris Ignited the Age of Modern Terror.* Boston: Houghton Mifflin Harcourt, 2009.

Michel, Louise. *The Red Virgin: The Memoirs of Louise Michel.* Edited and translated by Bullitt Lowry and Elizabeth Ellington Gunter. Tuscaloosa: University of Alabama Press, 1981.

Miller, Henry W. *The Paris Gun: The Bombardment of Paris by the German Long Range Guns and the Great German Offensives of 1918.* New York: Jonathan Cape & Harrison Smith, 1930.

Monet, Claude. *Monet by Himself: Paintings, Drawings, Pastels, Letters.* Edited by Richard R. Kendall. Translated by Bridget Strevens Romer. London: Macdonald, 1989.

Mouret, Jean-Noël. *Louis Renault.* Paris: Gallimard, 2009.

Mucha, Jiri. *Alphonse Mucha: His Life and Art.* London: Academy Editions, 1989.

———. *Alphonse Mucha: His Life and Work.* New York: St. Martin's, 1974.

Mugnier, Abbé (Arthur). *Journal de l'Abbé Mugnier: 1879–1939.* Paris: Mercure de France, 1985.

Murphy, Justin D. *Military Aircraft, Origins to 1918.* Santa Barbara, Calif.: ABC CLIO, 2005.

Murray, Gale, ed. *Toulouse-Lautrec: A Retrospective.* New York: Hugh Lauter Levin, 1992.

Myers, Rollo H. *Erik Satie.* Rev. ed. New York: Dover, 1968. First published 1948.

Newark, Timothy. *Camouflage.* New York: Thames and Hudson, 2007.

Nichols, Roger. *The Life of Debussy.* Cambridge, UK: Cambridge University Press, 1998.

Nichols, Roger, and Richard Langham Smith. *Claude Debussy: Pelléas et Mélisande.* Cambridge, UK: Cambridge University Press, 1989.

Nostitz, Helene von. *Dialogues with Rodin.* Translated by H. L. Ripperger. New York: Duffield & Green, 1931.

Olivier, Fernande. *Loving Picasso: The Private Journal of Fernande Olivier.* Translated by Christine Baker and Michael Raeburn. New York: Abrams, 2001.

———. *Picasso and His Friends.* Translated by Jane Miller. London: Heinemann, 1964.

O'Mahony, Mike. *Olympic Visions: Images of the Games through History.* London: Reaktion Books, 2012.

Orenstein, Arbie. *Ravel: Man and Musician.* New York: Columbia University Press, 1975.

Orledge, Robert, ed. *Satie Remembered.* Translated by Roger Nichols. Portland, Ore.: Amadeus Press, 1995.

Osma, Guillermo de. *Mariano Fortuny: His Life and Work.* New York: Rizzoli, 1980.

Ousby, Ian. *The Road to Verdun: France, Nationalism, and the First World War.* London: Jonathan Cape, 2002.

Palau i Fabre, Josep. *Picasso: The Early Years, 1881–1907.* Translated by Kenneth Lyons. New York: Rizzoli, 1981.

Penrose, Roland. *Picasso: His Life and Work.* Berkeley: University of California Press, 1981.

Perloff, Nancy. *Art and the Everyday: Popular Entertainment and the Circle of Erik Satie.* Oxford, UK: Clarendon Press, 1991.

Peters, Arthur King. *Jean Cocteau and André Gide: An Abrasive Friendship.* New Brunswick, N.J.: Rutgers University Press, 1973.

Picardie, Justine. *Coco Chanel: The Legend and the Life.* New York: itbooks, 2010.

Pissarro, Camille. *Letters to His Son Lucien.* Edited by John Rewald, with assistance of Lucien Pissarro. Translated by Lionel Abel. Santa Barbara, Calif.: Peregrine Smith, 1981. First published 1944.

Poiret, Paul. *King of Fashion: The Autobiography of Paul Poiret*. Translated by Stephen Haden Guest. Philadelphia: J. B. Lippincott, 1931.

Potter, Caroline. *Nadia and Lili Boulanger*. Burlington, Vt.: Ashgate, 2006.

Prestwich, P. F. *The Translation of Memories: Recollections of the Young Proust*. London: Peter Owen, 1999.

Proust, Marcel. *In Search of Lost Time*, vol. 1, *Swann's Way*. Translated by Lydia Davis. New York: Viking, 2003.

———. *In Search of Lost Time*, vol. 2, *Within a Budding Grove*. Translated by C. K. Moncrieff and Terence Kilmartin. Revised, D. J. Enright. New York: Modern Library, 1998.

———. *In Search of Lost Time*, vol. 3, *The Guermantes Way*. Translated by C. K. Scott Moncrieff and Terence Kilmartin. Revised, D. J. Enright. New York: Modern Library, 1993.

———. *In Search of Lost Time*, vol. 4, *Sodom and Gomorrah*. Translated by John Sturrock. New York: Viking, 2002.

———. *In Search of Lost Time*, vol. 5, *The Captive*. Translated by C. K. Scott Moncrieff and Terence Kilmartin. Revised, D. J. Enright. New York: Modern Library, 1999.

———. *In Search of Lost Time*, vol. 6, *The Fugitive*. Translated by C. K. Scott Moncrieff and Terence Kilmartin. Revised, D. J. Enright. New York: Modern Library, 1999.

———. *In Search of Lost Time*, vol. 7, *Time Regained*. Translated by Andreas Mayor and Terence Kilmartin. Revised, D. J. Enright. New York: Modern Library, 1993.

———. *Selected Letters*. Vol. 1 (1880–1903). Edited by Philip Kolb. Translated by Ralph Manheim. Garden City, N.Y.: Doubleday, 1983.

———. *Selected Letters*. Vol. 2 (1904–1909). Edited by Philip Kolb. Translated by Terence Kilmartin. New York: Oxford University Press, 1989.

———. *Selected Letters*. Vol. 3 (1910–1917). Edited by Philip Kolb. Translated by Terence Kilmartin. London: HarperCollins, 1992.

———. *Selected Letters*. Vol. 4 (1918–1922). Edited by Philip Kolb. Translated by Joanna Kilmartin. London: HarperCollins, 2000.

Quinn, Susan. *Marie Curie: A Life*. New York: Simon & Schuster, 1995.

Ravel, Maurice. *A Ravel Reader: Correspondence, Articles, Interviews*. Compiled and edited by Arbie Orenstein. Mineola, N.Y.: Dover, 2003. First published 1990.

Rearick, Charles. *Paris Dreams, Paris Memories: The City and Its Mystique*. Stanford, Calif.: Stanford University Press, 2011.

Renoir, Jean. *Renoir: My Father*. Translated by Randolph Weaver and Dorothy Weaver. Boston: Little, Brown, 1962.

Rewald, John. *Camille Pissarro*. New York: Abrams, 1963.

———. *Paul Cézanne: A Biography*. Translated by Margaret H. Liebman. New York: Simon & Schuster, 1948.

———. *Post-Impressionism: From van Gogh to Gauguin*. 3rd ed. New York: Museum of Modern Art, 1978. First published 1956.

Reynolds, John. *André Citroën: The Man and the Motor Cars*. Thrupp, Stroud, UK: Sutton, 1996.

Rheims, Maurice. *Hector Guimard*. Translated by Robert Erich Wolf. Photographs by Felipe Ferré. New York: Abrams, 1988.

Rhodes, Anthony. *Louis Renault: A Biography*. New York: Harcourt, Brace & World, 1970.

Richardson, John. *A Life of Picasso: The Prodigy, 1881–1906*. New York: Knopf, 2012. First published 1991.

———. *A Life of Picasso: The Cubist Rebel, 1907–1916*. New York: Knopf, 2012. First published 1996.

———. *A Life of Picasso: The Triumphant Years, 1917–1932*. New York: Knopf, 2007.

Roland, Gérard. *Stations de metro, d'Abbesses à Wagram*. Clermont-Ferrand, France: Christine Bonneton, 2008.

Rosenstiel, Léonie. *The Life and Works of Lili Boulanger*. Cranbury, N.J.: Associated University Presses, 1978.

Ross, Alex. *The Rest Is Noise: Listening to the Twentieth Century*. New York: Farrar, Straus & Giroux, 2007.

Rubin, William. *Picasso and Braque: Pioneering Cubism*. New York: Museum of Modern Art, 1989.

Sabartès, Jaime. *Picasso: An Intimate Portrait*. Translated by Angel Flores. New York: Prentice Hall, 1948.

Saint-Saëns, Camille. *Camille Saint-Saëns on Music and Musicians*. Edited and translated by Roger Nichols. New York: Oxford University Press, 2008.

Salmon, André. *André Salmon on French Modern Art*. Translated and annotated by Beth S. Gersh-Neš. New York: Cambridge University Press, 2005.

———. *Montparnasse: Mémoires*. Paris: Arcadia, 2003.

———. *Souvenirs sans fin (1903–1940)*. Paris: Gallimard, 2004.

Scheijen, Sjeng. *Diaghilev: A Life*. Translated by Jane Jedley-Prôle and S. J. Leinbach. New York: Oxford University Press, 2010.

Schmidt, Carl B. *Entrancing Muse: A Documented Biography of Francis Poulenc*. Hillsdale, N.Y.: Pendragon Press, 2001.

Scott, Kathleen. *Self-Portrait of an Artist: From the Diaries and Memoirs of Lady Kennet, Kathleen, Lady Scott*. London: Murray, 1949.

Secrest, Meryle. *Modigliani: A Life*. New York: Knopf, 2011.

Sert, Misia. *Misia and the Muses: The Memoirs of Misia Sert*. Translated by Moura Budberg. New York: John Day, 1953.

Shattuck, Roger. *The Banquet Years: The Origins of the Avant Garde in France, 1885 to World War I; Alfred Jarry, Henri Rousseau, Erik Satie, Guillaume Apollinaire*. New York: Vintage, 1968. First published 1955.

Shaw, Martin. *Up to Now*. London: Oxford University Press, 1929.

Shaw, Timothy. *The World of Escoffier*. New York: Vendome Press, 1995.

Sicard-Picchiottino, Ghislaine. *François Coty: Un industriel corse sous la IIIe République*. Ajaccio, France: Albiana, 2006.

Skinner, Cornelia Otis. *Elegant Wits and Grand Horizontals: Paris—La Belle Epoque*. London: Michael Joseph, 1962.

Spurling, Hilary. *Matisse the Master, A Life of Henri Matisse: The Conquest of Colour, 1909–1954*. New York: Knopf, 2007.

———. *The Unknown Matisse, A Life of Henri Matisse: The Early Years, 1869–1908*. New York: Knopf, 2005.

Steegmuller, Francis. *Cocteau: A Biography*. Boston: Little, Brown, 1970.

———, ed. *"Your Isadora": The Love Story of Isadora Duncan and Gordon Craig*. New York: Random House and New York Public Library, 1974.

Steele, Valerie. *Paris Fashion: A Cultural History*. 2nd rev. ed. New York: Oxford University Press, 1998.

Stein, Gertrude. *The Autobiography of Alice B. Toklas*. New York: Vintage, 1990. First published 1933.

———. *Gertrude Stein on Picasso*. Edited by Edward Burns. New York: Liveright, 1970.

———. *The Making of Americans: Being a History of a Family's Progress*. Normal, Ill.: Dalkey Archive Press, 1995.

———. *Three Lives and Q. E. D.: Authoritative Texts, Contexts, Criticism*. Edited by Marianne DeKoven. New York: Norton, 2006.

———. *Three Lives and Tender Buttons*. New York: Signet, 2003.

Stein, Leo. *Appreciation: Painting, Poetry, and Prose*. Edited by Brenda Wineapple. Lincoln: University of Nebraska Press, 1996.

Stravinsky, Igor. *An Autobiography*. New York: Norton, 1998. First published 1936.

Stravinsky, Igor, and Robert Craft. *Memories and Commentaries*. New York: Faber and Faber, 2002.

Studd, Stephen. *Saint-Saëns: A Critical Biography*. Madison, N.J.: Fairleigh Dickinson University Press, 1999.

Sturges, Preston. *Preston Sturges*. Edited by Sandy Sturges. New York: Simon & Schuster, 1990.

Sweetman, David. *Paul Gauguin: A Life*. New York: Simon & Schuster, 1995.

Thomas, Edith. *Louise Michel*. Translated by Penelope Williams. Montréal: Black Rose Books, 1980.

Tombs, Robert. *France, 1814–1914*. London: Longman, 1996.

Tuchman, Barbara. *The Guns of August*. New York: Ballantine Books, 1994. First published 1962.

———. *The Proud Tower: A Portrait of the World before the War, 1890–1914*. New York: Bantam, 1976. First published 1966.

Tuilier, André. *Histoire de l'Université de Paris et de la Sorbonne*. 2 vols. Paris: Nouvelle Librairie de France, 1994.

Varenne, Gaston. *Bourdelle par lui-même: Sa pensée et son art*. Paris: Fasquelle, 1937.

Villoteau, Pierre. *La vie Parisienne à la Belle Epoque*. [Genève, Switzerland]: Cercle du bibliophile, 1968.

Voisin, Gabriel. *Men, Women, and 10,000 Kites*. Translated by Oliver Stewart. London: Putnam, 1963.

Vollard, Ambroise. *Recollections of a Picture Dealer*. Translated by Violet M. Macdonald. London: Constable, 1936.

———. *Renoir: An Intimate Record*. Translated by Harold L. Van Doren and Randolph T. Weaver. New York: Knopf, 1925.

Walsh, Stephen. *Stravinsky: A Creative Spring; Russia and France, 1882–1934*. Berkeley: University of California Press, 2002. First published 1999.

Walter, Alan E. *Radiation and Modern Life: Fulfilling Marie Curie's Dream*. Amherst, N.Y.: Prometheus Books, 2004.

Watson, David Robin. *Georges Clemenceau: A Political Biography*. New York: David McKay, 1974.

Weber, Eugen. *France, Fin de Siècle*. Cambridge, Mass.: Belknap and Harvard University Press, 1986.

Wharton, Edith. *A Backward Glance*. New York: Appleton, 1934.

———. *Fighting France, from Dunkerque to Belfort*. New York: Charles Scribner's Sons, 1919.

———. *The Letters of Edith Wharton*. Edited by R. W. B. Lewis and Nancy Lewis. New York: Scribner, 1988.

Wildenstein, Daniel. *Monet, or the Triumph of Impressionism*. Vol. 1. Translated by Chris Miller and Peter Snowdon. Cologne, Germany: Taschen/Wildenstein Institute, 1999.

Williams, Charles. *The Last Great Frenchman: A Life of General de Gaulle*. New York: Wiley, 1993.

Wineapple, Brenda. *Sister Brother: Gertrude and Leo Stein*. New York: Putnam, 1996.

Winock, Michel. *La Belle Epoque: La France de 1900 à 1914*. Paris: Perrin, 2003.

Wolf, Peter M. *Eugène Hénard and the Beginning of Urbanism in Paris, 1900–1914*. The Hague: International Federation for Housing and Planning; Paris, Centre de recherche d'urbanisme, 1968.

Wolgensinger, Jacques. *André Citroën*. Paris: Flammarion, 1991.

Wullschläger, Jackie. *Chagall: A Biography*. New York: Knopf, 2008.

Index

Note: When there are multiple identical note numbers on one page, they are preceded by the chapter number, e.g., 296:9n2 refers to note 2 in chapter 9. Page numbers for illustrations are italicized.

~

About the Author

Mary McAuliffe received a PhD in history from the University of Maryland, has taught at several universities, and lectured at the Smithsonian Institution. For many years a regular contributor to *Paris Notes*, she has traveled extensively in France and recently published *Dawn of the Belle Epoque: The Paris of Monet, Zola, Bernhardt, Eiffel, Debussy, Clemenceau, and Their Friends*. She is also the author of *Clash of Crowns: William the Conqueror, Richard Lionheart, and Eleanor of Aquitaine—A Story of Bloodshed, Betrayal, and Revenge*, and *Paris Discovered: Explorations in the City of Light*. She lives in New York City with her husband.

~

For further insight into the Belle Epoque and Mary McAuliffe's other books, see her Facebook photo blog and her website: www.ParisMSM.com.

Dawn of the Belle Epoque

Now available in paperback, *Dawn of the Belle Epoque*, the prequel to *Twilight of the Belle Epoque*, traces the early years of the miraculous rebirth of Paris.

A humiliating military defeat by Bismarck's Germany, a brutal siege, and a bloody uprising—Paris in 1871 was a shambles, and the question loomed, "Could this extraordinary city even survive?"

Mary McAuliffe takes the reader back to these perilous years following the abrupt collapse of the Second Empire and France's uncertain venture into the Third Republic. By 1900, Paris had recovered and the Belle Epoque was in full flower, but the decades between were difficult, marked by struggles between republicans and monarchists, the Republic and the Church, and an ongoing economic malaise, darkened by a rising tide of virulent anti-Semitism.

Yet these same years also witnessed an extraordinary blossoming in art, literature, poetry, and music, with the Parisian cultural scene dramatically upended by revolutionaries such as Monet, Zola, Rodin, and Debussy, even while Gustave Eiffel was challenging architectural tradition with his iconic tower.

Through the eyes of these pioneers and others, including Sarah Bernhardt, Georges Clemenceau, Marie Curie, and César Ritz, we witness their struggles with the forces of tradition during the final years of a century hurtling toward its close. Through rich illustrations and evocative narrative, McAuliffe brings this vibrant and seminal era to life.